D1473418

# The Book of the British Rich

Philip Beresford

and *The Sunday Times* of London

# The Book of the British Rich

St. Martin's Press
New York

Library of Congress Cataloging-in-Publication Data

Beresford, Philip.
    The book of the British rich : the 400 wealthiest people in
Britain / by Philip Beresford and the Sunday times of London.
        p.    cm.
    ISBN 0-312-05163-8
    1. Wealth—Great Britain.    2. Millionaires—Great Britain.
3. Women millionaires—Great Britain.    I. Sunday times (London,
England : 1931)    II. Title.
HC260.W4B47    1990
305.5'234—dc20                                        90-37302
                                                        CIP


First published in Great Britain by George Weidenfeld and Nicolson Ltd.

First U.S. Edition: December 1990
10 9 8 7 6 5 4 3 2 1

# Contents

# Acknowledgements

This book would not have been possible without the support of all my colleagues at the *Sunday Times*, who have suggested names to me, helped with facts and figures. I should also like to express my appreciation of the time I was given free from the trials of journalism to concentrate on this project by Andrew Neil, the *Sunday Times* editor. Ivan Fallon, the deputy editor, inspired me to look into wealth in Britain many years ago when he was City editor on the *Sunday Telegraph*. His encouragement over the years has been crucial. Roger Eglin, the editor of the *Sunday Times* business section, was particularly kind and patient during my long absence from the ranks. Steve Boyd at the *Sunday Times* magazine has been a wonderful inspiration, editing the two issues of the magazine devoted to the rich in 1989 and 1990.

A special word of thanks to Eugene Weber and his staff at the Press Association Library, and to Brian Arrowsmith and the staff at the News International Library, who never lost their sense of humour no matter how late the hour or how difficult the request.

I have also had invaluable support from Kevin Cahill and Paddy Masters, who have toiled for many hours on my behalf, often well into the night, searching for a fact or checking entries. I cannot express my appreciation for their efforts too highly. My thanks to Kay Cahill, who did the indexing and checked the arithmetic.

Of course, nothing would have been accomplished without the encouragement of Della, to whom I dedicate the book.

*Picture acknowledgements*

The publishers wish to thank the following for their help and for the use of photographs:

Camera Press
*East Anglian Daily Times*
*Glasgow Herald*
*Indiamail*
*Jersey Evening Post*
MCA Records
Paul Francis
Press Association
Pressens Bild, Stockholm
The *Sun*
*Times* Newspapers Ltd

Picture research by Deborah Keeping

# Introduction

## Britain's richest 400
## *Ivan Fallon,*
*Deputy Editor, The Sunday Times*

Paul Getty used to say, 'No one is really rich if he can count his money.' In Getty's day, anyone with £1 million (or even $1 million) rated as 'rich' and anyone with more than £5 million was 'very rich'. Above *that* and you were in the 'super-rich' category, and when you got above the £50 million level, you rated as a 'can't count'. Nelson Bunker Hunt, who with his brother inherited a fortune even greater than Getty's, was a 'can't count' man before he tried to corner the silver market. Asked by a Senate committee how much he was worth, he snapped, 'Hell, if I knew that, I wouldn't be worth very much.'

In the United States for many years *Forbes Magazine* and *Fortune*, among others, have published lists of the very wealthy which have been eagerly awaited events in a society where wealth is a macho symbol, to be boasted about rather than hidden. In Britain, however, wealth is something best not talked about, and it has never been easy to establish authoratively just who owns what, and what they are worth.

In 1989 the *Sunday Times* broke with tradition by publishing the first real guide to Britain's wealthy, causing a considerable amount of unease among those who hated being on it, but remarkably few criticisms of our calculations. In 1990 we repeated the exercise, adding a further 70 names to the list and raising the minimum stake to £50 million. Both the 1989 and 1990 lists occupied most of one entire colour magazine, well-thumbed copies of which have both become collectors' items. The lists have since been widely discussed and copied by the rest of Fleet Street. They have also been used as ammunition by both sides of the Old Britain versus New Britain debate, quoted on the one hand to show how even in the Thatcher years old money has reinforced its power, and on the other hand to record the rise and rise of the new rich at the expense of the old.

Much work has gone into updating and refining the list which in this book runs to 400 people and families who are worth between them £54.3 billion, over 40% of it concentrated into the hands of the top ten. These 400 own 4.4 m acres of land, nearly 10% of the total land area of the United Kingdom and equivalent in size to 6 average counties.

The list includes one sovereign, 13 dukes (out of 24), 18 earls and one countess (out of 156), 12 viscounts (out of 27), 26 lords and one baroness. There are 103 aristocrats in the 400, just over a quarter of our total. We also have 31 knights, but some of them represent the wealth of the New Britain. The total number of inheritors is 162, most of whom have added to their wealth which accounts for 50% of the total.

The public schools are well represented. There are 78 Old Etonians, 11 Harrovians and 3 Wyckhamists. And if you want to know how clubbable the wealthy are, we have 36 members of Whites, 11 members of the Turf or Jockey Club, 6 members of Boodles and a single member of the Garrick.

When the *Sunday Times* published the first list in 1989, the paper commented editorially on its own study, mourning the fact that, after a decade of Thatcherism, old money still dominated and paternalism appeared to be making a comeback. Others of course took an entirely different view of the list, expressing astonishment at the amount of new money, at the relative *decline* of old wealth, and the degree of egalitarianism which had crept in. It started a debate which still goes on, and will be further fuelled by the extra material in this book which contains twice the number of names published in the newspaper.

Some who were on the 1989 list took pleasure from it, one for instance phoning from the Bahamas to announce himself to a competitor: 'This is number 48 ringing 64.' Others wrote or rang to request they be removed because their presence in such a list made their previously anonymous lives uncomfortable. Others still (not many, it should be admitted) rang to wonder why they had been excluded, and sent personal balance sheets to prove their worthiness. There were those who regarded the list as a significant contribution to understanding Britain's changing (or unchanging, depending on your point of view) social order; others who felt it was a gross invasion of privacy that the *Sunday Times* should reveal details which only accountants and taxmen (and preferably not even the latter) should know about.

However the list itself is interpreted, there is a consensus view, even among some of the wealthy themselves, that accurate and detailed information on Britain's very wealthy is much overdue. There is a positive correlation between great wealth and influence, and therefore a need to know who actually owns Britain, on the grounds that it may tell us something more about who really runs it. The list in this book is a contribution to the discussion, raw material for the social economists who will find in it a wealth of information to make of what they will.

We can however give them some nudges. In the year between compiling our first list and this book there were events which confirmed the relative fragility of the new wealth and the stability of the old. Most of the new money has been made through owning shareholdings in companies quoted on a booming stockmarket. 1989 was another excellent year for stockmarkets, which around the world rose an average of 96% from the bottom of the crash of October 1987 to their peak in January 1990, yet in that time there were spectacular dips in our table. Arundbhai Patel, millionaire newsagent in early 1989, and in 116th place with a fortune of £50 million, put his company into liquidation. Sophie Mirman, founder of Sock Shop and one of the brightest of the new generation of female entrepreneurs, also lost much of her fortune. Alan Sugar, the man behind the extraordinary rise of Amstrad in the mid-1980s, saw his wealth decline in a

single year by £314 million, or £6 million a day. By contrast, the Earl of Cadogan, roughly equal to Sugar in 1989, was still, a year later, worth the same £450 million. As Sophie Tucker might say, 'I've been rich and I've been poor; rich is better.'

The list of 400 features only 23 women, including the Queen – worth £7.4 billion between them. There are also 3 MPs, Michael Heseltine, Alan Clark and Bill Benyon; we could probably have included Peter Walker. In the list as a whole we have identified 215 who have declared a political allegiance, of which 206 are Tory, many of them staunchly Thatcherite; we have 1 declared Labour supporter (Robert Maxwell), 1 Green (Simon Fussell), 4 Liberals and 3 SDP. These political allegiances are of course not fixed: the rich are probably as fickle as anyone else in their voting intentions, although it would be no surprise to anyone to find a strong Tory bias. But it is no secret that Tiny Rowland, for instance, is actively opposed to Mrs Thatcher, or that David Sainsbury, the richest of the grocery family, has backed David Owen. Not everyone would agree with Voltaire's dictum that 'when it is a question of money, everybody is of the same religion'.

'What have you changed?' Mrs Thatcher was asked in 1979 when she became prime minister. 'I have changed everything,' she replied. By that she meant that, 100 years after Disraeli talked about Britain's Two Nations, she was reversing a century of decline by reviving the enterprise spirit. At the Tory Party conference in October 1985 Norman Fowler, the social services secretary, drew cheers when he reaffirmed, 'We could take no pride in the rebuilding of a prosperity that remained the privilege of the few.' A few months later, the Archbishop of Canterbury's Commission *Faith in the City* report pronounced, to Thatcher's fury, that rich and poor, privileged and deprived, 'have become more sharply separate from each other'. This table shows only the top end of that gap, and to support or disprove the commission's report one would have to take it much deeper down the wealth ladder; but it does leave an impression that despite the new arrivals on the list, nothing much *has* changed this past decade. Eleven years after Mrs Thatcher entered Downing Street, Peter Morgan, the head of the Institute of Directors, could get a standing ovation at a packed gathering in the Albert Hall with precisely that message. 'It is obvious that responsibility for the 100 years of decline of UK plc must be laid at the door of the Establishment.' Like all his generation at school, Morgan had learned of how Britain had once been the 'workshop of the world ... cotton, coal and iron, canals and railways ... and the heroes, Arkwright and Watt, Stephenson and Brunel,' their legacy all now gone, killed, he said, by 'intellectual opposition from an establishment that espouses a different culture'. One view of this list is that the same Establishment is still guiding the affairs of the nation, more entrenched and richer than ever.

It contains very few families one might associate with the Victorian and Edwardian might of Britain, or even of the industrial companies which came later: we have a single Lever, Lord Leverhulme, but no Geddes or Slazenger (of Dunlop), no Armstrongs, Siddeleys, Sopwiths, de Havillands, Fergusons, Lyons, Morrises or Rootes; none of the great shipbuilding families who controlled the Vickers, John Browns, Cammells, Lairds, Thorneycrofts, Vospers, Yarrows, Swans or Hunters. No Colvilles, Redmans, Dormans or Longs; no Courtaulds, Carringtons, Coats, Patons or Baldwins; no Hepworths or Wedgwoods. Gone, too, from the ranks of the very wealthy are the big shipping families, the Cunards, Ellermans, Andersons, Greens and Mackenzies, although we do still have the Inchcapes (Mackays) and Cayzers, neither of them now in shipping. The Swires and the Keswicks, who made their money in Hong Kong, still thrive, but the only old industrial family on our list is the Pilkingtons.

The nearest we have to a new self-made industrialist of the old school is Lord Weinstock, son of a Jewish tailor who arrived from Poland in 1906. Evan Cornish, whose packaging company is worth £190 million also possibly qualifies as an industrialist, but scarcely of the kind that once made Britain great.

Yet for those who prefer a more mobile social order, and welcome the injection of the new rich, there is hope too. Britain has more millionaires – 20,000 at the latest count in comparison with over a million in the US – than it has aristocrats, and 239 of the 400 started with nothing (or next to nothing) to build their fortunes in a single generation. There are even 21 Asian immigrants, several of them among the Ugandans so abruptly rejected by Idi Amin. There is a considerable smattering of other immigrants too, some of whom came to Britain as children: Robert Maxwell (born poor in Czechoslovakia), Sir James Goldsmith (born rich in Paris), Tiny Rowland (born in a British internment camp in India of German parents), Lord Forte (born poor in Italy), the Saatchis (born well-off in Baghdad), Sir Mark Weinberg (born in South Africa), and Sir David Alliance (born in Iran). Some of the billionaires were also born abroad: John Paul Getty II, George Livanos and Sighismund Berger. Many others are second generation British: who for instance knew that the Wham! pop star George Michael (worth £68 million) is the son of Jack Panayiotou, a millionaire restaurant owner who arrived in London penniless from Greece?

The list therefore, despite the fixtures of the landed aristocrats, reveals a considerable amount of movement and something which has probably been true of Britain for centuries: a continual state of renewal, with some of the new rich adding titles and land and becoming the Establishment several generations on, but a high proportion of them losing their fortunes before they have had time to consolidate it. By a curious trick of statistics, the balance in the top 200 is an almost equal one between establishment and self-made money: 102 Old Rich play 98 New Rich.

This is however at the end of a period which has almost uniquely – at least this century – favoured the new. A financial crash on a mid-1970s scale would amost certainly shift the balance back. It is all too easily forgotten that some of the most successful New Rich were almost wiped out 15 years ago: Jimmy Goldsmith, Robert Maxwell, Gerald Ronson and many others had a huge struggle through the property and fringe banking crisis. The Beckwith brothers, in the list at £80 million, once had losses of £1.5 million. The Old Rich on the other hand came through it all relatively undented, having had generations to learn to cope with adversity.

We do not pretend the list is either complete or perfect: it cannot be when works of art, and even land and property, are so difficult to value accurately even by full-time experts with access to all the details of the assets they are selling. Many of Britain's richest families have no idea of their true wealth, and there is no reason why they should have. Even five years ago, works of art were still regarded as ancillary furnishings, worth something certainly, but not enough to qualify as real wealth. Now Impressionist paintings sell for tens of millions of dollars, and a good collection of modern art, such as that built up by Charles and Doris Saatchi, can be worth far more. Even vintage cars, until recently an eccentric rich man's hobby, now represent serious money.

Putting a value on the wealth of the royal family is not only difficult but to some extent pointless: there are art treasures and jewels in the Queen's collection which are priceless and will never be sold. Queen Elizabeth II is the 63rd monarch in a line going back 1,000 years, each one of whom has added to the collection. By contrast, for instance, the Saudi Royal family – which features ahead of her in the international *Fortune* list – has not even ruled for a century. In 1971 the Royal Chamberlain told a parliamentary committee set up to look into her finances that Her Majesty was concerned by 'the atronomical figures bandied about in some quarters' suggesting that the value of her personal fortune 'may now run into £50m to £100m or more'. The Queen assured the committee that these estimates were 'wildly exaggerated' – the royal collections, she pointed out, were not at her private disposal. She has not, as far as we are aware, objected to the far higher estimates which have lately been put on her wealth. It should however be remembered that when Edward VIII abdicated, he was able to take only a modest fortune and worried about money for the rest of his life. The Queen cannot take it with her, not even if she were to retire abroad.

Nevertheless, because she pays no tax, the Queen's fortune accumulates faster than a private individual's in the same circumstances. On *Fortune*'s list she ranks fourth, well ahead of the Sultan of Brunei.

This list is essentially the work of Philip Beresford, formerly Associate Business Editor of the *Sunday Times*, who has spent much of the last decade compiling information on Britain's wealth, and now has on his computer files more information on the subject than anyone in the land, probably including the Inland Revenue. He has been assisted by Patrick Masters who has combed through hundreds of unpublished accounts in Companies House, checking and cross-checking details. They have been backed up by a team of researchers led by

Kevin Cahill who has managed a network of *Sunday Times* local correspondents to provide details of landowners and private millionaires, which have then been checked with estate agents, chartered surveyors and, in the case of works of art, with the leading auction houses. It is as accurate as we can make it, although it will obviously soon be out of date as stock market conditions change and as individual company fortunes wax and wane.

Lady Astor said that the only thing 'I like about rich people is their money'. On this list there are people of all sorts, some nice, some not so nice, some mean, some generous – in fact probably a typical cross-section of the population, except that they all have a great deal of money. Does that by itself make them different? As Oscar Wilde might say: 'When I was young I thought that money was the most important thing in life; now that I am old I know it is.'

---

# Asset Management
## *Gilbert de Botton*
*Global Asset Management Ltd*

A nineteenth-century definition of wealth was the ability to live well off the interest on the interest of one's capital. Twentieth-century taxation and the notion of total return on assets have contributed to making this concept obsolete. Nevertheless, in the UK much old wealth has survived the perils of mismanagement and taxation.

Forty per cent of the wealth of the people in this book – about £21.5 billion – is held in the form of financial instruments, mainly in company shares. The rich use the financial markets in two ways: either they invest, placing their money with others who make it work for them, or they are more actively involved. There is in the UK a great concentration of wealth through ownership of large shareholdings of companies by the descendants of the founders or by first generation entrepreneurs who have gone public.

Going public is the most spectacular way of capitalising on earnings and illiquid assets via financial markets. It is an approach much more common here than on the Continent. The UK Stock Exchange is old and has a long tradition of making funds available for companies and their backers and owners. In Germany, on the other hand, there is a smaller stock exchange, fewer shares are available on it, and many large companies are privately owned. The 1980s saw a move towards public flotation in the UK: the Body Shop, Rechem and Woolworth are examples of this. But the end of the 1980s saw a reversal of the trend, with Virgin Records and Andrew Lloyd Webber's Really Useful Group going private, albeit via the Stock Exchange.

Where very great wealth is involved, there is usually a move to incoporate it, or the trusts or foundations created with this wealth, into 'family' or corporate offices which usually engage in charitable and artistic work on a scale beyond the capacity of an individual. Examples of these are the Rockefeller Foundation and the Whitney Foundation in the US. In the UK much of the Sainsbury wealth is vested in a series of special trusts which are involved in educational and social charity on quite a large scale. The managers of these foundations are often financial professionals, unconnected with the families that may sit on the Trust boards. They operate the trust funds across a range of investment instruments, such as shares, bonds and government stock, and they will routinely invest in shares outside the boundaries of the founders' companies. For the individual, the financial markets of the 1980s provided a whole range of new instruments such as deep-discounted, high yielding bonds with which to engage in large scale corporate takeovers and mergers. People like Sir James Goldsmith and various aggressive entrepreneurs have made extensive use of these and other exceptional credit facilities to create the empires which are the foundation of the wealth which placed them in the list in this book. At the beginning of the 1980s UK businessmen were enormously helped by the abolition of exchange controls and they were able to better use the UK as a base for overseas expansion. Their operations and those of others on a smaller scale, together with the savings concentrated with pensions and institutions, have made the UK into one of the great capital exporters in the world. In the UK there is no wealth tax, but there is income, capital gains and inheritance tax. Trusts are one common method of making founders' wealth mobile and can legitimately defer certain liabilities until such time as remittances are make to UK resident beneficaries or the trust dissolved.

For the seriously rich, and there is no one in this book who is not, tax is still a problem, and advisors, usually accountants and lawyers, are employed to make the tax imposition as small as is legally possible. In a celebrated case in the late 1970s it emerged that the Vestey family had paid little or no tax for almost 60 years through the perfectly legal use of discretionary trusts. That loophole was closed in 1981, but expert advisors can still ensure that the bulk of wealth created through company growth and through inheritance can remain in the hands of founders and heirs with minimal tax loss. One example of careful tax planning is the Westminster estate, the inheritance of the second richest person in Britain. This is vested in 24 carefully structured trusts.

While the lesson of excessive taxation and its deleterious effects on enterprise seem to have been learned by most governments, nothing will remove the element of risk from the creation and use of wealth. Sir James Goldsmith's famous declaration that he had been out of the market before its horrendous crash in October 1987, led the unwary to do exactly what he had not done, which was to sell out in the middle of a price slide. Goldsmith had spotted the market peak and made his exit. Those who had the sense to hold on to their investments saw the value of most of their stock fully returned two years later. Inherited wealth, particularly land, tends to be more stable, yet in the course of the last 100 years the volume of land owned by the peerage has dropped by 80%, in many cases through the loss of an entire estate.

But, in spite of the surface appearance of quick riches or of sudden financial death, with the use of the better regulated, less imperfect mechanisms for the recycling of savings and wealth we can all transform our savings into investments and count ourselves rich.

## Property and Land
### John Ritblat
*The British Land Company PLC*

The ownership of land is visible proof of riches. Feudal barons fought for their territories – 'lack land' was then a term of contempt – but happily their descendents do not have to be so aggressive. Large estates are often inherited, a family tradition which passes through the generations. So the landed classes land on their feet.

The wealth of about 40% of the people in this book is based on land or property. Much was inherited, but nothing could more clearly illustrate the intrinsic attractiveness of land and good property than the fact that the majority of those people who have made their own money in recent times have bought landed estates or old houses. In so doing, they have conformed to a very British tradition: they have bought their way into an institution, that of land ownership, which carries more than a little history with it. Up to the seventeenth century the country was divided into manorial districts, each still virtually 'ruled' by a feudal land lord who held his title from the King. The marriage of one Mary Davies, whose dowry included the Lordship of Ebury and the lands which came with it, laid the foundations of the fortune of the second richest person in modern Britain, the Duke of Westminster. Wars, the growth of the population, and mergers, many of the type that created the Westminster fortune, eroded the importance of the manorial land divisions, but they did not necessarily destroy the buildings. Few of those now surviving go back to the Saxon originals, but many, such as Saltley Castle, occupied by Alan Clarke MP, stand on sites that have been occupied by houses for many centuries.

These ancient castles, manors and halls are seldom cheap to buy and never cheap to maintain. Yet for the most part their modern owners, often their new owners, devote a considerable part of their fortunes to maintaining and restoring them. Why? Land is permanent, irreplaceable, indestructible, and we all need somewhere to live. Each old property is unique and, for many people, a treasure comparable to a work of art. Like works of art, they can be hugely improved by conservation, giving them a significant investment potential.

Such property needs positive management, and most investors will have to look to someone else to do the work for them. It is possible to engage experts to investigate proposed property investments and then to look after them effectively as managers. *Caveat emptor* – let the buyer beware – is still a fundamental rule in the property world. This applies to choice of location, legal rights, security and changing tastes. Will the buildings of the 1960s ever be loved? Will Lord Holford's Paternoster Square survive at the vociferous request of a 60s revivalist, commended for its clean (if wind-inducing) lines, contrasting with the flamboyance of Wren's St Paul's Cathedral? Historical precedents suggest that, after a respectable interval of perhaps seventy-five to one hundred years, buildings once despised have a chance of returning to favour – that is, of course, if they are still standing.

As late as 1876 almost half the land in the UK, about 24 million acres, was in the hands of about 1,200 peers. Their heirs still form a significant group in this book, but their holdings, at 4.4 million acres, total no more than 9% of the land area of the country. It is from the gradual break up of these great estates that much of urban Britain has grown. However, it is noticeable that where estates held on to metropolitan land they have prospered very greatly, as have those people who bought the land they sold. It is no accident that modern property owners, developers and builders form the fourth most important element of the richest 400 people in Britain.

When we invest wealth in property we incur responsibilities to the community, for what happens to buildings and to land is of great consequence to everyone. The permanence of land and the long life of buildings together place environmental obligations on landowners, and those who find these restrictions unacceptable may decide that other forms of investment suit them better. But land and property provide the perceptive investor, in addition to financial success, with rewards other than financial profits. The majority of home dwellers in the UK, 65% of us, own our own homes. In this way we share the instincts of the newly rich and of the great landowners by investing our modest fortunes in that most enduring, rewarding and profitable investment, land and the homes which stand on it.

## The Rules of Engagement

1) This listing represents our analysis or estimate of the minimum wealth of the 400 people or families whom we believe to be

the richest in Britain. Some people's wealth could be and probably will be much higher.

2) We are measuring identifiable wealth, whether land, racehorses, art treasures, significant shares in publicly quoted companies or private companies. We do not include cash in the bank (to records of which we have no access) or small share-holdings in private share portfolios.

3) Many of the wealthy people – particularly the landowners – can rightly claim that they do not have great hordes of cash to spend on a life of luxury. Their wealth is tied up in the land. They cannot easily dispose of it and, indeed, are loath to do so. Their families have not become rich and remained so over the centuries by squandering their money. The Marquess of Bath, for example, admits that he is worth £200 million, but he lives a very frugal life. Selling land or paintings may also be difficult for legal and tax reasons.

4) Similarly many business people with large shareholdings in their own companies are very loath to sell the shares to raise cash. They could lose control of the company, and any sale may be interpreted as a sign of trouble by City stockbrokers, who will, therefore, lower the price offered for the shares. The only time that business men typically raise large sums of cash is in a takeover bid for their company, whether forced or agreed. Paper fortunes based on ownership of shares can also disappear quickly if a company crashes. Sir Clive Sinclair, the computer genius, used to be worth over £100 million five years ago. Today, he is worth a fraction of that. Every time Amstrad shares suffer a sharp fall on the stock market, millions are wiped off Alan Sugar's fortune, but always seem to recover at a later date.

5) Where an individual or family has sold their major stake in a company (whether through an agreed or forced takeover), we take their receipts from the sale to be an indication of their wealth. We assume that, if they were clever enough to build up a company worth millions of pounds, they will not fritter that money away when they sell it, but invest it wisely in the most tax-efficient manner possible.

6) We take a common-sense approach to every case but stick to some broad rules in identifying the wealth:

a) All share stakes in publicly quoted companies are valued according to the price quoted in the *Financial Times* on Tuesday, 2 January 1990.

b) The private company share stakes are valued at a ratio of 12.5 times their latest post-tax profit figures or the average for a similar company that is quoted on the Stock Exchange (whichever is most appropriate). The figure of 12.5 times profits is the average figure for the whole stock market on 2 January 1990, as reported in the *Financial Times*.

But in some cases, where the brands of the company are particularly prized (as in Drambuie, the Scottish liqueur company), the price will be higher. Good brands attract a hefty premium in the stock market today.

Also, where a company is investing in long term ventures such as forestry to minimise tax problems, we may use other yardsticks to value it, such as its net assets.

c) Family shareholdings are banded together as one grouping when it is obvious that the family members act together to defend the interests of their company. But we use the picture of the leading member of that family to illustrate the family wealth. In the case of the Sainsbury family, for example, Lord John Sainsbury, the chairman of the J. Sainsbury supermarket group, is shown as the head of the family, though his cousin David is the larger shareholder.

d) The Sainsbury fortune illustrates another rule: family trusts are included as part of the fortune.

e) Charitable trusts which give all their income to charities are not included. Sometimes, however, it is difficult to determine what is a charitable trust and what is one designed to minimise tax demands. We use our common sense and instincts to make a judgement here.

f) In one or two cases, where individuals have recently stated on the record or in print that they are worth more than other recent valuations of their wealth, we have taken them at their word, after checking. Christopher Moran recently claimed his fortune was £100 million or more, and he has a 45,000 acre estate in Scotland and other wealth to back up his claim. Similarly, Peter de Savary claims to be worth £100 million.

7) Land is valued on what and where it is. Most valuable is London land with planning permission, then other urban land,

then good farming, forestry, poor farming and, finally, desolate land. We took account of valuable shooting and fishing rights. We spoke to local agents and to four of Britains' major chartered surveyors/land managers (who did not want to be identified). They gave us their estimates of land values per acre for agricultural land. They differ considerably for various regions. Despite the fall in urban land values in the south of England in 1989/90, Scottish rural land, farmland and estates continued to increase in value, with an apparently unstoppable influx of 'settlers from the South', all with money to spend and little worry about interest rates, according to one estate agent in northern Scotland. As a result, land values per acre range from:

|  |  | (1990) | (1989) |
|---|---|---|---|
| Scottish | Poor – up to £300 | (£75) |
| Highlands | Good – up to £1000 | (£800) |
| Scottish | Poor – up to £600 | (£500) |
| Lowlands | Good – up to £2000 | (£2000) |
| North of | Poor – up to £1600 | (£1300) |
| England | Good – up to £2000 | (£2000) |
| Wales | Poor – up to £200 | (£100) |
|  | Good – up to £1700 | (£1300) |
| West | Poor – up to £1400 | (£1200) |
| Midlands | Good – up to £3200 | (£3000) |
| East | Poor – up to £1600 | (£1500) |
| Midlands | Good – up to £3125 | £2750) |
| East | Poor – up to £2100 | (£1500) |
| Anglia | Good – up to £4000 | (£2700) |
| South- | Poor – up to £1500 | (£1400) |
| East | Good – up to £2200 | (£2750) |
| South- | Poor – up to £750 | (£700) |
| West | Good – up to £2750 | (£2100) |

Note: These figures should be treated with care, for the land market became both volatile and highly differentiated as between parts of the country in late 1989 and early 1990.

The Strutt & Parker Land Index for December 1989, a published document, gives a breakdown of the mean price per acre of various categories of farmland throughout the UK:

|  | Dec 89 | (Dec 88) |
|---|---|---|
| Mainly dairy | £3410 | (£3015) |
| Mainly arable | £2335 | (£1960) |
| Mainly beef/sheep | £2390 | (£1755) |
| All commercial farms | £2445 | (£2200) |
| Mainly residential | £4635 | (£4425) |
| All farms sold | £2695 | (£2168) |

8) Fishing and shooting rights have seen the most radical changes in the last year or two. Salmon rivers, which sell on a basis of price per salmon caught, moved from an average in 1989 of £5,000 to £8,000 per fish caught per season to an average nearer £10,000 throughout the country. In Scotland, one salmon river was sold on the basis that each fish caught was worth £18,000. Trout rivers, where they came up for sale, and very few did, started to fetch almost double 1988's £100 to £150 per yard price. All trout fishing is sold by the yard, and needs a good record, but even humble feeder streams to major rivers, which in 1988 fetched £100 per yard, were fetching double that in late 1989. The best trout stream in England, the Test, at the last sale in 1987 fetched £404 per yard. Land with grouse shooting, which was making £500 to £1000 per brace shot in 1988, reached £1500 per brace in some areas. Again, a good record, well documented, is needed to sustain the best prices. Land with pheasant or partridge shooting went up from £750 per acre to over £1000. Shooting rights alone are valued at £50 to £100 per acre, against last year's £20 to £50. In Scotland, trout fishing is not normally sold separately from the land itself, as trout-fishing rights carry bank and river-bed ownership rights.

9) Art, porcelain, gold, and silver are valued according to expert advice. The last five years have seen record prices achieved at auctions for many artists, whose works grace the homes of many of our 400. For example, the highest price paid for a Canaletto up to the end of 1988 was £520,000. In December 1989, a Canaletto fetched £1.2 million.

10) Stately homes are valued according to location and notoriety/desirability. One estate agent reckons that he would have a queue of wealthy people willing to pay £25 million for Blenheim Palace.

11) The 400 include people who may not be British citizens, such as James Sherwood or the Rausing brothers from Sweden. But, in an increasingly cosmopolitan world, they live and work in Britain, so they are included. British citizens abroad such as Sir James Goldsmith are also included. But we have not included Rupert Murdoch, proprietor of the *Sunday Times* as he is an American citizen and he is based in America. *Forbes* magazine in 1989 esti-

mated his wealth at $1.7 billion. By the same token, we do not include Baron Heini Thyssen, the art collector, who, apart from his home in Britain, has several homes in Europe, including his main residence in Switzerland. Also, Alfred Taubman, the American billionaire, is not included despite owning 56% of that very British institution Sotheby's, because he is based in America.

12) Reference sources we have used include companies' own reports and accounts, Extel's financial information cards, McCarthy press cutting cards, *Jordan's Top 2000 Privately Owned Companies, Who's Who, Debrett's Peerage & Baronetage, Debrett's Distinguished People of Today, Who's Who in the City, Crawford's Directory of City Connections, The Directory of Directors, Acquisitions Monthly, Strategic Holdings for Takeovers* and *The Hambro Corporate Register* also provided invaluable information. We had a network of local correspondents finding local information for us. We have also found the P A library and the News International library to be invaluable sources of reference material, and we would like to thank the staff in both libraries for all their help.

## Faces of the Future

Wealth is a constantly moving feast. As stock markets and the price of art treasures and land fluctuate quite sharply at times, so a list of rich people will vary accordingly.

A slump in retail sales in 1990, for example, hammered the fortunes of several well-known figures who had prospered for most of the 1980s, including Sir Bernard Ashley, head of the Laura Ashley group and Sir Terence Conran, the Storehouse chairman. Fortunes have been won or lost when millionaires sell their firms or, in their quest for growth, over-extend themselves.

But there will always be new blood coming along, whether rising business stars, sportsmen and women at the peak of their careers, or pop and film stars.

Who are some of the people to look out for as potential candidates for the next edition of *The Sunday Times Book of the Rich?* Look out for: Michael Buckley, chairman of SelecTV, a television production company, is tipped as a future multi-millionaire. With several television hits, a link with 20th Century Fox, and Robert Maxwell as a major shareholder, SelecTV could go the way of Michael Green's Carlton Communications. In January 1990, it was still a minnow, worth just £10 million on the stock market.

Martin Sorrell, the former finance director of the Saatchi & Saatchi advertising agency, who left in May 1985 to buy a stake in a small Kent engineering company which he has turned into the world's largest advertising agency. His stake in WPP (which originally stood for Wire and Plastic Products) is now worth some £6 million. Though the advertising market is suffering a sharp-downturn now, Sorrell's management skills and his ability to keep a tight control on costs should enable him to emerge unscathed and, indeed, in a stronger position.

Shami Ahmad, one of the newest Asian millionaires, has built a £20 million fashion chain in Manchester called 'Joe Bloggs'. His toughest decision today is whether to take his £200,000 Ferrari Testarossa or the more mundane £100,000 Bentley Turbo to work.

Nigel Rudd, chairman of the Williams Holdings industrial group, is tipped to be the next Lord Hanson. Based in Derby, Rudd has already built Williams from a loss-making foundry business which he took over in 1982 to a £1 billion company seven years later. He is currently worth some £7.5 million.

Michael Slade, the chairman of the Helical Bar property group, made the headlines in 1987 when his pay shot up to over £1 million a year. Though it is back to a more modest £330,000 today, he owns some £12 million worth of the high-flying property group and a yacht in the Caribbean.

From the field of sports, Stephen Hendry, the young Scottish snooker star, looks set to join the multi-millionaire class. Hendry managed to take his prize money past £1 million in February 1990, when he was just 21. He is now regarded as the main challenger to Steve Davis, the world champion.

# THE
# BILLIONAIRES

---

## £1000m and more

# The Queen £6,700m

*Head of State*

dob 21/4/26

The richest woman in the world, the Queen's wealth stems from two fortunes. There are the Crown Estates, which contain much of her 267,000 acres of land, including 350 valuable acres of central London. She also owns virtually all the land round the coast of Britain, between the high- and low-water marks. This gives her the rights to land when it is reclaimed and any mineral rights, giving an annual income of £2 million a year.

All these assets of the Crown Estates were valued at £1,200 million in March 1987. But the Queen is really the custodian of these estates, rather than the direct beneficiary. She pays all the revenues to the Treasury (£29.4 million in 1987) in return for an annual payment from the Civil List. In 1990 the Queen received £5.09 million.

The Queen's second fortune, which is more clearly her own property, is hers to sell if she wishes, although this is thought to be a very unlikely eventuality. This fortune embraces the royal treasures such as an art collection, with works by all the Dutch and Italian masters, and several hundred drawings by Leonardo da Vinci. It also includes the royal antiques which require a 75-volume catalogue to cover them all. The royal stamp collection, started by George V, runs to over 330 albums. The Queen's jewel collection includes over 20 tiaras.

In addition, racing stables, stud farms and property in Britain (50,000 acres at Balmoral and 20,000 acres at Sandringham) are held by the Queen personally. There are also valuable properties on the continent and in America, though these are shrouded in secrecy. The total value of this portfolio has been estimated at nearly £3 billion.

The Queen has stocks and shares in an equity portfolio which is managed with utter discretion by blue chip banks and brokers in the City. This was valued after the 1987 crash at around £1.9 billion, but it increased in value by some 25% in line with the surge in world stock markets in 1988 and 1989.

She has a passion for horses and racing, but a disappointment is the inability of any of her horses so far to win the Derby.

# Prince Charles   + £200m

*Landowner and heir apparent*

dob 14/11/48

The Duchy of Cornwall dates back to 1337, when Edward III created the title Duke of Cornwall for his famous son, the Black Prince. The dukedom was no empty title and came endowed with huge estates in Devon, Cornwall and the Scillies.

Today that land stretches over 140,000 acres and includes the lease to Dartmoor prison. There are also flower farms on the Isles of Scilly which are almost entirely Duchy property leased to local landowners. But the jewel in the ducal estate is the 43 acres of London's Kennington, including the Oval cricket ground. This area is becoming increasingly fashionable with 'yuppies', the upwardly mobile youth of the Thatcher era, moving in.

All this is currently the personal property of the 21st Duke of Cornwall, His Royal Highness Prince Charles, who is also heir apparent to the throne of the United Kingdom.

The estates provided Prince Charles with a gross income of £1.9 million in 1987, less the 25% which he surrenders to the Treasury, retaining the balance in 'the family business'. Prior to his marriage he paid 50% as a voluntary remittance to the Treasury. However, unlike any other business in this country governed by the Companies Acts, the accounts laid before Parliament are reticent about the true value of the estates, including the valuable London acres. The auditor to the Duchy, Jeffery Bowman (the senior partner of the well-known accounting firm Price Waterhouse) has been doing the job since 1971. He writes in the latest accounts: 'the Duchy was instituted in 1337. It is therefore impracticable to arrive at the cost of the estates, many of which were acquired centuries ago, and no amount has been included for them in these accounts.' The fact is that all the Duchy's assets are quantifiable by professionally qualified people, but it would cost money to do so and, from Prince Charles's point of view, such a valuation would serve no purpose since there are no taxes to pay. However, Prince Charles clearly needs to have his estates managed efficiently and profitably in order to meet his living expenses, since he gets no money from the Civil List.

Owners of estates of this size are taught to think 50 years ahead and to measure their acts against the long-term probable results. The Prince is not

a profligate man and it is not likely that he would squander his birthright. But there are statutory constraints on his strategy for the Duchy. One is the Duchy of Cornwall Management Act, 1982, which slightly loosened the original Victorian Act giving the Treasury certain powers of veto over transactions affecting Duchy property. The Treasury can now give its approval after considering the effect on 'persons living on, or in the vicinity of' the land and, to be even-handed, having 'given regard to the interests of both present and future Dukes of Cornwall'. On the whole, the arrangement has worked well, as tenants of the Duchy's London properties agree; rents have risen, but not reflecting the surge in London property prices.

The Prince's personality has been another factor in the changes occurring in the management of the estates. The 'Green Prince' has shown consistent concern for the preservation of animals and plants, issuing nesting boxes free to West Country tenants and sending memos deploring the excessive use of chemicals on tenanted farms. His major experiment in guiding the Duchy's development along his own lines is the Poundbury Farm project, Dorchester, near the Iron Age fort of Maiden Castle. This is set in about 300 acres of Duchy-owned farmland in Dorset, where the Prince has appointed Leon Krier, an architect, academic and planner, to create a plan for building about 2,500 homes as an overspill for the nearby town of Dorchester, with light industrial units and playing fields on a human scale, which Prince Charles described in a television programme as the challenge of building in the countryside 'without spoiling it'.

He has also adopted a more commercial approach to his tenants than has been the case with many of his predecessors this century. He has raised some rents by as much as 90%, from levels set in the 1950s or earlier. They still remain lower than the rents set by other big landowners and estates.

£ The annual defence budget of the UK is approximaely £20 bn.

The 10 richest people could, if they liquidated their assets, pay for the defence of the realm for a year and still have £200 m in change each.

# Duke of Westminster   £4,200m

*Landowner*

dob 22/12/51

In his speech at the Farmers' Club annual dinner at the end of 1989, held appropriately at the Grosvenor Hotel in London's Park Lane, Gerald Grosvenor, the 6th Duke of Westminster, made a passionate plea for help for the emerging democracies in eastern Europe. A fellow peer, sitting near by, was heard to remark: 'I suppose this means that Gerald has just bought Prague.'

If any man in England has the wealth to buy whole cities, it is the Duke of Westminster, easily Britain's wealthiest man with a fortune of £4.2 billion. The Duke is descended from the Earl of Chester, chief huntsman to William the Conqueror and also his nephew. The dukedom itself is one of the last created in the UK. It was conferred by Victoria on the 23rd Earl of Chester in 1874.

The present Duke's fortune is traced to the marriage to Sir Thomas

Grosvenor in 1677 of Mary Davies, aged 12 and heiress to the Manor of Ebury and a small acreage of undrained marsh and bog on the edge of 17th-century London. Most of those acres, with the exception of Pimlico which was sold after World War II, are still in the hands of the Grosvenors.

Even in Victorian times, however, John Bateman, a chronicler of the great estates and landowners, said of the newly created 1st Duke: 'He owns what is commonly supposed to be the most valuable London estate held by any of Her Majesty's subjects.' Bateman added that an uncle of his had shot snipe within half a mile of Belgrave Square in 1822. Today the London estate includes 300 acres of Mayfair, some of the most valuable real estate in the world. The details of the estate, according to a brochure produced for the 300th anniversary of the wedding, read like an exaggerated version of Monopoly. Belgravia, Mayfair, Chester Square, Park Lane, Eaton Square, Oxford Street and Bond Street all figure in the portfolio.

The first Duke did not own anything approaching the same landholdings outside London as the 6th Duke does today. Nowadays the Grosvenor estates run to around 150,000 acres, making Gerald Grosvenor the sixth largest landowner in modern Britain. In the 1880s the estates ran to a mere 19,000 acres. Outside London the estate comprises 100,000 acres of Scottish forest, a large tract of Co. Fermanagh, and 13,000 acres around the Duke's home, Eaton Hall, in prime Cheshire countryside.

His international investments are made via Grosvenor International Holdings, based in Vancouver, Canada, where it owns over 12,000 acres. In real estate it owns over 70 prime commercial properties in the English-speaking world. The estate built and owns the Wailea Beach Hotel, the Davies Pacific Center and other properties in Hawaii. In Australia there are buildings and property in Sydney, Melbourne and a 10,000-acre sheep farm at Wagga Wagga. Since 1977 the Grosvenor estate has added real estate in Spain, Florida and other places to its holdings.

The present Duke lives in Eaton Hall, which is universally acknowledged to be an awful example of 1960s housebuilding. He is said to be planning to rebuild in a more tasteful style in keeping with the Prince of Wales's thoughts on modern architecture. He is also heading the Prince's new drive to help the rural poor.

The Duke was educated at Harrow, left with two O levels and is now a governor of the school. He wanted to be a footballer and had a trial for first division club Fulham. He has a shrewd business brain and commutes to his office in London by helicopter. He is patron or president, with his wife Natalia, of over 150 charities. His older sister, Lady Leonora Grosvenor, was formerly married to the photographer Patrick, Earl of Lichfield; his younger sister, Lady Jane, was formerly married to the Duke of Roxburghe (q.v.).

# Gad and Hans Rausing    £2,040m

*Industrialists*

dob HR 25/3/26

*Hans Rausing*

A clutch of millionaires have fled to Britain to escape higher tax rates elsewhere. The richest of these tax exiles, Gad and Hans Rausing, did in 1962. The two brothers live in London and Sussex respectively, having left their native Sweden to escape the tax regime there.

Their wealth stems from Tetra Pak, one of the world's biggest food packaging groups. It was founded by their father in 1951, using a special package he had invented which did away with the need to refrigerate liquids. When they took over the business, the two brothers expanded it into 100 countries.

Hans collects vintage cars on his Sussex deer farm. Gad, an avid patron of the arts, returns occasionally to Sweden to lecture at the University of Lund on archaeology. He is extraordinarily proud of the thesis he wrote for his PhD on bows and arrows. Hans is chairman of the company. He has degrees in economics and technology. Both are married with children.

# Garfield Weston £1,674m

## *Industrialist*

dob 28/4/27

Garfield Weston is chairman of Associated British Foods, which makes such household names as Sunblest bread and Twinings tea. The company is quoted on the Stock Exchange and the Weston family control 63% of the shares.

In 1882 Weston's grandfather, a Cockney, emigrated to Canada and began a door-to-door bread delivery service from a cart. Thirteen years later he sold out for $1 million and went into biscuits. The business never looked back.

In the 1930s a British business was established and the family went back into bread. About a third of all British bread now comes from ABF. At the beginning of World War II Weston's father wrote out a cheque for £100,000 to replace the first 15 Spitfires downed in the Battle of Britain.

The present chairman is renowned for his caution. In 1989 the company was sitting on a cash mountain worth £800 million. In the wake of the 1987 stock market crash, Weston pulled out of a takeover bid for S & W Berisford, owner of British Sugar.

An intensely private man who shuns the limelight, Weston lists his hobbies as gardening, tennis and walking. *Business* magazine describes him as one of the ten industrialists closest to the Prime Minister in 1989.

Younger brother Galen Weston (29/10/40) runs the American operations of ABF from Toronto, though he is active on the British social scene, playing polo with the royal family.

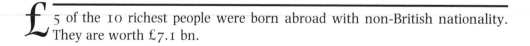

£ 5 of the 10 richest people were born abroad with non-British nationality. They are worth £7.1 bn.

# The Moores family
# £1,670m

## *Pools magnates*

dob JM 25/1/1896

*Sir John Moores*

Sir John Moores founded Littlewoods Pools in 1923. Today the business is the largest private company in Britain, making profits of £62 million in 1989, a small decline on 1987. It has branched out into 175 stores and mail order, but the pools, played by 12 million people every week, remains the base of the fortune. At the end of the 1980s the stores side of the business suffered severely from the Tory government's attempt to squeeze inflation out of the economy by increasing interest rates. Over 1,700 staff were made redundant in 1989.

Moores left school at 14 to work as a post-office messenger, later showing interest in telegraphy. In World War I he served as a wireless operator. The pools venture was started with two partners and paid out a £2.12s.0d dividend initially (against today's £1.5 million top prize). It was not an immediate success and Moores bought out his two colleagues. That was in 1923. By 1932 he had made his first million.

The Moores family of 4 sons and 19 grandchildren live in Merseyside. Sir John, a keen Everton Football Club supporter all his life, used to watch virtually every match. His brother Cecil, the driving force behind the pools side of the business, died in 1989. The second and third generation of the family are believed to be keen on floating the company on the stock market to realise some of their enormous wealth.

# Lord Sainsbury and David Sainsbury £1,568m

*Grocers*

dob JS 2/11/27   DS 24/10/40

Britain's biggest and most successful supermarket chain began in 1869, when John Sainsbury opened a shop in Drury Lane, selling milk, butter and eggs. The first supermarket was opened in Lewisham in 1955 when rationing, introduced during World War II, ended.

By the end of the 1980s, 6.5 million customers were using the 250

*Lord Sainsbury*

Sainsbury supermarkets every week. Annual sales were forecast to top £7 billion in 1990–1.

Sir John, great-grandson of the founder, is chairman while his cousin David, Lord Sainsbury, is deputy chairman. The family control around 39% of Sainsbury shares, which were floated on the stock market in 1973.

Sir John's other great passion is supporting the arts. He is chairman of the Royal Opera House, and is married to Anya Linden, a former dancer with the Royal Ballet. The family is funding the £50 million extension to the National Gallery.

David is a founder member of the Social Democratic Party, and remained loyal to David Owen after the split over merging with the Liberals. The continuing existence of the SDP depends largely on David Sainsbury's willingness to fund its operation, and that in turn appears to depend on David Owen's willingness to stay in politics. Tim Sainsbury, Sir John's younger brother, is Conservative MP for Hove and serves as a junior defence minister in the Thatcher government.

**£** The 10 richest people in Britain are worth £22.9 bn, or 41% of the total wealth.

4 of the 10 are peers; the 5th is a knight.

1 of the 10 richest people – the richest single person in Britain – is a woman.

# Lord Samuel Vestey and Edmund Vestey  £1,420m

*Food producers*

dob SV 19/3/41

The Vestey family fortune derived from mass-producing food for the burgeoning British population in the late 19th century. The Liverpool-based Vestey brothers built up vast cattle ranches and cold storage facilities round the world. They then acquired their own shipping lines to transport the food and, in Dewhursts, their own butcher's shops in which to sell it. Dewhursts' 1,400 shops are doing well with new investment and aggressive management. This has all helped to increase the Vestey fortune by some £200 million in 1989 alone.

*Lord Samuel Vestey*

*Edmund Vestey*

The two cousins, great-grandson and grandson of the founders, live in style. Twice married, Lord Vestey has a 4,500-acre estate, Stowell Park, in Gloucestershire. He is a keen player and patron of the game of polo, belonging to a select band of enthusiasts which includes Prince Charles. Edmund has three homes, including a 100,000-acre estate in Sutherland, which once belonged to the Duke of Westminster. He is joint master of the Puckeridge and Thurlow Foxhounds, and a keen huntsman.

The Vesteys caused considerable controversy in 1980 when a *Sunday Times* investigation revealed that they had paid virtually no tax for 60 years. In 1981 the Inland Revenue took steps to plug the loophole but a leading firm of tax specialists say that it is still possible to remit unlimited sums of money to UK residents, tax free and without breaking any laws, if proper provisions are made. As in the Vestey case, overseas trusts form the basis of the provision they would recommend.

*John Paul Getty II*

# John Paul Getty II  £1,350m

*Philanthropist heir to oil industry fortune*

dob 9/7/32

More English than the English, American-born John Paul Getty II is best known for his charitable work. In recent years he has given away around £100 million to various causes, including the National Gallery (£50 million) and the British Film Institute (£20 million). He loves watching cricket videos and his passion for the game is reflected in his donations to cricket grounds such as Lord's and Trent Bridge, to help with ground improvements. He has a box at Lord's and can boast membership of the Marylebone Cricket Club (MCC).

Mick Jagger, the pop star, introduced Getty to the game when they were neighbours in Chelsea's exclusive Cheyne Walk. Today, cricket stars like Alan Knott, Colin Cowdrey, Peter May and Derek Randall are frequent visitors at his 1,700-acre estate in Buckinghamshire.

Mrs Thatcher recognised his charitable work by awarding him an honorary knighthood in 1986. He would have taken up British citizenship had his accountants not advised against it for tax reasons.

Getty, eldest son of the legendary oil magnate of the same name, was born in California. He fought in the Korean War as an infantry corporal but later turned to drugs and was a heroin addict. In 1973 he came to Britain and has lived here ever since, gradually mellowing with age. He even enjoys a good English roast beef and Yorkshire pudding washed down with beer.

His fortune really prospered in 1984 when Texaco, the giant American oil company, bought Getty Oil, the company founded by his father, for over $10 billion. Getty's share was worth nearly £900 million in cash. Invested, this generates an income of over £100 million a year. Not even his huge charitable contributions can stop his wealth simply piling up, and he is now worth around £1,350 million. A recluse for many years, he is gradually coming out into the limelight and has started giving press interviews. Apart from cricket, his main hobbies are watching films and collecting rare books.

# Robert Maxwell   £1,100m

*Publisher*

dob 10/6/23

Son of a poor Czech labourer murdered by the Gestapo, Jan Ludwick Hoch escaped to Britain in the war. He joined the army, changed his name and, promoted to captain, won the Military Cross for gallantry. In 1948, he set up the Pergamon Press and later became a Labour MP.

Despite losing his Parliamentary seat in 1970 and once being branded by a government report as 'not a person who can be relied on to exercise proper stewardship of a publicly quoted company', Maxwell has thrived on an 18-hour day of tireless wheeling and dealing. Pergamon's scientific journals provided the basis for his fortune, but he is now building Maxwell Communications into one of the largest media conglomerates in the world, embracing everything from printing to newspapers and satellite television.

Home is Headington Hill Hall near Oxford, rented from Oxfordshire County Council; hence Maxwell's boast that he is a council tenant. He lists his hobbies as football and chess, but many suspect that it is the oxygen of publicity that keeps him going.

Recent years, especially 1989, have been good for Maxwell. He has revived the lacklustre *Mirror* newspaper group, acquired in 1984 for £113 million, to the point where it would be worth some £500 million if floated on the stock market. Maxwell intends to float the *Mirror*, though retaining a 50% stake himself.

He is a huge donor to charities in the UK, Israel, Africa and eastern Europe.

# Charles Feeney   £1,020m

*Retailer*

Charles Feeney, who moved to London in the 1970s, began his life as an entrepreneur while he was a student at Cornell University in New York, studying at the school of hotel administration. He supplemented his GI Bill (a Pentagon bursary for ex-army veterans) by selling sandwiches to fellow students in their halls of residence. In the late 1950s he joined a former classmate, Robert Miller, to start a business in Europe selling duty-free alcohol and European cars to American servicemen returning home. Later they expanded the same operation into the Far East. In 1961 and 1962 they made their most significant move by opening two duty-free shops at Hong Kong and Honolulu international airports.

When the US government changed the regulations on duty-free sales for servicemen, the pair came close to going out of business. But the two airport shops saved them, particularly after the 1964 Tokyo Olympics which resulted in a huge surge in Japanese tourism. Today Duty Free Shoppers is the largest duty-free retailer in the world and its several Hong Kong shops make it the biggest retailer in the colony. Sales of Duty Free Shoppers are thought to have passed the $2 billion mark, making it four times larger than any other group in the business.

By paying generous commission to Japanese tour guides to take their parties to his stores, Feeney has made a fortune from the growing purchasing power of the yen. By concentrating on well-known high-quality brands, they are able to achieve high profit margins and also wrest generous credit terms from their suppliers. The brands they market – Hermes ties, Gucci shoes, Fendi bags, Dunhill lighters, Wedgwood china and Chivas Regal whisky – are world renowned.

Since the early 1970s, Feeney and Miller have handed over day-to-day management of the Duty Free operation to professional managers, to concentrate their own efforts on investing their enormous profits in other ventures. Feeney's vehicle is a Bermuda-based company, General Atlantic Holdings, which has invested in dozens of businesses in Europe and Asia. He is considered a long-term investor and has recently targeted computer software companies. He shuns glamour stocks, preferring a company with steady sales and which he considers is undervalued. Recently Feeney took a near 10% stake in Management Science America, an Atlanta-based group.

Apart from the Bermuda company, he also runs hotel and clothes chains in America and the Far East, magazines and shops in Britain and has oil and gas interests. One of his investments, the Inter-Pacific group, runs the Pacific Islands Club, a sort of Club Med for youthful but wealthy Japanese holidaymakers.

Feeney left his Hong Kong base in the early 1970s to live in London, with his French wife and five children. A noted workaholic, he is also extremely frugal despite his wealth, and flies economy class round the world. He does not care a fig about his appearance and one business associate told *Forbes Magazine*: 'The first time I met Feeney, I recall he had a safety pin holding up his pants.'

 31 of the richest 400 were born abroad with non-British nationality. They are worth £11.1 bn or 19% of the total worth of the 400.

# Gopi and Sri Hinduja   £1,000m
## *International traders*

Four reclusive brothers control one of the largest and most secretive trading empires in the world, stretching from India via the Middle East to Switzerland and Britain. The Hindujas – two of whom live and work in London – inherited the business from their father Parmanand Deepchand Hinduja. Born in 1901, he started as a trader in Bombay, India's trading centre, and developed strong links with Iran, where he thrived under the Shah, supplying many of the country's import requirements and handling Iranian exports.

Parmanand lost his eldest son at the early age of 32, but the other four

*Gopi Hinduja*

*Sri Hinduja*

THE BILLIONAIRES

came into the business. When he died in 1971 they expanded it into
new industries and other parts of Asia. Among their Indian interests are
telecommunications and Ashok Leyland, the Indian bus and truck maker,
which they acquired in 1989. At the time the Hindujas believed that the
Ashok purchase would act as a cornerstone for future investment they
planned in the transport field, including cars, hovercraft, shipping and
airlines. They are also important players in the power industry in India, and
have signed an agreement with Bechtel, the giant American construction
company, for joint venture projects in electricity supply.

The brothers developed close links with Rajiv Gandhi, the former prime
minister of India (where influence at ministerial level is vital for winning
contracts). They also have access to the foreign exchange vital for re-
equipping Ashok's factories. In March 1989 the Hindujas also gained full
control of the Gulf Oil Trading Company, when they acquired a stake
previously held by Sheikh Yamani, the former Saudi oil minister.

The two brothers in Britain, Sri and Gopi, live in a large house in exclusive
Carlton Gardens in London. They have been photographed meeting Mrs
Thatcher and the Prince of Wales in recognition of their substantial work
for charities through their Hinduja Foundation. Another brother is based
in Bombay and the fourth in Geneva. They also have large homes in New
York and Tehran.

All the brothers are dedicated to business and hard work. Gopi's daughter
was married over Christmas 1989 in Bombay. There were some 3,000
guests at the week-long celebrations, which one observer said were conducted 'like money was going out of fashion'.

£ The total land area of the UK is about 49 m acres.
3.5 m acres is urban or metropolitan land under bricks and mortar. 56 m
people live on these 3.5 m acres, with a maximum of about .065 of an acre each.

An acre of rural Worcestershire is worth about £2,000. An acre of Kensington in
west London is worth close to £9.3 m. An acre of Mayfair in central London is
worth some £23.5 m.

The approximate value of non-urban and non-metropolitan land is £98 bn. The
estimated value of all urban and metropolitan land is £350 bn. Britain's GNP for
1990 is expected to be around £509 bn.

There are huge variations in the estimates. Ours are based on the figures in the
rules of engagement.

# 2

# THE
# SUPER-RICH

## £100m and more

# George Livanos  £930m
## *International shipping industrialist*

This Greek shipowner has lived in London for a number of years, though he also has a private Aegean island, a Swiss home and a villa in the Bahamas. Inheriting an estimated £150 million fortune from his father in 1963 in the shape of the largest Greek shipping fleet of 60 vessels, George has now expanded the fortune by shrewd investment in such areas as art.

Livanos, a regular Concorde traveller and devotee of exclusive nightclubs, caused a stir in 1966 when he married the 17-year-old daughter of a Greek tobacco millionaire in Paris. He met his wife-to-be by accident at the Athens villa of the late Aristotle Onassis, and they were married soon after. He had until then been a regular figure on the London social scene and was at one stage tipped to marry Princess Sophie of Greece. The first of his three daughters was born in 1968, but it was not until 1980 that his son and heir was born in New York.

Livanos's family has been struck by tragedy. In 1970 his sister Eugenie, the wife of Stavros Niarchos, another famous Greek shipping magnate, died suddenly on the island of Spetsopoula. His other sister, Tina, who was at one time married to Aristotle Onassis, married the Marquess of Blandford, heir to the then Duke of Marlborough, in 1961. But the marriage ended in 1971, just a year before the Marquess succeeded to the title. Tina later married Niarchos but she died in 1974 of a lung ailment.

In 1983 Livanos bought a 75% stake in the famous British firm of Aston Martin, whose cars grace James Bond films and are favourites of the Prince of Wales. In 1987 he sold most of this stake to Ford, retaining a small share in the business. He is now thought to be keen to sell some of his ships, with ship prices moving up sharply in recent times. Six large tankers, worth well over $210 million, were believed to be up for sale in early 1990 according to *Lloyd's List*, the respected shipping paper.

£ The shareholdings of the richest 400 are worth approximately £25 bn and they own works of art worth approximately £5 bn.
The market capitalisation of the UK Stock Exchange is about £2,000 bn on an average p/e ratio of 12.5.

# Sir James Goldsmith    £870m
## *Financier*

dob 26/2/33

Gambling, whether in a fashionable London club or on the world's stock markets, has been the *métier* of Sir James Goldsmith. The son of a wealthy Tory MP and a French mother, he left Eton at 17, having already made a small £8,000 fortune from betting on horses.

His first brush with the gossip columns came at age 20, when he eloped to Scotland to marry María Isabel Patiño, daughter of a Bolivian tin magnate and heiress to a £75 million fortune. She died four months later, giving birth to a daughter.

In the 1960s and 1970s he was active building up a food empire, but kept his fascination for the gossips with his gambling exploits at the Clermont Club. He ranked Jim Slater (q.v.), John Aspinall (q.v.) and Jacob Rothschild (q.v.), among his close circle of friends.

In the 1980s he became one of the stars on Wall Street, buying and selling large companies with the same energy he had spent on gaming tables, but far more profitably. In 1982 he bought Diamond Corporation for £246 million and sold it for three times as much two years later. Even when he failed to take over companies, he made a handsome profit on the deals.

Goldsmith shrewdly anticipated the October 1987 stock market crash by selling all his major holdings two months previously when the market had reached an all-time high. In the year 1989 Sir James made his mark on the British financial scene. Through his Hoylake consortium, he launched Britain's biggest takeover bid – the £13 billion assault on BAT. Though the bid lapsed at the end of that year, it demonstrated that Goldsmith's appetite for buying and selling companies had not diminished after a decade in America. Goldsmith formally abandoned the bid early in 1990.

Apart from his business activities in Britain, Goldsmith is also busy developing a huge complex on the western coast of Mexico. The estate, which includes tropical rain forests, unspoilt lagoons and a volcano, was the setting for the council of war early in 1989 at which Goldsmith and his two fellow BAT stalkers, Jacob Rothschild and Kerry Packer, planned the takeover bid.

His private life is colourful, with a former wife (he says his relationship with her has not altered 'one iota' since divorce) in Paris, a wife, Lady Annabel (formerly Birley, whose previous husband named a famous nightclub, Annabel's, after her), and a mistress in New York. He has had seven children by four women.

---

# Sir John and Sir Adrian Swire    £672m
## *Shipping*

dob JS 28/2/27    AS 15/2/32

In 1816 John Swire, a Yorkshireman, established his own company in Liverpool to take advantage of its growing world trade. By 1867 the company was established in the Far East and China. Despite extensive damage to their shipping, refining and dockyard interests in the World War II, the Swires rebuilt and reinvested.

Today the Swire business includes ships, the Cathay Pacific airline, insurance, property and hotels and it is one of the largest companies in Hong Kong.

In 1988 the still privately run John Swire group produced after-tax profits of

*Sir Adrian Swire*

nearly £91 million, a sharp increase on the figure for 1987. The two Swire brothers sit on the board and control nearly 60% of the shares between them directly or in trusts.

Sir John, the elder brother, is honorary president of the company and lives in Kent. Both brothers were educated at Eton and University College, Oxford. Sir John served in the Irish Guards in Palestine and, in 1950, joined the family business, working his way up to become chairman in 1966. He is married and has three children.

Sir Adrian served in the Coldstream Guards from 1950 to 1952 and later with the RAF Volunteer Reserves and the Royal Hong Kong AAF. He married Lady Judith Compton, eldest daughter of the 6th Marquess of Northampton (q.v.), in 1970. In 1980 he moved to an Oxfordshire manor house, and is a prominent member of his small village community. He attends services at the village church when at home and has supported various church projects in recent years, including landscaping and tree planting. Sir Adrian is a popular figure in the village and occasionally drinks in the local pub, the Star. He has a private plane which is often seen in the sky above the village.

# Gerald Ronson
# £548m

*Property and*
*petrol station owner*

Ronson's Heron group is Britain's second largest private company embracing self-service filling stations, house building and the HR Owen car dealership.

Ronson left school at 15 to work in a furniture business with his father Henry, the son of Russian Jewish refugees who fled tsarist pogroms. In 1956 they moved into property and later into petrol.

Ronson works a six-day week from his Marylebone headquarters, and has built Heron into a £1 billion per annum turnover business. In the year to the end of March 1989 the group made after-tax profits of £54.8 million, valuing Ronson at some £548 million. But City success has eluded him. In 1982 and again in 1983 he lost two bid battles by refusing to pay what he considered over the odds for companies.

He lives a quiet private life in a luxury north London home with his wife Gail, a former model, and four daughters. His only indulgence is a penchant for luxury cigars and Bentleys from HR Owen. He has a £10 million yacht called *My Gail III*, complete with an enormous 7-foot jacuzzi. It is based in the Mediterranean. In 1989 Ronson held his 50th birthday party on board surrounded by his close friends and trying to forget the problems of his trial over his alleged role in the Guinness affair. Ronson is a well-known supporter of charities such as the National Society for the Prevention of Cruelty to Children. He is no lover of publicity and is said to have shunned a stock market quotation for his company in order to avoid unwelcome media attention. He and his colleagues on the Heron board did, however, give themselves a 270% wage rise in 1989.

# David and Frederick Barclay   £500m
## Hotel and property owners

dob 27/10/34 (twins)

Known as Britain's most secretive business men, the Barclay twins were born in London of Scottish parents. They began as estate agents and later moved into property and hotels in the early 1960s. They specialised in converting Bayswater boarding houses into hotels. The small dapper twins survived the 1973–4 property crash and prospered in the 1980s. A series of quick-fire deals culminated in the takeover of the famous Ellerman shipping and property empire in 1983. They transformed the business and sold the shipping line back to its management.

In 1982 they bought a chain of temperance hotels. Within a year they sold it, apart from a large tract of land for housing, making a substantial profit on the deal. In 1983 they bought three railway hotels in London from British Rail for £17 million and sold two of them in 1985 for £37 million.

Today they employ over 4,000 people and own luxury hotels in London, New York and Monte Carlo, as well as breweries and a travel agency. They made a £12 million profit from the sale of a stake in the IC Gas business in 1987 when they abandoned plans to bid £750 million for the whole group.

David became chairman of the family business as he was born ten minutes before Frederick. They are identical twins, distinguishable only by having their hair parted on different sides. David is regarded as the dominant one and works in the business with his son Aidan.

In 1990 they offered to buy Canova's sculpture *The Three Graces* for £7.6 million to save it from being sold to a foreign buyer and shipped abroad.

# Richard Branson   £488m
## Music and entertainment entrepreneur

dob 18/7/50

The sweaters, jeans, flowing hair and beard, along with an office on a houseboat on the Regent's Canal, suggest a hippie locked in a 1960s timewarp. But Richard Branson – the man charged by Mrs Thatcher with cleaning up Britain – has a shrewd and tough business brain, despite not being able to work a calculator.

After a private school education at Stowe, which he left at 16 with just three O levels, he founded *Student* magazine. Businesses followed quickly: Virgin Mail Order in 1969, Virgin record shop in 1971 and the Virgin label in 1973. His first signing of a recording contract was Mike Oldfield's album *Tubular Bells*. This LP sold 5 million copies. In 1984 he started the cut-price Virgin Atlantic airline. He also owns nightclubs. In 1986 he took the Virgin group public, but, disenchanted with the City, has since made it a private company again.

Branson's unbusinesslike appearance did not prevent him making a deal in 1989 with the inscrutable and utterly conventional Japanese group Fukisankei, which enormously increased his personal wealth. For a sum of £96 million the Japanese took a 25% stake in Branson's Virgin group, valuing the rest of the company at nearly £300 million. Virgin Atlantic, Branson's highly successful airline, is also valued at around £200 million, with the Japanese again interested in taking a stake. Early in 1990 the Seibu Saison hotel group paid £36m for a 10% stake in the airline.

Branson lives in fashionable Ladbroke Grove, London, and has an Oxfordshire mansion complete with recording studio for the weekends. He even owns a Virgin Island in the Caribbean, which he will rent out for $3,500 a day.

He is a great practical joker and has tried a series of hair-raising stunts including ballooning across the Atlantic and a power boat crossing competing for the coveted Blue Riband. In November 1989 he planned to cross the Pacific by balloon but his dreams were shattered when the £3 million balloon ripped and caught fire. In December he finally married his long-time girlfriend Joan Templeman on their Caribbean island. Whether she can persuade him to 'settle' down to the conventional life is unclear.

# Earl Cadogan £450m
## *Landowner*

dob 13/2/14

The Cadogan family owns 90 acres of fashionable Chelsea in London. The holdings came as a result of the marriages of three families in the 18th century, families whose names will be familiar to Chelsea residents today: the Cadogans, the Cheynes and the Sloanes. But it was the 5th Earl, one of Queen Victoria's ministers, who turned Chelsea from a slum into a top residential area.

The present Earl has a distinguished war record, having won the Military Cross in the Western Desert in 1943. He fought single-handed in his tank after it was disabled and caught fire, then he helped evacuate wounded crew members under heavy German gunfire.

Today the Earl, who was a Jockey Club steward and owns some of the finest grouse moors in Scotland, is semi-retired. He lives in Chelsea and on the Scottish estates in Perthshire. The Cadogan estates are run by his son, Viscount Chelsea, formerly a merchant banker. He has homes in London and Oxfordshire. Chelsea re-married in 1989.

# Viscount Portman £400m
## *Landowner*

dob 22/4/34

The Portman fortune stems from 100 acres of London around Portman Square and Oxford Street. The estate was granted by Henry VIII to Lord Chief Justice Portman in 1533. It was further extended in Queen Mary's reign.

The 9th Viscount, who inherited the title from his uncle in 1967, is a Hereford-shire farmer with over 3,000 acres of farmland. He also enjoys music, and plays five instruments with considerable virtuosity.

Over the years the family estates have been gradually diminished by death duties. In the 1940s some £7.5 million had to be raised on the death of the 7th Viscount. This led to the sale of a 3,800-acre Dorset estate and 26 acres in London, including 221b Baker Street, the 'home' of Sherlock Holmes. In 1955 the Portman family trust was created with an initial value of around £4 million.

# David Thompson £400m

*Food processing industrialist*

dob 4/3/36

Until 1985 few people outside Smithfield meat market had heard of Hillsdown Holdings. But when it was floated on the stock market in 1985, 100,000 people wanted to buy the shares. This stampede made David Thompson, a shy north London business man, a multi-millionaire.

Hillsdown, which produces everything from Buxted chickens to Smedley peas, was founded in the mid-1970s, when Thompson merged the meat business he inherited from his father with some property interests of a solicitor, Harry Solomon. The business was named after Thompson's luxury north London home.

In April 1987 Thompson sold half his stake in Hillsdown for £145 million. Since then, he has sold his entire stake and moved into property companies. He is currently chairman of Glentree, a north London estate agency.

Outside work, his great passion is the turf and he owns two Newmarket studs, Cheveley Park and Sandwich. The best price Thompson achieved for a yearling

*Viscount Portman*

was 42,000 guineas. He also owns a controlling stake in the Royal Windsor racecourse, the Queen's favourite. The value of his racing interests alone is over £30 million.

His son Richard handles the family's finances when he is not chairing Queen's Park Rangers Football Club. The family are now the biggest shareholder in Quinta da Largo, a luxury holiday centre and golf course in the Algarve.

Richard, an extremely shy bachelor, is terrified of being pursued by a 'gold digger' and tries to hide his wealth from girlfriends.

# Viscount Cowdray   £352m

*Financier*

dob 10/2/27

Under heavy fire in the retreat to Dunkirk, Lord Cowdray took over from his wounded driver and, with a mangled arm, drove to the beaches. This was an early display of the dogged determination that characterises so many of the Pearson family.

The Cowdray fortune had been built up by his grandfather, Weetman Pearson, in the late 19th-century construction boom. Pearson built tunnels in New York and London, Dover harbour, and railways in Spain and China. He drained swamps around Mexico City and dredged channels in Egypt and the West Indies. Banking and newspaper interests soon followed.

The present Lord Cowdray took over the reins after the war and the family still controls over 20% of the Pearson Group, which is worth around £1.7 billion.

Lord Cowdray, formerly an expert shot and a keen polo player despite his wartime injury, lives modestly in Cowdray Park, his 17,000-acre estate in Sussex. He prefers beer to whisky and once said he hated fancy food, preferring 'cottage pie and meat and potatoes'. He also has a 60,000-acre estate in Aberdeenshire.

His sons and daughters have proved colourful. His heir, the Hon. Michael Pearson, was an active member of the London social and gaming scene, often betting for high stakes against the likes of James Goldsmith. His elder daughter Lucy was briefly married to the Argentine socialite Hector Basualdo while his younger daughter Rosanna, formerly *The Independent*'s inner cities correspondent, married a Jamaican reggae performer. Lord and Lady Cowdray did not attend the wedding.

The family business, which has been regarded as a prime candidate for takeover, has been described as a collection of priceless jewels. These range from *The Financial Times* to the merchant bank Lazards, and Royal Doulton, the china group. It is run by Viscount Blakenham, aged 51, Lord Cowdray's nephew. The group also tried to own the Château Latour vineyard.

# Lord Cayzer   £350m
*Finance and shipping magnate*

dob 21/1/10

In 1878 the Clan shipping line was launched by a one-time shipping clerk, Charles Cayzer. The line grew to take over Union Castle and diversified into finance in the 1950s and 1960s.

Lord Cayzer, grandson of the founder, heads the family which until recently had a 31% stake in the group (now called British & Commonwealth Shipping). This was reduced to 4.9% in June 1987, raising £427 million.

Cayzer is an ardent supporter of the Conservative Party, and lavishes thousands of pounds on party funds every year.

He has homes in Mayfair and Suffolk, and lists golf and shooting as his hobbies. In recent years Cayzer has been in the news over plans to redevelop his Redhill airfield into an executive jet base. The move infuriated the local Tiger flying club, whose membership includes Princes Charles, Philip and Andrew.

# Paul McCartney £350m
## *Musician*

dob 18/6/42

The golden touch which has made Paul McCartney allegedly the highest-earning pop musician of all time deserted him for the latter part of the 1980s. Apart from the hit 'Pipes of Peace', his only release in recent years was 'Flowers in the Dirt' in 1989. Yet McCartney can afford to rest comfortably on his laurels and on the revenue from the extraordinary string of successes he enjoyed with the Beatles and as a solo performer.

The key to McCartney's wealth lies not simply in the sales of his records, but in his activities as a songwriter and owner of music copyrights. He has always been mindful of the value of his songwriting. Until 1969, the rights to Beatles songs composed by Lennon and McCartney were owned by Northern Songs, in which both writers were substantial shareholders. In 1969, prior to ATV taking control

of the company for £10 million, John Lennon was surprised to find that while his holding in Northern was still the original 644,000 shares, McCartney had quietly built up his stock to 751,000 shares. 'It was a matter of investing in something you believed in instead of supermarkets and furniture stores,' McCartney explained at the time.

The ownership of Northern Songs subsequently passed to Robert Holmes à Court, and eventually, in 1985, to Michael Jackson for £47 million. Even without owning the catalogue, however, McCartney still collects composer's royalties amounting to some 3% of the retail price of every Beatles record sold, as well as Performing Rights Society royalties for radio plays of the songs. This, of course, also includes the countless 'cover' versions of Beatle hits: 'Yesterday', for example, is said to be the most recorded song ever, with 1,600 different versions made between 1965 and 1986.

McCartney continues, of course, to own the rights to all songs written by him since his Beatles days, and over the years he has invested in a portfolio of other publishing catalogues. Perhaps the most lucrative among these is the Buddy Holly song-publishing catalogue. But he also owns the copyrights to such Broadway musicals as *Grease*, *A Chorus Line*, *Hello Dolly* and *Mame*, as well as more obscure titles like *Lily of Laguna* and *Meet Me at the Cowshed*.

For all his wealth, McCartney leads a steadfastly modest and unostentatious life. He has a five-bedroom farmhouse in Sussex, known locally as Paulditz because of its security arrangements – and his three children, Mary, Stella and James, have been educated at state schools. His wife Linda places great store on the unassuming values of 'a good breakfast, and nice neighbours'. The family also own an estate on Mull of Kintyre, which inspired his hit record of the same name.

He commutes to London by train. He rarely goes out, preferring to eat home-cooked vegetarian stews and drink mineral water. He drives a battered Range Rover. The local hunt is banned from his 160-acre estate.

He is chairman of his own company, MPL Communications Ltd, which embraces 17 different companies responsible for song-publishing, films and video. MPL returned a profit of £234,444 for activities in the year ending December 1987, showing a retained profit of £3.8 million.

While his career has suffered setbacks in recent years, not least in the failure of the self-financed film *Give My Regards to Broad Street*, a report published in 1987 alleged that McCartney was continuing to accrue royalties at the rate of £3,750 an hour – £62.50 a minute – for an average 30-hour working week.

In the 1960s McCartney was a frequent supporter of 'underground' causes such as the newspaper *International Times*, as well as lavishing hundreds of thousands of pounds on ill-fated ventures through the Apple foundation. He continues to give away large sums of money each year to charity, but always with the condition of anonymity. The offer is withdrawn if there is the slightest hint of publicity – a fact, perhaps, which has contributed to a reputation for parsimoniousness.

His 1990 world tour, McCartney's first for 13 years, is estimated to have earned him £12 million profit, and he was expected to make £43 million, all told for the year.

# Sighismund Berger £330m
*Property owner*

dob 21/8/21

Reckoned to be Britain's largest residential landlord with 100,000 rented homes, the secretive Berger empire was founded by the late Gerson Berger. He was born in Poland and lived in Romania until he came to Britain when he was 30.

During the war, Berger made a fortune from making and selling torch batteries, which were then in short supply. He used much of the profits to buy the lives of Romanian Jews from the Romanian government at £2,000 each. Spared the gas chambers, many made their way to Palestine.

In the East End of London he was called the bean man because his first job was selling beans in the street. Later he was to become a leading member of the Sotmarer sect of Orthodox Jews.

His son, Sighismund Berger, came to Britain before the war and ran the torch factory with iron discipline. He now runs the Berger business empire which is based in north London. Berish Berger, his American-educated son, who is in his late 20s, is also in the business, part of which is now quoted on the Stock Exchange via a company called Palmerston Holdings.

In spite of the secrecy with which they surround their operations the Bergers have been personally criticised on several occasions by tenants' groups complaining about the management of their properties.

# Jack and Fred Walker £330m
*Ex-industrialists*

Jack Walker's father started a small sheet metal business in Blackburn in 1945. When he died in 1951, Jack took over the company at the age of 21 after little formal education. He had left school at 14. In the late 1950s he took the business, C. Walker, out of sheet metal and into steel stockholding. He never looked back. In 1956 sales stood at £46,000. In 1988, they were £623 million with £48 million profits. By then the company had 3,400 employees, spread around 50 British sites. In October 1989 the business was sold for £330 million to British Steel – the largest price ever paid for a private British company. The money goes to Jack, now aged 59, who lives in Jersey, and his elder brother Fred, aged 63, who still lives in Lancashire.

The Walker success was built on establishing a nationwide chain of offices in the 1960s. They also acquired the steel stockholding interests of GKN, which doubled the size of C. Walker. Before the sale to British Steel, the two groups had built up a close working relationship.

British Steel was said to give Walker special rates, and is believed to have helped in the purchase of the GKN operation after the government restricted its own steel stockholding plans.

The two brothers were very hard-working and 'made some shrewd moves. Jack had no inhibitions and got to big-name customers early. He got the taste to be biggest and he employed good people. He is very straightforward and down to earth,' one rival told *The Financial Times* just after the sale to British Steel.

Jack had already retired by this stage, and was simply a consultant to the group. Fred, the chairman, has indicated his intention of following his brother into retirement in the near future. The two will concentrate on building up Jack's airline which flies out of Jersey to the continent. The 50 Walker offices also remain with the brothers. Despite his wealth, Jack lives modestly and drives an old Renault round the island.

# Harry Hyams
## £320m
*Property owner*

dob 2/1/28

Controversy has always dogged Harry Hyams, son of an East End bookmaker. Owner of Ramsbury, a 600-acre estate in Wiltshire (bought from Lord Rootes, the motor magnate) complete with art treasures and some of the finest shooting in the country, Hyams is best remembered for one urban building, Centre Point in London. This remained unoccupied for 13 years and Hyams regularly sued – and won – if any paper dared to allege that it was being kept empty deliberately. The Centre Point saga fuelled Hyams' obsessive desire for secrecy. He used to hold annual meetings on New Year's Day and refused entry to the press. As a result, several financial journalists held shares in the company simply to be able to question him. But he does not always have his own way. Ex-employees have won cases of unfair dismissal against Hyams.

His yacht, *Shemara*, has also hit legal minefields. First Hyams tried to cancel the purchase from Sir Bernard Docker, the industrialist. That failed and later Hyams was locked in dispute over repairs carried out by the Vosper Thorneycroft yard. In fourteen years, the yacht did not leave the yard.

Hyams' major stake in Oldham Estates (bought in 1959 for £50,000) was taken over for £150 million in 1988.

---

# Lord Howard de Walden
# £310m
*Landowner*

dob 27/11/12

London's Harley Street and many of the consulting rooms around it are owned by Lord Howard de Walden through his private company, Howard de Walden Estates. The company owns 110 acres of prime London land and some 1,200 houses, which are mainly used as smart offices.

The London estate was acquired in 1710 and Lord Howard de Walden inherited in 1946. He is a member of the Jockey Club, and has been senior steward three times. The three studs he owns – in Yorkshire, Newmarket and Berkshire – reflect his passion for racing.

He lives on a Berkshire estate and also has a Mayfair flat.

With no male heir, his four daughters by Countess Irene Harrach, whom he married in 1934, are all named as co-heiresses. She died in 1975. Three years later he married his second wife Gillian, Viscountess Mountgarret.

Educated at Eton and Magdalene College, Cambridge, Lord Howard de Walden has a splendid country mansion set in its own estate at Avington, on the edge of Hungerford Common in Berkshire. He is a friend of Lord Carnarvon, the Queen's racing manager, who looks after her equine interests from his estate at Highclere Castle about eight miles away on the other side of Newbury.

Lord Howard de Walden's estate stretches over 3,000 acres of some of the best arable farming land in the Thames Valley.

A multi-millionaire, he bought the estate in the 1950s. When he took over, he ordered the bulldozing of all the historic and picturesque farm buildings and some cottages to streamline the farm and provide more land for crops. He pulled down the Manor House, which had a ballroom, and moved into one of the big farmhouses on the estate called Avington Manor, which became his country seat.

He keeps cattle and sheep but mainly concentrates on corn and other crops. The estate is one of the most famous in the area for top-class pheasant and partridge shoots during the November to January season. He employs his own gamekeepers and also controls a stretch of the River Kennet through the estate, one of the most sought-after trout-fishing rivers in Britain, where a rod can cost £1,000 a session. But he reserves most of the shooting and fishing for his wealthy friends.

He is described by locals as 'aloof' but they also say he can be charming.

# Viscount Rothermere    £308m
*Newspaper publisher*

dob 27/9/25

Britain's most private press baron enjoys the good life but still keeps a very shrewd eye on the family business founded by his grandfather, Alfred Harmsworth, the legendary newspaper man. Rothermere may not have the ego of a Beaverbrook or a Maxwell, but he has seen off both the *Express* and the *Mirror* publishers. The *Daily Mail* and latterly the *Mail on Sunday* (which Rothermere supported courageously through four years of heavy losses until it became immensely profitable) have carved out a dominant position in the middle market of the British press. Rothermere managed to sink Robert Maxwell's *London Daily News* by relaunching his own *Evening News* as a spoiler. Typically, this was a spur-of-the-moment Rothermere decision which he ordered to be put into effect instantly.

Rothermere's strong support for the Tory cause is reflected in the editorial columns of the *Daily Mail*. His coyness about publicity is in direct contrast to the high-profile party-going activities of his wife, known to gossip columnists as 'Bubbles'. Apart from his main Paris base, Rothermere also has homes in London,

New York, Sussex, Jamaica and Los Angeles. He lists painting, sailing and reading as his hobbies.

In 1989 the *Mail* group moved into its smart new offices in Kensington, and a high-technology printing operation has also been commissioned. The benefits of a lower cost base are now making his newspapers highly profitable again. As a result, Rothermere, through his controlling stake in the Daily Mail and General Trust, has seen his fortune rise sharply to £308 million.

---

# Joe Bamford  £300m
## *Construction equipment manufacturer*

dob 21/6/16

The bright yellow JCB diggers seen on construction sites around the world owe their existence to a down-to-earth Staffordshire business man, Joe Bamford.

He first tried to develop a rival to Brylcream but the problem with his Smartfix was that it turned hair green, 40 years too early for punks. But in 1945 he broke away from the family agricultural business and built odd bits of farm machinery until he hit on the idea of the backhoe loader, with its distinctive arm on the back and bulldozer-style excavator at the front. From then he never looked back.

Today the firm, still entirely controlled by the Bamfords, operates from a modern factory in Staffordshire. It is one of the few British industries to beat its Japanese and American competitors. The firm has never had to borrow a penny and regularly updates its model range. In 1988 it made profits of £15 million. It runs an impressive display team which performs amazing feats of simulated combat and the like with JCBs.

The business is now run by Anthony Bamford, Joe's son. Joe lives in comfortable retirement in Switzerland, though he still comes to England to keep an eye on business. The first digger he ever built is now on proud display at the new factory.

Anthony, a fervent admirer of Mrs Thatcher, recently bought Daylesford in Gloucestershire, one of Britain's finest stately homes, from Baron Henry Thyssen for £12 million. He also owns a 2,500-acre farm in the Midlands and a Barbados property that cost him £1 million in 1979. He beat Alan Bond, the Australian magnate, in the bidding for Daylesford.

Joe educated Anthony at Ampleforth and then at 16 put him to work as an apprentice on the shop floor at Massey-Ferguson. When he was 22 Anthony survived a 100 m.p.h. crash in his racing car.

# Duke of Buccleuch  £300m

*Landowner*

dob 28/9/23

Owning 277,000 acres of Scotland and Northamptonshire would on their own make the fortune of the Duke of Buccleuch, Britain's largest private landowner. But it is the art treasures in his four homes that make him super-rich. They include a Leonardo which is too valuable to insure, so the Duke takes it with him when he moves between houses every three months.

In his Northampton home, Boughton House, there is a set of 37 oil sketches by Van Dyck, as well as works by El Greco and Gainsborough. At Bowhill, near Selkirk, the Duke has more works by Van Dyck, Reynolds, Gainsborough and Canaletto. At the main family seat, Drumlanrig Castle, the single most valuable work is Rembrandt's *Old Woman Reading*. The art treasures are complemented by a superb array of French porcelain and furniture. His fourth home is in London.

The Buccleuch land goes back to the days of Robert Bruce. The Douglas clan, which the Duke heads, was given its land by Bruce as a reward for their support. The present Duke was Conservative MP for North Edinburgh until he succeeded to the title in 1973. The lands are owned through Buccleuch Estates Ltd and Boughton Estates Ltd, in which the Duke and his family own shares.

# Jack Dellal £250m
*Property and general trader*

dob 2/10/23

In 1972 Jack Dellal was paid £58 million by the City banking group Keyser Ullmann for his secondary banking group, Dalton Barton, based in Manchester. 'Black Jack', as he is called by his friends, joined the Keyser board as deputy chairman but resigned in 1974. Dellal had been active in the property finance field, backing such well-known figures as William Stern.

Known as a brilliant wheeler-dealer since his days in Manchester (where he was raised), Dellal has often emerged as a key stock market player, building stakes in groups which he then sells for a profit.

He married an Israeli air hostess in 1952, and they had a son and four daughters. Tragedy struck in 1981 when one daughter, Suzy, died of a drugs overdose. Another daughter, Gabrielle, is making a name for herself as an actress. Jack Dellal sent her to drama school in Los Angeles for four years.

Parted from his wife, Dellal has been spotted by the gossip columnists with attractive younger women on his arm. 'Black Jack' lives in London, and has a farm in Hampshire and a luxury yacht on the Mediterranean. He lists tennis, squash, music and art as his hobbies.

His money-making skills were again revealed in November 1989 when he sold Bush House, home of the BBC World Service, to the Japanese Kato Kagaku company for £130 million. Two years previously he had paid £55 million for the building.

# Richard George and family £250m

*Cereals and food distribution*

dob RG 24/4/44

The George family control Weetabix, the company that makes that famous breakfast cereal and also Alpen, the Swiss muesli-style cereal. Based in the Northamptonshire town of Burton Latimer, Weetabix is a highly profitable operation, making £7.5 million post-tax profits on sales of £139 million in the year to the end of July 1988. But it is the two brand names, Weetabix and Alpen, that really make the company an attractive target for large cereal groups such as Nabisco, who would be willing to pay up to £250 million for it.

Weetabix was launched in Britain in the 1930s by three men, an Australian and two South Africans. But it soon ran into trouble and Frank George, a former mill apprentice, bought them out. George built up Weetabix and also took over Whitworth Holdings, the dried fruit producer, which is based in nearby Wellingborough. His motto was 'make a noise quietly' and the company built up a 20% share of the British cereals market with few people knowing of its existence. He was also a dogged and stubborn manager who refused to take no for an answer. On his death in 1970 he was succeeded as Weetabix chairman by his son, Tony.

Today Richard George, Tony's son, is the chairman of Weetabix. Although the family maintain a very low profile, Weetabix recently launched a three-year sponsorship scheme worth £100,000 for young gymnasts.

£ The richest 400 and their families are worth a total of £55.3 bn. £33.3 bn of this money is inherited wealth. £20.9 bn is wealth made by the present owners in their own life time.

# Rothschild family: Sir Evelyn de Rothschild
## £250m
*Banker*

dob 29/3/31

and

## Lord Jacob Rothschild
## £150m

dob 29/4/36

*Sir Evelyn de Rothschild*

In 1804 Nathan Rothschild arrived in Manchester with £20,000 to start a textile business. By the time of the Battle of Waterloo in 1815, he had built his company into a commanding position in the banking heart of London. He learned, even before the British Prime Minister, of Wellington's famous victory. The bank that still bears his name N. M. Rothschild is run by his great-great-grandson Evelyn.

Evelyn's tenure at the bank has been marked by controversy, wholly at odds with the traditional Rothschild family unity and discretion of the past two centuries. In the mid-1970s the customary positioning of the Rothschild heirs in relation to the heart of their inheritance – the bank – changed. The chairmanship, held by Baron Edmond de Rothschild, had been expected to go to his nephew, Jacob. It went instead to Jacob's father, Lord Victor Rothschild, who died in 1990, then coming to the end of a long career as head of various Whitehall think-tanks and a spell as an intelligence officer. When the time came for Victor to step down, he nominated his nephew Evelyn, not his son Jacob, to succeed him. Evelyn also represented over 40% of Rothschild Continuity, the trust which controls the Rothschild bank. Jacob spoke for less than 10% of Rothschild Continuity.

In September 1980 Evelyn wrote to Jacob, then head of the corporate finance department at the bank, insisting that if he did not cease banking under his own name in any part of the world, steps would be taken to remove him from the board of N.M. Rothschild. Jacob left and took over the management of RIT, a small investment trust. He has parleyed this into a major financial institution and recently partnered Sir James Goldsmith in his ambitious bid to break up BAT.

Evelyn emerged from the cousinly confrontation with renewed energy and N.M. Rothschild Bank is once again a leading player in the City big league. Evelyn is a shy man, twice married, who avoids publicity at all costs, despite being chairman of the *Economist* magazine. He is also chairman of the key banking institution, the British Merchant Banking and Securities Houses Association. In 1988 his and Jacob's aunt Dolly, widow of James de Rothschild, died, leaving £92 million in her will, the largest sum ever left in a will in Britain. Much of that sum was represented by Waddesdon, a French château in Buckinghamshire which she donated, with all its treasures, to the National Trust. It has been described as by far the finest and greatest bequest ever made to a body already well endowed with castles and palaces.

A racing fan all her life, she left her stable to Jacob, who it is said cares little for horses, while Evelyn, who is chairman of United Racecourses, received 'not a leg', as one racing critic put it. Evelyn was educated at Harrow and Trinity College, Cambridge, and is known in banking circles as a traditionalist.

---

# Tiny Rowland    £231m
*Industrialist*

dob 27/11/17

Born Roland Fuhrop in a British internment camp in India, the son of a German trader and a British mother, Tiny Rowland's life has been dogged by controversy. He was briefly interned as an enemy alien in the war. He went to Africa in the late 1940s to become a farmer and trader, and at the request of Angus Ogilvie, took over the tiny London & Rhodesian Mining and Land Company (Lonrho) in 1961. Today it is Africa's largest food producer and publishes *The Observer* newspaper.

Rowland loves feuds and pursues his enemies remorselessly. When Edward Heath described him as 'the unacceptable face of capitalism' in 1971, Rowland retorted that 'it was the only notable thing he had ever said'.

Currently he is embroiled in a battle with the Al Fayed brothers, owners of Harrods. Rowland is bitter about the manner in which they acquired the store

and the House of Fraser chain, and he has put all his energy and *The Observer* columns into questioning the source of their wealth. He felt vindicated in 1990 when the long-awaited Government report into the House of Fraser takeover was bitterly critical of the Fayeds.

Over the last few years Tiny has stepped up the pace of his attacks against his enemies. A devastating onslaught on the Australian financier, Alan Bond, led eventually to the virtual collapse of the Bond empire, loaded down with debts. Bond had had the temerity to take an unwelcome stake in Lonrho.

Tiny's feud with the Fayeds continued to fascinate a bemused British financial establishment and Fleet Street into the 1990s. In 1989 in an unprecedented midweek edition *The Observer* published extracts from the then unpublished report by the Department of Trade and Industry into the Fayed takeover of the House of Fraser stores group. The report, which branded the Al Fayeds as 'liars', was finally published in 1990 and appeared to vindicate Rowland's position. The Government refused to take any action against the Al Fayeds.

Despite his advancing years, Tiny shows no sign of abandoning business or ending the feuds, which he appears to relish. His burning interest outside the company is Africa and African politics.

One of his proud boasts is that he owes no bank money, he belongs to no clubs and he has no entry in *Who's Who*. He lives quietly with his wife Josie in Berkshire on the banks of the Thames.

# Asil Nadir   £213m
## *General trader*

dob 1/5/41

In the early 1980s one name dominated conversations in City watering-holes: Polly Peck. City investors rushed to buy the shares of this former East End clothing company. Its share price rose from 9p to £35 by 1983, making a multi-millionaire of its major shareholder, Asil Nadir.

Nadir, the son of a wealthy Cypriot business man, came to Britain in the 1960s after studying economics in Istanbul. He joined his father, who had earlier arrived in Britain during the EOKA troubles in Cyprus. Together they ran an efficient clothing business called Wearwell which, when floated on the Stock Market in 1973, was 51 times over-subscribed. In 1980 Nadir took over Polly Peck and moved into a whole range of activities including packaging, fruit and even consumer electronics. Despite sceptical probing by investigative reporters, Polly Peck was not a seven-day wonder and has prospered.

Polly Peck was the best performing share on the stock market during the 1980s. Anyone who invested £1,000 in the group in January 1980 and kept it there would now (1990) be sitting on around £1.2 million. Nadir himself has not rested on his laurels; in 1989 he bought the American Del Monte fruit operation for some £557 million. He also became the first European business man to 'invade' Japan by taking a 51% stake in the Japanese Sansui group.

In his private capacity Nadir has given £5 million to the Spastics Society. He lives a quiet life, preferring to spend his evenings at home rather than out in nightclubs. His wife Ayesha is a noted Turkish beauty and they had a stormy relationship, separating twice but having 2 children, in their years together. Nadir told Stephen Aris in the *Telegraph* weekend magazine that 'the only thing I am passionate about is business'.

# Lord Forte and family
# £210m

*Hotelier*

dob CF 26/11/08

In 1913, Charles Forte left a remote hilltop village in Italy to come to Edinburgh with his mother. He later served milk shakes in his father's Alloa café. Today Lord Forte presides over the Trust House Forte empire employing over 70,000 people in 800 hotels.

A strict paternalist and ardent admirer of Mrs Thatcher, Forte built up THF in the 1960s and 1970s through a mixture of shrewdness and hard work. But one prize eluded him for many years: the Savoy group where he has a stake but, because of the voting structure, lacked control. Annual shareholders' meetings became a ritual battle. In 1989, a peace agreement was signed between the two sides and the war officially ended.

Rocco Forte, 46, his heir, is the only son among his six children. He worked in the business even while he was at school, washing dishes and making sandwiches. Once when he broke a tray of dishes, his father deducted the cost from his wages. He is now an able chief executive and led the assault on the Savoy. He still finds time to indulge in a passion for running and marathons.

Father and son are close, living on opposite sides of the same Mayfair street. Rocco's sister Olga is THF's design director, and holds shares worth over £80 million in the company.

# Marquess of Bath £200m
## *Landowner*

dob 26/1/05

Longleat – famous for its lions and other exotic creatures such as gorillas, white tigers and rhinos – is also the family home of the Marquess of Bath. Dating from the Elizabethan period, Longleat is also filled with priceless art treasures and has 10,000 acres of grounds.

The Marquess, who drives a small Japanese station wagon, is regarded as a modest man. He spends hours directing visitors around Longleat, weeds the gardens and will pick up any litter he sees left around.

The family wealth is tied up in trust funds, which means it cannot be spent. But in 1987 the Marquess had a public row with his son and heir, the eccentric Viscount Weymouth, over the sale of paintings. Four paintings were sold by the Marquess and replaced by identical colour photos mounted in similar frames. The Marquess said he had every right to sell them. His son did not agree.

# Viscount Hambleden and family   £200m
## *Newsagents*

dob VH Smith 2/4/30

William Henry Smith was only a month old when his father died in 1792, leaving his mother to struggle with a small newspaper delivery business. But he went on to lay the foundations for the present W. H. Smith empire. He designed light horse-drawn vehicles to send papers over a wider area and took advantage of the railway boom in Victorian Britain.

Today, with profits surging from £70 million in 1988 to nearly £90 million in 1989, the core of the business remains the same: newspaper distribution and sales. There are 379 high-street branches and 68 at airports or railway stations. The company has also diversified into record shops via the purchase of the Our Price chain and DIY with its Do-It-All shops.

The family has around a third of the voting shares and two Smiths, one a peer, sit on the board. The Smith peer is Viscount Hambleden who lives in the Manor House at Hambleden, near Henley-on-Thames.

The Hambleden family are close friends of the royal family and the Viscount's mother, the Dowager Viscountess, has been a lady in waiting to the Queen Mother since 1937. Viscount Hambleden himself is a close friend of Princess Margaret, and in the 1960s was part of what was known as the Annabel's set, centred on Annabel's club in Mayfair. He now farms extensively at Hambleden. He married the daughter of an Italian count in 1955, and they had five sons. He and his wife were finally divorced in 1988. Viscount Hambleden has since been romantically linked with Lesley Watson, a model.

# Malcolm Healey    £200m
*Furniture manufacturer*

Malcolm Healey's father started his own decorating business in Hull before World War II. After the war, he opened a shop selling decorating materials. Malcolm's two elder brothers (including Edwin, q.v.) joined the business and, eventually, he also joined.

While working for Status, as the business was called, Malcolm became increasingly disenchanted with late deliveries, poor workmanship and price rises from British manufacturers. In 1976 he decided to make his own kitchens and bought a 40,000-square-foot factory and second-hand machinery. Humber Kitchens was born. Experts said the machines would break down but Healey kept them in top working order. In 1981 he acquired the Hygena name and built it up to the point where it made £20 million pre-tax profits in 1987.  '

He then sold the company to the MFI group, netting £200 million in cash and shares. A private man, Malcolm Healey has now emigrated to America, where he is planning to 'take the American furniture industry apart'.

# Earl of Iveagh and family    £200m
*Brewers and landowners*

dob BI 20/5/37

Arthur Guinness, the Dublin brewer, created the famous stout on the banks of the River Liffey in the 18th century. Today the family still have links with the company, though its management is now in professional hands.

Lord Iveagh ('Benjie') presides over the Guinness family, which has had a run of bad luck in recent years, with the untimely death of several family members in unhappy circumstances. Benjie Iveagh lives in the Phoenix Park area of Dublin and sits on the Guinness board. In 1984 he was divorced from his wife Miranda.

He has a 23,000-acre estate at Elveden in Suffolk, worth an estimated £50 million. His grandfather, whom he succeeded, had revitalised the estate which in Edwardian days was regarded as the best shoot in the country. In 1984 the contents of Elveden Hall were auctioned by Christie's for £5.7 million in a four-day sale. The house has not been occupied since the war.

Members of the Guinness family went to court in 1988 to challenge the interpretation of the 1st Earl of Iveagh's will. The High Court decided that several million pounds left in a trust by the Earl, who died in 1927, could be inherited by his great-great-grandchildren, Dorian and Garech Browne, whose father, Tara Browne, died in a car crash in Chelsea in 1966.

For the rest of the Guinness family 1989 was a quiet year. But 1990, with one trial underway and another scheduled for later in the year, against some of the former senior management of the Guinness company and their associates who directed the takeover of Distillers in 1985, will keep the spotlight of public attention close to the family. Ironically, the main defendant, Ernest Saunders, the former Guinness chairman, was largely responsible for turning the company round in the early 1980s and reviving the family fortunes.

---

# Charles and Maurice Saatchi   £200m

*Advertising agency owners*

dob CS 9/6/43   MS 21/6/46

'You know Labour doesn't work' worked wonderfully for the Saatchi brothers. As the advertising agency employed by the Conservative Party in 1979, the Saatchis devised the controversial poster and slogan attacking Labour's record. It won Mrs Thatcher the election and the Saatchis national fame.

The middle sons of a north London textile merchant, the Saatchis started their own advertising agency in 1971. By the end of the decade they were the biggest agency in Britain. Until recently they were the biggest in the world. This has been achieved by a hectic takeover of rival agencies and by branching out into new markets such as management consultancy. They even considered bidding for the Midland Bank at one time.

The two brothers disdain personal publicity and being photographed. Maurice lives in a Sussex mansion and enjoys gardening, tennis and renovating cars. Charles and his wife Doris have what is acknowledged as one of the finest and most valuable collections of modern paintings in the world.

A disappointing year at work (1989), leading to a 30% pay cut in 1990 for the two Saatchi brothers, has only been relieved by the valuation put on the art treasures. The collection is now conservatively valued at £175 million. But the art cannot hide the disappointing performance of the advertising group that bears the brothers' name. The explosive growth that propelled Saatchi & Saatchi into the largest advertising business in the world began to peter out in 1989 when painful retrenchment became the order of the day. The results for the year to the end of September 1989 revealed a pre-tax loss of over £15 million. Robert Louis Dreyfus, a brilliant French business man, was appointed to revive the group's fortunes.

*Charles Saatchi*                              *Maurice Saatchi*

# Marquess of Tavistock   £200m
## *Landowner*

dob 21/1/40

Fate has dealt the Marquess of Tavistock a mixed hand. He was a reluctant inheritor of Woburn Abbey and its treasures, preferring that his father, the Duke of Bedford, tread the path of duty a little longer before fleeing to tax exile and freedom in Monte Carlo in 1974. Then, early in 1988, Tavistock suffered a devastating stroke from which he is only now recovering.

When his father transferred the family lands and property to his heir, Robin Tavistock was a contented 34-year-old City stockbroker. Educated at Harvard, he preferred the company of American friends and had little in common with the hereditary antediluvians of the House of Lords.

When the Marquess's wife, Henrietta, heard that the Duke was becoming a tax exile and that she and her husband would have to live at Woburn, she made her famous outburst: 'I never wanted to live there. It was extremely selfish of my father-in-law to go. My husband was enjoying his life. At 34, to be made a prisoner of an inheritance is very cruel.' She probably reflected her husband's view.

The Marquess is renowned among his peers for being a diffident, almost chilly, individual. 'I don't know why I'm so formal,' he once confessed. 'I just think some people are slightly more reserved than others. Some people are slightly shyer than others, too.'

Millions of visitors a year enter Woburn and its 13,000 sculpted acres. The Duke was practically the inventor of the stately home game as it is now played. In 1955 he opened his ancestral home to the charabanc trade largely to pay off the death duties with which his own father had saddled him. Since taking over, the Marquess has followed his father's example and Woburn is a top tourist attraction. Yet this is only the visible side of a two-pronged foray into modernising the Bedford assets. Twenty acres of Bloomsbury, one of inner London's most rapidly improving areas, came with the portfolio. The Bloomsbury acres have subsidised Woburn for many generations.

The first Earl of Bedford, a crony of Henry VIII, received a parcel of land just north of the Strand as his portion of the booty from the dissolution of the monasteries. In the 1680s his grandson commissioned Inigo Jones to develop Covent Garden. A marriage to the Southamptons secured another 100 acres and Bloomsbury was born. Unfortunately, in the early years of this century, the 11th Duke decided to sell off such choice items as Covent Garden and the British Museum site, netting £2 million that no one in the family really needed at that time.

# Evan Cornish and family   £190m
*Packaging manufacturer*

LinPac makes much of the metal, plastic and paper packaging we take for granted today. It is a private company based in the Lincolnshire town of Louth. The managing director and chairman is Evan Cornish. He makes most of the business decisions for the firm himself. It has around 4,000 employees worldwide and has a turnover of £400 million a year. It is a diverse packaging group dealing with anything from plastic cups to fast-food packets.

Evan Cornish founded the company 25 years ago and runs it from a small untidy office. In its first year turnover was in tens of thousands of pounds. By 1969 it had risen to £7 million, and in 1977 had jumped to £100 million. Cornish once said that 'We like to have small sites of no more than around 300 employees.' In its accounts for 1988 the group had sales of £468 million. The firm shuns publicity. Cornish lives in Woodhall Spa. His brother is a director of the company, at least one member of the next generation of Cornishes also works there, and the accounts show that the Cornish family have a sizeable stake of over 50%.

In the year to the end of 1988 the company made profits after tax of over £19 million and it has huge cash reserves of £116 million. As companies in the packaging business now sell at very high prices, LinPac could be worth nearly £500 million on the stock market. The Cornish family stake would be worth some £190 million at least. The company also owns racehorses which all have LinPac in their name. They are stabled with the trainer Charles Elsey at his North Yorkshire stables at Malton.

# Stephen Rubin   £188m
*Shoe manufacturer*

dob 3/12/37

America's fitness fad has made the Reebok running shoe a best seller. And that has made Stephen Rubin a rich man, with a home in north London, a flat in Florida and a yacht in the south of France. Rubin, who trained as a lawyer, has always seemed to have an uncanny eye for good deals, runs his father's old company, Pentland Industries, which started life as Liverpool Shoes in 1936. In

1981 it bought a 55% stake in the then struggling Reebok for $77,500. Today the stake is down to 32%, but it is worth over £430 million.

Rubin's best investment, however, was made in 1974 when Pentland bought 51% of Unicam, a home brewing business, for £51. In 1978 that stake was sold to Robertson Foods for £1 million.

In 1989 and 1990 so as to lessen Pentland's dependence on Reebok, which provides 75% of its profits, Rubin bought two greetings card companies. A restructuring of the group, in which Rubin holds 55% of the shares, also released some £50 million in funds to shareholders. Rubin himself collected £27.5 million which, added to his share stake, values him at £187.5 million.

Being a one-time Liberal candidate did not prevent Rubin from asking Mrs Thatcher to open Pentland's new headquarters in her Finchley constituency. But he has also been involved in controversy. In 1974 Pentland was caught up in the fringe banking crisis. In 1980 Rubin was acquitted of fraud charges arising out of the affair. In June 1990 Rubin put his stake in Pentland up for sale, with the expectation of a price of around £350 million.

---

# John Clothier and family    £180m
*Shoe manufacturer*

John Clothier is the great-great-grandson of James Clark, the J. of C. & J. Clark, now Britain's largest shoe makers. Clarks was founded over 150 years ago by Cyrus and James Clark in the Somerset town of Street, which is still its headquarters.

company now employs over 23,000 people. It is being groomed for a stock market float.

Oxford-educated Clothier has been with the business all his life. There are other Clarks on the board including Daniel, the great-grandson of James.

Recently the growth of imports has hit the business, and it has launched Project Thrift to cut out wasteful spending. But it still managed a healthy £30.3 million pre-tax profit in the year to the end of January 1990. However, in 1989 the company closed 2 older factories with a loss of 600 jobs. It has recently built a new factory near Bath to make children's shoes.

The Clark family are well-known local Liberals, and exerted a strong Quaker influence on Street, which had no pubs until 1975.

John Clothier, who lives near Taunton, is a keen sailor and farmer. He was in the 1979 Fastnet race which was hit by a severe storm that killed a number of the competitors.

# Antony Pilkington and family £180m
## *Glass maker*
dob AP 20/6/35

Founded in 1826, Pilks – as it is known in its St Helens base – is Britain's biggest glass maker. But it only became a world force in 1959 after the invention of the float glass technology used to make high-quality glass. This involves floating molten glass in a bath of hot metal. It took seven years and £7 million to perfect. Today it is the world's largest float glass company. The Pilkingtons still control over 10% of the company shares. Despite 10,000 redundancies in the recession of the early 1980s, the family has a paternalistic reputation in St Helens, one of the few company towns left in Britain.

Chairman Antony Pilkington, a fifth-generation family member, was educated at Ampleforth and later went to Trinity College, Cambridge, gaining an MA in history. He did his two years' National Service with the Coldstream Guards where he was commissioned with the rank of lieutenant. He is married, lives at Frodsham in Cheshire and has three sons and a daughter. His hobbies are cars – he used to race saloon cars, reading, skiing, sailing and squash.

He really gained his spurs in 1987 when he fought off a £1.2 billion bid for the company from the BTR group. The whole of St Helens, led by the Labour-controlled town hall, united behind the company.

In 1987 he was awarded an honorary law degree from the University of Liverpool and in the same year was presented with the Liverpool Publicity Association's Gold Medal Award for promoting Merseyside. In 1989 he became Deputy Lieutenant of Merseyside.

# David Rowland   £180m
## *Property developer and dealer*

dob 10/9/33

Wheeler-dealer and darling of the 1960s and early 1970s stock market, Rowland was a millionaire at 23. The son of a London scrap merchant, he left school before taking any O levels and started work at 16 in a stockbroker's office. He left because he couldn't see a way of making real money. He then went into estate agency and after a year – armed with a £9,000 inheritance from his father – set up on his own using his mother's front room as his office.

By the time he was 21 he had bought his first public company for £200,000. In 1970 he sold up and went to live in tax exile in Paris. He has made occasional forays into the London stock market, not all successful. He lost £3 million on a deal to buy 25% of Vickers in the mid-1970s and his main company collapsed in 1982 with losses of £25 million.

In the 1970s he invested heavily in the London casino business. He planned to become involved in a lucrative casino in Tehran, but the fall of the Shah put paid to those plans. In the early 1980s he owned Maxim's, the club in London's West End. Rowland sold his 30% stake in Edinburgh's Hibernian Football Club early in 1990. He now lives in tax exile in Monaco and has expanded his fortune by astute share trading.

# Albert Gubay   £170m
## *Supermarket owner and banker*

dob *c.* 1930

In the late 1960s a mud-spattered figure in a donkey jacket would often be seen building new supermarkets in Wales. This huge figure was no ordinary navvy. It was Albert Gubay, the boss of the Kwik Save supermarket chain, and he would quite literally muck in to build his new stores.

Born in the north Wales town of Prestatyn of an Armenian father and Irish mother, Gubay went into business on his own after doing his National Service in the navy. Spotting that a British public, tired of rationing, would want some luxuries in the drab postwar world, Gubay first went into business selling cut-price sweets from the back of a lorry. Borrowing £100, he bought an old cinema and converted it into a factory to make sweets, but by the late 1950s, with derationing, the big sweetmakers moved into the field and cut the ground from under him.

He then went into retailing and set up a cut-price store. This was the age of Resale Price Maintenance, when manufacturers could dictate the price of their goods. But Gubay managed to overcome this problem by buying his stock under different names, so that the manufacturers could not identify him and cut off his supplies.

Through the 1960s the Kwik Save group prospered as Gubay introduced new selling techniques such as late-night opening, car parking, out-of-town stores and a philosophy of selling cheap goods out of boxes, often without labels, 25% below the cost of well-known brands. He flouted local by-laws in Prestatyn to keep his store open until 9 p.m. and simply paid the fines and kept on trading. 'Every week we were summoned until it looked as though I was going to prison for contempt of court,' he said later. But the public loved it and coach parties used to come on shopping expeditions to his stores from all over Wales.

In 1972 Gubay sold all the shares in Kwik Save and moved to New Zealand, where he had a 290-acre stud farm, to breed trotting horses for harness racing, one of his hobbies.

The sale of the Kwik Save shares, which netted Gubay some £12.5 million, attracted considerable criticism in the City. But Gubay shrugged that off and went on to build up a large chain of modern supermarkets in New Zealand. In 1975 he returned to Britain to live on the Isle of Man, where he already owned a castle. Since then he has led a quiet life on the island, turning to property development and the Celtic Bank, which he bought in 1984.

In 1985, he claimed his master company Montrose Holdings would be worth £200 million if quoted on the stock market. He reckons to be worth £170m at a conservative estimate. He keeps in touch with his extensive business interests via his £2 million Gulfstream private jetplane.

---

# Paul Hamlyn    £164m
## Publisher

dob 12/2/26


No one in the English-speaking world is ever likely to forget the *Spycatcher* affair. Between 1985 and 1988 the British government, in courts across the world, sought to suppress the memoirs of a tired and embittered secret service man, Peter Wright. At vast cost to the British taxpayer, and at equally vast profit to Wright and his publisher Paul Hamlyn, the government lost the case.

Hamlyn, the son of a Jewish paediatrician who fled to London to escape Hitler's tyranny in 1933, and one of the most successful publishers in Britain, was approached by various 'friends' of the government while the case was in progress.

It was made politely clear to him that if he were to drop his attempt to publish the book, 'it would be viewed favourably by the government'. As the *Observer* tells the story, Hamlyn's reply was, 'Tell them that nothing less than a Dukedom will do.'

It was typical of the man who opted out of school and the intense middle-class respectability of St John's Wood, London, at the age of 16 to become an office boy at *Country Life* magazine. A lifelong Labour supporter, his form of national service sent him down a Welsh coalmine as a medical orderly. He combined this job with that of stringer for the *South Wales Argus* and driving a bus at weekends. His involuntary service to the nation complete, he rented a shop in Camden, then the Irish ghetto of London, and began the career as bookseller that was to see him earn two immense fortunes.

His first publishing venture, Paul Hamlyn Associates, specialised in cheap popular works: mostly hobbies, art, cooking and travel. He refused to join the Publishers' Association, and expressed antipathy for the Net Book Agreement, the trade's monopoly arrangement designed to protect the price of books. He was frowned upon as an iconoclast. Nobody in the business seemed to notice that his cheap popular Shakespeare had sold over a million copies and his pocketbook Kafka sold 73,000 copies.

In 1964 he sold out to IPC, then run by Cecil King, for the sum of £2.25 million, about £40 million in 1990 terms. For a while he dithered at News International as Rupert Murdoch's joint managing director, but soon left and later set up Octopus Publishing Group, based on the book options he extracted from Murdoch for £50,000. In 1987 he sold Octopus for £535 million, £214 million of that being his own stake in the company. He had always encouraged his staff to take up shares and his chauffeur made £200,000. Twice married, Hamlyn has homes in London and France. He is the brother of the poet Michael Hamburger, who bears the original family name. One of Hamlyn's first acts on completion of the sale of Octopus was to give £50 million to charity. He likes to gamble.

# Michael Hunt    £160m
## Car dealer

Michael Hunt is a major shareholder in one of Britain's most mysterious and profitable companies – Nissan UK. Founded by Octav Botnar, a reclusive German-born business man, Nissan UK has the sole rights to sell all the Nissan cars sold in Britain. With thousands of Nissans coming off the production line at its Sunderland plant, the profits have risen sharply. In the year to the end of July 1988 it made pre-tax profits of £132 million on a turnover of £1.2 billion.

Hunt, who has a 13.5% stake in the business in his own name and through family trusts based in Lichtenstein, worked with Botnar from the outset, and today is deputy chairman of the group which is based in Worthing. His stake would be worth at least £160 million if sold on the stock market, given the company's profitability.

Hunt lives with his family in an exclusive area of Hove in a luxury home. He has a huge swimming pool in the garden and all the trappings of a millionaire. In 1986 he received dividends of some £3 million from his share stake.

One of Hunt's passions is organ music and he is particularly keen to preserve pipe music. This passion led him into a bitter battle with his local council over plans to build a music room in his garden. Neighbours complained that the historic cinema organ he planned to install there would disturb the peace.

The council rejected the application, but Hunt appealed to the Department of the Environment and an inspector ruled in his favour. A three-year battle followed over the amount of compensation the council should pay, and a figure of £7,275 was agreed – small beer for Hunt.

By then, however, Hunt had changed his mind and he built his swimming pool instead.

# Ken Morrison and family   £155m
*Supermarket owner*

dob KM 20/10/31

The Morrison family still controls over half the shares of the Wm Morrison northern supermarket chain. The business was started in Bradford at the turn of the century by Bill and Hilda Morrison who sold eggs and butter to householders and then moved on to a market stall. The company opened its first supermarket in 1961. Today there are over 40 Wm Morrison stores and the business is run by Ken Morrison, son of the founder.

Enterprise Five is the Morrison flagship store in Bradford. It has its own mock Tudor half-timbered 'high street' and a Victorian arcade inside.

The group has been a perpetual takeover target but, with the family controlling over 50% of the shares, no realistic takeover bid can be mounted until 1990 when their holding its ultimately reduced to around 44%.

# Anita and Gordon Roddick   £152m
*Retailers*

dob AR 23/10/42   GR 27/4/42

As Britain sweltered in the 1976 heatwave, Anita Roddick opened her first Body Shop in Brighton, with a £4,000 overdraft. The hot weather made people more aware of their bodies and on the first day the stocks virtually sold out, netting £130. Despite being next to a funeral parlour which caused considerable confusion, she persevered. The Body Shop secret is to use natural products, no-nonsense packaging and refillable bottles. The Roddicks travelled the world looking for new products. It worked. By 1990 there were over 400 stores round the world, over half of them overseas. Anita Roddick had become the byword for British business women's success.

Husband Gordon is not as well known but is crucial. He dreamt up the idea of franchising the Body Shop to spread the business faster. In 1984, the Body Shop

*Gordon and Anita Roddick*

was floated on the stock market and its share price doubled within a week, such was the demand for the shares and the excitement the company generated in the City. The Roddicks between them still own around a third of the shares

The seal of royal approval came in 1986 when the Princess of Wales opened the company's new headquarters in Littlehampton in Sussex. The Roddicks live in the area. They are keen supporters of Third World projects. Anita used to work for the housing charity Shelter and supports CND. Her children went to private schools. The Roddicks have also acquired a 13,000-acre Scottish estate.

The Roddicks and their Body Shop proved to be the great survivor of all those stars of the mid-1980s retailing revolution. While other retailers were hammered by the slow-down in consumer spending of the late 1980s the Body Shop went from strength to strength. Its shops were packed over the Christmas 1989 period, as an increasingly 'green' British population sought out Anita's natural environmentally friendly products. Early in 1990 the Body Shop was worth £500 million on the stock market, while the combined net worth of Anita and Gordon Roddick rose to £152 million, nearly four times the level of a year ago. The Roddicks are now eyeing the newly liberated East European consumer market as a lucrative source of new custom for their wares.

# Bob Edmiston  £150m
*Car dealer*

dob 6/10/46

As a young married man in Dagenham, Bob Edmiston found it difficult to make ends meet on his salary as a bank clerk. So he did up old cars such as Morris Minors, and sold them for £50. Hooked on cars and trained as a cost and management accountant, he rose through the car industry to become finance director of the glamorous Jensen sports car company. But behind the glamour, Edmiston found a company that was on the verge of financial ruin. His first act was to lay off half the staff, and when the company eventually folded his last job was to pay himself a £6,000 redundancy cheque. He was then 29.

He used the money to launch International Motors in 1976, with the backing of a Californian business man. Initially it dealt with Jensen parts and served the loyal band of Jensen Interceptor owners. Later it was to become the United Kingdom concessionaire for Hyundai, the South Korean car manufacturer, and two Japanese manufacturers, Subaru and Isuzu. The company has a plush headquarters in West Bromwich.

Edmiston initially had 15% of the company, which he increased to 25% in 1980; by 1987 he was up to 50%. That year he spent £9 million acquiring the remaining 50%. In its latest accounts, IM Holdings, as it is called, revealed profits of over £21.5 million and had cash reserves of some £30 million. That would put a stock market value on the company of around £150 million at least. Much of the success of IM Holdings has been based on the British public's appetite for four-wheel drive vehicles from Far Eastern manufacturers.

Edmiston is noted as a big supporter of charities and also has a profit-sharing scheme for his 150-strong workforce. He lives in the countryside near Birmingham.

# Ian Bentham McGlinn  £150m
*Investor*

In 1976 Ian McGlinn, a Sussex garage proprietor, made the wisest investment of his life. He put £5,000 into the Body Shop – the fledgling cosmetics business being started by Anita Roddick (q.v.).

Today that investment represents nearly a third of the Body Shop's share capital and makes McGlinn a multi-millionaire. When the Body Shop was floated on the

Stock Exchange with the usual razzmatazz in 1984, the modest McGlinn was typically out of the limelight on holiday in Portugal. McGlinn himself has nothing to do with the day-to-day operations, merely collecting a huge dividend from his shareholding, which nearly quadrupled in value in 1989 due to City excitement over prospects for the Body Shop.

---

## Anant Rabheru    £150m
*Hotelier*

Rasik Rabheru and his son Anant run the Park Hotels Group, with 11 hotels. Rasik is the nominal head of the company, but Anant, a business studies graduate, seems to be taking the lead. The family came to Britain in 1970. Rabheru went into buying and doing up luxury country hotels. He believes the first generation of Asian immigrants in Britain had a high-risk, gutsy approach. They knew what they wanted and were not afraid to try to get it. The young have the professional management expertise, though the first generation were dealers and traders. He says that Asians have gone into hotels because they offer investment in property as well as good cash flow.

Their four-star hotels include: the Park International and the Burns Park in Kensington, London; the Eden Park and the Hyde Park Towers in Bayswater, London; the Royal Albion in Brighton; and the Cheltenham Park in Cheltenham.

Assuming £250,000 a room for a four-star de luxe, £200,000 a room for a four-star, and £100,000 to £150,000 a room for a three-star hotel, Rabheru reckons he has 1,500 rooms worth £225 million gross.

---

## John Asprey    £149m
*Jeweller*

dob 8/11/37

The Aspreys have been supplying jewels and expensive trinkets to the wealthy for 200 years, since they fled Huguenot persecution in 18th-century France. Today they are jewellers to the royal family and will supply individual diamonds costing

over £1 million to anyone who cares to enter their shop in New Bond Street, London.

In the past they have supplied solid gold collar stiffeners, a collapsible gold toothbrush and even a model of a bacon and egg sandwich worked in precious metal.

The Asprey family have around 46% of the equity and have staved off takeover bids in the past. In 1980 a long-running feud between rival Aspreys was finally settled when disgruntled family members were bought out, so preventing a takeover by Dunhill. The family claims to be more motivated by respect for tradition than money.

John Asprey, the present chairman, is a tall blond ex-Scots Guards officer. He lives in London and has three sons. After the bitter family feud over Dunhill which pitted him and his father against his uncle and cousin, he said he 'simply would not allow' a similar feud in the next generation of the family. Aspreys largely escaped the late 1980s recession in the retailing sector caused by high interest rates and a collapse in consumer confidence. Business is booming. It reported a 20% rise in pre-tax profits for the year ending in March 1990.

# Samuel Whitbread and family £148m
## *Brewer*

dob SW 22/2/37

The Whitbread brewing empire is run by a family member some 250 years after the business was founded by Samuel Whitbread, a Bedfordshire farmer who used a £2,000 inheritance to set it up.

Today Samuel Whitbread, his great-great-great-great-grandson, is chairman of what is Britain's third largest brewer, turning out 13 million barrels of beer a year. The family owns over 10 million shares in the group which was valued at around £1.7 billion in January 1990.

Before joining the Whitbread board in 1972 as one of the family directors, Sam was a farmer. He read farming and estate management at Cambridge and later worked for a year as a shepherd on the Duke of Buccleuch's estate. He then managed the Whitbreads' 10,800–acre estates in Bedfordshire. But gradually his interest in the family business grew. He took over as chairman in 1984, the first Whitbread to run the business since 1970 when his uncle, Col. William Whitbread, retired.

The family also owns a 32,000-acre estate in Ross and Cromarty, Scotland, and all the family members enjoy country pursuits such as shooting and fishing.

# Bruno Schroder and family   £147m
*Banker*

dob BS 17/1/33

Despite inheriting a German title conferred on his grandfather by the Kaiser, Baron Bruno Schroder has an impeccably English pedigree: Eton, Oxford and the Life Guards. He is the only Schroder on the board of one of the City's most prestigious and profitable merchant banks. His brother-in-law, George Mallinckrodt, is chairman.

The bank was started in 1804 when John Henry Schroder left Germany to set up the British arm of his brother's merchant bank. It merged with Herbert Wagg in 1962. It has survived and prospered in the cut-throat market since the City's Big Bang deregulation in 1987 by offering top-class advice and help to companies fighting big takeover battles. In 1988 it became embroiled in the £2.9 billion takeover bid by Minorco for Chartered Consolidated, the mining group. In 1988 it was also involved in the battle for Rowntree, the confectionary group.

Bruno has a home in London and another in Scotland: his hobbies are flying and shooting. The family still have a controlling interest in the bank.

# Ken Scowcroft   £147m
*Insurance broker*

dob 8/8/28

From modest beginnings in 1957, using the front room of his Manchester home as his office, Ken Scowcroft has built an insurance empire. At one time, only the Automobile Association insured more cars than his Swinton Insurance Services, named after the area of Manchester which was and still is his base. In 1988 he sold a 30% stake in the group to Sun Alliance and London Insurance for £30 million, retaining nearly 70% of the company.

The deal gave Sun Alliance one million customers, and enabled Scowcroft to indulge his hobby of breeding horses for carriage driving.

Scowcroft pioneered television advertising of insurance. Of his first year's commission of £227, he spent £73.4s on advertising. In 1964, he followed this by opening the first high street shop selling insurance over the counter. Today there are 300 branches and 200 staff employed at the head office. The budget for advertising has risen to nearly £3 million a year.

Scowcroft remains chairman, while his son Brian is managing director. His daughter Janet, a solicitor, is legal director.

In May 1990 Sun Alliance raised its stake to 49% at a further cost of £31.7m. This raised the Scowcroft family worth to nearly £147m.

# Sir Donald Gosling   £145m
*Car park owner*

dob 2/3/29

For a man obsessed with the sea, Sir Donald Gosling could hardly have chosen a more landlubbing job than running National Car Parks, which owns many of Britain's big city car parks.

He joined the navy as a boy signalman at 15, towards the end of the war, and, just after it, saw service in the Mediterranean on HMS *Leander*. He was seen as officer potential and promoted to leading seaman, but by 1949 the shrinking navy had no further need of his services. He loved the navy and described the day he left as 'the blackest of my life'.

There were compensations. Gosling, who had been born in Streatham, London, became a trainee surveyor with Westminster City Council and would have stayed there but for a chance encounter with Ronald Hobson (q.v.), an ex-soldier who wanted to clear one of the innumerable bomb sites in Holborn and set up a car park. He needed planning permission and Gosling told him how to get it. They became firm friends and partners. They are still together and the business has grown to become one of the Britain's largest private companies with a turnover of over £151 million.

But Gosling has never lost his passion for the sea. He runs a £3 million yacht in the Mediterranean called *The Brave Goose*, the third vessel he has owned bearing that name. The original name came from an incident when Gosling was visiting his son who was seriously ill in hospital, and called him a 'brave goose'; his son replied that that would be a good name for the boat Gosling was buying. The latest, in 1987, was the largest vessel ever to be built on the Thames, costing £3 million to build and around £300,000 a year to maintain. Equipped lavishly with gold thread carpet and a secure satellite communications system, *The Brave Goose* can be chartered for £34,000 a week. Gosling regularly holds board meetings on the yacht which is berthed at Port Gallice on the Riviera. The largest boat in the port, it can only dock by occupying three berths rather than one.

Gosling was knighted in the Wilson resignation honours list in 1976. He was a close friend of Harold Wilson though he is a staunch Conservative. His knighthood was awarded for services to the Forces. He is a leading figure in the White Ensign Association, formed to advise ex-naval and marine personnel on finances after leaving the forces.

But super-patriot Sir Don has run into problems with the British establishment. In 1988 he quietly withdrew his proposed membership of the Royal Yacht Squadron, where Prince Philip is admiral, fearing he would be blackballed.

He married a doctor's daughter in 1959. She is an heiress in her own right, as her father was a principal shareholder in the Palmer & Harvey confectionery business. Gosling is chairman of Palmer & Harvey and is credited with turning its fortunes round. In 1988 the couple parted.

---

# Ronald Hobson  £145m
*Car park owner*

London's frustrated motorists can thank Ronald Hobson for at least some relief from the chronic parking problems of Britain's capital city. It was his idea to start car parks in the late 1940s on old bomb sites that led to the chain of National Car Parks – complete with bright yellow signs – found off many city streets today.

Hobson, an ex-soldier, realised that postwar Britain would see a motoring explosion, and somewhere would be needed to park cars. He had a site in Holborn which he wanted to develop for a car park and went to see 20-year-old Donald Gosling (q.v.), a Westminster planner, about how to get planning permission. The two hit it off and went into business together with £200, offering a free car wash service to entice customers.

Today they remain firm friends. Hobson lives in Mill Hill, in north London.

---

# Duke of Atholl
# £143m
## *Landowner*

dob 19/6/31

'Wee Iain', the 6ft 4in Duke of Atholl, is the only man in Britain allowed to have his own private army, although it is limited to 80 soldiers who perform strictly ceremonial duties.

A confirmed bachelor, the Duke inherited the title at the age of 25 when his third cousin died. Despite the determined efforts of society hostesses, he shows no sign of wanting to marry their daughters.

He has no need to do so for money. The Atholl estates in rich Perthshire run to 130,000 acres; and his mother was sister to Lord Cowdray (q.v.), head of the Pearson empire. The decline of the family lands has been much less rapid than for many other Scottish aristocrats. One hundred years ago the Atholl estates covered 194,500 acres.

The Duke lives in Blair Castle, and is an active supporter of the Scottish Landowners' Federation and the National Trust.

# Sir Kenneth Kleinwort and family   £132m

*Bankers*

dob KK 28/5/35

Kleinwort and Sons started as a merchant bank in 1830 and later merged with Robert Benson Lonsdale to form the present Kleinwort Benson group. It has been quoted on the stock market since 1961 and is valued at over £530 million in 1990.

The Kleinwort family, headed by Sir Kenneth, a tax exile in Switzerland, still have a 24% stake in the business. He remains a director of the bank.

He list his hobbies as travel, photography, skiing, shooting and gardening. Despite his Swiss base, Sir Kenneth is also a committed supporter of the Slimbridge Wildfowl Trust and a council member of the World Wildlife Trust. His son, Richard, works as a banker in Germany.

# Benzion Freshwater   £131m

*Residential property owner*

dob 24/4/48

Osias Freshwater arrived as a Polish refugee in Britain three days before the start of World War II. He started out as a textile merchant during the conflict but turned to property. By the early 1970s he was London's biggest private landlord with 20,000 tenants.

Growth had been achieved with the help of his son-in-law, William Stern, who joined the business in 1960. They were neighbours in two luxury homes in Hampstead, London. Stern left in 1970 to start up his own business but that folded in the 1974 property crash with debts of over £200 million.

Osias Freshwater, who had been on the Angry Brigade hit list in 1971, died in July 1976 to be succeeded by his son Benzion.

Today the family has a near 80% share stake in a public company, Daejan Holdings, through which they control their property empire. This stake is worth around £131 million. In 1978 Benzion, who controlled a network of 200 companies, bought a modest flat in Hampstead for his wife and three children.

---

# Brian Thomson and family  £127m
## *Publishers*

dob BT 21/11/18

They publish the *Beano*, Britain's best-selling comic, with the legendary Desperate Dan and Dennis the Menace, but the Thomson family only entered publishing by chance. In the 1870s William Thomson, a Dundee shipowner, took an interest in a firm which published the local paper, and in 1886 he took complete control, putting his son D. C. Thomson in charge.

The firm is now dominated by Thomsons. Five are on the board and the family owns nearly two-thirds of the shares. In 1989 D. C. Thomson made profits of £13 million, after tax.

It has a reputation as a publisher of staid and conservative papers and magazines such as *My Weekly* and *The People's Friend*. It is a strategy that works. Both sell nearly 600,000 copies while *The Sunday Post* sells 1.4 million. The company is also looking to the future and has major television and cable interests.

Brian Thomson, the current chairman, who was educated at Charterhouse, joined the business in 1937. During World War II he served in the Fife and Forfar Yeomanry. He married in 1947 and has a son and four daughters. He lists his hobbies as golf and shooting.

OPPOSITE: *Lord and Lady McAlpine*

# Lord McAlpine    £125m
*Builder*

dob 14/5/42

The McAlpine family now run two separate and competing building companies, Newarthill and Alfred McAlpine, but they were once a united family.

Newarthill was the Lancashire town where, in 1847, a Robert McAlpine was born and started work as a miner at the age of seven, on the princely wage of one penny a week. Later he became a bricklayer and then started his own company

at the age of 22. By the time he was 28, he had 1,000 staff and two brickyards, but he later went bankrupt when a Glasgow bank collapsed.

He rebuilt his fortune, however. When he died in 1934 his second son William took over the family business; then his third son Alfred branched out on his own in 1935.

The two companies – Sir Robert McAlpine (later renamed Newarthill), run by William, and Alfred McAlpine, run by Alfred – used to divide the country up to avoid competition. But no more.

William died in 1951. His son Lord McAlpine of Moffat, who headed the Newarthill branch, died in 1990. Unusually, his son is also a life peer but is best known for being treasurer of the Conservative Party and a railway enthusiast, with a full-scale railway in the garden of his Hampshire home. His parties at Conservative annual conferences are always said to be most lavish. He resigned as Party Treasurer in 1990.

He also collects modern art and gave 60 sculptures to the Tate Gallery in 1971. He once boasted he had had 500 lunches at the Dorchester (then owned by the family) in five years.

On the other side of the family, Alfred McAlpine lives in Cheshire where the company is now based. His son, Bobby, is vice-chairman of Alfred McAlpine.

---

# Duke of Northumberland £125m
## *Landowner*

dob 1/7/53

Henry Percy inherited the title of Duke of Northumberland from his father, the 10th Duke, who died in October 1988. The new Duke's inheritance covers 80,000 acres in Northumberland, Syon Park in Middlesex and an estate in Surrey.

The family seat, Alnwick, which is about 20 miles from the Scottish border, is filled with art treasures. There is a fine collection of Italian paintings including three Titians and works by Tintoretto, Palma Vecchio and Canaletto. There is also a collection of English and Dutch paintings by Reynolds, Gainsborough, Turner and Van Dyck. Alnwick has been the seat of the Percy family since 1309; the dukedom was created in 1766.

The Duke is nephew of the Duke of Buccleuch (q.v.), who is the largest landowner in the United Kingdom. His mother, Lady Elizabeth, is the elder sister of the (late) 9th Duke of Buccleuch. He was eduated at Eton and Oxford where he read history and English. He is known to be a film buff and has expressed an interest in becoming a film producer.

He and his elder sister, Lady Caroline, live at Syon House overlooking the Thames and Kew Gardens. The Queen is one of his godparents. The Duke has been linked in society columns with Natasha Grenfell, the daughter of Lady St Just.

---

# Duke of Devonshire  £120m

*Landowner*

dob 2/1/20

There are some 3,000 drawings at Chatsworth, the 175-room Derbyshire seat of the Duke of Devonshire. These include works by Leonardo, Raphael, Veronese, Claude, Rubens, Van Dyck and Rembrandt. In 1984 a collection of surplus Old Masters raised £21 million for the Duke. Aside from his paintings, the Duke also owns 70,000 acres in Derbyshire, Yorkshire and Sussex, including most of Eastbourne's sea front.

Noted as a keen gardener and an SDP supporter who defected from the Tories, the Duke is married to one of the famous Mitford sisters. He is ever conscious of the need to preserve the Chatsworth inheritance. In 1985 he put Lismore, his 200-room castle in Eire, up for rental at £2,600 a week.

His pale yellow racing colours are the oldest registered in Britain, and he has been a member of the Tote board and Jockey club.

---

# Lord Hartwell and the Berry family  £120m

*Newspaper publishers*

dob MH 18/5/11

The Berry family is one of Britain's great newspaper dynasties. The first Viscount Camrose, son of a South Wales alderman, was the proprietor and editor-in-chief of the *Daily Telegraph*. From 1915 to 1936 he was also editor-in-chief of *The Sunday*

*Times.* He died in 1954, to be succeeded by his eldest son. But the family tradition in journalism was really carried on by his second son, Michael Berry, later Lord Hartwell.

Hartwell, who learnt his trade as editor of Glasgow's *Sunday Mail* in the Depression of the 1930s and later as managing editor of *The Financial Times* from 1937 to 1939, became a world-respected editor-in-chief of the *Daily Telegraph* and later the *Sunday Telegraph.* Under his hand, the *Telegraph* became the best-selling quality paper, reaching a circulation at one time of nearly 1.5 million. But in the 1980s it was beset by financial problems. Hartwell and the Berry family had to relinquish control of the paper to Conrad Black, a Canadian business man.

The family still have an 11% stake in the *Telegraph* group, which turned in a record profit of over £29 million in 1989 from its new Docklands home, where there is new technology and lower manning levels. But with increased competition from new quality titles such as the *Independent* and two Sunday newspapers, the *Telegraph* papers are under intense pressure. Advertising rates and volumes have also been hit, which would clip any stock market valuation of the group today. A flotation of the group would value the Berry stake at less than £100 million, which would cut the family wealth back to £120 million though it is protected by substantial private trusts which are unaffected by the economic climate. Lord Hartwell was educated at Eton and Christ Church, Oxford. He served in the army during the war, reaching the rank of lieutenant colonel, after twice being mentioned in dispatches. He lives at a country house near Aylesbury, and he has a London house. His wife, Lady Pamela, the younger daughter of the Earl of Birkenhead, was a noted society hostess. She died in 1982.

---

# Alan Sugar   £118m
*Computer manufacturer*

dob 24/3/47

A genuine East End barrow boy raised in a council flat, who left school at 15 to sell car aerials out of a car boot, Sugar now owns nearly 250 million shares in Amstrad, the company he founded in 1968.

Standing for Alan M. Sugar Trading, Amstrad sells computers, televisions, hi-fis and now satellite dishes more cheaply than anyone else. Sugar has a high-powered marketing and technical team at his Brentwood headquarters looking for niches in the consumer electronics market. They dream up new products and new attractive designs, which are then built in the Far East at a cut-price rate.

Thus far the formula has worked perfectly, with the exception of the economic downturn in 1989.

Sugar has no time for the old school tie network or the City. He tried to sue one stockbroker for hostile comments about Amstrad, and says that he is 'proud' to be called a barrow boy. He is married and has two sons and a daughter, with homes in Essex and Florida.

The year 1989 proved disastrous for Sugar. Problems with his computers, a slow-down in retail sales and high interest rates have hammered the group and his own shareholding. At one stage, his wealth was bleeding away at over £1 million a week. But it is too early to write off the tenacious Sugar.

His one innovation in recent times has been to install himself in a proper office rather than directing operations from a large armchair in the middle of his sales floor.

# James Miller and family   £111m
## Builders

James Miller, the son of an Edinburgh architect, was destined to enter the same profession as his father after some training with the family firm. But he elected to become a builder instead and started building homes and housing estates in the Pentland hills to the south of the city. The company prospered and branched out both into civil engineering and into England, with offices in Wakefield and London.

Knighted in 1953, Sir James retired in 1973 and handed over the running of the company to his son, also called James. Sir James died in 1977, but his group, now called the Miller Group, has prospered and is one of Britain's largest independent construction and property development companies. The shares are all held by 16 individual shareholders and 14 family trusts. Its 1989 results showed a steady growth, with pre-tax profits rising by 20% to £21.5 million and turnover up by nearly a quarter to £234 million.

James Miller, the chairman, is assisted by his brother Roger who runs the house-building division, and his cousin Keith (a keen sailor) who heads Miller Developments. The company is now heavily involved in open cast mining, as well as urban renewal projects in Scotland, a leisure complex at Perth, a section of the Edinburgh bypass and office building in the City of London. It recently won a contract to extract some 480,000 tonnes of open cast coal from the former Patent Shaft steelwork site at Sandwell in the West Midlands. The group is now expanding into micro-tunnelling and environmental services.

James Miller, described as shy and private by *Scottish Business Insider* magazine, has no intention of taking his company to the stock market for a flotation.

# David Wilson   £110m
## House-builder

dob 5/12/41

In 1960 18-year-old David Wilson joined his father in a housebuilding business in Ibstock, a gritty Leicestershire mining town. Twenty-seven years later, though the father had died, the fruits of that parternship were realised when their company, now called Wilson Bowden, was floated on the Stock Exchange. The share sale was oversubscribed four and a half times. In 1990 David Wilson's stake was worth £110 million.

Wilson Bowden specialises in building high-quality four-bedroom houses in the Midlands and the north of England, but not the south-east. It has also branched out into commercial development and is to build an eleven-screen cinema complex in Nottingham. The company possesses a large land bank.

Wilson himself has enjoyed the fruits of his success and bought a house costing £1 million in 1981. He has been married twice.

# Clark family  £109m
## *Property developers*

In 1938 Scottish business man Robert Clark founded his own company which was later to be called Equity Trust. In 1951 he teamed up with Joe Levy, a London bookie's son, to create one of the most successful post-war property companies, Stock Conversion. Clark died in 1984, and the family's stake in Stock Conversion was sold for some £58 million a year later.

The family still control Equity Trust (now renamed Taylor Clark) and have extensive interests in leisure, entertainments, forestry, farming, property and finance. Their shares are held either directly by the family or through family settlements set up over the years. A charity, the Underwood Trust, also has an 18% stake in the business.

Accountants who have examined the latest accounts of Taylor Clark estimate that the company is worth well over £100 million, with net assets of £126.5 million.

# Duke of Beaufort  £107m
## *Landowner*

dob 23/3/28

The 11th Duke inherited the title in 1984 from his second cousin, known to all as 'The Master', who was regarded as the greatest foxhunter of his time and who started the Badminton Horse Trials in 1948. On his death all full-time employees of the 52,000-acre Badminton estates in the West Country received £10 for each year of service.

The new Duke had to sell off some land to meet death duties. But this was not too much of a burden, as the Beaufort estates had actually grown, from the 19th to the 20th centuries, from 51,000 to 52,000 acres. Before moving into the 40-bedroom Badminton House he insisted on installing lifts and central heating in what was a notoriously uncomfortable home. The Queen Mother, a frequent guest, once asked for carpet to be laid on the stairs.

By profession the new Duke is a modern picture dealer in London and New York. Badminton itself is filled with art treasures bought mainly by the 3rd Duke in the 18th century. These include two famous paintings of Badminton by Canaletto, carvings by Grinling Gibbons, and portraits by Reynolds.

Beaufort came to prominence in 1988 in the course of Sir James Goldsmith's (q.v.) £13 billion takeover bid for BAT. Beaufort had been encouraged by his friend, Gianni Agnelli, the head of Fiat, to join a group of rich backers of the bid. With the prospects of huge rewards for splitting up BAT, the Duke was prepared to commit up to £10 million to the cause. In the event, the bid lapsed, and Goldsmith abandoned it, admitting defeat.

---

# Sir Bernard Ashley    £104m
## *Retailer*

dob 11/8/26

The kitchen table of a Pimlico house was the birthplace of the Laura Ashley legend in 1953. It was there that Bernard Ashley, newly demobbed from the army, and his wife Laura pioneered the flowery fashions with which the British – and latterly the American – middle classes fell in love.

A chain of shops named after Laura Ashley was formed. Bernard, a large ex-Gurkha, balked at having the flowery prints named after him.

Tragically Laura was killed in a fall in her Welsh home just weeks before the hugely successful flotation of the group on the Stock Exchange in 1985. Some £2 billion worth of money chased the £60 million of shares on offer. The family retain about 66% of the shares.

But in 1989 the business suffered a slump in sales brought on by the government's high interest rates policy. The Laura Ashley profits and share price were both slashed. At the end of 1989 the group was forced to do the unthinkable and axe 100 of its 1,500 workforce. To make matters worse, a month later the group stunned the City by announcing losses of £2.5 million when profits of some £15 million had been expected. Known throughout the group as B A, Ashley is now busy trying to save it.

Sir Bernard, knighted in 1986, lists his hobbies as sailing, swimming and walking. He is impatient of bureaucrats and turns up unannounced in his executive jet at European airports without a passport, demanding entry to the country under the terms of the Treaty of Rome.

He bought the derelict Llangoed Castle near Brecon for £150,000 and has spent £3 million on restoring it as the first of a chain of luxury £100-a-night country hotels. Today it is called Llangoed Hall. The £3 million conversion has been described by the National Forum, a Welsh conservation body, as 'Mammon masquerading as art'. One consolation for Sir Bernard will be his marriage to Madame Régine Burnell from Brussels.

He lives in a large Brussels town house and, apart from his executive jet (kitted out in Ashley prints), owns a French château, a 500-acre Welsh farm and a house in the Thames Valley. He also has the millionaire's obligatory plaything, a yacht.

# Michael Ashcroft £100m
*Entrepreneur*

dob 4/3/46

At first Michael Ashcroft had few advantages in his life besides a willingness to take risks and work very hard. Yet today he runs a £2 billion business empire based in Bermuda. He left Norwich Grammar School and took a Higher National

Diploma in business studies. After a spell as a management trainee at Rothmans, which he described as 'the two most boring years of my life', he joined Pritchards, the office cleaning firm, before branching out on his own in 1972.

First he became a consultant advising companies and then, borrowing £20,000, he bought a struggling cleaning company with just 200 workers. Within four years it employed 4,000 and Ashcroft pocketed £1.3 million by selling it to the Reckitt & Colman group. This gave him the capital to build what was to become a huge business empire. He searched for a publicly quoted company that was near to receivership and in 1977 alighted on the Hawley camping equipment manufacturer. He quickly acquired 25% of the company (a stake that has since been diluted to around 3%) and turned it round very quickly. Within a year, it had achieved profits of £22,000 and by 1984 it had made £31.4 million.

By 1987 Hawley was based in Bermuda, had made some 250 acquisitions and had 100,000 employees. He had taken over Pritchard, the group where he cut his teeth in cleaning. That year he also snapped up ADT, an American security group, for £440 million and renamed it Hawley-ADT.

For many years he ran a pub in Berkshire to relax from the pressure of business but now he lives in Bermuda with his second wife – formerly his secretary – and three children. He commutes regularly to London by Concorde from America and is a close friend of Denis Thatcher. ADT also sponsors the London marathon, though Ashcroft describes himself as only an occasional jogger. He enraged feminists early in 1989 when he remarked, 'You know what I always say ... the best place for a woman is either in the kitchen or the bedroom – and she shouldn't spend too much time in between the two.'

# Viscount Astor   £100m
*Landowner*

dob 27/12/51

Succeeding to the title at the age of 15, William Waldorf Astor became the 4th Viscount.

Waldorf, an Astor family name, refers to the village near Heidelberg in Germany from which John Jacob Astor emigrated to America at the end of the 19th century. He later bought up land around New York. His only son, William Waldorf, was American ambassador to Italy and eventually settled in Britain, becoming Viscount Astor in 1917. The present Viscount's grandmother, Nancy Astor, was the first woman MP. The family have a long link with the *Observer* newspaper and own the old printing works and offices in the City. These are worth around £100 million at today's prices.

Viscount Astor lives in Ginge Manor, near Wantage in Oxfordshire. He is now on the board of Blakeney Hotels, which leases the old Astor family seat at Cliveden from the National Trust and uses it as an hotel. Guests are served by butlers, valets and chambermaids rigged out in Edwardian costume. Cliveden was prepared for its new role at a cost of £1 million. Viscount Astor, who lists his hobbies as fishing and shooting, lives on the income from the family trusts. His wife is a jewellery designer.

# Stephen Boler    £100m
*Entrepreneur*

dob *c.*1944

At 16, Stephen Boler became a trainee with Unilever, but he left five years later to establish his own business in the tyre trade, inspired by his father who had worked as a garage mechanic. Armed with £1,000 and an old Nissen hut, he rapidly built up the business, and four years later sold out to another company, Albany Tyre, netting some £400,000. That was in 1969 and Boler immediately started another similar business.

His biggest business coup came in 1980 when he bought 36 of the troubled Kitchen Queen retail outlets for £2 million. A few months later he bought Wharf Mill, a furniture group. From these businesses he created Kitchens Direct, a group that specialised in selling fitted kitchens through an expensive advertising campaign in the national press. Within three years he had built up a turnover of £22 million. In 1984 he sold the business to the then Hawley group for £22 million. He diversified into different businesses, buying the exclusive Mere Golf and Country Club outside Manchester, a domestic and industrial security group and a £10 million-a-year conservatory business. He runs his business from an office overlooking the 18th hole of the £14m club.

Together with Peter Swales, the chairman, Boler also controls 60% of the shares in Manchester City Football Club. In April 1989 he bought back a much bigger Kitchens Direct group, which also included the Moben company. In October he reinforced his determination to become a major player in the fitted kitchens market by buying a subsidiary of the BET group, Farouche Cuisine.

Now single, he lives in considerable style, with a Warwickshire estate and a mansion in exclusive Knutsford. He keeps a very low profile, and relies heavily on the advice of his right-hand man, Ashley Lewis, an accountant. He commutes by helicopter between his various enterprises.

# Peter de Savary   £100m
*Financier*

dob 11/7/44

The bearded face, the bald head and the large cigar are the familiar trade marks of Peter de Savary. But so is his penchant for hitting the headlines and gossip columns. One moment he is buying up yet another chunk of Cornwall, the next he is negotiating the British challenge in the America's Cup. His lifestyle is luxurious and ostentatious.

He owns a £7 million estate in Berkshire, a 'semi' in South Kensington (London), a West Indies home, and three yachts including the 106-foot *Vagrant*, once owned by the American Vanderbilt family. He has 26 cars, including one that used to belong to Hermann Goering, and travels round the world by private jet.

Yet it all began fairly modestly. Born in Essex, de Savary was educated at Charterhouse where he managed only one O level in religious instruction. At 16 he went to Canada, working as a car and duplicator salesman. He returned home

at 21 and joined his father's furniture firm, only to leave after three years as production manager when he was refused a pay rise.

He went to newly oil-rich Nigeria in the mid-1970s and established a successful business by being a link to the world markets for oil and bringing in vital imports such as cement and bricks. In 1977 he took on a similar role in the Middle East, particularly in Kuwait. Based out of Nassau in the Bahamas, de Savary was a millionaire at 32. In 1980 he established the St James's Club, which he sold for £22 million in October 1987. He boasts that he started the 1980s worth little but ended the decade worth £100 million.

In his private life, de Savary caused a stir by parting from his long-time girlfriend and fiancée, Linda Paton, to marry his secretary. In a matter of days he had returned to Linda who became his wife.

He is busy increasing his fortune with a number of new deals, including a green skyscraper in New York, costing £200 million, which he claims will be the tallest in the city ever built by an Englishman. He is also building a floating methanol plant to be towed out to the Middle East, where it will convert natural gas into methanol.

Nearer home he is building a new hotel at John O'Groats to complement his work at Land's End. Some 4,000 houses are planned at a Canvey Island development and he is aiming to be the biggest ship repairer in Europe.

# Earl of Derby  £100m
*Landowner*

dob 21/4/18

The famous Derby horse race is named after the 12th Earl of Derby who instituted it at Epsom in 1780.

Today the 18th Earl is just as interested in horses. He has 18 in training and he owned a £250,000 stake in Shergar, the Irish horse valued at £10 million which was kidnapped in 1983 and never found again.

He owns 30,000 acres in Merseyside and also has a Newmarket estate. Part of Knowsley House, an ancestral home, is let to the local police.

It was the 17th Earl who really made the Derby name in the 20th century. Known as the 'King of Lancashire', he was a formidable figure on the turf with his racing colours of black silks and white cap. He also spearheaded the army recruiting drive across Britain during World War I.

The present Earl has no children and his heir is a nephew, Edward Stanley, a godson of the late Duke of Windsor.

# Lady Glover £100m
## *Landowner*

Eleanor Glover, British born, was first married to the Swiss financier Edwin Hurlimann, who died in 1966. He left her his magnificent Schloss Freudenberg estate on Lake Zug near Geneva, complete with 2,000 acres of parkland. In 1976 she married Sir Douglas Glover, the former Conservative MP for Ormskirk, following the death of his first wife of 42 years.

Sir Douglas, who was a prominent member of the Anti-Slavery Society and also an active supporter of the Commonwealth, died in 1982. But that was after he had introduced Margaret and Denis Thatcher to the delights of holidaying in Switzerland. In 1978 the Thatchers spent five days at Schloss Freudenberg and came back again in 1980 for a further ten days. After Sir Douglas died the Thatchers returned for further holidays, by which time Mrs Thatcher had struck up a firm friendship with Lady Glover. But in 1989, when Lady Glover was ill, Mrs Thatcher went elsewhere for her summer vacation.

Lady Glover herself has an apartment in Paris and a permanent suite at Claridge's hotel in London. She is famous for her house parties at Schloss Freudenberg, considered to be one of Switzerland's most sumptuous houses, with a particularly fine cellar. A motor yacht is kept permanently on standby on Lake Zug to take guests to nearby picnics and tours.

# Charles and Jocelyn Hambro and family £100m
## *Bankers*

dob CH 24/7/30 JH 7/3/19

The name Hambro conjures up the image of the charming, smooth and utterly British banker. And that is exactly what the various members of the family are.

Started in 1839 by the Danish Baron Hambro, the bank is now run by Charles Hambro (Eton and the Coldstream Guards). Cousin Jocelyn Hambro and his son Rupert are also well known in the City.

The Hambros used to own 49% of the bank through the Hambro Trust, but

*Charles Hambro*

this was dissolved and the shares were bought by the bank, releasing the family wealth.

Charles lives on an 800-acre farm near Cheltenham while Jocelyn has two homes, one in London's Mayfair and another on a Gloucestershire estate. His son Rupert lives a few doors away from him in London.

# Trevor Hemmings   £100m
*Builder and leisure operator*

Trevor Hemmings started as a builders' apprentice in the Lancashire town of Leyland after World War II. He first set up in business on his own building a pair of semi-detached homes. Today he controls 15 companies, ranging from property companies to one of Britain's largest ice cream makers.

But Hemmings' first break dates back to 1967 when he met Sir Fred Pontin, the holiday camp king. Hemmings was asked to build a Pontins' camp in Southport, complete with 3,000 beds. Those were the days of the Hi-di-Hi style holiday camps. Hemmings did the job in nine months. The partnership prospered and he built another camp in Wales. Eventually he ended up as Sir Fred's right-hand man when Sir Fred took over his building firm.

But when Pontins was taken over, first by Coral and later by the brewing giant Bass when it acquired Coral, Hemmings saw his opportunity. He felt that Pontins was languishing as part of a large group, and he assembled his own management buyout team which bought the business early in 1987. Within two years he had sold it to Scottish & Newcastle Breweries, netting nearly £100 million.

Hemmings stayed with Scottish & Newcastle. He runs their leisure division, as well as being their largest single individual shareholder, with over 5% of the shares, worth some £73 million.

He commutes regularly round his various operations, but his base is still firmly in Chorley in his native Lancashire, where Pontins provides employment for 150 people.

# Elton John £100m
## *Musician*

dob 25/3/47

Reginald Dwight from Pinner started work as a tea boy in Denmark Street, in the heart of London's music industry. He became a pub pianist and changed his name to Elton John after two famous musicians he had played with.

Today he is a world superstar with sales of 100 million albums worldwide. His hits include the classic 'Rocket Man', but he had to wait for his first solo number one hit until 1990. He lives in a Windsor mansion, complete with six Bentleys in the garage, a theatre with 100 seats and a chandelier over the swimming pool.

He counts royalty among his friends and played at Prince Andrew's stag night. He is chairman of Watford Football Club, and has seen it move from the fourth to the first division. He spent £1 million on improving the ground and training facilities. He tried to sell the club in 1987 to Robert Maxwell (q.v.) but the Football League thwarted the deal. He has also won £1 million in damages off the *Sun* newspaper for a serious libel, which they eventually settled out of court.

# Henry and Simon Keswick   £100m
*Financiers and traders*

dob HK 29/9/38   SK 20/5/42

*Noble House*, the recent television adaptation of James Clavell's famous novel, was supposedly based on the activities of Jardine Matheson, the Hong Kong trading group. Jardines was founded in 1832 by William Jardine, a Scottish doctor and sometime opium trader, along with his partner, James Matheson.

The Keswicks, a Dumfries family, married into the Jardines in the mid-19th century, and five have served as chairman.

The current *taipan* (Chinese for big boss) is Simon, who succeeded his brother Henry. The family has around 10% of the company shares, and also owns a substantial Gloucestershire estate.

Henry is now based in Britain. He is a keen follower of the turf (racing horses) and owned the *Spectator* magazine until 1981.

# Ian and John Marks
# £100m
*Confectioners*

*John Marks*

Trebor, the sweet group, was founded in 1907 at Trebor Villas in London's East End, by Robert Marks. Today, with four factories in Essex, Kent, London and Chesterfield, it is best known for its Extra Strong Mints, Refreshers, Wine Gums and, a favourite with the royal family, Sharp's Toffees. In 1988 Trebor made profits of £7.1 million but the heavy advertising and marketing costs in the confectionary business began to weigh the company down and it accumulated debts of nearly £40 million. As a result, in September 1989, Trebor was sold to the giant Cadbury Schweppes group for £146 million.

The deal netted over £100 million for the Marks family who still controlled the group 82 years after its birth. Two brothers, Ian and John, together with their sister, shared the proceeds of the sale. Though the family are particularly secretive, Ian Marks is known to live in an exclusive part of Chelmsford, where he is a well-known local figure. John collects valuable cars and has three Bugattis, kept in a special Cotswold garage. Though he also owns a special racing version, he does not race himself, believing it to be too dangerous. He has involved himself in the rebuilding of a rare Bugatti Type 59, of which only six were ever built. Two of those were scrapped and he managed to acquire their chassis, and is rebuilding them into one. He has funded the Applied Futures Institute, which has produced a report called *The World to 2010*.

---

# Christopher Moran
# £100m
*Financier*

dob 16/1/48

Leaving school at 16 with a few O levels proved no handicap to Christopher Moran, who then went to work in the Lloyds insurance market. In 1982, by the age of 34, he had been expelled, the first time in the 300-year history of Lloyds that the whole of its disciplinary machine had ever been used. The market stopped trading for four hours as members gathered to hear the evidence against Moran and a colleague. Their expulsion was later upheld by the Court of Appeal. But Moran was not to leave a poor man. He had built up a £3 million fortune.

Since then he has traded his way in and out of companies, buying them cheaply when he reckons they are undervalued and selling them on at a profit.

He anticipated the October 1987 crash and cut his exposure to the stock market. He lives in a Chelsea penthouse, owns the 45,000-acre Glenfiddich estate (of whisky fame) near Balmoral and has two personalised chauffeur-driven Rolls Royce cars. He is married to a former Miss Thames Television. He scored a notable coup in 1989 when the Court of Appeal decided that he had obtained squatter's rights over a £100,000 plot of council land near a Buckinghamshire home he owned.

# Earl of Stockton
# £100m
*Publisher*

dob *c.* 1943

Grandson of Harold Macmillan, prime minister from 1957 to 1963, the Earl of Stockton is the major shareholder in the publishing firm Macmillan. The family own 95% of the shares in the company, one of the country's largest and most profitable publishers. Its accounts for 1988 give profits of over £8.3 million after tax on a turnover of £159 million. Although this means a slight drop in after-tax profits, Macmillan would be highly prized by large publishing houses and could command a price of over £100 million.

The present Earl inherited the title in 1986 on the death of his grandfather. A former journalist, the Earl moved into the family business in 1970. He lives in Chelsea, having sold the Macmillan family home, Birchgrove in Sussex, for over £5 million in 1989. He enjoys country pursuits such as shooting and fishing. He also lists motor racing and conversation among his hobbies.

# David Sullivan
## £100m
*Soft pornographic magazine and newspaper owner*

The 'girlie magazines' found on the top shelves in newsagents have helped David Sullivan to a £100 million fortune. Britain's leading titillator certainly looks the part. Small, brash and, according to accounts of interviews with him, with absolutely no taste for the finer things in life (apart from a huge appetite for chocolates and chips) and completely unemotional about the women he uses.

Born of a father serving in the RAF, Sullivan led an itinerant life as a child including a spell at boarding school which he hated. After taking a degree in economics at Queen Mary College, London University, he went into advertising, working as an account executive on dog food. But soon the 'shy' Sullivan, who confessed to the *Mail on Sunday* that he lost his virginity only at age 21, was selling nude pictures by mail order through *Exchange & Mart*. 'I offered 20 nude lovelies for £1. I went from earning £88 a month to £800 a week and I only had to work three hours a day,' he recalled.

Thus was born one of Britain's biggest soft-porn empires which in the 1970s embraced 125 sex shops and 25 magazines. In 1982 Sullivan was convicted of living off the immoral earnings of prostitutes and was jailed for nine months and fined £10,000. Before the conviction was quashed on appeal, he spent 71 days in prison. He claims that the experience 'mellowed' him.

He changed the direction of his business after that, though still retaining a stable of eight magazines. He became a newspaper publisher through *Sunday Sport* and the twice-weekly *Sport*, which hit a new low in sleaze with its fantasy stories.

Sullivan, unmarried, lives in Chigwell in a nine-bedroom house which is covered in pictures of nude women. He has recently bought Birch Hall in Epping Forest for £1 million, and he has a Marbella home and a stud farm near Bishop's Stortford. Despite his magazines and papers, Sullivan claims to 'have very established views deep down. I believe in tolerance and moderation. Believe me, I am very law abiding, anti-violence, anti-hooligan and anti-drugs. I've never taken a drug or smoked a cigarette in my life.'

In May 1990 the Monopolies and Mergers Commission blocked his plans to take a controlling interest in the *Bristol Evening Post*.

# 3

# THE
# VERY RICH

—

# £50m and more

# Peter Tom and family  £99m

*Quarriers*

dob PT 20/7/40

Ten-year-old Peter Tom was nearly put off quarrying for life when he was crushed by a rail wagon at his grandfather's quarrying firm at Bardon Hill in Leicestershire. Luckily he survived the experience and still loves quarrying enough to head the Bardon group, now quoted on the stock market with a value of over £130 million.

His grandfather started the business by quarrying in Cornwall and sold out to Amey Roadstone, using the money in 1948 to buy Bardon Hill, a 136-year-old quarry in Leicestershire. In 1958, when the grandfather died, Peter's father Greg took the helm; Peter has been running the company since 1985. Today the Tom family own 72% of the shares.

Bardon Hill still forms the core of the operation and has some of the best hardstone in Britain, ideal for motorways and runways. The quarry is also ideally situated to take advantage of the big road construction programme in the south-east. There are known reserves of about 200 million tons of high-quality Leicestershire granite at the quarry, where some £20 million is being spent over the next five years to expand capacity and improve efficiency.

Since he took over, Peter Tom has been changing a management style heavily influenced by Methodism and a paternalist approach that, in the words of *Management Today* magazine, placed 'hard work and company loyalty among employees above the quest for profits and growth'. As a result, the company only expanded very slowly.

Peter Tom changed all that. In 1985 he bought the Isle of Wight Vectis group for £3 million, and followed this up with the purchase of an American aggregates business for £100 million and a British wholesaler of polished marble for £8 million.

Peter Tom, who has an 11.7% stake in the business himself, lives in an old farmhouse outside Leicester where his wife runs a fashion shop. When not working, he rides and plays tennis.

# Sir Hector Laing and family  £96m

*Biscuit manufacturer*

dob HL 12/5/23

Biscuits have always been part of Sir Hector Laing's life. His grandfather, the first chairman of McVitie and Price, concocted the famous 'Digestive' biscuit recipe at the end of the last century. Sir Hector, recently retired as chairman of the giant £2 billion United Biscuits group, jealously guards that recipe. In 1989 the company made 5 billion packets of various foods, including half the biscuits eaten in Britain.

A leading member of the Scottish establishment, Laing was educated at Loretto and served in the war with the Scots Guards as a tank commander, winning the American Bronze star. In 1947 he started his business career at McVitie's Harlesden factory in west London, humping sacks of flour. A year later, McVitie merged with Macfarlane

Laing to form United Biscuits, where Sir Hector has stayed, becoming a director in 1953, managing director in 1964 and chairman in 1972.

Sir Hector's management style is modelled on Field Marshal Montgomery's. He tries to visit half his 46,000 workforce every year, and the company is obsessive about communicating and training its staff. He also insists on being at work at 7.15 a.m. and does not take huge pay increases when his staff are being held down to modest ones. 'In army parlance, I am not an officer who sits back in headquarters while troops risk their lives and then decides I ought to double my salary', he told the London *Standard*.

In 1986 Laing lost a bruising £2.8 billion takeover battle for control of the huge Imperial group to Lord Hanson. The defeat seemed to sour Laing's feelings towards the City of London, and since then, though a strong supporter of Mrs Thatcher, he has been critical of the City's short-term approach to British industry.

'If too many of our major companies are taken over by non-British owners,' he wrote in *The Times*, 'and free market forces make that more rather than less likely, then the UK will become increasingly a satellite economy.... We have fought wars to keep Britain independent. Are we going to sell that heritage for instant cash gratification?'

Laing, who is regularly invited to lunch and dinner by Mrs Thatcher, advises her on industry. In 1982 he lent a plane to help in the search for Mark Thatcher, missing in the Sahara. He has been a joint treasurer of the Conservative Party. He also helped establish a fund to support the legal expenses of miners fighting against the 1984 strike call by Arthur Scargill.

His links with government do not stop Sir Hector having a finely developed social conscience. He is chairman of Business in the Community, an organisation that helps small businesses and other job-creation schemes. He also started the Per Cent Club, which is busy persuading the top British companies to devote not less than 0.5% of their profits to the community.

Outside work – from which he retires in 1990 – Sir Hector lists his hobbies as flying, gardening and walking. He enjoys piloting his company plane round Britain.

# Lord Hanson    £95m
*Industrialist*

dob 20/1/22

If any business man represents the style of Thatcherite Britain, it is Lord James Hanson, head of the £5.7 billion empire that bears his name and straddles the Atlantic.

Hanson started out running his father's haulage business. In his youth he was well known to gossip columnists and was once engaged to Audrey Hepburn. But from the moment he started the Hanson Trust in 1965 with his partner Gordon White (q.v.), the accent has been on hard work, making his assets sweat and on an ability to

buy up companies cheaply and sell the bits off one by one for more than the cost of the whole. It is a strategy that came into its own in the 1980s – in America as well as Britain. Food, typewriter, battery, brick companies were swallowed up almost effortlessly. The City loves what Hanson has achieved.

He showed his superb timing in 1989 by taking over Consolidated Goldfields for £3.5 billion. With the skill and timing of a chess player, Hanson saw that ConsGold was vulnerable and

struck quickly to sew up an agreed deal, which turned out to be the biggest and most successful takeover in British history so far.

In 1990, with his consummate skill in selling businesses, he should emerge with a handsome profit from breaking up ConsGold. He is thought to be looking for one last big deal to crown his 25-year business career.

In his private life he is now more subdued. He has homes in London, Berkshire and America. He is a passionate supporter of the Conservative Party and was created a life peer in 1983.

# Sir Kirby and Sir Maurice Laing  £94m
## *Builders*
dob KL 21/7/16   ML 1/2/18

Some 140 years after the first Laing house was built in the Carlisle area, the Laing construction business is now one of Britain's leading building companies.

The business started around 1800 when David Laing drove cattle from Scotland to England and settled in the village of Sebergham, near Carlisle, to take up a job repairing buildings. His son branched out into new work and the business never looked back. After the war it went international and has carried out construction work in the Falklands.

Both Sir Maurice and Sir Kirby have been chairmen of John Laing plc, but Martin Laing, Sir Kirby's son, now runs the business, which also includes a valuable property company. In January 1990 this was the subject of a £441 million takeover bid from Elliott Bernerd (q.v.) and Sir Jeffrey Sterling of the P&O group.

Sir Kirby's first wife died in 1981 and left £1.5 million in her will. He married a doctor in 1986. The Laing brothers both live in north London and have had honours heaped on them by the civil engineering fraternity.

---

# Lord Weinstock and family £91m

*Industrialist*

dob AW 29/7/24

Arnold Weinstock has built up the General Electric Company from near bankruptcy to become Britain's biggest and most successful electronics combine, with profits of nearly £800 million and 145,000 employees. But to

the young Arnold Weinstock, running a large business seemed unlikely. Born of a Polish tailor who emigrated to Britain in 1906, he grew up in the Jewish community of north-east London, where he was a shy and bookish child. His father died when he was five. Four years later his mother Golda also died, leaving him to be raised by his elder brother, a hairdresser. Despite being evacuated to Warwickshire at 15 when war broke out, he was able to win a scholarship to the London School of Economics where he took a degree in statistics.

At the end of the war he was working as a £420-a-year clerk for the Admiralty in Bath, supplementing his income by lecturing for the local Workers' Educational Association.

In 1947, when he was demobbed, his brother persuaded a client, Louis Scott, a West End estate agent, to give Weinstock a job. He became Scott's personal assistant, and found he liked the cut and thrust of the commercial world.

Scott later introduced him to Netta Sobell, daughter of Sir Michael Sobell, founder of Radio & Allied Holdings. They were married in 1949 and Sobell, with no son, saw in his young son-in-law the qualities needed to run the business which thrived in the 1950s television boom.

In the early 1960s a successful Radio & Allied Holdings acquired the ailing and much larger GEC through a reverse takeover. Soon Weinstock was running the whole show. He instituted a ruthless pruning operation that was to be his hallmark. The head-office staff was cut from 2,000 to 200, and 35 regional offices were shut. This was typical of Weinstock, who had always loathed waste. Much more was to follow. In 1967 he took over the lumbering AEI group in a bitterly fought takeover. Among his first acts was the cancellation of one of the two copies of

*The Financial Times* ordered by the AEI headquarters, asking, 'Why do they need two copies?' Even today GEC staff religiously turn off all the lights when a room is empty to save electricity.

Later he took over English Electric to create the basis for the modern GEC. He was, and remains, a tough manager. In the first two years after the AEI and English Electric mergers, 20,000 jobs were lost. Hugh Scanlon, then the leader of the Engineering Union, dubbed him 'Britain's largest unemployer'. But the City loved him, as did the Labour government in the 1970s. Whole industries such as telecommunications and power generation were virtual monopoly preserves for GEC.

The onset of Thatcherism proved a blow to Weinstock. At first he was a close confidant of Mrs Thatcher and was part of a small group of senior industrialists advising on economic and industrial policy. But he found the increasing emphasis on competition applied to GEC's key defence and telecommunications markets hard to bear. He alienated the government by publicly condemning the privatisation plan adopted for British Telecom. He also appeared to make GEC a haven for Tory wets by appointing a succession of them to the post of chairman.

In the 1980s GEC was criticised for its caution in not investing its profits in new equipment, preferring to leave them in the bank as a notorious cash mountain that reached £1.5 billion at one stage. Weinstock was also stung by the government's cancellation of the Nimrod early warning aircraft project in 1986 after £1 billion had been spent on developing its GEC radar. But subsequently Weinstock proved his critics wrong with a string of alliances and deals, the like of which had not been seen since he created GEC.

With Siemens, he finally took control of Plessey, run by Sir John Clark (q.v.), his bitter rival for many years. He has steered GEC into a series of European alliances with French and German partners, not to mention a link-up with the American General Electric Group. He even saw off a half-hearted takeover attempt from a Plessey-led consortium.

In private, Weinstock is still a shy person but is charming and amusing, though he relishes heated debate where he can bring a powerful intellect and superb memory to bear. He has a wealth of anecdotes about people in power, and has many of them on his board as non-executive directors. He sits as an independent peer in the Lords.

Outside GEC his main passions are racing and opera. His spartan office at GEC is dominated by a portrait of Troy, his 1979 Derby winner, and he has been known to interrupt meetings to find out racing results. The family has a 300-acre racing stud in Ireland.

When he comes in to work from his London flat or Wiltshire estate, Weinstock spends the first few minutes listening to and even conducting his favourite Mozart operas before getting down to work. He frequently attends the Royal Opera House in Covent Garden.

Simon, his son, is as sharp as his father. He was educated at Winchester and Oxford and is a main board director of GEC. It is thought by some that he is being groomed as Weinstock's successor.

£ 172 of the richest 400 went to public schools
78 went to Eton
11 went to Harrow
3 went to Winchester

# Jasminder Singh and family £90m
## *Hoteliers*

Jasminder Singh came to Britain from Nairobi in 1970. Four years later he had qualified as a chartered accountant. But after a spell working with a City firm and in his own practice, he sought the advice of an uncle on what career to pursue. His uncle, Satinder Vohra (q.v.), a well-known hotelier, gave him a thorough insight into all aspects of hotel operations.

The two went into partnership and bought the Edwardian Hotel in London's Harrington Gardens. After 18 months they sold it and bought another, the Vanderbilt. Soon after, Singh acquired the Savoy Court on his own and bought out his uncle's interest in the Vanderbilt. They are now friendly rivals.

Today Singh has nine hotels in central London, all part of the Edwardian Hotels group, with 1,769 rooms in total. They are all four- or five-star, except for one three-star, and they aim to 'recapture some of the glamour of that more gracious age by the careful restoration and refurbishment of some of the best located hotels in central London', as one brochure recently put it.

The strategy appears to be working. In 1982 Singh bought three old properties from Grand Metropolitan. One of these was the old Stratford Court hotel. In 1987 it was closed and refurbished at a cost of £6 million, to reopen later that year as the Berkshire Hotel. In 1989 the Berkshire was named hotel of the year by *Caterer & Hotelkeeper* magazine.

Another Edwardian hotel, the Hampshire, was opened in April 1989 in what was the former Royal Dental Hospital building in Leicester Square. It was refurbished for a total cost of £25 million, bringing it to five-star status.

Singh's latest venture has taken him out of central London. Edwardian has bought the Skyway Hotel at Heathrow from Trusthouse Forte for £35 million. They plan to upgrade the three-star 450-bedroom Skyway to five-star status. That will cost a further £25 million. More hotel purchases are in the pipeline.

Singh lives a very low-profile life. He was once apparently offered over £200 million for the group but he rejected the overture. Singh's family own around 64% of the shares in Edwardian Hotels.

# Stuart Lipton £89m
## *Property developer*
dob 9/11/42

Lipton is one of the handful of property developers giving London its biggest facelift since Sir Christopher Wren. The huge Broadgate office complex around Liverpool Street Station is his most spectacular work to date. He started in the property market as an estate agent in the 1960s and had made his first million before he was 30. He sold his company, Sterling Land, for £28 million a month before the property crash in 1973. 'I was simply lucky,' he says of that time.

He was the first to realise that the 1960s City office buildings could not cope with the modern computer dealing rooms demanded by the post-big bang Stock Exchange. Broadgate's success helped Lipton's latest company, Stanhope Properties, raise profits from £12.5 million to £15.5 million in the year to the end of June 1989. Lipton owns a third of the equity in Stanhope and the Reichmann brothers, the Canadian developers of the huge Canary Wharf office project in London's Docklands, own another third. Yet such is the City's disenchantment with property companies that the shares nearly halved in value from 1988 to 1989, cutting Lipton's personal fortune from £150 million to £89 million. Despite this City view, Stanhope is pressing on with new developments, and recently announced plans for a new village near Cambridge with 3,000 homes.

Lipton, a very private married man, lives in north London. He drives a red Ferrari and has a luxury Mayfair office. He is a keen patron of the arts, recently joining the board of the National Theatre and becoming a Royal Fine Arts Commissioner.

His son, Connolly, succeeded him in the family business. Lynn Wilson, his grandson, became chairman in 1981. Despite the difficulties in the house-building industry, the company remains profitable and in 1988 built 2,160 homes. Around 30% of the company shares are in family hands. The stock market values Wilson (Connolly) Holdings at around £294 million.

Lynn Wilson is an ardent cricket fan and is chairman of Northamptonshire Cricket Club.

# Lynn Wilson and family   £88m
*Builder*

dob LW 8/12/39

Fortunes are not always made in America as Thomas Wilson, a Northampton shoe maker, found when he went out to Massachusetts in 1905. Although he met his wife there and had a son, times were hard and he returned to Northampton, but not to the shoe industry. He entered the building trade and made a house from a windmill. The house still stands as a testament to his workmanship.

# Duke of Argyll   £87m
*Landowner*

dob 28/8/37

In 1877 the Argyll estates covered 175,000 acres. Today they are down to 81,000 acres. But the 12th Duke,

1975. It has now been restored and a magnificent Armoury Hall has a fine display of muskets, axes and Highland broadswords. The Duke married the daughter of a baronet, Capt Sir Ivan Colquhoun, in 1964. She is an expert shot and has competed at Bisley.

---

## Captain Alwyn Farquharson £87m
*Landowner*

dob 1/5/19

Head of Clan Farquharson, Captain Alwyn Farquharson inherited the Invercauld estate from an aunt in 1941 after her death in an air raid. He was on active service in the Royal Scots Greys at the time.

After the war he took over running the land which stretches over 100,000 acres in Aberdeenshire, Perth and Argyll. He became Clan chief in 1949. His American wife, a former fashion editor of *Vogue* and *Harper's Bazaar*, obviously enjoys life in the Highlands. She organises theatre, film and music evenings in the local village and has established a craft gallery.

Balmoral is the neighbouring estate to Invercauld. Once the Queen Mother came to stay when her own house was being renovated.

The estate's best assets are the 24 miles of River Dee, one of the finest salmon rivers in Scotland, and extensive grouse moors.

The family were given the estates in the 14th century by Robert Bruce after being ejected from the Speyside landholdings by a rival clan.

Chief of the Campbell clan and Keeper of the Great Seal of Scotland, has done a lot to preserve and develop what is left.

The Duke sold the island of Iona to the Fraser Foundation for £1.5 million in 1979 to pay off duties owed since his father's death in 1973. Beginning in the mid-1980s, tourists were invited to spend up to £1,000 a week for the privilege of deer stalking with the Duchess of Argyll. The Duke also sells his own brand of 21-year-old Argyll single malt whisky to the Japanese for around £245 a bottle. There is a caravan park and a wildlife park on the family estate.

The Duke's home is Inverary Castle, which was nearly destroyed by a fire in

# Wilf Corrigan £85m

*Electronics engineer*

dob 21/3/38

Wilf Corrigan is the most successful of the British high-tech boffins who went across to Silicon Valley in California to make their fortunes.

The son of a Liverpool docker, Corrigan was one of a large family. After taking a degree in electronics engineering from Imperial College, London, he headed for America on graduation. Later he justified his decision, saying 'There was no future for enterprising people in the UK, even in the early 1960s.'

He worked for a number of the leading American electronics companies such as Motorola. By the early 1970s he had been recruited to Fairchild, then a leading electronics group, which was going through a bad patch. Les Hogan, an ex-Motorola man, who was trying to rescue Fairchild, thought that his former protégé, Corrigan, was just the man needed to help him. They formed a team, nicknamed Hogan's Heroes by other Fairchild employees.

But it did not work out quite as Hogan wanted. Corrigan disagreed violently with him over the strategy and went above his head to the Fairchild family trustees, who largely owned the company. They supported him, and Hogan was ousted, with Corrigan taking his job. 'That guy has ice water in his veins,' said one American broking analyst at the time.

In 1980 Fairchild was sold to another large American group and Corrigan, who had built up a sizeable share stake during his tenure as chairman, received around $60 million and $4 million of bonuses.

He had developed a reputation as a tough hire-and-fire man, and was even reputed to sack people over the company tannoy. He also had close links with several leading venture capital funds. Out of one such link he set up LSI Logic, a specialised electronic chip maker in 1981, with a personal stake of around 40%. That stake is now worth at least $170 million.

Married with three children, Corrigan lives in Silicon Valley's millionaire belt. He is a very keen family man, and his old image as a tough business man has softened ever since he nursed his mother who was dying of cancer. He is president of the Semiconductor Industry Association, the supreme accolade that can be given to a leading electronics engineer in America.

LSI Logic has two large subsidiary companies in Britain, and Corrigan serves as chairman of both, maintaining his links with his homeland.

# Earl of Inchcape
## £85m

*Landowner and industrialist*

dob 27/12/17

The Inchcape family have had a long association with the sea. The grandfather of the present Earl created the modern P&O shipping group. The Earl, who no longer runs P&O, collects City directorships. At one stage, he had at least 30.

The family wealth came from both P&O and the Inchcape group, which is valued at over £700 million on the stock market. In the early 1970s the family owned 40% of the Inchcape shares. The Earl, who was chairman from 1958 to 1982, is now life president of the company.

He is a keen follower of field sport. But he can no longer stalk the red deer at his 14,000-acre Scottish estate of Glen Isla as he has had to sell it. In 1968 he bought a 1,500-acre Essex estate for £500,000 and sold it in 1980 for £5 million.

He still has another home in Scotland and a manor house in Bucks.

# Peter and John
# Beckwith   £80m

*Property developers*

dob PB 20/1/45   JB 19/3/47

Many of the stylish new buildings in the City are the work of the Beckwith brothers, John and Peter. Sons of an army colonel from Hong Kong, they had a conventional upper-middle-class education at Harrow and Cambridge. They set up their own property company, London & Edinburgh Trust, in 1971. But they were badly hit in the property crash of 1973–4, when they each suffered a £1.5 million loss.

The two brothers used their training as a solicitor and chartered accountant respectively to fight back. They paid off all their debts and today have the smooth, sleek look of the successful property developers they have become. They branched out in recent years from building City offices to business parks. They were also very active in Europe and America.

Between them, the Beckwith brothers owned around 29% of the company. Both are fanatical sportsmen, enjoying tennis, football and skiing. They are both heavy supporters of charity; they both live in south-west London.

The brothers became increasingly disenchanted with the stock market and in April 1990 sold their joint stake to a Swedish company for £80 million.

Peter Beckwith recently put his luxury mansion in London's exclusive Hyde Park Gate on the market after less than a year of occupation. The asking price of £2.5 million did not deter would-be buyers. Some 20 would-be purchasers inspected the property in the first month of the sale. Beckwith, who bought the house for £1.9 million, never intended to live there long-term.

*Peter and John Beckwith*

# Terry Curry and family £80m

*Former retailer*

dob TC 5/3/39

As the great-grandson of the founder of Curry's electrical chain, Terry Curry seemed in a safe job for life. The family controlled up to 35% of the company which was well run and highly profitable. But they reckoned without the boss of rival Dixons, Stanley Kalms and his main adviser Roger Seelig, then a star merchant banker at Morgan Grenfell. In December 1984 they managed to wrest Curry's from the family in a bitterly fought £250 million takeover battle. One consolation was the £87 million payout for the family's stake. The victors' lot has not been particularly happy: Seelig was caught up in the Guinness affair and has left Morgan Grenfell, while Dixons' profits have suffered as the consumer boom of the 1980s came to an end.

Since the takeover, Curry has kept a low profile. The family invests in the stock market, but Curry has no other known business interests. In the years before the takeover, he distanced himself from the City. His home is near Maidenhead; his children are now grown up.

# George Moore £80m

*Furniture manufacturer*

Having left school at 14, George Moore later regretted that 'I missed my way educationally and felt I could not make the grade, but I loved creating things,' as he told the *Yorkshire Post*.

The lack of education proved no barrier to Moore, however. His first job was to rent a shop in the north Yorkshire town of Knaresborough where he repaired toys. He then trained as a joiner and moved to Bingley, where at the age of 17 he bought an old henhouse for £45, which he converted into a joinery workshop.

A year later Moore was able to afford to hire a skilled tradesman, allowing him to finish his own apprenticeship.

The business prospered and in the mid-1960s he was able to buy up a huge old munitions factory site at Thorp Arch, outside Wetherby in Yorkshire, for £200,000. He converted it into a trading estate, building around the huge reinforced concrete ammunition bunkers where he couldn't afford to demolish them. He established a Moore's Furniture factory there and in the late 1970s sold off a large part of the site to a Greek shipping group based in Jersey called Kuliam Investments, netting some £8 million. But Moore kept the furniture factory and other choice sites on the estate. The business went from strength to strength and, with another factory in Co. Durham, it had 900 staff by the mid-1980s. It also claimed 15% of the market for kitchen furniture, selling to DIY stores, local authorities and private housebuilders.

While the business prospered. Moore's health did not, and in late 1986 he decided to sell the furniture company, a decision that was reinforced by a heart attack he suffered in January 1987. Neither his son nor his daughter wanted to carry on with the business.

Though Moore made a good recovery, he still determined to sell and bids were invited from potential purchasers. His managing director, Fred Davies, who had been at Moore's since 1974, led a management buy-out in October 1987. Originally this had been ruled out because of the price demanded, but the nine managers involved did not want to work with any of the four or five prospective purchasers. In the event a deal was arranged in ten days. Moore now lives in the smart commuter village of Linton, though he is rumoured to be interested in buying a large estate in Yorkshire. His daughter runs a local financial company, while his son is not associated with the furniture company at all.

# Nazmu Virani £80m
## Property owner

dob 2/3/48

The biggest Asian-owned company in Britain is run by Nazmu Virani, a Ugandan Asian refugee, who set up his first supermarket in Dulwich 17 years ago.

Today he heads a business with a stock market value of nearly £175 million, embracing 16 hotels and 265 pubs. He deals as an equal with property magnates such as Gerald Ronson (q.v.).

An Ismaili Moslem, Nazmu professes a fanatical dedication to hard work and loyalty. He claims to be 'more married to my business than my wife'. He worked 18 hours a day for seven days

*Nazmu Vivani*

a week at the Lordship Lane supermarket in London's smart Dulwich suburb, which he dubbed 'hardship lane'.

The move into hotels and pubs came by chance. His father had a heart attack while helping run the supermarket chain that had grown to 19 by the mid-1970s. So Nazmu bought a hotel for him, hoping it would be less demanding. Within a year his father had the hotel running smoothly and was bored. So more hotels followed.

Before the stock market crash in 1987, shares in his master company, Control Securities, were in huge demand, but they suffered a sharp downturn after Black Monday. Nazmu calls that day 'golden' Monday as he was able to buy up more shares in the business at a much lower price. His family now own 47% of the shares, which are also widely held by other members of the Asian community.

father, Robert, and based in Northampton. The share offer was oversubscribed by nine times, as pension funds sought to grab shares in the highly efficient group.

Horne, who was still active in the group six years later though he had relinquished the post of chairman, controlled over half the shares. He also presided over a huge expansion in the business. In five years the tonnage of paper it handled rose by 60%, turnover trebled and profits quadrupled.

But early in 1990 Horne decided to sell to a Dutch group, and in March that year accepted a £154 million offer. This valued his family stake at £79 million.

Horne, educated at Haberdashers' Ashe's School and London University, lists his hobbies as his family and gardening. He has three sons and four daughters.

## Kenneth Horne and family  £79m

*Paper merchant*

dob 6/5/13

In the mid-1980s, the men who made their millions on the stock market were normally in their thirties and computer boffins to boot. But Kenneth Horne was the exception who proved the rule. His company, the Robert Horne Group, was a major paper merchant, and when it came to the Unlisted Securities market in 1984, Horne was 71 years old.

But that did not stop eager City investors scrambling to invest in the business founded in 1925 by Horne's

## Lord Rayne  £79m

*Property owner*

dob 8/2/18

Max, now Lord, Rayne has been a London property man since the 1940s. The son of an East End tailor who moved to Oxford Street, Lord Rayne worked for his father before the war. After wartime service with the RAF he moved into property and found he could make more money letting his father's showroom than as a tailor.

He specialised in buying sites in areas that were unfashionable, developing them and watching as prices and rents soared. He was the first to spot the potential of the Angel, Islington (known to all Monopoly buffs), five

biggest soft-porn empires in Soho. His father was a haulage contractor, while his mother was a fierce Roman Catholic and daughter of a police superintendent. Up to the age of 13 he was all set to join the priesthood, but his mother stopped him entering a seminary. His interest found other outlets and he would often dress up as a priest, playing with holy statues and pretending to say Mass. On the outbreak of war he was evacuated to Glossop in Derbyshire, where he remained until his early twenties.

During the war he started work as an office boy with a Manchester estate agency by day, and at night he alternated between spells as a firewatcher and as a drummer in a local band. Eventually he went full-time as a drummer. He was called up by the RAF but managed to find a nice cushy billet there. He was able to spend his days buying and selling second-hand cars

minutes north of the Bank of England. His company, London Merchant Securities, is interested in oil and leisure industries as well as property.

He has been married twice and his second wife is the daughter of the 8th Marquess of Londonderry. His son, the Hon. Robert Rayne, is now also active in the family business.

Lord Rayne is a patron of the arts. For 16 years he was chairman of the National Theatre, retiring at the end of 1989. His office wall is dotted with valuable paintings; he gave £250,000 to the National Gallery to help it buy Cézanne's *Les Grandes Baigneuses*.

---

# Paul Raymond £78m

*Publishing and theatre*
*entrepreneur*

Paul Raymond, born Geoffrey Quinn in Liverpool, had a strong dose of religion and law and order in his youth. But it did not stop him developing one of the

and organising local dances at a big profit. 'I suppose you could say I was a spiv,' he said in the 1970s.

After the war Raymond continued in show business. In 1947, he started work at Clacton-on-Sea funfair, where a palmist gave him a mind-reading code. He learnt this by heart and started doing a mind-reading act in Llandudno. In 1951 he left Glossop for good and came to London, where he played the drums again and started a revue show, which toured the country for six years. He started nude shows when a Manchester theatre owner would only give him a booking if he had nude dancers. Raymond paid two girl dancers 10 shillings a week extra to go topless. The show was exactly the same otherwise, but takings went up fivefold.

But as British theatres gradually closed down for financial reasons, Raymond realised that he would have to have his own place, and in 1958 he opened Raymond's Revuebar. It was an immediate success. He also invested in other theatres and ran two well-known soft-porn magazines, *Men Only* and *Club International*.

His wife – a former stage con-tortionist – divorced him in 1974 and received the then record British settle-ment of £250,000. She named Fiona Richmond, a star of the sex revues staged by Raymond, as co-respondent in the divorce action.

Today, Raymond has toned down his magazines and has tried hard to clean up Soho. He has branched out into lucrative property development. His daughter Debbie helps run his organ-isation, which showed £6.3 million profits in its latest accounts. He lives alone in a luxury flat in the St James area of London which was once the home of Lord Beaverbrook, a very different media magnate.

# Antony Crosthwaite Eyre and family £77m
*Former publisher*

dob ACE 22/8/40

The Crosthwaite Eyres have been con-nected with publishing since the days of Charles II through Eyre & Spot-tiswoode, their family firm.

This became part of Associated Book Publishers in the 1960s and the family took a 37% stake in the business. A few weeks before the October 1987 market crash, International Thomson took over ABP and bought the Eyre holdings for £77 million in cash, nearly three times their value a month later. Had either party waited until after the crash, the price could well have been reduced by around £14 million as the value of many publishing company shares fell by nearly 20% in the débâcle.

The Eyres are a well-known New Forest family, and have owned a 1,000-acre estate near Lyndhurst for centuries. Antony's father, the late Sir Oliver Crosthwaite Eyre, was MP for the area. The family has had con-nections with publishing since the sev-enteenth century. In the eighteenth century, one of the Eyre family paid £10,000 for the right to be the Queen's printer for 30 years. This royal patent was later extended and gave the family a virtual monopoly to print the Bible in England. Anthony, the present head of the family, is a leading British Roman Catholic. He married a Belgian count-ess in 1960, but they later divorced. They have five children.

# Sir Peter Michael  £76m

*Industrialist*

dob 13/6/38

The clever graphic illustrations seen on television news bulletins and the like come from a device called the Paintbox, designed by a high-tech company in Berkshire. UEI is the company responsible and its former chairman, Peter Michael, is the archetypal 1980s electronics entrepreneur. He works from four half-timbered 18th-century cottages overlooking the Kennet and Avon canal, flies a helicopter, and relaxes by playing squash or tennis or listening to opera. He has recently bought a large farm in Wiltshire.

He was born in Croydon, the son of the 'Mick' Michael who built up the Stanley Gibbons stamp chain. He had a comfortable upbringing in the Croydon stockbroker belt, and went to private school followed by an electronics degree at London University.

After working in British industry and being depressed by its lack of vision, he branched out on his own to form a company called Quantel which merged into UEI in 1982. He became chairman the same year.

A former member of Mrs Thatcher's think-tank, Michael was knighted in the Queen's birthday honours list in 1989. Equally significant was his complete change of career from running UEI, a successful company, to becoming a company doctor, nursing an ailing company back to health.

In 1989 he agreed to merge UEI with Michael Green's Carlton Communications, in a £526 million deal which netted Sir Peter some £76 million personally. At the time he planned to stay on as joint chairman but he later decided to leave the group. He moved into the troubled Cray Electronics group, where he took a 5% stake along with two other ex-UEI colleagues. Their plan is to turn the company around in a move which could earn Michael another fortune of up to £15 million, according to City experts.

# Charanjit and Satinder Vohra  £76m

*Hoteliers*

dob CV 12/2/42   SV *c.* 1948

The Vohra family, led by brothers Charanjit and Satinder, are rapidly building up one of the biggest hotel chains in London. They currently own some 1,500 London hotel rooms in six, mainly three- or four-star, establishments. Among the hotels run by their private Crysanta chain are the Washington in Mayfair and the Rubens in Victoria.

Ironically, the Vohras gave a big boost to their major rivals, their cousin Jasminder Singh (q.v.) who runs the Edwardian Hotel group. When Jasminder arrived in Britain from Nairobi, he sought the advice of Satinder Vohra on what career he should pursue. Vohra took him under his wing and gave him an 18-month training course in all aspects of the hotel business. They went into partnership and bought the Edwardian Hotel in London's Harrington Gardens. Eighteen months later, they sold up and bought another. But they have since parted and are now friendly rivals.

Both Charanjit and Satinder were born in Nairobi and later came to Britain to make their fortunes. Charanjit, who arrived in 1960, lists his hobbies as golf and swimming, and supports various religious, social and welfare organisations.

---

# John Brotherton-Ratcliffe and family £75m

*Property owners and developers*

Born in the London suburb of Ealing and later moving to Purley, John Brotherton-Ratcliffe went to Oxford University before the war, where he served in the university air squadron. He was commissioned in the RAF Volunteer Reserve in 1939, serving in South Africa and the Middle East. In August 1944, by then a squadron leader, he was awarded the DSO for displaying 'outstanding determination to complete his missions regardless alike of enemy opposition or adverse weather'.

In December 1943, the citation continued 'Squadron Leader Brotherton-Ratcliffe was forced to leave his aircraft by parachute and, early in this year, he was involved in a very serious crash. Despite these harassing experiences, his keenness for operational flying is undiminished and by his skill, courage and devotion to duty this officer has set an inspiring example to all.'

After the war he founded Croudace, a small family building company. Today it is one of the largest builders and developers in the country still in private hands. In 1988 it reported after-tax profits of over £15 million on a turnover of £113.5 million. All the shares in the company are owned by Brotherton-Ratcliffe or his four children, who are now all grown up. If the company was floated on the stock market, it would be worth around £150 million. In the early 1960s he moved from South Godstone to a large Sussex mansion, which was completely gutted by fire in 1977 and has since been rebuilt.

The company is based in the Surrey town of Caterham and undertakes housebuilding, construction work and property development mainly in the London and Home Counties area. In the year to the end of September 1988, Croudace built 1,062 homes and was planning a major shopping centre in Sutton. But the group could not avoid the effect of high interest rates on housebuilding, and Brotherton-Ratcliffe warned in his annual report that, 'Because of changes in market conditions, we expect the margins on sales to be reduced from the 26% level to more normal levels.' But he also saw a boost to general construction work, which 'is looking more promising than it has for several years, so we are now planning to expand in that area, building upon a current 18 months' workload'.

# Peter Greenall and family   £75m

*Brewers*

dob PG 18/7/53

Though not yet into middle age, Old Etonian Peter Greenall has few heights left to conquer. As a Cambridge undergraduate he took a year off his studies to try to become a champion amateur jockey. He succeeded. Today he is busy making his way in the business world as chairman of the Aintree racecourse and in the brewing field where he is being groomed to take over the helm of his family's Greenall Witley company.

Based in Warrington and famous for its Vladivar Vodka, Greenall Witley started by the Greenalls in the 18th century is one of the largest independent brewers left in Britain. Peter Greenall is now the only family member on the board, through his younger brother John also works for the group.

Apart from his business interests, Peter is a keen skier and frequently entertains younger members of the royal family such as the Prince and Princess of Wales and the Duke and Duchess of York at his luxury chalet at Klosters. John Greenall and his wife Gabrielle are also close friends of the Duke and Duchess of York, and Gabrielle is a godmother to Princess Beatrice.

Peter Greenall will one day inherit the title Lord Daresbury, currently held by his octogenarian grandfather who lives in Ireland.

# Sir Phil Harris   £75m

*Carpet merchant*

dob 15/9/42

When his father died, Phil Harris, a 15-year-old Streatham Grammar School boy, took over running the family's three lino and carpet shops in south London. Thirty-one years later, Sir Phil is worth a fortune, having sold his Harris Queensway company to James Gulliver (q.v.), the Scottish entrepreneur.

Until mid-1987 the Harris career had been a glittering success, with headlong expansion. New stores were opened, other companies acquired and Harris was regarded as one of Britain's brightest young business men.

But then profits began to slide and eventually Harris sold the company retaining only a soft furnishing business. Sir Phil seemed almost a beaten man.

*Sir Phil Harris*

But it is too early to write him off. While Harris Queensway (now called Lowndes Queensway) has lurched from one crisis to another, leading to the resignation of Gulliver, Sir Phil has begun a new business called Carpet-right. He will compete directly with Lowndes and plans to have nearly 40 outlets in operation in 1990. He has already poached key executives from Lowndes.

Outside work, his great love is show jumping. He gives large amounts of his money to Guy's Hospital, the res-toration fund for Westminster Abbey and charities such as Birthright.

# Mick Jagger    £75m
*Pop singer*

dob 26/7/43

A lithe figure, pouting lips and gyrating hips were Mick Jagger's hallmarks on stage as he belted out hits like 'Jumping Jack Flash' or 'Honky Tonk Woman' to adoring female audiences for over 20 years. After a seven-year gap, the Rolling Stones – with Jagger at the helm – decided on a world tour in 1990 which was expected to gross £100 million.

Raised in the London dormitory town of Dartford by his father Joe, a PT instructor, Mick went to the London School of Economics but dropped out and turned to music. After a time in small clubs, the Rolling Stones finally achieved their first hit in 1963 and never looked back.

In the early days, Mick was a distinctly anti-establishment figure, swearing and, on tour, indulging in drugs and orgies at hotels with the inevitable groupies who followed the Stones.

But since the early 1980s Mick has mellowed and devoted himself to his family and Jerry Hall, the equally lithe American model who shares his life. She is wealthy in her own right, owning a Texas ranch.

There have been many women in his life and he has four children: a daughter by Marsha Hunt, the former star of *Hair*, another daughter by his former wife Bianca, and a son and daughter by Jerry Hall. In 1979 Bianca picked up an estimated £1 million in a British divorce settlement with Mick.

He was considered lucky to have escaped so lightly. In America she would have been awarded much more.

Today Mick numbers Desmond Guinness and Jacob Rothschild (q.v.) among his friends. He collects paintings and houses. He owns a £2 million château in the Loire Valley, a £1.5 million Manhattan town house and a £5 million Caribbean retreat. Drugs and drink are out now as Mick pursues a punishing physical fitness regime to stay in trim and keep his weight at a constant 10 stone. 'It's horrible to be called the Grand Old Man of Rock,' he says.

Mick tried a solo career and earned £3 million for five concerts in Japan. But the magic was missing without the other Stones, so they agreed on the world tour, spending weeks in the Caribbean practising and recording.

He has had a stormy relationship with Keith Richard, the Rolling Stones guitarist, who resented Mick's assumption that he is leader of the group. They nearly split the group permanently, but finally buried the hatchet at a meeting in Barbados in the summer of 1989.

# Simon Miller   £75m
## *Property developer*

Simon Miller runs the Charter Group, one of London's most profitable private development companies which in its accounts for 1989 made profits of £16 million after tax on a turnover of £105 million. With large cash reserves and small borrowings, the group should really be valued at some £100 million, though the early 1990s downturn in the property market could push that down to £75 million.

Miller's success came from spotting the development potential of London's Docklands at the right time. He undertook three major projects in the Isle of Dogs Enterprise Zone in the mid-1980s. Among his schemes was a Business Efficiency Centre and the 1.25 million square foot Harbour Exchange. The group also undertakes interior design work for offices and supplies office furniture.

Simon Miller and his family own all the shares in Charter, and they live in a manor house north of London.

---

# Earl of Radnor    £75m

## Landowner

dob 10/11/27

In 1714 an eminent London merchant, William des Bouveries, was created a baronet by the Walpole government. Succeeding generations managed to rise in the ranks of the British aristocracy until one was created the first Earl of Radnor in 1765. The family name may be Welsh, but it is Salisbury in Wiltshire with which the family has long-standing links. William des Bouveries' son sat as MP for New Sarum, and a later earl sat as MP for Salisbury and Wiltshire South in the 19th century.

Today Jacob Pleydell-Bouverie, the 8th Earl, lives in Longford Castle near Salisbury, where he has a 10,000-acre estate. His father, a noted expert on forestry and farming, died in 1968. His estate was then valued at £4.3 million. The present Earl was able to satisfy death duties on the estate in 1970 by selling a portrait by Velázquez which fetched £2.3 million. The loss of the picture barely dented one of the finest collections in Britain. This includes a Holbein portrait of Erasmus, a Claude landscape and two pictures by Franz Hals. One Hals and other paintings were stolen in 1969 but were recovered the following year. Even then, the stolen paintings were valued at £75,000.

Despite installing an elaborate alarm system, the Earl – family motto: 'My country is dear, my liberty is dearer' – refuses to open Longford to the public. He once said: 'The people who come around here might be very nice, but you wouldn't want to see and hear them all the time. I am told that you can even smell them, and eventually your house takes on an odour like a railway station.'

Apart from land and paintings, the Radnor family also has valuable London holdings. The Bouverie name gives the clue: this famous street – just off Fleet Street – contains two invaluable properties, Harmsworth House and Northcliffe House West whose freehold is owned by Radnor's son, Viscount Folkestone. With former newspaper buildings in that area changing hands for up to £100 million, the two properties are worth at least £50 million. The family also own substantial property in Folkestone, which is expected to appreciate considerably in value once the Channel Tunnel opens in 1993.

The Earl, who has been married twice and divorced twice, has two sons and four daughters. His heir, Viscount Folkestone, was educated – like his father – at Harrow. He then went to the Royal Agricultural College in Cirencester. He lives near Salisbury.

OPPOSITE PAGE *Peter Thomas*

# Stanley and Peter Thomas £75m
## Food producers

Pies and savoury snacks have always been in the Thomas blood. In 1952 Stanley Thomas senior decided to launch a pie business in Merthyr in the heart of the South Wales coalfields. He had taken over a local bakery in 1947 and concentrated on making bread and cakes until meat rationing was lifted in 1952. Stanley junior and Peter Thomas joined their father in the business aged 15 and 18 respectively.

The recipe for the pies had been concocted by their grandparents in their kitchen, years before. The business prospered mainly because of the hard work and the personal touch that the Thomas family put into it. Peter Thomas used to scrub pie tins until his hands bled and he also went out selling the pies: 'You might make as many as 23 calls in a single street. I remember travelling all over the valleys around Merthyr, starting at six in the morning and finishing at six at night. I might make 170 calls in one day,' he told the *Western Mail*. The business prospered so much that in 1965 it was sold to the Avana group.

In 1970 Stanley Thomas junior decided to launch his own business and he was joined by his brother Peter, with Stanley senior and sister Mary as directors. The company, called Peter's Savoury Products, gained a reputation for providing the solid fare needed by South Wales miners and their rugby clubs. Its pies were also sold in the Italian and Greek cafés in the valleys. In 1976 the company spent £1 million on building a modern pie factory in mid-Glamorgan and opened depots in

Bristol and the Midlands. Later it took over other sausage and bacon manufacturers and built a £2 million sausage and beefburger factory.

In November 1988 the company was sold to Grand Metropolitan for £75 million, the largest sum ever paid for a private business in Wales.

Peter Thomas stayed on to run it under Grand Met, while Mary and Stan planned new careers. Peter lives in a five-bedroom Merthyr house with 16 acres of grounds and drives a Mercedes, while Mary, a Jaguar driver, lives in a similar Cardiff house with 2 acres, Stan, who also lives in Cardiff, said after the sale: 'I've just ordered a Bentley and I wouldn't mind a little sailing yacht.'

# Christopher Wates and family £75m
*Builder*

dob CW 25/12/39

Wates' progress from a small house-builder to a large-scale developer in London was mainly the work of the late Sir Ronald Wates and his brothers Norman and Allan. The firm is still in family hands, with Christopher Wates, Norman's son, running Wates Holdings.

The family floated their property business on the Stock Exchange in 1984, but they retain a 25% stake.

The Wates family have considerable bloodstock interests. Michael, Sir Ronald's son, runs the Bloodstock Breeding Company and is a successful breeder himself. Michael's brother Andrew, another director of the company, has ridden 24 winners under National Hunt Rules and is a member of the Jockey Club. He lives in Dorking.

Christopher lives in Sussex, while Michael's home is a Dorset manor house.

# Sir Gordon White £75m
*Industrialist*

dob 11/5/23

In 1940 17-year-old Gordon White left his job selling advertising space for his father's publishing business and went into the army, where he served in Force 136, a unit of the Special Operations Executive, the forerunner of the CIA and the SAS. It was there that he made friends with Bill Hanson, the younger brother of the future Lord Hanson (q.v.). After the war the friendship continued when Bill went back to work for his family haulage business, Oswald Tillotson, while White became chair-

man of his family business, Welbecson, in 1947. In 1954 Bill Hanson died of stomach cancer, and White got to know James, the elder brother, who described him as a 'surrogate brother'.

They were to become partners when their respective businesses were taken over by the Hull-based Wiles Group. But later, Hanson and White bought out Wiles, which was later renamed the Hanson Trust. Today Hanson is one of the largest and most successful British companies, with huge interests ranging from food to building materials, batteries and typewriters. It buys and sells businesses like any commodity, but always at a handsome profit. White never visits the companies owned by Hanson, preferring to leave their smooth running to top-class managers.

The 6ft 6in 'Gordy', as he is called, runs the American side of the operations called Hanson Industries from a Park Avenue address. He enjoyed a certain notoriety as a playboy, not marrying until he was 35. By then his name had been linked in gossip columns to Ava Gardner, Rita Hayworth and even Marilyn Monroe. Eventually Gordon settled down with a Swedish wife who produced two daughters; his second wife, a former starlet, Virginia North, produced a son.

He currently shares his life with Victoria Tucker, a model some 40 years younger than him. She has been pressing him to marry, but to no avail. One of his favourite phrases is: 'Never marry a young girl – they want babies.'

Apart from business, White finds time to relax aboard his 176-foot yacht, *Galu*. The yacht is now on the market, with offers invited of over £8.5 million. He has homes in New York, London and California. He also has extensive bloodstock interests and backed the English Derby through sponsorship. He lists his other hobbies as skiing, riding, tennis and, as a qualified helicopter pilot, flying.

# John Whittaker £75m
*Property developer*

In 1986 John Whittaker burst into national prominence when his company, Peel Holdings, tried to take over the old Manchester Ship Canal Company. One of the most bitter takeover battles in recent times then ensued. While Whittaker was able to buy up a majority of the shares, the voting structure of the company prevented him taking full control. Accusations and counter-charges flew from one side to another as the old management tried to resist Whittaker, who was attracted by the property potential alongside the canal. There were even reports of door-to-door canvassers out in Lancashire towns like Blackburn seeking to buy up small parcels of shares.

Whittaker never gave up, and nearly two and a half years later he finally obtained control of the canal. The deal is believed to have netted him a £20 million profit. It was typical of the opportunism that has made him one of the north's most successful property developers. With a farming background in the Rochdale area, the thrifty Lancastrian is a devout Catholic who once considered entering the priesthood but went into business instead. He started in quarrying when the trans-Pennine motorway M62 was being built in 1962. The quarrying profits financed his expansion into demolition, knocking down redundant factories and mills.

Whittaker soon saw that he could make more money by taking over the ailing companies, rationalising them to develop their successful operations and then redeveloping their surplus factories. By the time the bid for the canal was launched he employed 1,000 people in ten different companies around Liverpool and Manchester. He also became one of the most successful out-of-town shopping and leisure park developers.

He saw the potential goldmine in the canal in the shape of 300 derelict acres at Barton Dock, on the edge of Manchester. With access to four separate motorway junctions near by, it was an ideal site for a £100 million 'shopping city' able to draw on a customer base of 5 million people, all living within a 40-minute drive.

Whittaker is a secretive and elusive man. He bought up many of the run-down companies via his parents' Isle of Man company, Largs Ltd. Largs owns half the shares in the quoted company, Peel Holdings, based in Rochdale.

Whittaker has surrounded himself with a young team of executives whom he allows to get on with the job, though he is said to pay low salaries. He is proud to be British and his favoured

recreation is said to be going to the pub for a pint with the lads. He does not display any of the ostentation of a millionaire. He is known to turn up late to meetings with City analysts because he insists on travelling by tube. He has a home on the Isle of Man and a farmhouse near Rochdale.

---

# Leonard van Geest and family £72m
*Fruit and food seller*

dob 1/4/50

Leonard van Geest, a 6ft 7in multimillionaire, had a textbook training to take over the family business, best known for its bananas and other exotic fruits. First he went into management consultancy, then worked for a top London accountancy firm before moving on to Marks & Spencer.

In 1976 he finally joined Geest and moved up the organisation to succeed his father, also called Leonard, as chairman in 1980. His father was one of three Dutch brothers whose family were horticulturists. In the 1930s they started exporting bulbs to Britain and in 1935 the three brothers came over to set up their own British company. With only £2,000 capital they began importing Dutch bulbs and selling them to commercial growers in Britain. The breakthrough came in 1952 when Geest negotiated a franchise to distribute the banana crops of the Windward Islands. Geest now handles half the bananas sold in Britain.

Today the company that was responsible for introducing avocados, red

peppers and kiwi fruit to this country is tempting British taste with new exotic fruits. It sells its products to major supermarkets and has moved into new areas such as prepared foods. It recently bought a manufacturer of chilled pizzas and it is spending heavily on new warehouses. Geest was floated on the stock market in 1986 and profits have been rising sharply. In 1989 the company made £20 million pre-tax profits, a rise of 9.5 on 1988's figure. The company imported 266,000 tons of bananas in 1988, an increase of 43% over 1987. The family owns 38% of the shares.

Leonard van Geest lives in a Regency farmhouse near Spalding, Lincolnshire, surrounded by the firm's bulb fields. His wife Gillian is a physiotherapist and they have a young son, Ross.

He is a keen rugby and tennis player. The family are enthusiastic followers of horseracing, and have several horses at a Newmarket stable.

# Sir David Alliance  £71m

*Textile industrialist*

dob 15/3/32

From running his first textile business in Iran at 16, Alliance has graduated to a business with 100,000 staff in 30 countries.

The son of a Jewish merchant, Alliance came to Britain in 1951 looking for supplies, and instead stayed on to move into the British textile industry. By 1953 he had bought his first mill for £8,000 and was on the way to a fortune. Today he runs Coats Viyella, and after a series of mergers in the 1970s and 1980s made it one of the world's largest textile companies.

But his luck has not always held up. Alliance was one of the biggest victims

*Sir David Alliance*

# John Apthorp and family £71m

*Former frozen food entrepreneurs*

dob JA 25/4/35

The television dinner taken straight from the freezer owes its success in Britain to John Apthorp, a business man noted for his distinctive bushy beard. In 1968 he started Bejam, a specialist retailer of both frozen foods and the freezers themselves, named after the initials of all his family members. The first store was in a Middlesex banana warehouse.

By 1975 there were 100 stores and, five years later, Bejam had sold 500,000 freezers.

Apthorp and his brother Brian, a Hong Kong doctor, were the principal shareholders in the group, and the

of the 1987 stock market crash. His shareholdings plunged in value by £73 million during 1988 – £200,000 a day. But they had slightly recovered by 1990 and, from a low point of £65 million, the Alliance fortune is now worth around £71 million.

Sir David Alliance lives in Manchester and London, and is an avid collector of L. S. Lowry paintings.

family at one time owned 30% of Bejam. In late 1988 they lost control after a bitter takeover battle to the rival Iceland Frozen Foods chain who paid £238 million for Bejam.

John Apthorp lives in Hertfordshire, enjoying shooting and fine wines.

## Earl of Lonsdale  £71m
*Landowner*

dob 3/11/22

Four times married, Lord Lonsdale owns 80,000 acres of Cumbria. His family gave boxing the Lonsdale Belt. His grandfather was known as the 'Yellow' Earl both because of his extravagant lifestyle in Edwardian society and for his yellow carriages. His vast wealth came from rich undersea mines off Whitehaven in Cumbria. This enabled him to keep two large yachts off Cowes and entertain in style. He spent £3,000 a year on cigars alone and King Edward VII called him 'almost an emperor, not quite a gentleman'.

The present Earl has totally revitalised the estates, which were nearly bankrupt when he inherited in 1949. He is chairman and major shareholder in Lakeland Investments, which has extensive farming and forestry interests. Showing a practical turn of mind, he has installed an electronic sawmill on what was once the site of his own private railway station. Lowther Park, on his estate, is a mini-Alton Towers theme park.

In 1987 he made £400,000 by selling up to 30 Lords of Manor titles,

which are the original form in which English land and titles were expressed. In 1988 he sold a further 30 at an average price of over £13,000.

## Chris Blackwell  £70m
*Record producer*

Harrow-educated, Blackwell comes from an old-established Jamaica plantation family, the Delissers, who made their fortune in the 18th century. But Blackwell made his money more recently – and well away from the plantation business. After leaving school he went to New York in the late 1950s,

where he developed a love of jazz. He went on to try his hand at watersports, real estate and accountancy, but boredom drove him out of those businesses. Combining his interest in jazz with the Jamaican music he had picked up in his childhood, he went on to found Island Records in 1962. He toured Britain's inner cities selling his records from the back of an old Mini Clubman. At last he had found his true vocation.

In 1964 his first hit came with Millie's 'My Boy Lollipop', which reached number two in the pop charts. By the end of the 1960s Island was Britain's leading independent record company and Blackwell branched out into the hippie market with groups like Traffic, Fairport Convention and Jethro Tull.

His biggest coup came in spotting and promoting an obscure Jamaican singer called Bob Marley in the early 1970s. Later, after some hesitation and an initial rejection, he signed the Irish super-group U2.

Blackwell was offered £6 million for Island Records in 1969 by Warner Brothers, but he turned down the offer. It was not until 20 years later – and at a price that had risen to £200 million – that he finally sold out to Polygram, collecting some £70 million for his share stake.

Blackwell has homes and considerable real estate around the world. These include Ian Fleming's old Caribbean house, Goldeneye, a Paris flat, two London homes and an Oxfordshire mansion. He also has a permanent suite in a New York hotel and a Los Angeles home. Intensely shy, he dresses informally in track suit bottoms and flip-flops, and prefers the company of musicians to sober business men.

# Tony Clegg   £70m
*Former property developer*

dob 8/4/37

Northern grit, determination and sheer hard work were rolled into one in the shape of Tony Clegg, an ex-property developer with the build of a Rugby League player.

Clegg, a bluff Lancastrian (born and raised in Manchester) who has defected to the other side of the Pennines, worked a reputed 18-hour day on multi-million-pound property deals for his Mountleigh company, one of the stock market stars of the 1980s. He rushed from appointment to appointment and even missed his own 50th birthday. Clegg was well known in property circles, dealing with such stars as Elliott Bernerd (q.v.) and Stuart Lipton (q.v.). He regularly commuted by plane from his Pudsey headquarters to his Mayfair head office and was renowned for having one of the longest list of mobile car telephone numbers to keep in touch with his multitude of deals.

Success brought Clegg a private plane, a Rolls Royce Camargue with personalised number plates and a large house near Wetherby, as well as a strong following among City investors. But he has now left that life behind him and has retired to Yorkshire with some £70 million to enjoy the fruits of his 1980s dealmaking skills.

Clegg attributed his business acumen to his mother who, left to fend for herself when her navy husband went off to the war, bought and ran a small corner shop which stayed open all hours. Later, his parents prospered and opened two restaurants. Clegg was sent to boarding school but left at 16 to become a general dogsbody for his parents' business, before the army claimed him for National Service.

In the Pay Corps, Clegg spent his time handing money over to others. But that soon changed. In 1961 he joined a Glossop textile manufacturer. By 1963 it had been taken over by Mountain Mills, a worsted suit maker based in Bradford. Ernest Hall, the Mountain boss – now a well-known developer in his own right – saw Clegg's potential and asked him to come to Bradford as his right-hand man. A strong partnership was born, and through sheer hard work Clegg and Hall built up Mountain Mills, and took it to the stock market through a reverse takeover of another textile manufacturer, Leigh Mills, in 1966.

Despite the hard work, Clegg and Hall could not stave off the recession in the textile business in the 1970s. They looked around for new areas and alighted on property. It was a call from Conrad Ritblat, the top London estate agent, that made Clegg see the potential of property. Ritblat phoned to ask about buying a piece of land adjacent to one of Clegg's sites. Clegg decided to buy it himself for £24,000. He got the money back by levelling part of the site and letting a 12,000-sq. foot building for £1 per square foot per year.

Deals followed deals through the 1970s and into the 1980s, when Clegg started to be noticed by the City. By this stage Leigh Mills had been renamed Mountleigh, and Hall had branched out on his own, leaving Clegg at the helm. In 1985 he took on Paul Bloomfield (q.v.), an experienced property dealmaker with scores of contacts, as a consultant.

Clegg specialised in spotting the hidden assets in properties, snapping them up and selling them on quickly for substantial profit. In 1981 he bought 800 houses in Suffolk from the Post Office for £5.25 million. By April the following year, he had arranged a 10-year lease on them to the American government for £2 million a year. In 1986 he bought the United Real Property Trust for £117 million and quickly sold on the individual properties it owned for a total of £140 million.

In 1987 it appeared likely that he would take over Sir Terence Conran's (q.v.) Storehouse group, but Clegg backed away from a hostile bid.

But the pressure of hard work took its toll. In 1988 Clegg was found to have a brain tumour and was forced to undergo an operation and ease up on his business life. But he could not remain inactive for long and took up the reins at Mountleigh again. His stake in the business, which had been around 9 million shares in 1988, jumped to over 30 million early in 1989 as he re-established his presence in the business. This enlarged stake, which represented around 14% of the share capital, was worth nearly £60 million at the time.

The return to work proved too much for Clegg's health and within six months he had sold his shares for £70 million to two Americans and retired to his Yorkshire estate to attend to his

Highland cattle, one of his main passions. He also finds time to do charitable work, sitting on the committee raising funds for Ripon Cathedral and working for the Home Farm Trust, which helps disabled and handicapped people.

# Len and Nigel Jagger £70m

*Trader and business man*

dob 24/6/25

Channel Islands-based entrepreneur Len Jagger used to deal in Ford cars in Essex but sold his business in 1972. Since then he has built up a fortune by astutely investing in fledgling companies which grow into multi-million-pound businesses.

He invested in UEI, a high-flying electronics company, where he built up a sizeable stake. With his son Nigel, an America-based financier, he made £64 million out of the sale of a stake in Atlantic Computers, a computer leasing company run by the late John Foulston. Foulston, a racing car fanatic who was killed in a high-speed accident in 1987, had met Jagger on a beach in Barbados some years previously. Within months of their first meeting Jagger had put £8 million into the business.

# David Kirch £70m

*Property dealer*

dob c. 1938

In 1958, at the age of 20, David Kirch was left £5,000 by his father, a wholesale meat trader. Today he is worth £70 million and lives in Jersey, home of tax exiles.

His money-making skills started at Tonbridge School where he had a small business selling stamps. 'I wasn't clever enough to go to university. I went into Lloyds in insurance for a while,' he told the *Evening Standard* in 1970. He did not enjoy Lloyds and, when his father died, he joined the family meat business then run by his uncle. But Kirch could not get on with his uncle, and set up on his own, buying a cold store in Kingston and getting up at 5.30 every morning to choose meat at Smithfield market. The business was taken over

after a year by a Dutch company who wanted the property, not the business.

That convinced him that the future lay in property and he bought a half-share in a Hampshire estate agency. He gave that up to concentrate on property dealing, working out of his mother's house in Esher until 1962, when he went into partnership with his older brother, Peter. They formed a company, Crown Lodge Estates, and they managed to borrow enough money from a bank and insurance company to buy up 23 houses near London's Gloucester Road. They expanded and, by 1970, had around 1,000 tenants. They also bought the Shaftesbury Theatre, which they threatened to demolish until a preservation order saved it.

The Kirch brothers survived the property crash in the 1974–6 period by turning their extensive interests private. David Kirch went to live in Jersey at the time and conducted his property dealings from there, taking control of the Channel Hotels and Properties group in the 1980s. In September 1988 he sold his last UK residential properties for £30 million.

Kirch lived a modest life in Britain until his Jersey exile. As the *Evening Standard* put it: 'Often at weekends, he takes his mother down to his cottage at Shoreham-on-Sea, otherwise he sits alone in his 15-room mansion in Hyde Park Gate and watches colour TV after eating his solitary dinner served by his Spanish butler.' In Jersey, Kirch is busy refurbishing his impressive mansion.

# Peter Rigby   £70 m
*Computer distributor*

Born in Liverpool, 46-year-old Peter Rigby has made his fortune in the computer industry, a rare feat for a Briton. Even rarer, he has managed to hold on to it and prosper in a highly competitive industry.

But there is little about the industry that Rigby does not know intimately. He started his career at the age of 18 working for the NCR group as an apprentice where he stayed for 5 years. He then moved to Honeywell, the giant computer company. At 28 he was a branch manager. But by then he reckoned it was obvious that a British national's career path was blocked in the American computer giant, and 'I wasn't prepared to see my career path flattened,' he says.

Having raised £2,000 capital he branched out on his own in the early

1970s. He chose the computer recruitment business as his field and, with the growing skills shortages in that field, he prospered. As the money poured in, he invested it in new areas of the computer industry, establishing his own computer bureau in the early 1980s.

Known as Specialist Computer Holdings, the business grew on the back of sales of IBM and Honeywell machines and Rigby's attention to detail. That was demonstrated when, in 1988 and 1989, SCH won what Rigby calls 'the badge that really matters' – the IBM dealer of the year award. The success was apparent in financial terms also. In the year to the end of March 1989 SCH's sales totalled £47m, producing a £3.4m profit. A year later sales had risen to over £70m, with profits of £4.7m. In the 1990–1991 year, Rigby estimates that sales will exceed £100m. With few borrowings and all the shares in his family hands, he says that he would not contemplate selling SCH for less than £75m. Rigby lives in the smart West Midland commuter belt with his wife Patricia.

---

# Duke of Roxburghe £70m

*Landowner*

dob 18/11/54

It was billed as the romance of the decade when Guy Innes-Ker, Duke of Roxburghe, married Lady Jane Grosvenor, the beautiful sister of the Duke of Westminster (q.v.). They met in 1975 at a party on the Duke of Westminster's Fermanagh estate (he owns much of the county) when Roxburghe was serving with the army in the elite Blues and Royals cavalry regiment. The gossip columnists had a field day, discussing the combined fortunes. That was in 1977.

In March 1990 the Duchess filed her divorce papers. She moved out of beautiful Floors Castle on the Scottish Borders and into a six-bedroom Georgian house a few miles away, taking her three children with her. It was said that the reason for the split was the Duke's 'roving eye'. The Duchess clearly hinted at such in an interview with the *Daily Express*: 'All I will say is that boys will be boys. And sometimes a busy mother with three children has to expect a little flirtation from her husband.'

Floors sits among 56,000 acres of good-quality farm and sporting land. It includes some priceless Tweed salmon-fishing rights. By selling a part of them off in 1974, the Duke was able to satisfy the death duties owing on the estate after his father's death. The Duke, educated at Eton and Sandhurst, where he took the Sword of Honour, the Academy's top award, later took a degree in land economy at Cambridge after he left the army.

Both the Duke and Duchess are close friends of the royal family who enjoy staying at Floors. The Duchess was godmother to the Duke and Duchess of York's first daughter.

The castle is filled with fine Brussels tapestries, many purchased by the wife of the 8th Duke, Mary Goelet, heiress to a 19th-century American magnate.

# Colin Sanders   £70m

*Computer engineer*

dob 23/2/47

As a 21-year-old, Colin Sanders deafened his parents with the sounds from his hi-fi. But what was then a hobby for the bright Oxford graduate who loved tinkering with electronics has turned into a multi-million-pound business.

It started in 1969 when Sanders – armed with £13 capital – invented an electronic device for use in organs to switch the air from the bellows down the right pipe. The device was snapped up by organ players and owners round the world. Some 12,000 were installed in places as far apart as Westminster Abbey and the Sydney Opera House, at a cost of £10,000 each.

Music-loving Sanders followed this up by inventing a computerised recording console in 1975, with some 9,000 separate controls to help in the making and mixing of records, another of his favourite hobbies. In 1979 the BBC gave a boost to his company, Solid State Logic, by ordering £200,000 worth of equipment for its Manchester studios. In 1984 there followed a £250,000 order from the China Record Company for recording-studio systems.

By then Solid State had an annual turnover of £20 million and 330 employees at its premises, a former convent school. By 1986 Solid State was able to boast some 50% of the world market for recording-studio equipment and was growing at around 25% a year. At this point Sanders decided to join forces with UEI, a similar but much larger high-technology business. Sanders received UEI shares worth nearly £30 million at the time of the sale, which represented around 14.4% of the total share equity. Three years later, when UEI agreed a friendly £492 million merger with Michael Green's (q.v.) Carlton Communications group, Sanders' shares were worth over £70 million.

# John James Fenwick and family   £65m

*Department store owner*

dob JJF 9/8/32

It may not be Harrods but the Fenwicks chain has built up a solid reputation and turnover. In 1988 it made profits of over £14 million.

John James Fenwick founded the first store in Newcastle in 1882, followed by another in London's exclusive Bond Street in 1891. Today the group has branches dotted round the country and is run by another John James Fenwick, great-grandson of the founder. The family still own most of the company's shares. But with the downturn in retail spending in 1989 and 1990 the value of the business, if floated on the stock market, could be clipped back to £65 million against £95 million in 1988.

John Fenwick was educated at Rugby and Pembroke College, Cambridge. In 1957 he married Gillian Hodnett, a physiotherapist at the Newcastle General Hospital. They have three sons. He is a member of the Marylebone Cricket Club and the Garrick Club and lists travel, theatre and shooting as his hobbies. Though he lives in a fashionable area of Chelsea, he has strong links with the North East and is a governor of the Royal Grammar School in Newcastle and a director of the Northern Rock Building Society.

# Cameron Mackintosh £65m
*Impresario*

Every time a theatre-goer sees *Cats* or *Phantom of the Opera* or *Les Misérables*, Cameron Mackintosh gets that little bit richer. The youngest and most successful impresario in the history of the British theatre, he is the son of a business man who ran a timber firm and a half-French, half-Italian mother. At 18 he became a stage hand at the Drury Lane Theatre, supporting himself by doing extra cleaning work in the mornings. By the age of 21 he had become a producer in his own right. He started out with a job in the musical *Camelot* and later toured with *Oliver* as an assistant stage manager. He once appeared nude on stage in Glasgow in the hippie musical *Hair*.

Though his first West End musical, *Anything Goes*, was a flop, his next two were minor successes. Finally his fourth, *Side by Side*, made money. But it was when he joined forces with Andrew Lloyd Webber (q.v.) in 1981 to produce *Cats* that the cash started rolling in. For a £450,000 initial investment, the show grossed over £500 million in 20 countries. Since then the money has kept coming in. In 1990 *Les Misérables* is running in 12 countries, and has grossed over £200 million, while *Phantom of the Opera* has made about £1 million in Britain and taken £106 million abroad. Mackintosh's next production, *Miss Saigon*, was voted best musical of 1989 by the London *Evening Standard*.

Though he now has a large London house, a cottage in Hampshire, a villa in the south of France and a small croft in Scotland, he has not always enjoyed such affluence. When describing his early days on the road, he said: 'There was a wonderful system called "putting a cheque on the road" whereby you had four or five bank accounts, at least one of which had to be in the Outer Hebrides, and one in Ireland, so your cheque would take two or three weeks to go through the system and by then you'd have put in another cheque to cover it. Hopefully, by the end of a 26-week tour, you'd be able to pay off all your bouncing cheques. I had no money at all. I used to get up very early on tour in order to draw my dole before the actors because it would upset them to meet their producer in a dole queue.'

Today Mackintosh commutes by helicopter from London to Scotland and is a generous supporter of charities. He offered Oxford University £2 million in July 1989 to endow a professorship of drama. He also supports charities for children and for AIDS. He is renowned for dressing casually in jeans and T-shirt.

---

# George Michael   £65m

*Pop star*

dob 26/6/63

His father gave him an ultimatum: 'You've got six months to make it or leave home.' That was enough to spur Georgias Kyriacos Panayoitou to take the plunge and enter the pop world with his school friend Andrew Ridgeley. The pair had first met as 12-year-olds at Bushey Meads comprehensive school. Thus was born Wham, with George changing his name to Michael and becoming the slickest pop star of the 1980s.

It is a classic rags-to-riches tale. George's father, Jack Panayoitou, arrived in London from Cyprus with little money and few prospects. But this Greek Cypriot moved into a cramped flat in Finchley and started work as a waiter, ending up as owner of a restaurant chain which made him a millionaire.

George left school in 1981 with two A levels and orders from his father to find work. He was certainly not going to be spoiled. Three days on a building site and a spell in British Home Stores convinced George that this sort of work was not for him.

But pop music was. A £20 demonstration disc, 'Wham Rap', led to a recording contract in 1982 for the unlikely pair. For the next four years, they toured the world and sold over 35 million records. Screaming fans pursued them and the Princess of Wales once described George as 'gorgeous'.

In 1986 the pair split, but George continued his solo career and was even more successful. His debut solo album, *Faith*, sold 15 million copies. In 1987 and 1988 his earnings totalled £24 million. Early in 1989 he earned £1 million for a day's work doing a Coca-Cola advertisement.

He spends the money as fast as he earns it. His homes include a £1.4 million mansion near his parents' Hertfordshire house, a £500,000 Knightsbridge flat near Harrods, a £350,000 mews house in St John's Wood and an £80,000 Soho flat plus three more

overseas. In total he has spent nearly £5 million on the homes and £3 million on a plane.

George started out as a socialist, appearing at a benefit concert during the 1984–5 miners' strike. But he came round to the view that Mrs Thatcher 'has given kids new drive'. He has not been happy with the fame and fortune, often appearing the worse for drink at awards ceremonies and lashing out at friends and photographers after the Wham breakup. He still remains good friends with Ridgeley.

thinly veiled attack on the Prince by claiming that in the past the great patrons of architecture had been royals, but today they were entrepreneurs.

Despite these differences Palumbo is a friend of royalty and a godfather to Princess Beatrice, elder daughter of the Duke and Duchess of York. He plays polo with Prince Charles. He lives in a manor house in Berkshire. His second wife, Hayat, presented him with a daughter in the summer of 1989.

## Peter Palumbo    £65m
*Property developer*

dob 20/7/35

A man with an obsession: for nearly 20 years Peter Palumbo has wanted to build a skyscraper on a valuable 6-acre City site built up by his father.

Although he received conditional planning permission in 1969, he could not get final approval until the 1980s when the last of the leases covering the Mansion House site had expired. By then the climate had changed and the City wanted to preserve the old Victorian buildings intact.

Old Etonian Palumbo may never see his lifelong ambitions realised. In March 1990 the High Court upheld efforts by conservationists to stop eight listed buildings being demolished on the Mappin and Webb site opposite the Mansion House.

The Prince of Wales thought the design looked like a 1930s wireless set, and this led to a rift between the two. Palumbo, the newly appointed chairman of the Arts Council, replied with a

# Raymond Slater  £65m

*Entrepreneur and property developer*

Born in Huddersfield just after the worst ravages of the Depression in 1934, Slater was brought up by his mother and grandmother after his father died. They ran a corner shop and young Raymond managed to get into the local grammar school before training as an estate agent in Bradford.

He showed early entrepreneurial talent by starting his own surveying and estate agency specialising in commercial property around Stockport. That was in 1959, a time when big property developers such as Jack Cotton and Charles Clore were doing deals in Manchester. Slater often acted for them and developed a taste for the business. He gave up his estate agency work and started dealing. Within a few years he was director of 34 property companies.

In the 1970s he was in the news over his efforts to wrest the then sleepy Norwest Holt property company from its controlling Le Mare family. It took a bitter eight-year battle for Slater to win in 1980. After that Slater bought out his former partner, John Lilley, sparking off another bitter row. But by the mid-1980s Slater had completely transformed Norwest Holt. A 1980 loss of nearly £2 million turned into a profit of £6 million in 1985. The group was planning a stock market flotation, but the dispute between Lilley and Slater killed that off. Instead, a management buy-out took place and Slater received some £40 million for his shares.

He sold his Cheshire home and went into tax exile in Guernsey, where he still lives. He retains substantial property, oil and gas interests in America. Apart from a passion for music – he was a regular at the Hallé Orchestra and a Friend of Covent Garden – Slater's main interest is in sport. He supports Manchester United Football Club, is a good tennis player and also plays golf and skis.

# Donald Bilton and family  £64m

*Property development heir*

dob DB 28/7/21

Making lubricating oil in his Ormskirk back garden and cycling round Lancashire selling it to farmers started Percy Bilton on the way to a fortune. In 1919 he went further and set up the Vizgol Oil Company, which covered Britain, South Africa and America. Later he moved into property and construction. By 1939 he had pulled together his extensive housebuilding and industrial development operations under his own name. In 1962 the oil interests were sold to Standard Oil of Indiana, and in 1972 he took the company on to the stock market.

His designated successor, who had been deputy chairman, fell out with him in 1976 and left, amid bitter disputes over the company accounts. Percy was forced to soldier on until he was nearly 80 while he drafted his son Donald on to the board as his successor. In 1979 there was another problem when Percy's wife sold £840,000 worth of shares the day before the company announced disappointing results. Percy claimed he was as surprised by what she had done as everybody else.

Though he stayed on as chairman and was planning his retirement, he died early in 1983 in Cape Town, South Africa. His dream of being succeeded by Donald did not materialise. Though Donald continues to sit on the board he prefers instead to concentrate on his vineyard in South Africa. He is also a round-the-world sailor.

Shortly after Percy's death, a British property group launched an opportunistic takeover bid for the group but was defeated. New management was installed and the group's fortunes improved markedly. Pre-tax profits increased by 38% in 1988.

Bilton family trusts, covering Percy Bilton's three children and their families, control over a third of the company. Percy Bilton lived in Virginia Water in Surrey, and left £1.8 million in his will. He left all his property to his second wife, Margherita.

owner of the British Midland fleet. When he took over the airline in 1978 he could not get any financial backing in the City and went to America for the finance. With a growing demand for airline travel, profits are soaring. In 1988 the group made £7.75 million profits on a turnover of £183 million.

Michael Bishop has half the shares in the airline, which has recently teamed up with SAS. The business is based in the beautiful Donnington Hall, near the Castle Donnington racecourse in Derbyshire.

# Michael Bishop £60m

*Airline operator*

dob 10/3/42

Airline passengers on the London-to-Glasgow route can thank Michael Bishop for the improvement in the quality of service.

Before he started a rival service, meals on the shuttles were rare. Today they are standard and of high quality, such is the level of competition from British Midland, Britain's second largest airline.

Bishop, formerly with Mercury Airlines, now runs Airlines of Britain, the

# Tony Budge £60m

*Construction contractor*

dob 9/8/39

In 1956 Tony Budge decided he did not want to be a bricklayer in his father's business, so he joined the local council highways department in Lincolnshire and became a junior engineer. After three years' apprenticeship, he went back to work for his father and built up the firm's civil engineering business. From then he never looked back, winning road contracts in the expansionist 1960s and 1970s.

Today AF Budge (Contractors) is in the big league. In 1988 its after-tax profits reached £9.3 million, valuing the Budge family stake at around £60 million if the company were floated on the Stock Exchange.

Tony Budge, a member of the Turf Club, lives in Retford where he is known for his passion for collecting old army tanks. A tank museum next to the Budge headquarters boasts 100 vehicles, including 30 Soviet tanks. Tanks line the approaches to the headquarters. An open day at the museum in 1988 attracted a crowd of 3,000, with the funds raised going to the Army Benevolent Fund.

Budge travels extensively and uses his own private aircraft based at a local airport.

# Marquess of Bute £60m

*Landowner*

dob 27/2/33

The 3rd Marquess of Bute developed Cardiff into a full-scale industrial port to exploit the coal trade in the 19th century. That built up a family fortune which still flourishes. The present 6th Marquess, a Roman Catholic, inherited the title in 1956. He was divorced and remarried in 1978. His second wife, Jennifer Percy, is the ex-wife of a Lonrho director.

He owns much of the isle of Bute and other islands off the west coast of Scotland. The family also has extensive landholdings in Spain, where they spend a good part of every year.

The family home on Bute, Mount Stuart, described as a Victorian Gothic pile, has a magnificent collection of books in its library. Some have been sold in recent years. In 1983 a collection of Bute manuscripts made over £730,000 at Sotheby's.

# Peter Cameron-Webb £60m

*Former underwriter*

There are a lot of people in Britain who would like to meet Peter Cameron-Webb again, preferably on British soil and in a court of law. A former star underwriter on the Lloyds insurance market, Cameron-Webb and his partner, Peter Dixon, fled to America in 1982 with over £130 million of their clients' money. The list of clients reads like *Who's Who*, and includes the Duchess of Kent, Lord Portman, the Duchess of Marlborough and Virginia Wade, the former tennis star.

Over a number of years Cameron-Webb and Dixon simply siphoned off the money from various Lloyd's syndicates, known as PCW syndicates after Cameron-Webb's initials. This money went into offshore tax havens, disguised as reinsurance contracts. It took years for the British authorities to unravel the complex case, by which time it was too late for the pair to be extradited to Britain to face justice. Although both have reached a settlement with Lloyd's involving hefty fines, they continue to be out of reach of the long arm of British law.

Cameron-Webb lives in some style in the Clipper Condominium in Miami, and is a well-known local figure in the expatriate British community. His former partner, Dixon, claims he has no money left.

# Earl of Cawdor    £60m

*Landowner*

dob 6/9/32

There really is a Thane of Cawdor: he is not just character in *Macbeth*, and he does live in Cawdor Castle, where King Duncan was killed in the Shakespeare play. Historically a thane was a minor noble with certain duties to the Crown. The title became baron in feudal times, and later earl.

A real incident did occur in 1498 when the wealthy daughter of the 8th Thane was abducted by the Campbells and forced to marry a younger son of the Earl of Argyll. Fortunately the marriage worked out rather well.

In 1976 the present Earl was forced to sell 36,000 acres in Wales to pay death duties. It was as owner of these estates that a previous Earl accepted the surrender of the last army to invade Britain – a French expeditionary force that landed in Fishguard in 1797. There are still 56,000 acres left in Cawdor hands around Nairn in Morayshire, including farms, forestry and moorland.

Cawdor Castle is being developed as a tourist attraction by the Earl's second wife, Angelika, a Hungarian countess in her own right.

# The Grant family    £60m
*Whisky distillers*

In 1887 William Grant and his nine children built the Glenfiddich distillery at Dufftown in Banffshire. Today the family still control the distillery, which turns out the quality single malt bearing that name. The distillery uses traditional equipment and distilling techniques. It is full of gleaming copper rather than modern electronics. But it works. In the late 1950s around 500 cases of Glenfiddich were sold annually. In 1987 the figure was over 500,000. Sales rose a record 18% in 1988 and it is the best-selling wine or spirit in duty-free shops throughout the world.

*Grant Gordon*

# Wensley Haydon-Baillie £60m

*Pharmaceutical manufacturer*

dob 7–11–43

The son of a Nottinghamshire surgeon, Wensley Haydon-Baillie read economics at Exeter University in the 1960s. He then went into the City to work for the Slater Walker bank which collapsed in the early 1970s. But Haydon-Baillie had secured enough wealth to buy a controlling interest in a small engineering company which was then in the doldrums. Together with his partner Tony Gover, a Cambridge law graduate, he turned the business round in spectacular fashion. Watsham's, as it was called, was renamed Optical & Medical, and it moved into high technology fields such as defence electronics. By 1989 it was producing profits of £7m on sales of £55m.

This venture so impressed the City that Haydon-Baillie had little trouble in gaining backing for his most spectacular coup. In 1985 he persuaded Kenneth Clarke, then health minister, to allow a new company he had formed to enter an exclusive marketing agreement with the Centre for Applied Microbiology & Research at Porton Down. Porton International attracted some £76m in City funds. Haydon-Baillie, who owned over 2m of the 4.8m shares issued initially, sold 294,000 in 1986, collecting some £24m for them. At the time, that would have valued his remaining shares at over £142m.

But Porton International has yet to fulfil its early promise of exciting new drugs. While its investors are content to wait for what they hope will be a big

The company celebrated its centenary in 1987 by flying 650 of its staff and salesmen in from round the world to the Scottish Highlands for a two-month series of Scottish country house parties.

The company is private and made £9.3 million after-tax profits in 1986. At least two family members sit on the board – David Grant and Grant Gordon. Both are great-grandsons of William Grant, the founder.

pay-off, its value as a business will have fallen sharply from its heady early days, and the £142m stake belonging to Haydon-Baillie would fetch much less today.

In his personal life, Haydon-Baillie is described as extremely charming but very secretive. His personal wealth extends to two large country estates, a collection of vintage cars, planes and boats. These are housed in a private museum in Southampton. One of the estates is in the New Forest. In March 1989, he acquired Wentworth Wood-house near Rotherham, the 17th-century seat of the Marquess of Rockingham. Haydon-Baillie is intent on restoring the 300-room house which is one of the largest stately homes in Britain.

sold paint and wallpaper. His eldest son John joined him in 1954. A year later Edwin joined at the age of 16. Eventually Malcolm (q.v.), the youngest son, also joined.

Edwin became the driving force of a family team. In 1972 he floated Status on the stock market and spent the next eight years building it up before agreeing a £30 million takeover by MFI. He stayed for three years and then branched out on his own, shunning the limelight and building up his property group, Stadium Developments, which he intends to keep as a private company. He became a leading force in building retail warehouses and in 1987 built 1 million square feet. Currently he is developing the huge Meadowhall site in Sheffield with fellow Yorkshire property man, Paul Sykes (q.v.). The latest accounts for Stadium Developments,

---

# Edwin Healey    £60m
## *Property developer*
dob 1938

Edwin Healey's roots are in the home-decorating business in Hull. His father Stanley started the business in 1931, pushing a handcart loaded with ladders, paint and decorator's tools and knocking on doors for work. During the war, while Stanley was in the army, his wife Sarah carried on the business. Back home, Stanley concluded that selling the materials was better than decorating. Healey Brothers, as the business was called, opened its first shop in Hull, paying a rent of just £1 a week.

In the 1970s Stanley Healey moved into the former Dance De Luxe ball-room and, trading as Status Discount,

where Healey and his wife Carol own all the shares, show after-tax profits of over £15 million.

Today Edwin lives in Hull's exclusive executive belt west of the city, an easy drive from his business base at Melton. In April 1988 he had a splended party to celebrate both the 21st birthday of his daughter Anne and his own 50th birthday on the same day. The party for 400 guests cost an estimated £250,000. The band of the Royal Artillery played in a mock castle in the 20-acre grounds and there was a firework display which was seen five miles away.

Edwin Healey, like his father, is a very private person, devoted to family and the business. He plays no part in local or county politics, and is regarded as a nice quiet man with 'no side', a Yorkshire expression meaning that he has not changed with success. He is occasionally seen in the village pub not far from his home and it is said that he has private invitations from royalty in recognition of the help he has given to various good causes.

# Michael Heseltine £60m

*Politician and publisher*

dob 21/3/33

The flowing blond locks and firm jaw helped earn him the nickname Tarzan. His impassioned oratory has made him the darling of the Conservative Party conference, though not of the party establishment since his abrupt departure from the Cabinet in 1986.

Although his chances of becoming leader of the Tory Party improved in 1990, the prospect still looked remote.

He doesn't need the money. The son of a Swansea business man, he went to Oxford where he was something of a dandy (his suits and ties are still the sharpest in the Tory Party). He became president of the Union, the prestigious university debating society, and even then was tipped as a future prime minister.

In the London of the 1950s he became a property developer and was a millionaire at 26. But his political career came first and he was elected to Parliament while embarking on the road to more wealth as a publisher. He founded the Haymarket Group, which publishes glossy trade titles such as *Campaign*. His family owns about 51% of the shares in the group which is highly profitable.

Today Heseltine lives in a £1.5

million Belgravia house and he has a £2.5 million 18th-century estate in Oxfordshire with 400 acres, a lake, stables and a swimming pool.

Heseltine waited until 1989 to begin his public pitch for the Tory leadership. He said it would be an 'honour' to serve as leader should Mrs Thatcher go. In his book, *The Challenge of Europe*, published in May 1989, Heseltine criticised the government line, calling for Britain to embrace its European destiny. In December 1989 a Gallup poll found that he would do more than any other Tory MP to attract wavering voters back to the Conservative Party, showing that his long-term campaign to win the leadership was paying off.

## Lord Iliffe and family   £60m
*Publisher*

dob 25/1/08

The Iliffe family founded and for many years owned the principal Birmingham and Coventry newspapers. The grandfather of the present Lord Iliffe started the *Coventry Evening Telegraph*; his father built up the publishing business with such journals as *Autocar*. One of the early employees of the firm was Alfred Harmsworth, later Lord Northcliffe, who edited a cycling paper for the Iliffes.

The present Lord Iliffe inherited the title in 1960. He also inherited a considerable estate and properties round the world. The Yattendon estate near Newbury in Berkshire, which was just 1,000 acres when his father bought it, had grown to 9,000 acres in 1960. His father had also bought a nearby 3,000-acre estate in 1929.

Lord Iliffe's first act was to rationalise his inheritance. In 1961 he sold his splendid Bahamas house to Jack Cotton, the legendary 1960s property dealer. Ten years later he sold one of his two St James's Place flats which overlook Green Park. In 1978 he gave his 18th-century house, Basildon Park, to the National Trust, with a six-figure endowment for its upkeep. He had purchased this 30-room house overlooking the Thames in 1952, and it was agreed that he would retain one wing but the public would be allowed to visit the rest of the house. His other residence is the mock-Tudor Yattendon Court.

Lord Iliffe married in 1928 but has no children. His heir is his nephew, Robert Iliffe (dob 22/11/44), who lives in Kenilworth. He has been directing the family newspaper and publishing operations in recent years, through the family investment company, Yattendon Investment Trust, which produced £5 million post-tax profits in the year to June 1988.

In November 1987 Yattendon sold its Birmingham papers to the American publisher, Ralph Ingersoll II, for £60 million. Robert Iliffe recently bought a new £2.5 million motor yacht, an 80-foot craft called *Dalvina*. He is a member of the Royal Yacht Squadron.

## John James   £60m
*Retired business man*

dob 25/7/06

'Easy come, easy go' could be John James's motto for money. The son of a miner, he showed early determination by picking enough blackberries to buy the coveted football boots his parents could not afford. Later he lied about his age to join the RAF, where he saved two-thirds of his wages and learnt as much about wireless development as possible. After leaving the RAF in 1934 he went to work in a radio shop in his native Bristol, drawing up plans to open his first shop in 1938.

But the war postponed those plans and he was called up to the RAF again, emerging as a squadron leader. He opened his first shop in 1946 and within a year had built a chain of ten. At the end of 13 years he had built the largest radio and television retailing group in the world, with 300 shops. In 1959 James, who had lived in the same modest suburban home since the war, sold the business for £6 million. He agreed to stay on, though allowing himself the luxury of a new home and a Rolls-Royce. But by 1961 he had severed all ties and started out afresh.

He determined to make another fortune and started looking for business opportunities. He founded the John James Group of companies which made furniture. He sold that business for £25 million in 1979. But perhaps his most remarkable coup was to be one of the first investors to spot the talents of Lord Weinstock (q.v.), the creator of the modern GEC. As an early television dealer, James often dealt with Radio & Allied Holdings, run by Michael Sobell and his young son-in-law, Arnold Weinstock. Impressed by Weinstock's ability, James took a 10% stake in Radio & Allied. When Sobell and Weinstock made a reverse takeover of GEC, James ended up with 20.4% of the GEC shares and stayed as an investor for some years, adding considerably to his fortune.

James moved to Ascot in the mid-1960s. He has become a huge benefactor to charities. By the early 1980s he was busy giving money away as fast as possible. He gave £4.5 million to Bristol schools, and over £1 million to major hospitals to help fund equipment or keep vital services running.

---

# Andrew Lloyd Webber £60m
*Composer*

dob 22/3/48

The man who almost single-handedly revived the British musical was born into an artistic family in South Kensington, London. Money might have been short – but not music. Andrew Lloyd Webber's father was director of the London College of Music, while his mother was a music teacher.

By the age of nine his prodigious musical talent was apparent. He was

composing his own songs and staging shows by himself. At 12 he went to Westminster School, where he was obsessed by musicals such as *South Pacific* and *The Sound of Music*. He won an exhibition to Magdalen College, Oxford, but left after one term to team up with Tim Rice, who had written to him hearing that he wanted a lyricist. Although *The Likes of Us*, their first musical about Dr Barnardo's children's home, was a flop, the second, *Joseph and the Amazing Technicolour Dreamcoat* was a hit. That persuaded David Land, a West End estate agent, to pay them £30 a week to allow them to concentrate on writing. They came up with *Jesus Christ Superstar*, which brought them outstanding success. *Evita* followed in 1976. Then the partnership foundered.

But Andrew kept going with a string of bigger box-office hits including *Cats* which has grossed more than £50 million in nine years in London alone, making it the most successful musical in history. The latest, *Aspects of Love*, took £4 million in advance bookings.

The Midas touch has allowed Andrew to live in style, though he hates spending money on himself. His Berkshire estate, Sydmonton, complete with 1,200 acres, is next door to that of one of the Saatchis (q.v.) and the famous Watership Down. He hosts an annual Sydmonton festival to try out new musicals. He has a Belgravia flat, a house in the south of France and an apartment in New York's exclusive Trump Tower. He also owns one of the greatest collections of Pre-Raphaelite paintings in the country as well as a private publishing house, Aurum Press. His main source of wealth is his large stake in the Really Useful Group, which controls his theatrical management operations. It came to the stock market in 1986 valued at around £36 million. In 1990 he began moves to reprivatise the

company: he proposes to buy back all the outstanding shares valued the group at £77.4 million.

His second wife, the singer Sarah Brightman, starred in his *Phantom of the Opera*. In June 1990 he announced that this marriage had ended. He still maintains a cordial relationship with his first wife and their two children. He is also an active supporter of charities, and recently gave £400,000 to support research into diabetes. His first wife is a victim of the disease and he is haunted by the fear that their children may have inherited it.

---

# Sir Peter Shepherd and family £60m
*Builders*

dob PS 18/10/16

In 1890 Sir Peter Shepherd's grandfather started a building business in York. Today the Shepherd Building Group is one of the largest building firms in the north of England and, under Sir Peter's leadership, it has built hospitals in York, Leeds and Lincoln, and other buildings at York university, as well as extensions to Leeds and Durham universities. The group is also noted for its high-quality houses and it has built a garden village estate for 2,000 residents at Woodthorpe in York. But it was the restoration work on York Minster between 1967 and 1972 that won Shepherd worldwide acclaim.

Sir Peter, whose father was an alderman of York, became a director of the then Shepherd Construction Company in 1940 and chairman in 1958. He retired in May 1988 to become presi-

dent of the group. Colin Shepherd, his younger brother, took over as chairman.

A lifelong passion for training and education led Sir Peter to head the Construction Industry Training Board and similar bodies for other industries. In 1982 he warned the CBI conference that regional pay bargaining should be introduced to reflect inequalities in local prosperity and labour demand. He also criticised educationalists who know little about industry's needs.

Sir Peter lives in retirement in York, and lists sailing as his hobby. His sons, who are all connected with the company, also live in the city. With their relations, they own most of the equity in the group, which produced £16.2 million after-tax profits in the year to the end of June 1989. The group has negligible borrowings and was recently tipped to win the contract for a large development in Manchester's old dock area.

# Ivan Twigden   £60m
*Builder*

dob 10/1/38

Running a housebuilding firm in East Anglia, where house prices were soaring by over 50% a year in the 1980s, proved to be a profitable business for Ivan Twigden. His building firm, Twigden plc, increased its after-tax profits from £3.9 million to £8.7 million between 1987 and 1988. In spite of the fall in house prices and slump in the market in 1990, this would give the Twigden company a stock market value of some £80 million. With 85% of the shares, Twigden's own stake could fetch some £60 million.

Twigden lives on a farm in Kimbolton in Cambridge and lists his hobbies as tennis, golf and bridge. He is a former county squash men's singles winner and he played tennis for Bedfordshire. He also owns racehorses, trained by Josh Gifford and Geoffrey Huffer. His best horses have been called, appropriately, Show Home and Showhouse.

# Peter Waterman   £60m
*Pop producer*

Born next to the Jaguar factory in Coventry, and later working as a coal miner, Peter Waterman had a tough early life. The rags to riches story really began when he became involved in the music industry in the early 1970s. He ran a shop selling obscure imported American records. He also worked as a disc jockey in a club.

Real success came after he teamed up with two moderately successful pop stars Mike Stock and Matt Aitken in 1984 to start a record production company. With his marketing savvy and his own company, PWL, which now has a £60m turnover a year, Waterman thrived in the partnership. Recording studios were established at a cost of £4m in the scruffy Borough area of South London. In five years, a stream of hits followed, 95 in all including 13 number ones. Their stars are household names to millions, led by Kylie Minogue, the teenage Australian singer and her co-star from 'Neighbours', Jason Donovan. Other singers discovered by Stock, Aitken and Waterman include Sinitta and Rick Astley.

Waterman enjoys his wealth. As well as a large 1,500-foot warehouse attached to the studios, he has a house on Merseyside, a former British Rail diesel train, a Firestreak heat-seeking missile, a carp farm in Japan and 48 classic cars, including Ferraris and Jaguars, worth at least £100,000 each.

---

# Peter Wilson and family £60m

*Publishers*

dob PW *c.* 1932

Peter Wilson runs what is probably one of the most profitable magazines in the world. *Estates Gazette* monopolises the commercial property advertising market in Britain, and every week it is packed with glossy adverts, making it the 'bible' for the business. It has also

made Wilson a multi-millionaire. With after-tax profits of £4.3 million up to the end of 1988, and a reputation as the most profitable business magazine in Britain, it would be a prize that any large publishing empire would like to get its hands on. Wilson could easily demand – and get – £60 million for the business if he were to sell or float it on the stock market.

Wilson inherited the magazine some 20 years ago and he believes in a hands-on management style at its Wardour Street office, though eschewing all personal publicity.

He lives with his wife Audrey and daughters in a large Surrey mansion. He also has two other homes, one in Portugal and the other in the French Alps where he is able to pursue his favourite outdoor hobby of skiing.

A close estate agent friend, Clive Lewis, says Wilson is a friendly man who is dedicated to his business. 'It's a very impressive magazine and has had a monopoly market for some time. He is in the office all the time and involved in the day-to-day running of the business. As a suryeyor, I can tell you that anyone who has a commercial property to sell will automatically expect an advert in the *Estates Gazette*. It has a lot of kudos and respect,' he added.

---

# Maurice Wohl £60m

*Former property investor*

dob 4/1/17

So enraged was Maurice Wohl when corporation tax was introduced by the Labour government in 1965 that he suggested winding up his property company, United Real Property Trust.

Instead, 11 years later he chose to become a tax exile.

He owned over 51% of the shares of United Real, which had 14 prime West End and City properties. Other London property men continually sought to lay their hands on the business but Wohl would not sell until 1986.

By then he lacked the time or inclination to enter the wheeler-dealing world of redevelopment. So he sold the company to Tony Clegg (q.v.), a fast-moving Lancastrian, for £117 million.

Wohl has a love of the arts and recently gave a discreet donation to the National Gallery to transform the dingy vestibule.

It has used the proceeds from the sale of 25% of its shares to buy overseas companies and to fund expansion out of its northern and Midlands heartland into London and the south-east. Within weeks of its flotation it had bought a Belgian confectioner for £2 million, followed a year later by the £7.6 million purchase of a French sweet and ice cream retailer.

# John Thornton and family £59m

*Chocolate manufacturers*

dob 30/1/44

In 1911 Joseph William Thornton opened his first sweet shop in Sheffield. He aimed to have the best shop in 'Steel City' and he succeeded. Within two years he had started making his own chocolates and the business has never looked back. Today Thorntons, where the family still control some 70% of the shares directly, has expanded to over 330 stores round Britain. It also produces many of the upmarket chocolates to be found in Marks & Spencer.

The company owns three factories and, in 1988, moved production out of Sheffield to a new £9 million purpose-built site at Belper in Derbyshire. At the same time the company came to the stock market, where its shares proved very popular. There were eight times as many applications as shares available.

Two grandsons of the founder, John Thornton and Michael Thornton, run the company today. John, the chairman and chief executive, was educated at Repton and Trinity College, Cambridge. He went to work for a year at Baker Perkins, the manufacturer of food processing equipment, before coming into the family firm. He was made managing director in 1967 and reached the chairmanship in 1982. He lists his hobby as sailing. Michael, his deputy, has been with the firm all his working life. He is interested in rugby and supports several local charities in the Derbyshire Peak District area.

# Michael and David Green   £58m

*Video and television production*

dob DG 14/2/46   MG 2/12/47

For a boy who left school half-way through his A level economics course because it was too boring, Michael Green has not done too badly.

Born into a comfortable north London family, with a textile business which he did not join, he had his own photographic and printing operation by the time he was 20. Today his Carlton Communications is worth nearly £1.5 billion on the stock market and he has just bought Technicolor, the world-famous American film processing business.

Green, an unassuming man, is determined to build Carlton into one of the world's major television and entertainment businesses for the 1990s. He has the right connections. He used to play poker regularly with one of the

Saatchi brothers (q.v.), plays bridge with the financier Jim Slater, and was married to a daughter of Lord Wolfson (q.v.), the stores magnate, although they are now separated. (Lord Young, the former Secretary of State for Industry, is a cousin of the Wolfsons.) He lives in a comfortable Mayfair flat, drives a Mercedes and has a mill house in the country.

David, his elder brother, is still on the Carlton board but devotes more of his energies to Colefax and Fowler, the upmarket wallpaper and home furnishings group, in which he has a 40% stake.

Carlton's position as the major force in servicing British television companies was confirmed in 1989 when Michael Green took over the rival UEI group in a friendly bid worth £513 million. In view of deregulation of television, he could make an even bigger mark on the broadcasting scene in the 1990s.

# David McErlain   £57m

*Coal mine owner*

dob 7/11/47

Leaving Durham University in 1970 with a master's degree in business administration, David McErlain went to work in his family's plant hire and road haulage business. After three years he branched out on his own and started McErlain (Plant) Ltd. His big break came in 1974 when, working for a pottery company searching for clay, he came across an ideal site for opencast coal mining. Borrowing £31,000 –

'not from my old man' – he bought an option on the site in Chesterfield and obtained planning permission to exploit it. With more borrowed money, he exploited the coal reserves so successfully that in 1981 he was able to sell the concern – now called Northern Strip Mining – for £12 million.

McErlain described the secret of his success as an ability to obtain the planning permission for the open-cast sites. He told *The Times* recently: 'You have to find a reason, like getting the clay out underneath the coal to secure continuity of employment at a local pottery or to create a cricket pitch for the community, something of that sort. And remember, wherever you've got coal you've got Labour-controlled councils.'

Working briefly for Burnett & Hallamshire, the group which bought his coal business, McErlain set it on the right track with typical speed and opportunism. He then acquired a new open-cast mining company operating in Derbyshire and South Yorkshire.

His new company, Coal Contractors, acquired some American interests and was poised to join the stock market in 1984, when the miners went on strike. That pushed the group into losses as coal sales were hit sharply, but after the strike recovery was swift.

In 1988 McErlain was back at Burnett & Hallamshire, leading a complex restructuring following some huge losses it had piled up, mainly as a result of ill-timed property speculation in California. He slashed overheads and closed 12 subsidiary companies without losing any turnover.

In May 1989 he mounted an audacious raid on the Coalite group, run by Eric Varley, a former Labour cabinet minister. Coalite was eight times larger than McErlain's group, but such was the respect he had earned from the rescue of Burnett & Hallamshire that the banks were eager to support the bid, which was ultimately successful.

This was likened almost to a by-election, as McErlain is an active Tory fund raiser. None the less, the soft-spoken McErlain has always been able to get on with the Labour politicians in his native Derbyshire. He is a good friend to some of the other wealthier Britons such as David Thompson (q.v.), the founder of Hillsdown Holdings. He is also very close to the powerful Kuwait Investment Office, which channels Kuwaiti funds into British companies.

He collects vintage cars and is thought to have been the under-bidder for a Bugatti Royale that was auctioned for £5 million at the end of the 1980s.

# William and Frank Brake £56m
*Food distributors*

dob FB 21/11/33

Raised above a London pub, the three Brake brothers saw at first hand the

British love of a pub lunch with a good pint of beer. All three developed their knowledge and skills at catering college in the late 1940s and early 1950s. When William, the eldest, married and moved to run the Bull Inn at Lenham in Kent, his two younger brothers Frank and Peter went with him.

As a sideline started in 1958 they rose at dawn to run a business killing and plucking chickens for sale to local pubs, villages and restaurants.

Chickens awaiting delivery began to pile up at their premises, so they built a cold store to freeze them in 1963. As the store was so big, they filled it with other foods to freeze and sell. In 1969 the brothers opened a purpose-built factory in Lenham to produce frozen prepared meals.

By the early 1970s the sale of frozen food was going so well that it supplanted the poultry business, which was discontinued in 1974. The Brakes were quick to spot the potential of computers in running their business and now boast of being able to supply customers within a few hours of receiving an order.

By 1986 the company was supplying 35,000 customers round the country from 16 cold store depots. The company was floated on the stock market that year. The two brothers, who are chairman and managing director, each kept 25% of the shares. Peter, the youngest brother, who was purchasing director, died in 1987, but the combined family shareholding is worth £56 million.

# Tony Bramall    £55m
*Car dealer*

dob 29/12/35

Charles Bramall started a successful car dealership in Bradford in 1957. His son Tony, who trained as a chartered accountant, joined him in 1963 after working in a Sheffield estate agency. He later took over the reins, and the company was floated on the stock market in 1978. A period of steady growth followed, with the company holding important Ford and BL dealerships. In 1987 Bramall agreed to a £79 million takeover by Avis. The family controlled 57% of the shares and received around £45 million for them.

Bramall took up an executive directorship in Avis but resigned a few months later in June 1988. He subsequently took a 20% stake in Lyon & Lyon, a Ford main dealer based in nearby Batley. Lyon & Lyon was taken over by another group for £13.6 million. That valued the Bramall stake at £2.7 million.

Bramall is now involved with a Harrogate company, Gregory Properties, where he has been a director since 1983.

Sheffield-born Bramall now lives in the Yorkshire Dales. His wife Susan is a horse trainer and they have three daughters. Known as a hard worker, he relaxes by playing golf to an 18 handicap. He also shoots and has owned some racehorses. A very private person, he is devoted to his family.

# Ronald Diggens  £55m

*Property owner*

dob 26/11/11

Starting after World War I as a £1-a-week surveyor's lad with the property magnate Major Alfred Allnat, Ronald Diggens took over the business when his boss retired. He then served in the army as a bridge-building engineer during World War II, reaching the rank of Lt.-Colonel.

After the war he shrewdly built up two property groups which owned large numbers of factories in north and west London. He was noted as a generous employer and many of his staff had shares in the companies. He is now a large shareholder in the Slough Estates property group, which runs the famous Slough trading estate.

He lives comfortably in Northwood in the north of London, and he has a cottage in Cornwall. A shy bachelor, he took up flying at the age of 48 and sails a dinghy for relaxation.

# Michael Hollingbery  £55m

*Retailer*

dob 16/4/33

In the 1930s George Hollingbery founded a Hull department store which his son Michael took over in 1958. He branched out into television rentals and later started the Comet chain of discount warehouses. Comet was finally taken over by Woolworth in 1984. The Hollingbery family stake of 30% was sold for £54 million.

Comet still operates under its own name and Hollingbery still runs the business with a seat on the Woolworth board. He lives in a picturesque village near Beverley on Humberside.

He drives an Aston Martin car with the personalised number plate MH1. He remains a private person. He has a close circle of influential business friends and maintains a keen interest in local Conservative Party activities but he remains politically and socially in the background.

His hobbies are shooting and fishing and he has a deep interest in the Round Table.

# Lord Lovat    £55m

*Landowner*

dob 9/7/11

The actor Peter Lawford played Lord Lovat in *The Longest Day*, the film about D-Day, but the glamorous portrayal did not go down well with the original. One of Scotland's three top landowners with 190,000 acres, he hates pomp and fuss. He boycotted the 40th anniversary celebration for D-Day in 1984, saying it was a jamboree.

Lovat's early years were relaxed: private school at Ampleforth, Magdalen College, Oxford, and the Scots Guards. In his autobiography *March Past*, he records: 'My youth positively reeked of privilege.... It will be no surprise to learn that my politics remain strictly feudal!' He sits in the Lords and takes the Tory whip.

Lovat raised a regiment of commando troops during the war and was decorated with the DSO, MC, the Croix de Guerre and Légion d'Honneur for his exploits during raids on Dieppe and Norway and later on D-Day, where he was badly wounded. The Soviet Union made him a member of the Order of Suvarov. David Stirling, knighted in the 1990 New Year's honours list, the man who founded the SAS, is a first cousin.

Lovat's war exploits were in line with family tradition. During the Boer War his father raised and commanded the Lovat Scouts comprised of members of the Fraser Clan, of which he is the head. In the 18th century a previous Lord Lovat was the last peer to be beheaded by the axe for treason on Tower Hill for supporting the 1745 Scottish revolt. His lands were confiscated, but his son distinguished himself as a British general and had the lands restored.

Lovat has made occasional forays into Parliament to speak on salmon fishing and deer stalking (and more often on the poaching thereof, a traditional obsession of Highland lairds). Today he no longer lives at the family seat of Beaufort Castle outside Inverness, having passed occupancy to his eldest son and heir Simon (also ex-Ampleforth and the Scots Guards). Simon, known as the Master of Lovat, sold one of the family salmon rivers in 1990 for a record-breaking £15 million. The deal also included a 30,000-acre deer forest.

Lovat's daughter, the Hon. Tessa Keswick (formerly married to Lord Reay), contested the Inverness-shire constituency for the Tories in the last General Election and came third. She has been appointed special policy adviser and 'strategic thinker' to Health Minister Kenneth Clarke.

# James Sherwood    £55m

*Shipping and hotel owner*

dob 8/8/33

Jim Sherwood may be the Yale-educated son of a Kentucky attorney, but he is a confirmed anglophile. He lives and works in London, and has run the Sea Containers shipping business since he founded it in 1965.

While doing his military service with the US Naval Reserve he was one of the first people to spot the potential of container traffic. Today Sea Containers is one of the largest container leasing businesses in the world. But Sherwood, increased. Sherwood plans to use the proceeds of the sale to buy more hotels and start another luxury train service in the Far East. The takeover bid helped increase the value of Sherwood's 7% stake in the business by £10 million to £55 million.

---

# Nat Somers   £55m
*Airport and property owner*

dob 1908

John Nathaniel Somers, now a Jersey-based tax exile, has made a fortune out of flying. Known simply as Nat, he has been involved with airports and aeroplanes almost all his adult life.

But his biggest financial coup came late in life. In 1988, at the age of 80, he sold Southampton airport for £50 million to Peter de Savary, the financier (q.v.). The deal was struck in secret via Somers' Jersey-owned company, Saipur Investments, and Findhelp, an off-the-shelf de Savary company. Somers had originally bought Southampton airport from the city council in 1961 for a few thousand pounds. He built its present concrete runway in 1966. Saipur Investments made some £2 million after-tax profits in its accounts to the end of 1986. Certifying these, the accountants included a note to the effect that the properties were substantially undervalued.

Somers had a great love for the airport and said that selling it was 'a very great wrench'. He also once owned Halfpenny Green Airport near Wolverhampton, but sold out to Midlands business man Maurice Collis in 1971. An expert pilot, he first flew in 1936, during a holiday in Bognor.

who lives in the exclusive Boltons area of South Kensington in London and an Oxfordshire mansion, has built up an impressive array of luxury businesses. He revitalised the Orient Express, turning it into a de luxe service between London and Venice. There is an Orient Express hotel chain, including the Cipriani in Venice and the Villa San Michele in Florence.

He also took over the Sealink ferry business from British Rail and fought a long campaign against the Channel tunnel, which is expected to hit the ferries in 1993. But he will be looking for new opportunities in 1990, having sold virtually all of Sea Containers' assets to two rival groups for $1.1 billion. The two companies, Tiphook and Stena, had been trying to take over Sea Containers for several months against fierce resistance from Sherwood, who finally agreed to the takeover only when the terms were

During the war he served as an instructor with the RAF, and won the Air Force Cross. He later won the King's Cup air race at Elmdon in 1949 with a Miles Gemini aircraft flying at an average speed of 164.25 m.p.h. Somers realised his 'lifelong ambition' to fly a Spitfire in 1988, at an age when he could draw a pension and have a bus pass. He described it as 'a wonderful experience'.

Somers first visited Southampton when he ran away from home on a bike. He was 14 and keen to get a job on a ship. He arrived in Southampton after three days, only to find there was no work available. Hungry and dishevelled, he was questioned by police and spent the night in the cells before being sent home.

---

# John Zochonis and family £54m
*Soap and overseas traders*

dob JZ 2/10/29

Cussons Imperial Leather, the quintessential British soap, is actually made by Paterson-Zochonis, a family-controlled company with Greek origins, based in Manchester. It is run by chairman John Zochonis.

As well as making soap and toiletries, it trades with Nigeria. This was very profitable when the Nigerian economy was flush with oil revenues, but as a big debtor nation it now has little room for trade. Every time there is a coup in Nigeria, the Paterson share price immediately drops.

Manchester-born John Zochonis is the grandson of the Greek entrepreneur who co-founded Paterson-Zochonis,

the West Africa-based merchants, in 1884. He was educated at Rugby School where he excelled at cricket, and he studied law at Corpus Christi College, Oxford. He completed two years' National Service in 1950, gaining the rank of second lieutenant.

In 1953 he joined Paterson-Zochonis as a junior executive, working in West Africa and England. Four years later he was appointed a director and in 1970 he became chairman. In 1975 he masterminded the takeover of Cussons, then valued at £8.6 million.

Zochonis, whose father is now dead, has never married and lives in Altrincham, Cheshire. He is a member of the Travellers' Club and the Marylebone Cricket Club. He chairs the Council of Manchester University and is president of the Greater Manchester Youth Association. He is also a liveryman of the Tallow Chandlers Company and a freeman of the City of London. His hobbies are cricket and horse racing and he owns at least one racehorse.

---

# Esmond Bulmer and family £53m
*Cider maker*

dob EB 19/9/35

The serious business of cider making started in 1887 when Percy Bulmer, the son of a Hereford vicar, made 4,000 gallons with apples from his father's orchard. The first batch was sold for £157. By contrast, in its 100th year, H.P. Bulmer made £12.5 million profit. Percy's brother Fred joined the business in 1888 after turning down the post of tutor to the King of Siam's children. The family are still heavily represented on the board, and own over half the shares.

Esmond Bulmer, the present chairman and Percy's grandson, was educated at Rugby and King's College, Cambridge. He was commissioned in the Scots Guards in 1954. He was the Conservative MP for Wyre Forest in Hereford from 1974 to 1983, but then stood down to concentrate on his business interests. He lives in an old rectory house and also owns a small private cider-apple farm. He and his wife Morella parted in June 1988 after nearly 30 years of marriage. They had met originally on a blind date when she needed an escort for a Conservative ball, and they married three years later.

His brother and cousin are also on the board. Esmond is a member of the National Trust's executive and enjoys gardening and fishing. He is also involved in local public and charitable work.

# Lord Clinton    £52m

*Landowner*

dob 12/7/31

It took an eight-year fight for Lord Clinton to establish his claim to his title. In 1957 he inherited the Devon estate of the 21st Lord Clinton, his great-grandfather, but it was not until 1965 that he became the 22nd holder of the title, after his aunt Mrs Fenella Bowes-Lyon petitioned her niece, the Queen, on his behalf.

The title had gone into abeyance on the death of his grandfather as there were no direct heirs in the next generation. But after a long and ultimately successful fight, Clinton took his seat in the Lords in 1965. He has spent the intervening years tending the 26,000-acre estate with considerable skill, as befits a trained land agent. The estate is on the Devon coast near Exeter, and it has always been regarded as one of the most efficiently run in Britain. Under a settlement designed to minimise tax liabilities, Clinton is in effect a tenant for life on the estate, enjoying all the privileges and responsibilities of a great landowner. The estate boasts fine Italian gardens designed by Le Nôtre, who created the gardens at Versailles for King Louis XIV of France. The gardens were constructed by a pupil of Le Nôtre in 1735, using prisoners of war from Napoleon's armies.

Clinton is well known in local farming circles, where he is a vice-president of the Devon Agricultural Association. He is also a former Justice of the Peace and Deputy Lieutenant of the county. Unsurprisingly, he lists his hobbies as shootin' and fishin'.

# Eric Grove £52m
*Property developer*

dob 30/4/30

A Midlands builder, Eric Grove started his own company, Canberra, in 1968 after working for a Stourport, Worcestershire, company. He built high-quality middle-price homes along the M1 corridor to Milton Keynes, along the M5 to Bristol and in the Southampton area.

Based in Solihull, Grove expanded Canberra to the point where it made £8.3 million pre-tax profits on a turnover of £51 million in 1988. In November that year Grove and his family sold 60% of the company to Alfred McAlpine and there are plans to float the group on the stock market where it is likely to be valued at £100 million. Under the terms of the deal, Grove and his family were paid special dividends of £3 million per year for two years, with more to come when the group is floated.

Bobby McAlpine (q.v.), the chairman of the group, said at the time of the purchase, 'We have had our eye on Canberra for some considerable time and we have followed them with admiration. Of all the companies we have followed, they have made the shrewdest purchases of land.'

Under the takeover, Grove is responsible for all the land deals in the combined operation. He lives in the Lapworth area of Birmingham.

# Peter Birse £51m
*Builder*

dob 24/11/42

Peter Birse's first job as a contractor earned him £3,000 in 1970. It was to re-lay tarmac on a footpath at a Humberside oil refinery which a firm of contractors had bungled. He told his boss at the giant Foster Wheeler group where he was a young engineer that he could do the work better. He was awarded the contract.

Quitting his job at Foster Wheeler, Birse took three weeks to do the job and lost a stone in weight. Before long he was winning more work at the refinery and the Birse group was in business.

Today, still based in Humberside, the group is an important contractor building roads, docks, bridges and water projects. Its future looks rosy in the light of the huge spending plans by the water authorities and the road programme authorised by the government. Birse already works for seven out of the ten

water authorities. The group is building Felixstowe harbour's Terminal 2 in a £20 million contract.

In 1989–90 Birse made £13.6 million pre-tax profits. Six years before the figure was just £1 million. The company was floated on the stock market in 1989 and is now valued at £80 million. Prior to the flotation Peter Birse owned 93% of the shares, 15% of which were sold to his West German partner, Bilfinger & Berger, while Birse himself realised about £10 million cash from the sale. Displaying the caution and prudence which one would expect from the son of a small shopkeeper from the Scottish golfing town of Carnoustie, Birse told the *Sunday Express* that some of the money would be earmarked for charity, though his wife Helen 'would give it all away if she could. In fact, I'm giving £2 million to charity as Helen is very interested in handicapped children. For myself, I have most of what I want already and I'm not a jet-setter. I have a yacht, a set of golf clubs, a lovely wife and three children. What more does a man want?'

---

# Stanley Clarke   £51m

*Property developer*

dob 7/6/32

In 1954 Stan Clarke, a Staffordshire plumber who had had ambitions to be a farmer, started his own village plumbing business with capital of £100. He later moved into housebuilding and some 33 years later sold the business to the giant BICC group for £51 million. Clarke himself owned 80% of the shares in his Clarke Securities, which by then was one of Britain's largest private housebuilders. In 1986 it sold more than 600 homes at an average price of £52,000 under the name 'Clarke Quality Homes'.

Clarke moved out of housebuilding but kept the property development side of his business, called St Modwen Properties (after the patron saint of beer). Through St Modwen he is actively developing sites as far apart as Plymouth, Sheffield, London and Manchester. But he is particularly active on his home patch in Staffordshire and in 1987 he pulled off his biggest coup by beating off a fierce challenge from rival developers to win control of the former National Garden Exhibition site in Stoke for over £7 million.

In 1988 work started on a £100 million redevelopment of the site, which included a huge Toys'R US store. Clarke took the controls of the first excavator on site, promising that over 2,000 jobs would be created on what had been a derelict area before the garden festival.

He was educated at the Burton-on-Trent technical high school, lists his hobbies as farming, horses and building heritage. He chairs the appeal for the restoration of Lichfield Cathedral. At a meeting of leading industrialists to raise the £1.25 million funds needed, he said: 'Sweat, blood and tears built the cathedral. We are the captains of industry and it is part of our responsibility to help sustain this building in the most substantial way.'

Reflecting his interest in training point-to-point racehorses, Clarke took over Uttoxeter racecourse in early 1989, saying: 'Uttoxeter's future as a jumping course is secure. We have no high-falutin plans for flat or all-weather tracks – just to improve the racing and the course and make it better for owners, trainers and jockeys as well as the public.' As he was buying the course, his wife Hilda's horse,

Honest Word, had just given trainer Martin Pipe his 107th win of the season.

# Gordon Baxter and family £50m
*Food manufacturer*

In 1877 George Baxter gave up his job as gardener to the Duke of Richmond and with a borrowed £10 opened a grocery shop in the Grampian town of Fochabers. Customers who were short of cash would pay their bills with fruit and other produce from their gardens. George's wife Margaret would turn this into jam. His son William, encouraged by the Duke, later built a small factory on the banks of the Spey to make jam, and Baxter's was born.

Today those high-quality soups and jams with the well-known brand label are coveted by virtually every major food company. But the members of the Baxter family, led by Gordon Baxter, grandson of the founder, have so far resisted all overtures (150 so far) and can do so as they hold 96% of the shares. Though the company only makes a £2 million profit on a £22 million turnover and employs only 500 people, the brand name alone would command £50 million. Among the hopeful bidders have been Colgate-Palmolive, Campbell Soups, Heinz, Unilever and Nestlé. Gordon usually takes potential buyers fishing on the Spey, then sits them down in front of a roaring fire with a whisky before saying no.

The family feel they have a social responsibility to their staff as the area's biggest single employer. Gordon be-lieves that any of the would-be pred-ators would simply destroy the firm and local jobs if successful. He joined the family firm in 1946 after doing wartime research on explosives for ICI. He was first introduced to the business when, at the age of five, he would get up at 5.30 a.m. to light the fires at home and then go out to hand over the factory keys to the manager. After school, his favourite job was to stick the labels on the jam jars. Gordon's mother who invented the first soup and pion-eered a method of canning raspberries.

Today his wife Ena comes up with new recipes in her own kitchen which are first tried by the family before going into production in the 50-acre factory. His three children are all either working for the business or are destined to do so. Gordon himself tends his prize Highland cattle and is a prominent backer of the Scottish Conservative Party.

# Lord Beaverbrook £50m
*Banker and financier*

dob 29/12/51

The *Sun* newspaper was charac-teristically blunt when Max Aitken, having revived his grandfather's peerage in 1985, was given a govern-ment job: 'Beaverbrook is not a chip off the old press baron, who created a newspaper.'

Whether stung by what the *Sun* said, or through natural reserve, Max Aitken no longer appears amongst the junior ranks of the Thatcher government. Educated at Charterhouse and Pem-broke College, Cambridge, he is married to a niece of Lady Cowdray (q.v.),

whose husband heads the Pearson family.

They have three children and he is the head of a small successful venture capital company and chairman of the Beaverbrook Foundation. He is a member of White's club and the Royal Yacht Squadron.

The original Beaverbrook fortune was created by William Maxwell Aitken, the son of a Canadian Presbyterian minister. He made his money in Canada and came to Britain in 1910, determined to enter politics. When hostilities broke out in 1914, he became the Canadian government representative at the front. By the end of World War I, he was Chancellor of the Duchy of Lancaster and Minister for Information. He later founded the Express Group of newspapers, which made him yet another fortune. In the inter-war years, as his British papers made him richer, he moved in the most exalted establishment circles while, according to his daughter, involving himself in endless love affairs with a

variety of women. During World War II he was, successively, Minister of Aircraft Production, Minister of State and Minister of Supply, member of the war cabinet and finally Lord Privy Seal. He had been made a peer in 1917. He married his second wife in 1963, a year before he died. She is one of Britain's top racehorse owners.

Beaverbrook's son, also called Max, disclaimed the peerage but used the baronetcy which had preceded it. Sir Max, who spent his life at his father's newspapers, was one of the air aces of World War II. He had enlisted in the Air Reserve in 1935 and when war broke out in 1939 he was already a pilot in the crack 601 Squadron. He finished the war as a group captain, having downed 16 enemy planes, and won both a DSC and a DSO. He was not a success as a newspaper proprietor and ownership of the Express Group passed to Victor Matthews. Sir Max died in 1985.

# Elliott Bernerd    £50m
*Property dealer*

dob 23/5/45

One of the major figures in the London property market today, Elliott Bernerd started young. He left school at 16 and joined the estate agent Michael Laurie & Co. becoming its youngest ever partner while still in his early twenties. By the age of 24 he had already built up a substantial personal property portfolio.

Today he runs a private property company called Chelsfield, which at one time owned the old *Times* building in London's Gray's Inn Road. He sold

He manages to include a wide variety of outside interests in his hectic life. He is chairman of the council of the London Philharmonic Orchestra, sits on the board of the National Trust and is an avid collector of modern and Chinese art. He lives in Belgravia, London, and has a selection of black luxury cars.

---

# Lord Bolton    £50m
*Landowner*

dob 11/7/29

Eton and Oxford educated, the 7th Lord Bolton has been described by the *Evening Standard* as 'Yorkshire Royalty'. He owns one of the largest estates in the county, the 17,000-acre Leyburn, which is famous for its grouse shooting but equally for the careful manner in which he has managed it over the years. A former Chairman of the Yorkshire Agricultural Association, one of the biggest in Britain, he has combined his landed interests with business by chairing the Waterers Group and acting as a director of the Yorkshire General Life Company.

Twice married, first to a daughter of Lord Forester, and then to the daughter of a deputy chairman of the *Yorkshire Post* newspaper, Lord Bolton revived the family's long-dormant racing interests and runs his own stud at Park House on the estate. The present Lady Bolton, Marsha Ann, is also a keen horsewoman and runs her own string of racing horses, in her own colours, from the family seat at Leyburn Hall. The estate includes the ruins of the medieval Bolton Castle, open to the public; until 1979 it displayed Bluebird

shares in another property company called Stockley in May 1987 and picked up over £21 million. In its accounts for 1989, Chelsfield made after-tax profits of £14.7 million compared to just £568,000 in 1987. The company is controlled from Panama, and Bernerd owns 80% of its share capital. In January 1990 Bernerd joined forces with his old friend Sir Jeffrey Sterling, the boss of the P&O group, to mount a £441 million takeover bid for the Laing property group which succeeded in April 1990.

Bernerd is a keen skier and regularly spends Christmas at St Moritz. He likes to go to the south of France during August. He has powerful international contacts in New York, Hong Kong and Tokyo.

He works an 18-hour day. Though not a qualified chartered surveyor, his business is built on experience and an innate feel for markets.

1, the boat in which Sir Malcolm Campbell won the world water speed record for Britain in 1937.

A dedicated and active Conservative, Lord Bolton was an occasional intermediary in the crisis that preceded Zimbabwe's independence.

---

# Sir Neville and Trevor Bowman-Shaw £50m

*Industrialists*

dob NB-S 4/10/30

Educated by a private tutor and with a commission in the 5th Royal Inniskilling Dragoon Guards, the young Neville Bowman-Shaw appeared to be the perfect example of the 1950s upper-class playboy. He had joined the cavalry because he did not know what else to do. However, while in the army and working on farms, he acquired a taste for machinery, which took him into the infant British mechanical handling industry in the early 1950s. But initially there was a clash of cultures. In two years he went through three jobs. He was either sacked or left of his own accord after pointing out how the companies making mechanical handling equipment could be improved.

He then decided to put his theory into practice and set up his own forklift truck operation with his brother Trevor. Called Lancer Boss, a name which harked back to his cavalry days, it started in a small room in Tite Street near the Chelsea Hospital in 1957. Initially the brothers acted as agents for a Dutch forklift company. But when they had sold their entire allocation of vehicles very quickly, 'we started looking around and suddenly realised we could buy the components and make them ourselves for less than we were paying the Dutch', Neville Bowman-Shaw told the *Sunday Times* in 1966.

So, armed with a £20,000 loan raised on an uncle's security, they spent the autumn of 1958 building their first machine. This was sold to Montague L. Meyer, a timber importer, and was delivered to his Manchester operation as soon as the agreement with the Dutch ended on 1 January 1959. 'It worked, Meyer paid us on the 20th and on the 21st the front axle fell off. But we screwed it on again and it's working in Manchester to this day,' he was able to boast eight years later. Meyer came back for another five machines.

In 1960 Sir Neville moved Lancer Boss to Leighton Buzzard, where the group is still based. By 1969 the busi-

ness was booming and they were making 200 vehicles a month. Neville paid well for good managers, but insisted on a tight financial control with budgets thrashed out monthly. 'We're a provincial Weinstock organisation when it comes to that,' he later said.

In the 1960s Neville Bowman-Shaw realised that the fragmented industry would have to expand. He approached Sir Emmanuel Kaye (q.v.) of Lansing Bagnall suggesting collaboration, but he met with a lukewarm response.

Though the business flourished, it was not until 1983 that he was able to find his partner. He took over an ailing German company, and applied distinctly British or even Thatcherite medicine to revive it. Financial controls were tightened and the workforce pruned. Within seven months it was back in profit.

Today, following the takeover of Kaye's business by another German company, Boss as it is now called is the largest British-owned forklift truck company. Sir Neville Bowman-Shaw (knighted in 1984) remains at the helm with Trevor. He lives in a large manor house in Toddington, near the M1 motorway, and is known to be a fervent admirer of Mrs Thatcher.

But the Earl, who had a reputation as a deb's delight and a trencherman of some renown, settled down to pay off the duties while saving the family estates.

He opened Weston Park, the family pile, to the public through Weston Park Enterprises. Art treasures worth £5.5 million were sold and the family estates reduced by 1,000 acres to 13,000.

But the Earl is still left with paintings worth over £30 million at today's prices, including works by Van Dyck, Reynolds, Holbein, Stubbs and Gainsborough. He no longer lives in the 17th-century house, but instead uses an eight-bedroom home on the estate. In his youth the Earl could call on a full-time staff of 15 in the house; today this has been reduced to two nannies, a gardener and some daily help.

# Earl of Bradford £50m

*Landowner*

dob 3/10/47

When Richard Thomas Orlando Bridgeman, 7th Earl of Bradford, inherited the title in 1981, he also inherited death duties of £8 million.

# Godfrey Bradman £50m

*Property developer*

dob 9/9/36

Godfrey Bradman's multi-million company Rosehaugh is one of Britain's most imaginative and wealthy creators of office complexes. Broadgate, at London's Liverpool Street Station, is one of his babies, as is the regeneration of the King's Cross area. This slight, bespectacled property developer had been content with anonymous success until 1981, when he met the campaigner Des Wilson at a lunch for those concerned about atmospheric pollution, and the Campaign for Lead-Free Air was born, seed-financed by Bradman. It was no road-to-Damascus acquisition of a social conscience: 'Godfrey always had an acute social awareness. But, apart from some considerable anonymous donations to charity, he didn't have the time or the knowledge to get involved,' says Wilson, a thorn in the flesh to those in authority since his time with Shelter in the 1960s.

Since that day Bradman has blossomed. He provided funds for legal aid to the victims of the discredited drug Opren, founded the Campaign for Freedom of Information and is president of the Society for the Protection of Unborn Children. Citizen Action, of which he and Wilson are now co-directors, is a permanent umbrella group which initiates and develops campaigns on issues of social concern – a more modern version of the Rowntree Trust. Yet this work is done from behind the safe anonymity of a grey suit and highly polished black shoes. 'He is very conservative in the way

he dresses and behaves,' comments Wilson, who clearly has enormous affection for Bradman and regards him as a great deal more than just a cheque book. 'Godfrey can be modest and self-effacing to an infuriating degree but he is extremely radical in his ideas.'

His willingness to stand convention on its head extends to finance. 'He is the most creative fund-raiser I have ever encountered in the City,' said one former colleague. 'He can raise new kinds of paper on buildings that are only a gleam in his eye.' Perhaps it goes back to the era that Bradman does not include on his personal cv, when he was one of the most successful names in tax avoidance. He now points out that taxation at a real level of £1.37 in the pound was perhaps itself anti-social.

The son of a Willesden shopkeeper, he was evacuated to rural Suffolk at the beginning of the war. There he encountered poverty and, so he told the *Jewish Chronicle*, rife anti-Semitism. 'I learned to fight all right. I was on my own.' His most cherished project is the Rosehaugh Selfbuild Housing Initiative. It gives homeless youngsters in London's Bethnal Green area a chance to create their own homes. Prince Charles had suggested to Bradman at one of their regular lunches that he might employ his creativity on the problem of homelessness.

Although Bradman lives comfortably in London and Sussex, there is no chauffeured Jaguar at the office door. He keeps a London cab on permanent hire because it can use bus lanes. The last year, with the City property slump, has been a difficult one.

---

# Robert Carter £50m

*Builder and contractor*

Robert Carter is the third generation of the Carter family to take the helm of the fast-expanding family firm, RG Carter Holdings.

The company prides itself on being called 'East Anglia's construction company with the national reputation'. With 2,000 employees and a turnover of over £104 million, it is also one of the largest private construction groups in Britain. With no borrowings, a huge cash surplus and healthy after-tax profits of £3.7 million, the Carter group would be worth some £50 million if floated on the stock market today.

It was Carter's grandfather, Robert George Carter, who founded the company in 1921 in a tiny office in the Drayton district of Norwich. It is still based there though in a much larger building.

Robert Carter began by taking on simple repairs and renovations of buildings before winning larger contracts from private and public clients. In 1989 in Norwich alone the company built new headquarters for the Norwich Union insurance company and a new Sainsbury's superstore.

In recent years the company has built banks, building societies, hotels, office blocks, shops and a television studio development for Anglia TV in Norwich. Contracts from the public sector have included building Wayland Prison in Norfolk over 70 acres, and the main ward block at the Norfolk and Norwich Hospital. Smaller developments include a church and a swimming pool. The group has not forgotten its roots and still tackles small jobs in people's homes despite its size today.

The company grew by acquiring other family-run businesses in East Anglia and now has some 25 subsidiaries, ranging from large construction firms in Ipswich, Colchester, Norwich and Grimsby to a small interior design company in Norfolk's North Walsham.

The original Bob Carter was joined by his son, R.E. (Bob) Carter, in 1938 and they worked together at the head of the organisation for the next 25 years. When Robert Carter, the founder, died in 1966, his son took over as managing director and chairman. But he died in 1974 and so the third Robert Carter rose to prominence.

# Lady Anne Cavendish-Bentinck   £50m

*Landowner*

dob 6/9/16

One of Britain's largest landowners, Lady Anne has homes and estates in Scotland, Northumberland, Nottingham and Ireland.

The daughter of the 7th Duke of Portland (known as 'Chopper' after his exploits in Eton's carpentry workshop), Lady Anne spends much of her time at Welbeck, near Worksop. The 16,000-acre estate has a magnificent palace with miles of underground corridors and a huge ballroom created by the 5th Duke. Despite his interest in the building work, he was a recluse who stayed in his quarters, having a letter box in his bedroom door as a means of communication. The family seat, Welbeck Abbey, is now a pre-Sandhurst army training college. The Welbeck Estate Company owns the surrounding land. Lady Anne is one of three directors of the company along with her late sister's son William Parente and Commander Philip Franklin, a family friend.

Lady Anne, who has never married, does not like being called by the name Cavendish. She has spent a large part of her life in charity work, holding numerous posts with, for example, the Royal Midland Institute for the Blind and regional branches of the National Deaf Children's Society and the NSPCC.

She is a keen huntswoman and for many years had her own private pack of hounds, the Rufford Forest Hunt, disbanded on the death of one of its leading members Stan Worthington. She still rides most mornings and has developed an interest in horse racing.

She owns four horses, trained by Jeremy Clover at Carburton, near Worksop.

She once appeared with Sir Michael Nall, Lord John Manners and Rupert Spencer in a local version of the BBC's antiques programme *Going for a Song*, staged at Welbeck Abbey.

In 1983 Lady Anne put a George III gold font commissioned by the 3rd Duke of Portland in 1797 from the master goldsmith Paul Storr up for sale at £1 million.

# Jonathan Clague   £50m

*Casino and hotel owner*

dob *c.* 1948

Hong Kong in the postwar period was the place to make a fortune and the late Douglas Clague was the one to make it. An ex-military man, he escaped from a prisoner of war camp in the Far East and spent 18 months fighting the Japanese from behind their lines. This gave him an invaluable network of contacts who were to prove very useful after the war. In 1952 he became chairman of Hutchison, the local Hong Kong trading house, and over the next 20 years he built it into a huge international trading house to rival Jardine Matheson. Among the friends he helped were Y.K. Pao, then a local merchant. Clague helped him build his first two ships and, today, Sir Y.K. Pao is one of the top shipowners in the world.

Clague also had links with Jim Slater, the 1970s financier, and he formed a Far Eastern merchant bank with Slater Walker. A noted racehorse owner with extensive houses in both Britain and Hong Kong, Clague owned around 10% of Hutchison's stock when he died.

Apart from his business interests, Clague was also a well-known local politician, public servant (as head of the auxiliary police) and chairman of the influential Hong Kong Jockey Club.

His son Jonathan inherited the extensive interests plus the Palace Hotel and Casino in the Isle of Man, from where he now operates. Brought up in Hong Kong, Jonathan lives quietly in a large farmhouse near Douglas with his wife and four children, and is well liked locally.

His working life revolves around the Palace group, which comprises a hotel, casino, ballroom and cinema complex. There is also some land and a golf links hotel, with an 18-hole course. Clague is seeking to build a second golf course at his hotel but has run into strong opposition from local conservationists.

His extensive racehorse interests are based in Ireland, where he owns the prestigious Collinstown Stud, winner of the top breeder's award in 1984 and 1985. He also has business interests in Hong Kong and Australia. He spent a lot of his youth in Ireland on the family stud farm. Apart from racing, his other main interest is golf.

# Viscount Coke  £50m
*Landowner*

dob 6/5/32

Heir to the Earl of Leicester who lives in South Africa, Viscount Coke runs one of the largest estates in England at Holkham, near Sandringham in Norfolk.

The 25,000 acres were subjected to £500,000 (equivalent to £20 million in 1990) worth of improvements in the 18th century by the great agricultural innovator, Coke of Norfolk. But he ran Holkham Hall along traditional lines. At Christmas, 18 large turkeys would be roasted on a spit in the kitchen, while it was the duty of the housemaids to sleep in all the beds in the house to give them a good airing.

Viscount Coke has had to sell paintings to meet death duties. In 1980 he sold a Leonardo da Vinci manuscript to Dr Armand Hammer for £2.2 million, which was described as a bargain price. Later, he sold a Raphael cartoon to the Washington National Gallery for £1 million. But that still leaves him with works by Rubens, Claude, Poussin, Van Dyck and Gainsborough. The furniture and sculptures at Holkham are equally impressive.

# Martin Dawes  £50m
*Communications entrepreneur*

Martin Dawes was born into the communications industry. The son of a television and radio engineer, he started his business career in the 1960s by opening his own television rental shop in Stockport. By a combination of aggressive advertising and good high-street sites, the business has prospered despite the general decline of the television rental market. Today there are 22 outlets with a turnover of nearly £20 million.

But Dawes' great strength is his expanding mobile communications business. He claims to have been one of the first people to spot the potential of the mobile phone and Martin Dawes

Communications, based in Warrington, is one of the largest independent
mobile communications retailer's in
Britain. It has also recently expanded
into Germany and France, while it is
signing up new subscribers at the rate
of 1,000 a week. Dawes aims to gain
up to 15% of the European market. Last
year the Racal telecommunications
group paid £7 million for a 20% stake
in the business, leaving Dawes and his
family with the rest, then worth £28
million. He is planning a stock market
flotation of the business.

The opportunities for growth seem
limitless as *Business* magazine noted:
'Martin Dawes recently installed a computerised billing system that can
handle 200,000 subscribers, six times
its present customer base. If it and the
other service providers can tap successfully into the corporate market,
their licence to print money could run
and run.'

Dawes is a popular man with the
Manchester financial community. A
fervent Northerner, he believes that
businesses in the South have it easy
when getting backing from the City of
London. He is also renowned for his
willingness to try out new ideas and is
said to have a strong sense of humour.

He lives in considerable style in mid-
Cheshire with his family of two
children. He expects them to carry on
the family business.

---

# Mary Foulston  £50m
## *Computers and property heiress*

Mary Foulston's husband John was
killed in 1987 when his 1969
Maclaren racing car crashed at
150 m.p.h. on the Silverstone racing
circuit. He was a computer engineer
who had built up a huge computer
leasing business, but racing his collection of 15 vintage cars was his chief
passion. A year before his death he
bought Brands Hatch and two other
major circuits – Oulton Park and Snet-
terton – for over £5.25 million.

He had married at the age of 19 –
against much parental opposition on
both sides. He was then earning the
princely sum of £97 a month designing
new computer systems. By the time he
was 21 he and Mary had two daughters
and life was a struggle. For nine years
he toiled, making so little money that
at one stage he and Mary had to use
vegetable crates for chairs and
maternity allowance to cover their
bills.

But Foulston joined a young American company where he discovered he
had a talent for selling. He broke every
sales record and within three years was

UK managing director. He then decided to branch out on his own and after two failures struck gold in 1975 when, armed with a £50,000 loan from the Midland Bank, he founded Atlantic Computers to lease IBM machines to British customers.

It was a huge success, coming to the stock market in 1983 with a value of around £40 million. Four years later, when he died, the value had risen to £540 million, and his own stake was worth around £90 million. His life was insured for £8 million when Atlantic was floated as a public company.

Foulston certainly relished the life of a tycoon although in the first three years of building Atlantic he never took a day off. He commuted between London and his seven-bedroom Tudor house on the Surrey/Sussex border in a £250,000 helicopter, painted in his racing colours. A private plane at Gatwick, flown by Foulston, enabled the family to go for skiing weekends or to their house in the south of France.

While Foulston ran the computer business, Mary ran their racing garage in Haslemere. She shared his passion for racing cars.

Foulston left £15 million in his will to Mary, also £10,000 to his lawyer 'in appreciation of his many tax victories on my behalf'. Today his elder daughter Nicola, in her early twenties, runs the racing circuits for her mother, who heads Brands Hatch Leisure, the parent company. In 1988 the circuits made £1 million profit.

# Paul Green and Martin Harrison    £50m each

*Leasing agents*

dob PG 28/1/49    MH 11/8/51

In the late 1970s Martin Harrison and Paul Green decided to set up their own leasing company. Working from home to cut costs and using what they called 'their well-used gold cards', they started Sovereign Leasing in Manchester, leasing equipment to British industry. From these humble beginnings they have built a company which produced £5.6 million profits in the year to the end of June 1989 on a £42.9 million turnover. They have over 120 top-flight customers now, including ICI, British Airways and J. Sainsbury. Green and Harrison own exactly 50% of the shares each, and they value the company at around £100 million, though they do not want to sell. 'We thoroughly enjoy it. I can honestly say that our main hobby is work,' Harrison says.

Harrison and Green are both from the north-west. Green was born and raised in Rochdale, while Harrison comes from Stockport. They have been in finance all their working lives and met while managing another leasing company where they found they had similar ideas and that the chemistry between them was right for branching out with their own business.

Their strong roots in the area are one reason why they have built the new Sovereign headquarters in Deansgate, in the heart of Manchester. The new office has been widely praised for its sensitive blending of a listed frontage with a new building behind.

*Paul Green* (right) *and Martin Harrison* (left)

Sovereign is a tightly run company. No employee smokes and alcohol is banned during working hours. Advice is given on appearance and dress, while time-keeping is paramount. By 8.00 a.m. 'there is already a "buzz" throughout the company,' Harrison says. The staff are carefully chosen and, since they are well paid, none has defected to rival companies.

Although they worked a seven-day week of 12 hours a day to set the business up, Green and Harrison now confine themselves to five days a week, though still working 12 hours a day each. Green's main passion is his family, while Harrison loves sport and is a keen Manchester United follower, but says he has 'more sense than to invest in a football club'.

# James Gulliver   £50m
## *Retailer*

dob 17/8/30

The son of a Campbeltown grocer, Jimmy Gulliver rose to build the Argyll group into one of Britain's largest supermarket combines, which now owns the Safeway chain.

He was also the unwitting victim of one of the biggest City scandals for many years, when his efforts to take over Distillers, the Scottish drinks group, were thwarted by allegedly dubious tactics employed by Guinness.

Gulliver has never lost his love for Scotland or his Scottish roots, despite living in London. He went to Glasgow University and took a first-class honours degree in engineering. After that, he became a management consultant before stepping into the grocery

trade at Fine Fare in 1965. Fourteen years later, he formed Argyll.

He has now left Argyll in the hands of Alistair Grant, a long-time business partner and friend. Gulliver was reputed to have left with £55 million.

He tried to revitalise the Harris Queensway carpets group, which he took over from Sir Phil Harris (q.v.), and renamed Lowndes Queensway. Unfortunately, high interest rates and a sharp drop in consumer spending undermined his strategy and, in January 1990, he resigned from the ailing group. Gulliver has his wealth safely tucked up in a number of ventures including hotels, the Waverley Cameron packaging and paper business and, until recently, a prominent City public relations company. Still, he will not be happy with the way Lowndes has performed. Look out for a come-back.

When not working, Gulliver can be found urging on Manchester United football team, skiing, sailing and driving fast cars.

# Earl of Harewood   £50m

*Landowner*

dob 7/2/23

Everything about George Henry Hubert Lascelles, 7th Earl of Harewood, reeks of aristocratic grandeur. Tall and distinguished in appearance, he went to the traditional school, Eton, and from there to King's College, Cambridge. A cousin of the Queen, he was one of the most famous of the British prisoners held in the Colditz Castle prisoner-of-war camp during World War II. As he was 18th in line to the throne, the Germans considered him a unique prize. He was captured after being wounded while fighting as a Grenadier Guards captain in Italy in 1944.

After the war he served in various appointments as an ADC to the Governor General of Canada and as Counsellor of State during the absence abroad of George VI and later Queen Elizabeth.

But he made his lasting mark on contemporary Britain as an arts patron and administrator. He was a director and executive of the Royal Opera House at Covent Garden and is chairman of Sadlers Wells Opera, now the English National Opera. He was also editor of the magazine *Opera.*

In 1967 he divorced his first wife Marion, and she later married the Rt. Hon. Jeremy Thorpe, former leader of the old Liberal Party. The same year he married Patricia Tuckwell, an Australian. He has four sons by the two marriages.

He owns Harewood House, one of England's finest historic buildings, which contains a genuinely priceless collection of the very best paintings by Hoppner, Gainsborough, Reynolds, Titian, Tintoretto, Veronese, El Greco and Turner. In addition there is a valuable collection of Sèvres and Chinese porcelain and some of the finest furniture ever made in Britain. Most of the wealth came from the 2nd Earl's involvement in the slave trade at the end of the 18th century. In the late 19th century the estate ran to just under 30,000 acres, though this is thought to have slimmed down during the 20th century.

# Sir Jack Hayward   £50m

*Financier*

dob 14/6/23

Despite living in the Bahamas, Hayward is intensely British. Not for nothing is he called 'Union Jack' Hayward.

He lists his recreations as promoting British endeavours and preserving the British landscape, keeping all things bright, beautiful and British. Today he is president of Wolverhampton Wanderers Football Club. He also has a home in Sussex. He served in the RAF during World War II. He has operated from the Grand Bahamas since 1956. His father, Charles Hayward, was chairman of the Firth Cleveland Group which developed Freeport in the Bahamas. Hayward bought the Firth interests in Jamaica and the Bahamas in 1970.

Hayward has been a substantial benefactor to various causes. In 1969 he gave £150,000 to the National Trust, enabling it to buy Lundy Island with the Landmark Trust. He gave £1 million for the care of the elderly of the Falklands and also bought Brunel's ship, the *Great Eastern*, for the nation.

He frequently buys into British companies and he was a long-time backer of the Liberal Party.

---

# Clive Hunting and family £50m

*Engineering and oil executive*

The Hunting family own a third of the Hunting Group, a medium-sized engineering and oil company. But their roots go back to the coal industry in the North East, where Charles Hunting, an astute Geordie, supplied equipment to the booming coal industry. He had side interests in shipping and, in 1874, set his son up as a shipowner with two sailing ships. Recognising that oil would replace coal as the fuel of the future, the Hunting group switched rapidly from sailing ships to oil tankers.

But it was Sir Percy Hunting, grandson of Charles, who between World Wars I and II steered the company into new fields such as aviation. He also moved down from the North East to London during the Depression. Sir Percy retired in 1960 at the age of 75; he died in 1973 after a very active life. His nephew, Clive Hunting, was chairman for many years, but now Sir Percy's grandson, Richard, is chairman. He has all the right qualifications. After schooling at Rugby, he took an engineering degree at Sheffield University and an MBA from Manchester. A sporty type, he lists his hobbies as skiing, swimming, languages, travel and choral singing.

For years Hunting was one of the most complex companies in the City, with different bits of businesses controlled by different members of the family. It was also prone to several reorganisations, as it gradually shed its old businesses to move firmly into the high technology end of defence.

Finally, in 1989, all the businesses were brought together as the Hunting Group. This is now worth around £150 million on the stock market with its headquarters in London's Knightsbridge.

In the reorganisation the family share of the business fell from a controlling 50% to 33.4% which, they admitted, was a wrench after more than a century of total control.

## Nurdin Jivraj   £50m
*Hotelier*

Nurdin Jivraj first set up in business as a 19-year-old in the Tanzanian capital of Dar es Salaam. That was in 1959 and was the start of his first business empire. Wisely he invested in Britain in the 1960s, so that when his private assets were nationalised in Tanzania in 1967 he had the resources to start again when he arrived in the UK in 1971.

He acquired hotels in the Kensington area of London and then moved into residential property. By 1984 Nurdin had bought the London Park Hotels group for £13 million and his son Nick had also joined the business.

Since then companies and stakes in them have been regularly bought and sold for a profit. In January 1989 father and son took over Leisuretime International from the Beaverbrook family. They have turned round Leisuretime from loss to profit and renamed it Buckingham International.

Nurdin and Nick Jivraj have not been slow to look for new opportunities, acquiring a Portuguese property group and later a new hotel in Lisbon. The hotel cost them some £14.7 million in cash. They have also moved into the British retirement home business by buying a 5% stake in Anglia Secure Homes.

Despite their addiction to work and wealth, the Jivraj father and son live modestly in a London flat.

## Peter Jones   £50m
*Builder*

Peter Jones, a former bricklayer, set up as a housebuilder in Cheshire in 1959. 'PE', as he is always known, had a reputation for taking risks which netted him big rewards, and he showed this flair early on. Buying a waterlogged site in the exclusive village of Alderley Edge for a very low price, he was able to drain it, build some houses and make a considerable profit.

He followed this success in the 1970s and early 1980s by buying up as much land as he could in the then unpopular South Manchester area, where there is now great demand for land. His latest venture is an office park on the outskirts of Moss Side, a site rejected by many other developers.

His main company, Emerson Holdings, is called after his second name – the E in PE. The various subsidiaries operate in housebuilding, construction and office development. In the year to the end of April 1989, Emerson Holdings made £3.6 million after-tax profits on sales of £40 million. The company, which is owned by Jones and his family trusts, has a property portfolio with a value of up to £50 million.

Recently the group has expanded into the south with projects around Heathrow, and it also has property interests in Portugal and America.

Now in his fifties, Jones lives in a £1 million mansion in Alderley Edge which he built himself. He drives a Rolls-Royce and is a fanatical snooker follower, having started a snooker league with some of Manchester's leading developers. Matches are generally played in his purpose-built snooker room.

He is regarded as a tough business man and a perfectionist, personally negotiating all the business development plans and agreements himself.

## Viscount Leverhulme £50m

*Landowner*

dob 1/7/15

Grandson of William Lever, who founded the Lever Brothers soap company and the Port Sunlight model village, Viscount Leverhulme has shown no direct interest in the family business, now Unilever, a multinational company. He inherited the title in 1949 and since then has devoted himself to his 90,000 acres in Cheshire and to racing.

A country lover, he took a course in estate management to prepare himself for farming. He is a former Jockey Club steward and prominent racehorse owner. Among his horses were Fascinating Forties, winner of the National Hunt Chase in 1968, and Hot Grove, runner-up in the 1977 Derby. In 1972 he bought the late Earl of Sefton's 4,200-acre Altcar estate, where the Waterloo Cup, Britain's main hare-coursing event, is run.

It was his father, known in Unilever as The Governor, who guided the company to multinational status with 300 subsidiary companies. He was also known as a generous employer, concerned about the welfare of his staff.

## Bernard and David Lewis £50m

*Fashion retailers*

dob DL 2/6/24

Bernard Lewis started trading out of the back of a fruit lorry after the war. With his brother David he later progressed to open the Lewis Separates shop in Hackney, which in the 1960s became the trendy Chelsea Girl chain. Today the Lewis Trust group still owns this well-known fashion chain and has also acquired property interests. The business has its headquarters in West London.

There are four Lewis directors on the board and the family control around 80% of the shares between them. Bernard is still the chairman, and his son Leonard deals with the marketing. In 1988 the Lewis Trust declared an after-tax profit of £8 million on a £195 million turnover. The family are particularly secretive about their wealth. But they are planning a major revamp of Chelsea Girl, masterminded by Leonard. The group's 260 shops are being renamed 'River Island'.

## Dr Daniel McDonald £50m

*Retired industrialist*

dob 1905

A device for changing records on the old record-players of the 1950s and

1960s made a fortune for Dr Daniel McDonald. The son of an Inverness grocer, McDonald was an unusual industrialist. For a start he took a degree in medicine, though he never practised as a doctor. Instead, he became rather good at making money.

Born in 1905, he first went to Glasgow University where he took a first class honours degree in engineering. In 1932, when Britain was still gripped by recession, he went into business in a shed in the Blackheath area of Birmingham with £300 of capital and one apprentice, making top-quality hi-fi and electronics equipment. Later, just before the war, to extend his knowledge he embarked on his medical degree, while working at a full-time job. When he qualified as a doctor from Birmingham University in 1942, the army wanted him as a medical officer and the Admiralty wanted him to keep making electrical equipment. The navy

won and he never looked back. He worked on defences against the V bombs and acoustic mines.

In 1951 he decided to make some real money and determined to make Birmingham Sound Reproducers – his company – into the Ford of the record-player business. He shrewdly anticipated the boom in records brought about by the advent of rock and roll, and determined to make his equipment at a price teenagers could afford. Through the 1950s he enjoyed a huge success. By 1958 BSR was the second largest maker of record changers in the world. Nearly half its output was exported to America and Canada. The BSR record changer was incorporated in all the major record-players such as Ferguson, Fidelity and Alba.

In 1957 BSR came to the stock market and McDonald was a millionaire overnight. Within a year he was worth nearly £3 million as profits rocketed. He expanded into new factories, opening two in Londonderry and one at East Kilbride New Town.

A paternalist and regarded as fiercely anti-union, McDonald ran into problems with the British trade union movement when it was at its most obdurate and powerful. In 1967 he shut his Londonderry factories on the grounds that the unions were pressing for recognition. He had another long and bitter strike at East Kilbride over recognition in 1968.

This dispute convinced him of the need to sell the business, but while he was preparing to sell to Plessey, it recognised unions and he changed his mind. In the end he sold his stake in 1970 for £16 million, and his wife and son later realised another £5 million by selling their shares. In 1971 his personal fortune was estimated to be well over £20 million.

He prepared his 1970 sale carefully, and moved into tax exile in a villa overlooking Lake Geneva. He also had a home in Bermuda, a large estate in Ireland and a small executive jet to flit between the three.

In 1971, bored with retirement, he bought a small German vacuum cleaner factory and invented a much cheaper and lighter cleaner. Though he flirted with the idea of coming back to do business in Britain, he was so frustrated by British inefficiency compared to the efficiency of Germany and Switzerland that he stayed away.

Now in his eighties, Dr McDonald lives a quiet life with his wife in the Isle of Man. They have one son and two grandchildren. He has built up a 1,000-acre estate and has won over the ever suspicious locals by his careful conservation and restoration of old farm buildings. He has also been a generous local benefactor. Early in 1989 he donated £1 million to the Manx Education Board to build a new village school at Sulby where he lives. He has also given £10 million to Cambridge University to fund the McDonald Institute of Archaeology.

Apart from his passionate interest in gardening, McDonald loves breeding cattle. He won two major awards once at the Royal Show for two bulls he had entered. He also loves art and in 1966 gave a collection of seven paintings valued at £500,000 to the nation. He also bought Turner's painting of Folkestone Bay for £7.2 million, then a world record.

£16 of the richest 400 people inherited their wealth. This constitutes 60% of the total wealth of the 400.

# John and James Macdonald-Buchanan  £50m
*Landowners*

Heirs to the Buchanan Black & White whisky fortune, John and James's mother left some £17 million when she died in 1987 at the age of 92. Lady Macdonald-Buchanan was a noted racehorse owner, proprietor of the Lavington stud, founded in 1904 by her father, Lord Woolavington. Under his daughter's control the stud produced Owen Tudor, winner of the 1941 Derby and sire of the winners of over 400 races.

Lady Macdonald-Buchanan herself had inherited what was then a huge fortune of £3 million when her father died in 1935. Following her death in February 1987, there was considerable controversy over the way a Constable painting, *Stratford Mill*, was handed over by the family to the nation in lieu of inheritance tax of £5.5 million. The board of the Museums and Galleries Commission, which normally oversees the transfer of paintings from private to public hands, was furious at the speed with which the deal was done. It was concluded in a record three weeks as opposed to the normal six to nine months. The family wanted the deal worked out fast to prevent a hefty interest charge building up on the tax debt. The painting, then the most important Constable in private hands, was given to the National Gallery. It was valued at £10 million and formed part of a large collection built up in the 1940s and early 1950s by her husband, the late Sir Reginald Macdonald-Buchanan.

The collection included other masterpieces such as Stubbs' *Gimcrack*. *Stratford Mill* itself had been bought for £50,000 in 1951. Today John Macdonald-Buchanan, the eldest son, lives in the family home of Cottesmore Hall in Northamptonshire. James lives in Scotland on the 71,100-acre Strathconan estate. The family connection with Buchanan's whisky has long ended.

# Norman Mackinnon £50m
*Liqueur manufacturer*

Every bottle of Drambuie Liqueur carries the slogan 'Prince Charles Edward's Liqueur. A link with the '45.' This refers to the personal recipe that Bonnie Prince Charlie gave to the Mackinnons of Skye to reward their services during the Scottish '45 rebellion.

The family claims the secret has remained with them ever since and, while others doubt this story, it has served the family well. The Drambuie Liqueur Company, now based in Edinburgh, remains in family hands. The link with the '45 rebellion is still kept up. One of the company conference rooms is decked out as a French frigate cabin, to commemorate the ship that took the Young Pretender into exile after the defeat at Culloden and his flight through Skye.

The present head of the business is Norman Mackinnon, who owns over half the shares. His son, Duncan, is also a director. The business is very profitable and its latest accounts reveal after-tax profits of some £2 million. But given the high prices being paid for well-known branded products, the company could command a price of well over £50 million.

Norman Mackinnon is described as a good old-fashioned manager, who knows exactly what he wants and can make decisions quickly. He has not attempted to change or adapt Drambuie, preferring to stick to its tried and tested formula. In 1988 he was the second highest paid director in Scotland, earning £359,940, a rise of 20% over the previous year.

# Brian Morrison and family £50m
*Whisky distillers*

The Morrison family company, Morrison Bowmore, is one of Scotland's leading whisky producers, with fine malts such as Bowmore, Glen Garioch and Auchentoshan. It is also one of the most profitable, with £3 million after-tax profits on a £23 million turnover in 1988.

The business was founded in 1951 by Stanley Morrison who teamed up with a young accountant, James Howat. Morrison had done an apprenticeship with a Glasgow engineering firm, which took him out to the Far East. On his return in the early 1920s, he joined a whisky broking firm, where he learnt the business.

In the 1950s Stanley Morrison acted as a conventional broker. But in 1963, hearing that the Bowmore distillery on Islay was for sale, he managed to buy it. In 1970 he bought the Glen Garioch distillery, which had lain empty for two years because of its poor water supplies.

By tapping into new water sources, he managed to increase capacity sixfold on its previously dormant period. In 1971 Stanley Morrison died and his son Brian took over. He followed his father's expansion and acquired the third distillery at Auchentoshan in 1984.

In 1989 he relaunched the company as Morrison Bowmore and brought the Japanese group Suntory in as a partner. The aim is to give the three malt brands a much higher prominence, rather than relying on selling bulk malt to overseas markets, particularly Japan. Many Scots regard that as simply selling Scotland's birthright. Morrison also has a brother, Stanley, in the business. They both live in Ayrshire. The company has a reputation for clever conservation, and at the Glen Garioch distillery there are 2 acres of greenhouses, fed by waste heat from the whisky plant and fertilised by surplus carbon dioxide from the distilling process, which aids photosynthesis. In 1989 the company harvested 40 tons of tomatoes, and from 1990 onwards there are plans to increase this to 600 tons.

# Charlotte Morrison £50m

*Landowner*

dob 16/4/55

When Viscount Galway died, his 15-year-old daughter Charlotte Morrison became a millionairess. He left her 3,000 Nottinghamshire acres, and she also inherited 15,000 acres of Dorset and an area round exclusive Holland Park in London from her mother, Lady Teresa Agnew, who left £40m in her will.

Charlotte lives in the 15th-century Melbury House near Dorchester, and also owns another country house near Doncaster.

Charlotte married Guy Morrison, an Old Etonian art dealer, in 1983. They met while out exercising their dogs in St James's Park one lunchtime. There were 1,200 people at the wedding service at Sherborne Abbey; Charlotte was 30 minutes late because her car broke down. She has a son, Simon, but is now divorced from her husband.

She spends most of her time in Dorset and is keen on hunting, being joint master of the Cattistock Hunt. She is active in a number of charities.

# Mickie Most  £50m

*Pop music promoter*

Every day Mickie Most goes down into the basement of his £20 million dream house in the exclusive Totteridge area of London to do a series of punishing exercises. This is followed by a 4-mile run and 50 lengths of the indoor pool. 'It's one of the best things you can do with your clothes off,' he says.

He then heads off on his 1500cc motorbike to his studios in St John's Wood. 'I don't do any work. I oversee what is going on.' But Mickie has a lot to oversee at Rak Records, the company he founded in 1970 while working as a pop promoter. By the age of 24 he had made his first million, and between 1964 and 1984 he sold 400 million records, with 22 American number ones and 15 in Britain.

The son of a soldier and raised in north-west London, he originally planned to become an actor, but the thought of rising at 6.00 a.m. for filming put him off. So with rock and roll sweeping Britain, he bought a guitar and started a career as singer and guitarist in a skiffle group.

At the age of 19, at a pop concert at the Chiswick Empire, he met his wife Christina, then a 16-year-old. She was on holiday from South Africa with her parents at the time. Five days later he proposed and they were married just after her 17th birthday. For four years Mickie worked in South Africa learning all about record studios and production. Then he came back home just in time for the era of the Beatles. He guided groups such as the Animals, Herman's Hermits and Hot Chocolate to success.

He discovered the Animals in Newcastle upon Tyne and financed their first top twenty hit, 'Baby Let Me Take

You Home'. But it was their second, 'House of the Rising Sun', recorded in just fifteen minutes, which really put him on the road to success.

Mickie still lives with Christina after some 30 years of marriage, and they have three children. His eldest, Calvin, plays in a band. His two young daughters live at the dream mansion which, he claims, is the largest private house to have been built in Britain since the war. It took seven years to build and has 33 rooms, including eight bedrooms and nine bathrooms. The swimming pool is the largest indoor/outdoor pool in Europe and has an underwater stereo system. Outside there is a five-a-side football pitch and a floodlit Astro-turfed tennis court. If he gets tired of London, the family can always move to their 11-bedroom house in Cannes, where he keeps his 36-foot boat.

---

# Marquess of Northampton   £50m

*Landowner*

dob 2/4/46

Inheritance has been the controlling influence on the Marquess of Northampton's colourful life. While admirers of the British aristocracy tend to stress the concept of *noblesse oblige*, the ethos of 'Do what you choose' is at least as strong. Spenny Northampton acquired from his father, the 6th Marquess, two stately homes in the Midlands, the freehold of much of Islington in London and an apparent lack of luck with his partners in marriage.

Where his passionate interest in spiritualism originated is unclear,

although a mutual concern with the Other Side led him to him fourth wife, Fritzi. She was previously married to Michael Pearson, heir to the Pearson empire. Northampton's previous wives, in chronological order, were: Henriette Bentinck, the Dutch-born niece of the Thyssen steel dynasty who gave him an heir and a daughter; Annette Smallwood and, thirdly, Rose Dawson-Damer. The third Marchioness turned out to have a head for the fashion business and created the enormously successful Northampton wellington boot. This chic mixture of canvas and rubber was seen on such high-profile calves as those of Princess Michael of Kent.

Northampton's father, universally known as Bim, was married three times. In the 1920s he lost a breach of promise case with damages of £50,000, worth over £1 million today. In 1985 the Marquess's sale of Mantegna's Renaissance masterpiece, *The Adoration of the Magi*, caused controversy. It went to the Getty Museum in California for £7.5 million amid protest from the art conservation lobby that it should stay in Britain – where it had been since its acquisition by a Northampton ancestor in the mid-19th century. The Marquess was unmoved, saying at the time, 'As far as the loss of heritage is concerned, I'm afraid I'm not very patriotic, because I believe we've got to think more globally. Art has shuffled around the world since the year dot.'

The Marquess maintained that the money was needed for the maintenance of his two homes. Castle Ashby, the grander of the pair, now operates as a superior conference centre. It is also available for commercial promotions, such as the launch of a new car. Although his Warwickshire house, Compton Wynyates, regarded as the world's finest example of Tudor architecture, is nominally the

Northampton family's private home, that too is rentable if the mood takes 'Spenny'. Michael Winner used it as the location for his 1982 remake of *The Wicked Lady*. Spenny is currently trying to sell a magnificent collection of Roman silver, which Sotheby's reckon could fetch some $40 million, but legal problems have cropped up, which may delay or even prevent a sale.

## Anwar Pervez   £50m

*Retailer*

dob c.1934

The big name in cash and carry is Anwar Pervez, head of Bestway, which he started in 1976. Group turnover in the year to the end of June 1989 was £340 million (18% increase on the previous year), giving a profit of £7.2 million (16% increase on the previous year). This has been increasing at the

rate of 20% a year. He has contributed £140,000 recently to the fund set up by Prince Charles to regenerate industry. His first shop was in the Park Royal area of west London. His operation is now highly computerised. He drives a Mercedes.

## Robert Sangster   £50m

*Racehorse owner and heir to a pools fortune*

dob 23/5/36

Horses and women characterise Robert Sangster's indulgent life. But originally his father, Vernon, made him work at the family business sorting pools' coupons during holidays from his public school.

That was enough for Sangster. Since then he has dedicated himself to the turf. With 1,200 horses, at first he won nearly every single classic, including the Derby and the Prix de l'Arc de Triomphe in 1977. But the uncrowned king of British racing has since had more difficulty. Arab sheikhs have swept all before them on the British racing circuit, leaving Sangster to pick up the odd consolation prize. But his commitment to racing has been so great that it halved the £110 million fortune he inherited from his father. Early in 1989 he was forced to put his lavish Manton stud on the market. Described as Europe's 'finest private training complex', the 2,050-acre farm has a price tag of around £15 million. Sangster also wants to close Pheonix Park racecourse in Ireland, where he is

a part owner, because of heavy losses.

Thrice married, Sangster is rarely out of the gossip columns. His first wife was a Lake District hotelier's daughter. His second, Susan, was the ex-wife of Australian politician Andrew Peacock. He married Sue Lilley, 20 years his junior, in 1985 after a brief romance with Jerry Hall who is now Mick Jagger's (q.v.) girlfriend. Sangster lives a luxury life in his Isle of Man home, inappropriately called the Nunnery. He also has a Barbados retreat.

---

## Paul Sykes  £50m

*Property developer*

Barnsley, at the heart of the so-called socialist republic of South Yorkshire, does not produce many Thatcherite entrepreneurs – and even fewer who are miners' sons. But Paul Sykes is one. He left school at 16, and a year later had already had six jobs 'because I didn't agree with the way the businesses were managed – I was that arrogant,' he told *Business* magazine.

He then decided to enter the vehicle-breaking business and, armed with £170, he bought some cutting gear, a pick-up truck and a scrapped double-decker bus. Breaking the bus up and selling the scrap metal gave him a profit of £31, which was three times his previous weekly wage.

Six years later he had made his first million. By then he was employing 17 men and breaking down 30 buses a week, selling the scrap metal locally and exporting the engines and other working parts to the Far East for use in powering fishing boats. He moved into all the ex-British colonies, and he started sending truck parts over as well. At one stage the operation involved moving two complete container loads of parts a day, and soon complete buses followed.

But the remorseless march of the Japanese eventually hit the business in the mid-1970s. The supply of sturdy old British buses also began to dry up. So Sykes diversified into coach distribution in Britain and supplying earth-moving equipment to the oil-rich Arab states, as well as some industrial property development. These various businesses were never as lucrative as the bus-breaking enterprise. In 1984 he sold them, only retaining a stake in the bus business, and moved wholeheartedly into property.

His most spectacular development has been the £200 million Meadowhall shopping centre in what was the devastated Lower Don Valley in Sheffield. He had to overcome ferocious resistance from the local Chamber of Commerce and also from a rival developer, Eddie Healey of Stadium Developments (q.v.), who was planning a rival centre in Rotherham. Eventually, after Sykes threatened to bring in London developers, Healey abandoned his Rotherham plans and joined Sykes in Sheffield. Sykes followed the Sheffield development up with a £50 million shopping mall near York.

He became embroiled in controversy in 1980 when, as chairman of the Barnsley Conservative Association, he claimed that local left-wingers were threatening him. He also sought to sponsor Roy Mason, the tough but independent-minded Barnsley Labour MP, when the local Labour Party was taken over by the left. Mason refused the offer. At the time Sykes lived within 300 yards of the council house where he was born. He has retired and spends his time planting trees. He and his wife own all the shares in his company, which is based in Leeds.

He hit the headlines in 1989 when it was revealed in *The Sunday Times* that he was the highest-paid business man in Britain, taking home a salary of £6 million in the previous year.

# Richard Tompkins   £50m
*Green Shield stamp dealer*

dob 15/5/15

In the mid 1960s 24 million Britons were collecting Green Shield stamps in the hope of saving enough to buy a Ford Cortina or expensive cutlery.

They made Richard Tompkins, a quiet and friendly business man, a £50 million fortune in the process. Born and bred in north London, Tompkins, who was once described as looking like a middle-ranking executive, left school at the age of 13, a self-confessed 'dunce'.

He went into a series of jobs including running a café and working in a

laundry. On his 17th birthday he passed his driving test and within three hours had a job as a van salesman. But the young Tompkins wanted more, and took a correspondence course to become a draughtsman. As a result, he spent the war years, 1939–45, in a reserved occupation.

After the war Tompkins took over a small London printing company, complete with some worn-out machines, which he managed to repair himself. In the drab postwar world he built up a thriving business based on his reputation for good delivery and reliable products.

But the big break came when he went on a holiday to Jamaica and met a Chicago business man who told him that half the output of the American cutlery industry went to gift stamp companies. Intrigued, Tompkins went over to America and saw for himself the popularity of the stamps. Stopping on a freeway outside four gas stations, he noted that the three selling stamps were full while the fourth – without stamps – was empty.

Tompkins determined to bring stamps to Britain on a large scale (up to then there had been over 30 small-scale operations). Green Shield was born in 1958. It was tough going at first. Operating from a converted Lyons tea house in Archway, it took Tompkins seven years to put Green Shield into profit. But offering high-quality prizes and with an expensive catalogue (the first cost £12,000 to produce), the operation eventually proved a huge success.

Typically, a supermarket with Green Shield stamps would have to add around 2% extra in costs, but in the first year turnover would be boosted by 50%. The big break came when Tesco decided to support them following the decision of rival Fine Fare to stock Pink Shield (an American venture that

Tompkins was easily able to see off). Tompkins himself owned over 97% of the shares in the Green Shield company, which in its heyday employed 5,000 people.

Success transformed Tompkins' life. He moved into a flat in the exclusive Carlton Towers block in London's Belgravia and had a holiday home in the south of France. A fanatical admirer of James Bond films, he had a Rolls-Royce with the number plate 007. He also had another Rolls and a private executive jet.

In May 1968 he bought the last private residence in Belgrave Square, which he turned into a 22-room, 9-bathroom home. In 1973 his pay and dividend payments totalled £1 million.

By the late 1970s consumer interest in Green Shield stamps was waning, and in 1977 Tesco appeared to deliver a body blow to the idea by withdrawing from the scheme. Tompkins finally wound up the operation in 1980, but by then he had made £25 million from the stamps. Shrewdly, he had also anticipated the waning interest and in 1973 he set up the Argos chain of discount stores. Six years later he sold Argos to BAT for around £25 million.

Tompkins married his first wife during World War II and they had two daughters. They parted in 1962. In 1970 he married the model Elizabeth Duke, a cousin of Neville Duke, the test pilot. The wedding reception at the Dorchester cost £7,000. In 1973 they had a daughter. They still live in Tompkins' Belgrave Square house. In 1978 he bought a Berkshire stud from Peter de Savary (q.v.) for £2 million. He has recently put it on the market.

Tim Jefferies, his grandson by a daughter from his first marriage, hit the headlines in 1984 when he was briefly married to Koo Stark, the former friend of Prince Andrew. They were divorced in 1989.

# Hon. Vincent Weir and family £50m
*Shipping owner*

dob VW 8/2/35

Andrew Weir, later the 1st Baron Inverforth, built up Andrew Weir and Co. into a powerful shipping and insurance group in the late 19th and early 20th centuries. The company controlled the Bank shipping line, Invertanker Ltd and the Inver Transport and Trading Company. Like other Scottish magnates such as Carnegie and Andrew Mellon, he had a passion for commerce, hard work and thrift.

Today the business is run by the Hon. Vincent Weir, son of the 2nd Baron, and it has branched out into investment, property, insurance, hotels and fine art dealing.

In the mid-1980s it was hit by the slump in shipping and moved into loss, but it has since recovered. In 1989 it achieved post-tax profits of nearly £5 million. The business has huge assets valued at around £128 million. It remains in the hands of the Weir family, who appear to be generous employers. During its 1985 centenary each member of staff received an extra month's wages. Vincent Weir lives in Mayfair, London; his interests are natural history and wildlife conservation.

The Bank line recently announced that it was going back into carrying passengers on its container ships at a cost of £50 per passenger a day for the five-month round trip to the South Pacific.

# George Williams £50m
*Double glazing manufacturer*

In the early 1960s George Williams was working as a chicken farmer in Norfolk, determining the sex of chicks for the likes of Bernard Matthews (q.v.), the poultry millionaire. But in 1966, just when double glazing was becoming popular in Britain, he started work part-time in the infant double-glazing industry. Initially, with £450 capital, he had just six staff and worked from a garage at his Norfolk home, but two years later he opened his first showroom in Ipswich.

George proved to be a strong-minded boss who motivated his staff and salesmen by paying well for results. And these were achieved. Battling hard for customers in the 1970s, he built up the company, Anglian Windows, to be the second largest double-glazing firm in Britain. It had 118 showrooms and 49 branches round the country, with over 1,400 full-time employees.

In 1984 Williams sold a controlling stake in the business to the giant BET group for £25 million, which left him and his family holding the rest. He stayed on as chairman of Anglian.

In 1985 his first wife separated from him and their four children. In 1986 George married a Chilean girl whom he had met in a King's Road shop. They live in a Norfolk mansion set in 70 acres and have three other homes in Devon, America and the Virgin Islands. George also has a private plane and a helicopter.

# Lord Wolfson    £50m

*Mail order dealer*

dob 11/11/27

Lord Wolfson's father, Isaac Wolfson, started work in his father's furniture business in Glasgow and then built up his own larger one in Manchester, where he came into contact with Great Universal Stores, a mail order business which he subsequently joined in 1931.

A consummate deal-maker, Isaac Wolfson was renowned for making an offer on everything and anything.

Today GUS is a £2.5 billion business which stretches from Burberry raincoats to furniture. In the first six months of 1989, GUS profits rose 5% to £171 million. It is now moving into property and plans to develop its £1 billion portfolio with George Wimpey, the building group.

Leonard, Sir Isaac's son, was created a Conservative peer in 1985, and has been GUS chairman since 1966. He lives in Portland Place and lists history and economics as his hobbies.

Leonard is renowned as a tough business man, but also makes large donations to medical and scientific bodies through the charitable Wolfson Foundation, which controls over £200 million worth of GUS shares.

Both men are obsessed by secrecy. Sir Isaac, who was once compared to Spencer Tracy, has a strong Glasgow accent. He once said that the secret of his success was that 'I worked with all my fingers.'

His son Lord Wolfson took over from Sir John Nott as trustee of the Imperial War Museum and has strong links with the Conservative Party.

£ Of the 77 peers entitled to sit in the House of Lords

6 have not taken their seats at all
1 has disclaimed his title
5 have not declared political allegiance
7 sit as independents
2 support the SDP
51 take the Tory whip
2 are women

None is identified as Liberal or Labour

# 4

# THE
# MILLIONAIRES

## £20m and more

## Peter and Ronald Goldstein   £48m

*Former chemist's shop owners*

The Goldstein brothers started working with a barrow for their father in London's East End, but eventually the business was taken over by Tesco. Peter and Ronnie Goldstein then branched out on their own, setting up their first chemist's shop in an old barber's premises in Putney High Street. That was in April 1966. The office was so small there that any conversations with sales reps had to take place standing up.

By 1983 they had established 143 of their cut-price Superdrug stores. The company was then floated on the stock market and the brothers became millionaires overnight. In 1987 they sold the chain – then 300 strong – to Woolworth and accepted 16 million Woolworth shares in payment. These are worth over £48 million today.

The brothers are part of a close-knit family. Neither smokes or drinks, and they work 120 hours a week between them. Peter is a keen tennis player and Ronnie sings for relaxation. They live within walking distance of each other in Croydon.

## John Hall   £48m

*Property developer*

dob 21/3/33

For a fourth-generation miner, John Hall is not doing badly for himself. He is the man who has turned 120 acres of derelict and muddy land in depressed Gateshead into the Metro Centre, described as Europe's most ambitious retail and leisure complex. People come from miles around to shop at the centre, and others are planned in Edinburgh, Glasgow and Birmingham.

He escaped from underground mining to work for the Coal Board's estate depart-

ment. After qualifying as a fully-fledged chartered surveyor, he became a partner in a Sunderland firm of surveyors. He survived the 1974 property crash and then planned the Metro centre.

Today he is busy drawing up plans for Wynyard Park, the 4,500-acre estate and former ancestral home of the Marquess of Londonderry, which he has just bought. Ironically, the Londonderry family used to be one of the largest mine owners in the country. John Hall plans to live in the house while creating a business centre, luxury hotel and three golf courses on the estate.

John Hall's family own the Cameron Hall development company in which they all play an active role.

## Joe Levy  £48m
*Retired property developer*
dob 27/1/06

Brothers Joe and David Levy went to work for Jackie Phillips, a West End property agent, in 1924. Phillips, a heavy gambler, had been asked by the Levys' bookmaking father to give them a job.

He duly obliged, and when he died Joe and David took over the business. David died in 1952, by which time Joe had bought a 'shell' company called Stock Conversion, which had links with the great railway building boom in the 19th century.

With a new partner, Scotsman Robert Clark, Joe built Stock Conversion into one of the major London property companies in the 1960s. It was responsible for buildings such as the Euston Centre.

His son Peter Levy came into the business. But when Robert Clark died in 1984, his share of the business was sold. In 1986 Stock Conversion was taken over by P&O, the property and shipping group. The Levy shares were worth over £48 million.

Joe Levy, though retired, has a home in Grosvenor Square, a villa in Antibes, a yacht and racehorses. He formed the Cystic Fibrosis Foundation to research into this disease because a client's child had suffered from it.

## Nigel Wray  £47m
*Financier*
dob 9/4/48

Singer & Friedlander is a very traditional merchant bank in the City. 'My main reaction was that it was a very weird name but I thought merchant banking had a nice sound to it,' recalls Nigel Wray. Eighteen years ago he joined the bank as a trainee. Bored with the conventions of that world, Wray left after four years, only to rejoin in 1987 as deputy chairman and part owner.

In between he made his fortune several times over, having what he terms 'an eye for an opportunity'. Wray's big 'punt' was to take over the *Fleet Street Letter*, an ailing tip sheet, for £6,500 in 1975. Although his family had owned a small north London printing company, Wray showed no ready talent for the family business. 'The whole of 1976 was a minor disaster. Things were going nowhere and I had £98 in the bank,' he says.

Among the lessons he learnt the hard way were to double the price and send the *FSL* out fortnightly instead of weekly.

The *FSL* came to the Unlisted Securities Market in 1981 and in 1983 Wray merged it with the phenomenally successful Carlton Communications, founded by Michael Green (q.v.).

'I just met Green at a party and we got on well,' explains Wray. 'I'm good at assessing opportunities but I would never describe myself as someone with a vision like Michael. All I can do is add up and spot downside risk at a considerable distance.'

Wray's next coup was to spot the potential of a sleepy property company, Gilbert House. He bought control for £3 million and eventually, through a series of deals,

# Richard Biffa  £46m
*Waste disposal entrepreneur*

Where there's muck there's brass, as Richard Biffa has found out. Chairman of Rechem, the waste disposal firm, Biffa has made a £50 million fortune out of disposing of toxic waste materials in his highly efficient plants in Southampton and Pontypool. He has been in waste disposal for all his working life. He joined the family firm, Biffa Ltd, in 1958 and was appointed to the board in 1971 when it became a subsidiary of British Electric Traction. From 1979 to 1985 he was chairman. He was also on the board of Rechem (Reclamation and Disposal Ltd), another BET subsidiary. BET had bought Rechem in 1971 from two business men, Arthur Coleman and David Thomas, but sold out in 1985, disappointed with the low margins in the business. Rechem was snapped up by its management for £1.8 million and came to the stock market in 1988 with a market value of £50 million. Biffa has now over 7 million shares in the business.

Under Biffa and Malcolm Lee (q.v.), his managing director, who has 6.8 million shares, Rechem has moved up-market and is concentrating on handling and disposing of specialist toxic wastes through high temperature incineration. For this it can charge a higher price. As a result, in the half year to the end of September 1989, Rechem's pre-tax profits rose 29% to £4.6 million. Biffa himself is regarded as a hands-on manager who likes to be involved in all aspects of the business.

Despite having Graham Searle, a founder member of Friends of the Earth, on the board, Rechem has run into severe criticism from residents around its Pontypool plant in Wales, who have voiced fears about pollution in the locality. The Torfaen Council in Wales claimed that the level of toxic waste around the plant was 88 times higher than normal. Rechem disagreed with the findings and have issued extensive reports contradicting the Torfaen con-

got back into banking. On lending he is now a conservative – although in the past he had borrowed routinely and was in difficulties in the 1974 property crash.

'Once you get creative in banking – like pouring money into Mexico because "a country can't go bust" – it all goes wrong. The big trend of the moment is always a disaster a few years down the track,' he says firmly.

Wray lives modestly with his wife and child, deploring yachts and racehorses. 'Having a lot of money means I can drive a decent car, go on holiday occasionally and go to the theatre without saving up.... Tycoonery is anathema to me. I don't know many, thank goodness.'

His convictions are strong. 'I have very strong views on how to run a company. I don't think directors should have perks. There should be no corporate donations to politics or charity. If you feel *that* strongly, spend your own money.'

clusions. It has announced plans to improve the Pontypool facility with a new £500,000 electric hearth. It has bought 16 acres next to the plant for expansion. Rechem also plans to spend £8 million improving efficiency at its Fawley works.

In September 1989, Liverpool dockers refused to handle a shipment of polychlorinated biphenols from Canada which were destined for Pontypool. They were returned to Canada, leading Biffa to comment, 'Rechem firmly believes that it can and should fulfil both national and international responsibilities in the provision of a safe method for the disposal of highly toxic waste.'

Biffa owns a villa in the south of France, where he holidays at every available opportunity with his wife and three children. He is a connoisseur of wine and French cooking.

John Menzies group is now one of the country's leading newsagents. In 1989–90 it made £29 million pre-tax profits despite problems in America. Compare that to the first bookshop which made £100 profit in its first year on sales of under £1,000.

The business remains in family hands and the current chairman, John Menzies, is a pillar of the establishment in Scotland where it is still based. He is a director of the Bank of Scotland and the Guardian Royal Exchange group.

Eton educated, Menzies served in the Grenadier Guards. He is married with four daughters. He lives on a 1,250-acre estate in Berwickshire and lists his hobbies as farming, shooting, reading and travel. He is a member of the Royal Company of Archers, the Queen's bodyguard for Scotland.

## John Menzies   £46m

*Newsagent*

dob 13/10/26

Founded in 1843 as a bookshop in Edinburgh's fashionable Princes Street, the

## Gerald and Vera Weisfeld   £46m

*Fashion retailers*

In 1971 Gerald and Vera Weisfeld set up a ladieswear shop in Glasgow. By 1990 they had built up a chain of 37 shops, of which 28 were in Scotland. Trading under the banner 'What Everyone Wants' or 'What Shoppes', the group known collectively as WEW made £6.64m profits in the year to January 1990. Some 80% of its sales were clothes, but it had also branched out into jewellery, toys and consumer goods.

But having reached the age of 50, the Weisfelds decided that they wanted to devote more time to other activities. Vera, in particular, wanted to have more time for charitable work. So they contacted Noble Grossart, the leading Scottish merchant bank, to find a suitable partner for a takeover.

After four months of negotiations they sold the business to Philip Green, chairman of the fast-expanding Amber Day retailing group, for £46.7m. The Weisfelds took £8.2m of the sale price in cash, with the rest in loan notes and some 14.5m Amber shares. Gerald Weisfeld remained chairman of WEW and Vera a consultant. All the shares of the group had been in family hands.

# John Aspinall  £45m

*Game conservationist and former casino owner*

dob 11/6/26

Before gaming was legalised, John Aspinall used to host floating chemmy and poker games round Belgravia for his rich chums, with the police hard on his trail. They broke up one game. Hard up on one occasion in France, he won a £3,000 bet by agreeing to stand naked in the street for a minute.

Gambling has always been in his blood, and it is a way of paying for his other great obsession – saving wild animals.

He founded his first casino, the Clermont, in 1962 but sold out ten years later. This was the centre of a social set which included Lord Lucan and Sir James Goldsmith (q.v.). In 1978, he returned to casinos to support the upkeep of his two private zoos, at Canterbury and Romney Marsh, which cost up to £4,000 a day to run. Here he breeds exotic creatures such as Siberian tigers, leopards, rhinos and buffaloes.

At the end of 1987 Aspinall Holdings, the casino business he owned with Sir James Goldsmith, was sold for £90 million. He has homes in London and Kent and a £550,000 mansion outside Cape Town.

# Marquess of Cholmondeley £45m

*Landowner*

dob 27/6/60

# Greta Fenston and family £45m

*Business woman*

dob GF *c.* 1935

The 7th Marquess of Cholmondeley, the honorary Lord Great Chamberlain of England, has two fine houses in Cheshire and Norfolk. He also owns over 12,000 acres of prime land in those two fast-developing counties. He inherited the title from his father, the 6th Marquess, who died in March 1990 at the age of 70.

Cholmondeley, educated at Eton and the Sorbonne, was a page boy to the Queen from 1974 to 1976. For much of the 1980s the Earl was a tax exile in Monte Carlo and the south of France, but he came home to help run the family estates in 1987.

His father had a distinguished war record with the Royal Dragoons in the Middle East, Italy, France and Germany, where he won the Military Cross. The 6th Marquess inherited the title from his father in 1968. No death duties were payable because his father had placed much of the estate in the hands of a private company, the Rocksavage Estate Company.

Houghton Hall, the Norfolk home, was built by Sir Robert Walpole. It is described as a 'magnificent Palladian mansion' by one expert. Another calls it a monument to Walpole's passion for art and architecture. Family portraits by Reynolds, Kneller and Batoni are on display together with fine French furniture and porcelain. There are also 20,000 model soldiers on parade.

£ 23 of the 400 richest people are women. They are worth a total of £7.4 bn or 13.2% of the total.

In 1963, at the age of 28, Greta Borg, the daughter of an army colonel, married Felix Fenston, then one of London's richest men who had made a fortune from buying and selling property. Fenston, the son of a theatre impresario who wanted to be a concert pianist, lost a leg and was invalided out of the Intelligence Corps during the war.

Starting with £100, he moved into property, with his first deal in Watford. Later he was to move into central London and he bought the St James's Theatre in 1957, which he turned into an office block despite the protests of the actress Vivien Leigh. He was also active abroad and pulled off what was then the biggest property deal in the Commonwealth with a large development in Montreal.

In the 1960s he gave up work and announced plans to travel and shoot big game. Within two years he was back in business but he finally relinquished his position in 1968. He died in 1970 at the age of 55, leaving one of the biggest estates for some years, worth £12.6 million gross. He also owned one of the finest houses in Mayfair, bought from the Duke of Devonshire.

Some of his funds were invested in the property and construction world; this was revealed in August 1989 when Kyle Stewart, one of the biggest private construction groups in the country, was sold to a Dutch company for around £50 million. Some 90% of the shares in the group were controlled by two trusts: one, with 30%, was controlled directly by Mrs Fenston; the other, with 60% of the shares, was another Fenston family trust, but under the trusteeship of Sidney Morris, the family solicitor.

Felix Fenston married three times. He

divorced his first wife during the war, and married a French woman almost immediately, in 1943. They had three children before divorcing in 1959.

## Lord Margadale   £45m

*Landowner*

dob 16/12/06

John Morrison, MP for St Ives in the 1830s, ran a thriving London drapery business. He cornered the market in black crêpe – much in demand for funerals – and left a £3 million fortune.

His great-grandson, Lord Margadale, was MP for Salisbury and rose to become chairman of the 1922 Committee of Conservative backbenchers in the early 1960s. He was reputed to be the richest MP in the Commons in those days. He inherited £500,000 on his 21st birthday, and a £15 million fortune all told.

Today, with the Islay estate on the Isle

of Islay, large tracts of Wiltshire and a collection of art including Ming vases, he is worth much more.

He has three sons, two of whom are Conservative MPs, including the Hon. Peter Morrison, a junior minister and deputy chairman of the Conservative Party.

## David Ogilvy   £45m

*Advertising executive*

dob 23/06/11

In the 1950s an advert appeared in the *New Yorker* magazine which gained a cult following and established David Ogilvy as one of the giants of the advertising industry. Entitled 'The Man in the Hathaway Shirt', it depicted a bewhiskered man in an eye patch wearing a particular brand of shirt. The shirt sales tripled and readers of each new issue of the magazine would turn to the advert to discover where the model, Count Wrangel (the son of a tsarist general), would be wearing the shirt next.

Ogilvy entered the world of advertising almost by default. The younger son of genteel Fabian socialists, he was born in London and educated at one boarding school that he hated and then at Fettes. In his early years he felt a sense of failure compared to Francis, his elder brother. 'I grew up thinking I was a boob,' he later said.

He overcame this feeling to win a scholarship to Christ Church, Oxford, but despite the best endeavours of his tutors, he could not pass any exams and left; 'I abandoned the cloistered serenity of Oxford and sought my place in the gutter,' he later recalled.

The gutter turned out to be working ten hours a day for six days a week in a Paris hotel as a cook. His first assignment was preparing meals for the customers' dogs, particularly poodles. Later he became a door-to-door salesman pushing cooking stoves in Scotland and learning the art of salesmanship.

His brother Francis then managed to get him a job with the advertising agency Mather & Crowther. By his mid-twenties Ogilvy had at last found his *métier* and he immediately began learning everything he could about the industry. Fascinated by American advertising techniques, he persuaded Mather & Crowther to send him to New York for a year in 1938. The year stretched through to his retirement in 1973.

During the war Ogilvy worked for British Intelligence in America, and after the war he briefly left advertising to become an Amish farmer, but the heavy work was too much for him and he lacked the mechanical and animal husbandry skills needed.

In 1948, with £3,000, he went back into advertising, launching his own agency with the backing of Mather & Crowther and S.H. Benson, another London agency. Hewitt, Ogilvy, Benson & Mather was born.

Ogilvy cut a strange figure on Madison Avenue, with his impeccable English style and the appearance of a history professor. Every day, at 4.30p.m., he took tea in his office. In winter he wore tweeds and in summer a light-coloured suit. He preferred the company of Boston intellectuals to his Madison Avenue peers, but in front of his clients he would always deliver a brilliant presentation for an exact, allotted time-span.

In 1951 came the first big break with the Hathaway shirt adverts, dreamt up by Ogilvy himself. Other campaigns with equal appeal followed, including 'the man from Schweppes'. For Rolls-Royce, he used the headline, 'At 60 Miles an Hour the Loudest Noise in this New Rolls-Royce Comes from the Electric Clock.'

Through the 1960s Ogilvy snapped up a whole raft of blue chip clients, starting with Shell in 1961. He broke new ground with the Shell account by working for a flat fee rather than on the prevailing commission basis.

In his summer vacation of 1962 he wrote a book, *Confessions of an Advertising Man*, which became a best seller and helped win the agency more business. But by 1964 Ogilvy was writing virtually no advertising copy, describing himself as 'an almost extinct volcano'. He bought another farm in the Amish community and also a beautiful French château. In the same year the agency merged with the British company Mather & Crowther, which had backed him at the beginning. Tragically, his brother Francis had died eight months previously.

David Ogilvy finally retired to his château in 1973, but continued to bombard the expanding group with telexes throughout the 1970s and 1980s. In 1988 his picture appeared on the front of the Ogilvy annual report, dressed typically in an elegant shirt, braces and muddy wellingtons. In 1989 he emerged briefly from retirement when Ogilvy & Mather came under a takeover threat from the aggressive British WPP group, run by Martin Sorrell. At first Ogilvy refused to have anything to do with Sorrell and was publicly critical of him. But Sorrell's persuasive tongue and high financial clout finally won through. Ogilvy somewhat reluctantly agreed to the bid and became non-executive chairman of the combined group.

It was an ironic ending to his career. For years he had railed against the very globalisation of advertising which had been pushed to its limits by the likes of Sorrell and the Saatchi brothers (q.v.).

# Swraj Paul   £45m

*Industrialist*

dob 18/2/31

A degree from the Massachusetts Institute of Technology and a spell at the Harvard Business School have helped Swraj Paul build one of Britain's most successful industrial groups.

Paul, who was born in the Punjab, worked in his family's steel, shipping and hotels business from 1953 until 1966 when he came to Britain. He came originally to seek treatment, unsuccessfully, for a daughter who died of cancer. Paul recovered from the tragedy by drowning himself in work. He bought a small steel-making firm in Huntingdon and then established a steel tube-manufacturing plant in Wales, which was to be the start of his Caparo empire. For most of the 1980s he specialised in buying up old and apparently dying British companies or doomed factories and turning them into highly profitable concerns. Old steel mills, Midland metal bashers and the like have all

responded to the Paul touch. He still retains his links with India and he was a firm friend and biographer of the late Mrs Gandhi. She in turn saw him as someone capable of modernising the creaking Indian economy and its bureaucracy.

As well as Caparo, Paul has substantial property and hotel interests in Britain and he owns Indian tea plantations.

Today he employs 5,000 people, and Caparo has a £400 million turnover. Like many other tycoons he hires the best British management experts available for huge salaries. 'God,' Paul, a devout Hindu, is fond of saying, 'has been good to me.' He insists that for Asians the most important business value is 'integrity'.

Paul is now looking beyond the confines of Britain to Europe, America, Australia and other countries. His twin sons, Ambar and Akash, also play a key role in the business today. He sent them to The Hall, a preparatory school in north London, and then to Harrow. This was topped with spells doing business studies in the United States. His youngest son, Angad, who was also at Harrow, will join the family business after finishing his studies in the United States. Like many Asian tycoons, Paul believes an American education gives children an extra edge over others.

Paul gives his sons considerable independence to run their bits of the business (the turnover of the 'bits' totals £100 million each for Ambar and Akash).

Ambar, for example, persuaded his father to let him run Clydesdale Engineering, a firm based in Dudley in the Midlands, which was about to be sold. Within three years, Ambar had increased a £30,000 profit on a turnover of £1.7 million to a £500,000 profit on a turnover of £4.1 million. 'My father leaves me to myself. He likes to be informed and I use him as an adviser,' Ambar comments.

Akash is based at Scunthorpe, supervising United Merchant Bar, a joint steel-rolling venture with British Steel. 'Dad', he says, 'is in charge of America and strategic planning.' Board meetings are conveniently held on Friday or Monday, so that the boys and their families can be with their parents for the whole weekend.

# Viscount Petersham   £45m
*Landowner*

dob 20/7/45

Heir to the Earl of Harrington, Viscount Petersham was briefly a tax exile in Ireland in the 1970s. His father still lives there, but the Viscount now has a Chelsea home and a Wiltshire estate.

His father moved to Ireland in 1963 when he sold Elvaston Castle and 4,500 acres in Derbyshire for over £1 million. He is a noted bloodstock agent.

Petersham is a keen sportsman, listing sailing, hunting, shooting, skiing and fishing as his hobbies. He spent two years circumnavigating the globe on the yacht *Surama*. He is married to Anita Robsham, formerly the wife of the Earl of Suffolk. It is his second marriage.

The family fortune derives from their ownership of a large chunk of London's fashionable South Kensington and Gloucester Road.

# Duke of Richmond   £45m
*Landowner*

dob 19/9/29

Charles Lennox, the 1st Duke of Richmond, was the bastard son of Charles II and Louise de Keroualle. He acquired Goodwood in Sussex in 1695, but it was the 3rd Duke who built it up into a full-scale ducal estate.

Today the 10th Duke, who inherited the title in 1989, presides over a 12,000-acre estate. He has been able to make considerable sums of money by selling estate properties. In 1984, 11 cottages fetched

£472,000. There are 200 left on the estate.

Goodwood has a long association with horse and car racing, through the race-course above the house. The 'Glorious' Goodwood race meetings are held there.

The Duke's art treasures include four Canalettos, together with portraits by Reynolds, Lely, Kellner, Hoppner and Lawrence. There is also some magnificent French furniture, tapestries and porcelain acquired by the 3rd Duke when he was ambassador to the court of Louis XV of France.

# Duke of Rutland   £45m

*Landowner*

dob 28/5/19

The Duke came to public notice in 1977 when he threatened to lie in front of a bulldozer if British Coal started trying to exploit the coal reserves under the Vale of Belvoir in the north of England. He owns 18,000 acres of the vale and, claiming the mineral rights, said he did not want any pits dug there. But it was a campaign

doomed to failure, and British Coal is currently developing a super-pit in the area, to produce low-cost high-grade coal for the 1990s and beyond.

Lady Teresa Manners, his youngest daughter, has also hit the headlines. She was once discovered passionately embracing a man while driving along a motorway. She was a lead singer in a pop group made up of aristocrats, including the heir to the Duke of Beaufort (q.v.).

Belvoir Castle, the Rutland home, is built on the foundations of a Norman stronghold. A fire necessitated rebuilding in 1816. The art collection includes works by Van de Velde, Gainsborough, the younger Teniers, Holbein, five Poussins and a Murillo.

# Lady Willoughby de Eresby   £45m

*Landowner*

dob 1/12/34

Lady Jane Willoughby de Eresby is the sole surviving child of the 3rd Earl of Ancaster, who died in 1983. Twenty years earlier her brother, Lord Willoughby de Eresby, had tragically vanished while sailing from the south of France to Corsica. Regarded as a black sheep, he had been convicted of illegal gambling in 1958.

Just before his disappearance he had opened Wips, a Leicester Square nightclub. It later changed its name to Ad Lib and launched the London disco boom. He left some £400,000 in his will.

The Ancaster estates are substantial. In Lincolnshire, there are some 12,500 acres around Grimsthorpe, a beautiful 100-room castle built by Vanbrugh, the architect of Blenheim Palace. It also has a fine art collection including works by Canaletto and Holbein. There are also some 30,000 acres in Perthshire, and valuable properties in Wales.

In 1978, five years before his death, Ancaster put much of the family wealth into a private charitable trust, with the aim of preserving the estates intact after his death. As a result, he left just £1.4 million in his will, and Lady Jane was able to live on at Grimsthorpe. She was a well-known member of London's swinging sixties set. She has never married and there are two elderly heiresses to the estate, both in their eighties. The title is likely to go to a niece, of whom there are several. Lady Jane was one of the Queen's train bearers at her 1953 Coronation.

# Malcolm Lee  £44m
*Waste disposal entrepreneur*

Graduating from Leeds University in 1967 with a degree in fuel science, Malcolm Lee spent ten years learning all there is to know about the disposal of toxic waste and liquids. After spells with Tarmac, developing a new waste division, he joined BET, working in their waste disposal business. In 1985 he led the management buy-out of Rechem along with Richard Biffa (q.v.). He is currently managing director and owns some 6.8 million Rechem shares.

Under Biffa and Lee, Rechem has moved up market and is concentrating on high-temperature incineration of toxic wastes at its two plants situated near Southampton and Fawley. Graham Searle, a founder member of Friends of the Earth, sits on the Rechem board, but it still runs into fire from environmentalists, particularly over its Pontypool plant. Early in 1989 the Torfaen Council in Wales claimed that the level of toxic waste around the plant was 88 times highter than normal. Rechem took issue with the findings and has submitted its own contrary findings to the European Commission in Brussels. It had already fought a successful libel action

against the BBC which had alleged in a 1985 *Newsnight* programme that toxic waste at Pontypool had not been properly incinerated. The company and Lee were awarded a complete apology and their legal costs of £50,000 were paid by the BBC. Rechem has announced plans to expand the Pontypool facility.

But controversy surrounding the plant and toxic waste refuses to die. In September 1989, Liverpool dockers refused to handle a shipment of polychlorinated biphenols from Canada which were destined for Pontypool. They were returned to Canada. Lee accused Greenpeace, which alerted the world to the Canadian cargo, of promoting pollution. 'The only safe way to destroy this difficult waste is by high-temperature incineration. There are no alteratives,' he told the *Sunday Times*. The Pontypool plant was given a clean bill of health by the Welsh Office in November 1989.

# Earl of Stair  £44m
*Landowner*

dob 9/10/06

In the 1870s the estates of the Earl of Stair ran to 116,000 acres and produced an annual rental of nearly £62,000. Today the 13th Earl still owns a hefty 45,000 acres in the area around Stranraer and he has his seat at Lochinch Castle. The estate comprises farms, forestry and sporting lands.

Educated at Eton and Sandhurst, the Earl, then known as Viscount Dalrymple, went into the army and served in North Africa, Syria and Italy during the war. He retired in 1952 as lieutenant colonel commanding the Scots Guards.

He became a member of Wigtown County Council in 1958 and served until 1975 when the council was abolished in local government reorganisation. He married Davina Katharine, daughter of Sir David Bowes-Lyon, and a cousin of the

Queen, in 1960. A year later he inherited the Earldom which dates back to 1703. They have three sons.

The royal connections are also maintained through the Earl's position as Captain General of the Queen's bodyguard for Scotland, the Royal Company of Archers. Lord Stair is now virtually retired and spends most of his spare time shooting and fishing.

# The Howard Family  £42m

*Landowners*

dob SH 26/1/56

Castle Howard, the setting for the television series *Brideshead Revisited*, is the magnificent home of the Howard family. It was designed by Sir John Vanbrugh at the beginning of the 18th century for John Howard, the 3rd Earl of Carlisle, to replace a partially burnt castle on his Yorkshire estate.

Today Simon Howard, the third son of the late Lord Howard of Henderskelfe, runs the 10,000-acre estate. He took over the management when his father, chairman of the BBC, died in 1984. His two elder brothers did not want the responsibility. Simon went to Eton and then did an estate management course. In 1983 he married Annette, Countess Compton, the former wife of the 7th Marquess of Northampton. He lists his hobbies as photography, wine and country sports.

Castle Howard is filled with art treasures. There are works by Rubens, Holbein, Van Dyck, Lely, Murillo, Reynolds, Vermeer and Gainsborough. Priceless porcelain, furniture and sculptures complement the paintings. Recently a bust by Bernini was sold to raise £3 million for death duties.

Simon Howard's forebears include the formidable Rosalind, Countess of Carlisle, in the 19th century. She made her daughters walk barefoot outside in the Yorkshire winter. She was also accused of taking her obsession with temperance too far and pouring wine and beer from the Howard cellars into a lake. She dismissed all the menservants and replaced them with burly parlourmaids when the footmen were too drunk to rescue an equally drunken guest who had slid under the table at dinner.

# Earl Spencer  £42m

*Landowner*

dob 24/1/24

Earl Spencer is best remembered for his dignified presence at the wedding of his

---

£ There are 103 aristocrats among the richest 400 in Britain. they are worth £23.3 bn of which £21.8 bn was inherited.

78 of these are entitled to sit, unelected, in the House of Lords.
The members of the Lords are
   13 Dukes out of 24
   7 Marquisses out of 27
   18 Earls and 1 Countess out of 156 Earls and Countesses
   12 Viscounts out of 102
   26 Lords and 1 Lady out of 850 Barons (Lords) and Baronesses.

daughter, Diana, to the Prince of Wales in 1981.

The 8th Earl lives on the 15,000-acre Althorp estate in Northamptonshire. It has been home to the Spencers since 1508 and contains some of the finest collections of paintings, furniture and porcelain in Europe. There are 700 paintings, acquired since the end of the 17th century. Some have been sold off in recent years to meet the cost of Althorp's upkeep and death duties. In 1977 four Van Dyck works were sold, breaking up one of the finest collections in the country.

Recently Earl Spencer was given permission by the Department of the Environment to develop some land for housing. He is married to Raine, the daughter of Barbara Cartland (q.v.), the romantic novelist. His first wife, Princess Diana's mother, is now Mrs Shand Kydd. His heir, Viscount Althorp, who now works for American television, was married in 1989 in what was called the society wedding of the year.

*Sir Owen Aisher*

# Sir Owen Aisher and family    £40m

*Building supplier*

dob OA 28/5/1900

There can hardly be a British handyman or DIY enthusiast who has not used Marley tiles or other bits of Marley equipment in his time. Marley was founded by Sir Owen Aisher in 1934 and the family still control around 10% of the shares. Though still president of the company, Sir Owen has now retired from day-to-day control, devoting himself to his passion for sailing. He was president of the Royal Yachting Association from 1970 to 1975. In 1958 he was named Yachtsman of the Year.

He lives in Surrey and when not sailing he is fishing or shooting. He regularly attends Cowes week, and in 1989 Prince Philip borrowed his boat *Yeoman XXVIII* to race.

# Viscount Allendale £40m

*Landowner*

dob 12/9/22

A lifelong friend of the royal family who played with the Queen and Princess Margaret as a child, Viscount Allendale is one of the great landowners of the north of England. He has a 20,000-acre estate in Northumberland and two large houses, Allenheads and Bywell Hall. There is a large art collection at Bywell with works by Rembrandt, Turner and Gainsborough.

His early childhood was dogged by accidents. In 1927 he was rescued from a fire. In 1936 he was nearly electrocuted in the bath and a year later he was injured in a shooting accident. He was an RAF pilot in the war. He was shot down in 1942 and imprisoned in Stalag Luft 111.

In 1948 his wedding to Sarah Ismay, daughter of the former chief of the General Staff, was attended by the Queen, Princess Margaret and Clement Attlee, then prime minister. But he was divorced in 1986. He was a steward of the Jockey Club from 1963 to 1965.

He inherited the title from his father in 1956, and saved the main family estates by selling a large Yorkshire property. In 1986 he indicated that he was preparing to marry a divorcee, but family pressure forced him to cancel the wedding plans.

# Sir John Barlow and family £40m

*Financiers*

dob JB 22/4/34

When the British Empire was at its most powerful, and the world map was largely coloured red, the Manchester trading firm of Thomas Barlow and Brother was a major beneficiary. Barlow owned huge rubber and tea estates in the Far East with offices in Calcutta, Shanghai and Singapore. At the turn of the century the head of the family, John Emmott Barlow, was a senior partner in the firm, as well as an active Liberal and MP for Frome in Somerset from 1892 to 1918. He was created a baronet in 1907. When he died in 1932, he was succeeded in the baronetcy by his son John Denman Barlow, who was first a Liberal National MP, and later a Conservative MP until the 1966 General Election.

During his time as an MP, Sir John continued to play a part in the family firm. He was also chairman of the Tory Party Trade and Industry Committee. In 1958, while on a visit to Singapore, he made an offer to buy the City Council's mace, in recognition of the 100 years in which the Barlow family firm had been linked to Singapore. His last major action came during the Falklands war in 1982, when he published a letter he had received in 1968 from Denis Healey, the then Labour defence minister, arguing that the small marine garrison in Port Stanley was big enough to deter aggression. Barlow had been chairman of a Falkland Islands emergency committee set up in 1968.

In 1986 Sir John died, to be succeeded by his eldest son, John Kemp Barlow. The new Sir John Barlow does not sit in Parliament, concentrating instead on running the family businesses. In 1982 the Malaysian government took over many of the Barlow plantations, and Sir John reinvested the compensation funds in property and other areas. He also streamlined the business into one company, Majedie Investments, with three Barlows on the board. Apart from Sir John, his younger brother Mark is an executive director, while his cousin Henry is a non-executive director. Between them they have over 14 million shares in the company.

Sir John lives in Cheshire, and lists his hobbies as steeplechasing, hunting and shooting. He is a steward of the Jockey Club and has four sons. He was High Sheriff of Cheshire in 1979.

# Lord Barnard   £40 m

*Landowner*

dob 21/9/23

The 53,000-acre Raby estate in Durham forms the basis of Lord Barnard's wealth. It is centred on two homes: Raby Castle and Selaby Hall.

Harry John Neville Vane is the 11th Lord Barnard. Educated at Eton and later at Durham University, he married Lady Davina Cecil, daughter of the Marquess of Exeter, in 1952. He is a former joint master of the Zetland Hunt, with which Prince Charles has ridden. His daughter married a villager in 1982.

The Vane family has owned Raby since 1626. In 1714 the entire contents of the castle were sold by the 1st Lord Barnard, because he disapproved strongly of his son's choice of bride. But an extensive art collection was built up after that date. This has portraits by Van Dyck, Reynolds and Batoni.

The estate includes some grouse moors with good shooting and up to 14 miles of fishing. At one time the estate boasted its own full-time mole catcher, who was paid 2d an acre by Raby tenants.

# Vivien Duffield   £40m

*Heiress*

dob c. 1946

Daughter of the late Sir Charles Clore, the property tycoon and business man who built up the Sears chain, Vivien is making a name for herself as a philanthropist.

In May 1989 she was named Benefactor of the Year by the trustees of the National Art-Collection Fund. In 1980 she gave £6 million to the Tate to build the Clore gallery and in 1987 she enabled it to acquire Con-stable's *The Opening of Waterloo Bridge*. These gifts came from the £56 million left after the taxman had taken a record £67 million from her father's estate.

Her expenditure is not confined to charities. In 1987 she bought the Earl of Dalhousie's 18,000-acre estate near Brechin for £2.5 million. In 1986 she chartered the *Sea Goddess*, a 4,000-ton luxury liner, to host her 40th birthday party for 110 people: the cost – £400,000. She also spent £150,000 on a birthday party in the fashionable Swiss resort of Gstaad for her long-time friend Jocelyn Stevens, the former director of Express newspapers, known as Piranha Teeth to readers of *Private Eye*. She lives in Switzerland as a tax exile, but also has a house in London.

Her success contrasts with the recent crash of her playboy brother Alan Clore, disinherited by his disapproving father. At one stage he had built up an American fortune of $150 million through corporate raiding on Wall Street. But he lost a great deal in the October 1987 stock market crash, though not all of his 300-odd thoroughbred racehorses.

# Sheena Easton   £40m

*Singer*

dob c. 1959

The first singer ever to have had hits in all five of the American *Billboard* magazine's charts was born in a Lanarkshire council house outside Glasgow. Sheena Easton was the youngest of six children, whose father died when she was ten. Raised by her mother who worked in a factory to support the family, Sheena showed academic ability and became a drama student, graduating from Glasgow University in 1979.

Prompted by her then husband – a folk-singer called Sandi Easton – whom she married at 19, she entered *The Big Time*, a BBC television talent-spotting show hosted by Esther Rantzen. The experts on the show

said she would never make the big time, but she proved them wrong. A string of hits followed, including the 1981 Bond theme, 'For Your Eyes Only'. She became the first girl to have two hits in the British top ten at the same time.

It was in America, where she went in 1982, that Sheena's career took off. She topped the charts with what was dubbed the secretaries' anthem, '9 to 5'. She became equally popular in Japan.

She bought a huge 1930s Hollywood house set in 2 acres and, divorced from her first husband, married again. But that marriage to Hollywood agent Rob Light lasted just 13 months.

Her career has been helped by her association with the top singer Prince. In 1987 they had a big worldwide hit called 'U Got the Look'. She has also turned to acting and appeared in the popular television series, *Miami Vice*, as the wife of Sonny Crockett, a detective played by Don Johnson.

Regarded as a shrewd business woman in her own right, Sheena has bought a home for her hard-working mother by the English seaside as a thank you for all the years of struggle. She told one interviewer that her mother is her 'role model', adding: 'Being brought up the way I was in Scotland, I saw hardship throughout my early life. My mother was left to raise six of us by herself. I was a selfish little teenager, insisting, "I've got to have a new dress and a pair of high heels for the school dance or everyone will laugh at me," but she always pulled through. Maybe the Christmas dress wouldn't be paid off until August, but she never fell apart.'

# Nicholas van Hoogstraten £40m

*Property owner*

Nicholas van Hoogstraten was once described by a judge as 'a sort of self-imagined devil'. The judge, sentencing

Hoogstraten at the time to a four-year sentence for a grenade attack on a synagogue, went on, 'He thinks that he is an emissary of Beelzebub.'

It is an image that Hoogstraten has periodically reinforced with interviews in the press. Anyone who crosses him 'will come well unstuck but I do not want it traced back to me. It is all well down the line,' he told the *Independent*.

The aura of violence which surrounds the black-suited Hoogstraten has been good for his business as one of Britain's largest residential landlords. His tenants have frequently complained of a reign of terror – including forcible entry to remove their belongings and even the removal of a staircase for one unfortunate tenant. He is on record as saying that his tenants are 'absolute filth', and after one operation when he and a gang entered a tenant's house and hurled the furniture into the road, he said, 'It's the best bit of fun we've had for some time.'

Although Hoogstraten's violence has resulted in a number of convictions and brushes with the law, they have not hindered his money-making skills. The son of a Sussex shipping agent, he made his first fortune through stamps: by the age of 15 his collection was worth £30,000. At 16 he went into the navy for a year, during which he bought land cheaply in the Bahamas. At 17 he entered the property business by buying up four houses in Brighton. All were tenanted, but he managed to sell three with vacant possession at a huge profit and was on the way to his millions. At 22 he was described as Britain's youngest millionaire with 350 properties in Brighton and Hove alone.

Today there are about 450 properties, of which a third are in west London. He has a £4.5 million mansion in Sussex, built on the site of an old people's home where – predictably – the last old residents were persuaded to leave. The water and electricity were cut off and eventually the old people were removed by the social services department.

At the time Hoogstraten was living in Liechtenstein for tax reasons, having just paid £5 million, the biggest ever personal tax bill, to the Inland Revenue.

Apart from the house, Hoogstraten also owns the finest collection of French antiques in Britain, two Turners and a Holbein, and he has extensive overseas property interests.

He is very much a loner. His parents hardly have anything to do with him. He has never married, preferring the company of four mistresses who can't get their hands on his fortune, as he sees it. He has two children by different women. Few people ever visit him at his home or get close to him. One close associate, Rodney Markworth, who met Hoogstraten in prison, became his strong-arm man. But Markworth, who had a long reputation for violence, owed Hoogstraten nearly £9,000 in 1979 and simply disappeared. Hoogstraten was quoted in the press at the time as saying of his former associate: 'He wasn't the cleverest of blokes. I think he stepped out of line and was dealt with.'

£ 31 of the richest 400 people in Britain are knights. They are worth £6.1 bn of which £2.4 bn was inherited.

# Sir Anthony Jacobs £40m
*Industrialist*
dob 13/11/31

Thousands of Britain's learner drivers have a link with Sir Anthony Jacobs, though few will actually know it. Jacobs, a prominent supporter of the Liberal Party and latterly of the Liberal Democrats, owned the British School of Motoring group until April 1990, when he sold the business for £40 million.

Born in London, Sir Anthony was educated at Clifton College and London University, where he took a degree in commerce. He is a chartered accountant by profession but in 1961, after six years' practice, he started his own fashion business called Tricoville.

Twelve years later he became chairman of BSM and, in 1978, with a group of associates, he took over the business for £3.5 million. Founded 80 years ago, the BSM has a strong brand image, and the Jacobs family retains £5 million worth of shares in the business, which was sold to its management.

Apart from his business career, Sir Anthony (knighted in 1988) lists his hobbies as golf, theatre, riding, opera and travel. He stood as Liberal candidate for Watford in the two 1974 elections. He was a prominent fund raiser for the party, appealing to industry for support at party conferences. BSM gave £188,000 to the Liberals in 1983 and £20,000 in 1987.

# Ron Jelley and family £40m
*Builders*

In 1889 a builder called Jelley started his own firm in Leicester. It was taken over by his son Herbert Jelley in the early 1920s, when it developed into a local house-builders with a reputation for good-quality work. In the 1960s and 1970s the company built nearly 20,000 homes for local councils and the private sector. Today it is still very much a quality firm, building everything from starter homes to £250,000 executive houses. It has also built many commercial and industrial buildings over the years in the east Mid-lands.

In its 1989 accounts, the business (now called Jelson Ltd) produced healthy after-tax profits of £5.1 million on a turnover of £38 million. With large cash reserves and relatively small borrowings, the firm would fetch around £40 million on the stock market. Most of the shares are very tightly held by the Jelley family.

Ronald Jelley, grandson of the founder, is chairman of the business, and his two sons are now working in the firm. One, Robert, is managing director.

Ronald Jelley lives in a large house with 40 acres of woodland in Leicestershire. He also farms locally and is known for his generous support for local causes. In 1969 he financed a new £12,000 village hall in a Leicester village, saying, 'I hope this will make the village tick.'

## Roger Levitt   £40m

*Financier and promoter*

Roger Levitt is aiming to be Britain's answer to America's famous sporting agent, Mark McCormack. Levitt now manages the finances of the leading sports personalities in the country and he is well on the way to his target: he looks after the fortunes of the likes of Sebastian Coe, and jockeys such as Steve Cauthen and Pat Eddery.

For Levitt, fascination with sport – and boxing in particular – came at the age of four, when the legendary boxer, Freddie Mills, held him up at the ringside to watch a fight. Now in his early forties, he still loves the sport and has just signed an extra-ordinary deal with Lennox Lewis, the holder of the Olympic superheavyweight gold medal. Under the terms of the deal, Lewis received a six-figure signing-on fee, £500 a week living expenses, a company BMW, a house in suburban London, and a job for his mother on the Levitt payroll. The total package will cost Levitt £500,000 before Lewis can expect a world title fight.

But the money is mere peanuts for Levitt, who started the Levitt Group in the late 1970s, dealing with all the financial affairs of wealthy individuals. A former Imperial Life assurance salesman, he quickly learnt all there was to know about pensions and financial consulting, knowledge which he has put to good and profitable use ever since on behalf of his 3,700 clients, both corporate and individual.

Today he lives in Highgate in north London, and drives a Bentley Turbo and an Aston Martin. He is also known for his flashy appearance, his snappy bow ties and the large cigars he is never seen without. One colleague says of him, 'He works at four million miles an hour.'

A fanatical Arsenal fan, he has been reported to be buying shares in the club, which have been trading at £2,000 each in 1990.

Levitt teamed up with Adam Faith, the 1960s pop star turned financier, in 1988. Under the deal, Faith, operating out of Levitt's Great Portland Street offices, was to introduce new clients from his wide contacts to Levitt.

But another link-up with the LIT financial group run by Christopher Castleman fell through in November 1988, barely a year after it had been set up. LIT originally took a 24.5% stake in Levitt, worth £11 million. This was later increased to 33% before Castleman decided to sell. It is valued by LIT at £17.8 million.

---

# Sir William Lithgow £40m

*Industrialist*

dob 10/5/34

The Clyde used to be the cradle of Britain's heavy industry, and the ships built on its banks were proud advertisements for its engineering and shipbuilding expertise. Lithgows, based at Greenock at the river mouth, were regarded as one of the best shipbuilders under the careful management of Sir James Lithgow, the 1st Baronet. In 1908 he had joined the shipbuilding business Russell and Co. of Port Glasgow, of which his father was one of the three founding partners. Later it became Lithgows, and Sir James, at the age of 29, was chairman of the Clyde Shipbuilders Association.

He continued to play a prominent role in shipbuilding in both world wars right up to his death in 1952. His son William, then a 17-year-old schoolboy at Winchester, inherited the title and an estate valued then at £1.9 million. Sir James had been preparing for the handover for some years. In 1937, at the age of three, William was left a quarter share in the Lithgow group with his two elder sisters. By 1950 some two-thirds of the business and two large estates were in trust for him.

On his father's death, Sir William continued his education at Winchester while his mother ran the family empire. He intended to take a degree at Glasgow University, but his studies were interrupted by illness and he went up to Oxford instead to read engineering. He had to leave the university to do national service, but when an army medical board rejected him, he started work in the shipyard as a 35-shilling-a-week apprentice. In 1956, at the age of 21, he was made a director of the company and three years later he took over from his mother as chairman.

During the halcyon years of the 1950s and 1960s he transformed the yard into one of the most modern shipbuilding facilities in Europe. But the rise of Far East competitors from Japan and then Korea hit the British and European yards heavily in the 1970s. In 1978 the yard was nationalised by the Labour government and Sir William ended a family association that had lasted 100 years.

For years after the takeover, Lithgow fought a campaign right up to the European courts over the £3.5 million compensation given for the loss of the yard. But this was rejected. Despite building up a new and thriving business in farming, marine engineering and electronics, which in its last accounts produced £2.29 million after-tax profits, Sir William never forgot the way he had been treated. In the latest accounts of Lithgow Holdings, he said: 'We could have done without the present government's oppressive behaviour in minimising the amount of our capital returned to us following the expropriation of the Scott Lithgow companies. I regret the ends the government has gone to in justifying their part in this sorry affair.'

Sir William, who earns a salary of £554,000 as chairman of Lithgow Holdings, lives on the 14,400-acre Ormsary estate, famous for its herd of Highland cattle. A keen shot and amateur photographer, he is anxious to promote viable

*Sir William Lithgow*

employment projects in the Kintyre peninsula. He suffered a personal tragedy in 1964 when his first wife died within a few months of their marriage. He remarried three years later and has two sons and a daughter.

# Jim and Bob McNeil   £40m

*Blind manufacturers*

The first sign of entrepreneurial spirit from the two McNeil brothers came when as boys they sold mice they had bred to local hospitals. Breeding animals was something they had learnt from their father. He first bred mink at the back of his Scotstoun tenement in Glasgow before moving to Aberdeen and becoming the country's top mink farmer. Though the business eventually folded, it helped nurture the same entrepreneurial spirit in his sons.

Later the pair went their own ways for a while. Bob worked in a Fort William pulp mill, while Jim, after initially working in an Aberdeen insurance office as an executive, moved to London to work for a mail order company. One of their product lines was blinds and Jim noticed how many of the orders came from north of the border, where there was no significant manufacturer. Risking everything, he teamed up with Bob in Fort William, using the garage of a local transport company. They soon moved to a small factory at Hillington in Glasgow and within nine months their company, Apollo, had built up a turnover of £250,000.

Their first shop was in Glasgow's Union Street. Before long they had hit on the idea of franchising, to remove the risk of disappointing potential customers. They reasoned that a shop manager would be more motivated if he had a stake in the business. The idea came to them when 'one of our self-employed salesmen said he would like to have a shop and would like to run it himself,' Apollo's franchise director said recently.

The franchisee, who is accepted by Apollo after a battery of interviews and aptitude tests (only one in four passes), invests some £20,000 in the business. As this business expands, it develops its own manufacturing capability, with Apollo providing the tooling, fabrics and fittings.

By 1989 Apollo had 25% of the British blind market, worth around £150 million a year and projected to grow to £500 million by 1992. The group also sells to 15 countries, from Bangladesh to Australia.

In May 1989 they sold the company to the London-based Ashley group (though staying on as executives) for a sum that will eventually reach £54 million, provided they can generate £10 million pre-tax profits by 1992. Even before the sale, the two brothers were doing well. In 1988 they received £3.75 million dividends and sold some investment properties for over £6 million.

## Stephen Morgan £40m

*Property developer*

dob 25/11/52

Despite his name and his base in Clwyd, Stephen Morgan is not Welsh. He is a Scouse – a Liverpudlian – through and through and a fanatical Liverpool fan to boot. He now runs one of the biggest private building companies in Britain, Redrow, which produced £10 million after tax profits on a £100 million turnover in 1989.

Morgan started his career as a labourer on a building site, earning £10 a week after he had walked out on his A level studies.

In 1974, at the age of 23, he took out a loan from his father to start a civil engineering company. He did bread and butter jobs, including laying new sewers and extending Manchester's Strangeways Prison.

When recession bit in the early 1980s and work dried up, he turned to house building. He built his first house in 1983 and in 1988 he completed 1,104. He aims to build 2,000 a year. A healthy reserve of building land able to provide 3,000 sites for homes has helped Redrow's developments.

At Redrow's headquarters in Alltami, outside Mold, Morgan has a workforce of 150, but nationally that figure can rise to 3,000 according to the building work on hand. From its base in Lancashire, Morgan has expanded Redrow into the Midlands and the south. In 1988 he announced plans to build a prestige office development at Ashford in Kent, the centre of operations for the Channel Tunnel. In October of that year he also announced plans for a new 'village' for up to 8,000 people in Cheshire to be built over the next three years between Knutsford and Holmes Chapel. Redrow had bought 500 acres on a greenfield site for the village and had also taken over a small Manchester construction group which had had direct experience of building a complete standalone community from scratch. In 1988 Redrow acquired a 5% stake in John Maunders, a quoted Manchester housebuilder. The stake was later sold.

Morgan and his wife Pamela live in Ruthin in Clwyd. Pamela plans the interior decoration of the Redrow homes.

## David Murray £40m

*Industrialist*

In 1976 David Murray's life seemed shattered. Returning from playing outside half for Dalkeith Rugby club, his Lotus sports car crashed and he lost both his legs.

*David Murray*

'I had a blowout at 70 miles an hour and struck a tree. Both legs were smashed below the knee,' he told the *Glasgow Herald*, adding, 'I don't consider myself disabled. I swim every day in the pool at home and I play snooker and get involved with the sports teams which the company sponsors. I'm very lucky really. I could be in the graveyard.' Murray, the son of an Ayr coal merchant, did not give up. 'You could say that the accident concentrated my mind on business from then on.' At the time he had just taken out a second mortgage on his home to set up Murray International, in which he owns 90% of the shares.

Initially he bought and sold metal from a modest Edinburgh base. In the first year he made a £100,000 profit on a £2 million turnover. With the advent of North Sea oil, he moved to a bigger site near Livingston and became Scotland's biggest supplier to the newly developing industry.

Between 1977 and 1989 turnover in the business – converting property, metal and office equipment – soared from £2 million a year to £70 million, with profits of around £5 million. He runs the operation from 17th-century Bonnington House near Livingston, which used to be the home of the Salvesen family, once one of the richest families in Scotland.

Sport has been a continuing passion and he is chairman of Glasgow Rangers, one of the country's richest football clubs. In 1988 he bought 75% of Rangers for £6.5 million. Earlier he had failed in a £450,000 takeover bid for Ayr United, a Scottish second division club. Murray also owns a sports complex near Livingston, where his top basketball, indoor hockey and volleyball teams are based.

He is planning to redevelop a large area of Edinburgh near Princes Street. The £80 million Port Hamilton scheme aims to create a London Docklands setting in the Scottish capital. Murray's business acumen has been recognised. In 1984 he became Young Scottish Businessman of the Year, and he heads the government anti-litter campaign in Scotland as chairman of UK 2000 there. He still drives a sports car – a Ferrari – but with hand controls.

# Earl of Pembroke   £40m

*Landowner and film-maker*

dob 19/5/39

Wilton House outside Salisbury is regarded as one of the finest English country houses. It has been home to the Earls of Pembroke since the days of Henry VIII. Today the 17th Earl is best known for his work as a film director. He has his fully paid-up ACTT union card and has made several films under the name Henry Herbert. These include *Emily*, starring Koo Stark, and the BBC series *By the Sword Divided*, about the Civil War.

The Pembroke estates cover 16,000 acres. But the family's real wealth is the art collection, which includes works by Van Dyck, Claude, Rembrandt, Lorenzo Lotto, Andrea del Sarto and Reynolds.

In 1984 the Earl turned down a bid for some of his art treasures from the Getty Museum in California. One painting, *The Card Player* by Lucas van Leyden, was esti-

mated to be worth £3 million on its own. In 1964 the Earl married Claire Pelley, daughter of the former High Sheriff of Essex. They had four children, but she left him to live with a neighbouring landowner. They were divorced in 1987, and the Earl married a London kindergarten owner in 1988.

## Marquess of Salisbury £40m
*Landowner*

dob 24/10/16

The Cecil family have long had a distinguished record of public service. In the late 16th century they were ministers to Elizabeth I. Later the family acquired the title of Marquess of Salisbury. The 3rd Marquess was prime minister in the 19th century, and more recently the Salisbury family have played a decisive role in the Conservative Party.

The family own 13,000 acres in Dorset and two homes: the Manor House at Cranborne and the magnificent Hatfield House in Hertfordshire. Completed in 1612, this house contains numerous treasures including paintings by Dahl, Mytens, Wissing, Reynolds, Romney and Lawrence. Portraits of Elizabeth I by Nicholas Hilliard have pride of place in the collection.

Much of the family wealth has been held in a nominee company, Gascoyne Holdings, based in London's Charing Cross Road. This enabled the estate to avoid crippling duties when the last Marquess died in 1972.

The present Marquess was seriously injured in an aircraft accident during the war but recovered sufficiently to fight the 1945 election as a Conservative. He lost, but he won the Bournemouth West seat in 1950, giving up in 1954 due to ill health. He was a long-time president of the Conservative Party Monday Club and a promi-

nent supporter of the Smith regime in Rhodesia.

One of his sons was killed in the Rhodesian insurgency while reporting on the fighting for the *Daily Telegraph*. Lady Salisbury took an HGV licence in 1982 to enable her to drive relief supplies to Poland during the period of martial law and food shortages. She is also a highly respected gardener and helped Prince Charles design his gardens at Highgrove House in 1982.

## Peter Savill £40m
*Publisher*

This tough, self-made man comes from the Yorkshire resort of Scarborough. He went from there to study law at Cambridge. He later worked with John Bentley, the financier who made his name with what were termed asset-stripping deals in the early 1970s and would probably now be called 'demergers'.

Today Savill's business interests span publishing and real estate in Grand Cayman and the United States. His main American company is International Voyager, which publishes tourism guides and company magazines for cruise ships. His other companies include P&D International, based in Cayman, and Biscayne Holdings. He employs some 70 people, mainly in America.

Savill has three homes: in Cayman, Miami and London's Battersea. Though single, his live-in companion is an air

£ The 400 richest people own around 4.4 m acres or the equivalent of 6 countries.

If their land holdings were split up between them they would each have over 11,000 acres.

The value of their metropolitan holdings in the UK and abroad is approximately £15 bn.

hostess with Eastern Airlines. A devoted fan of the Miami Dolphins American football team, he will travel anywhere to watch them. A loner, his other main passions are gambling and the turf. He is reputed to bet $10,000 a game on the Dolphins. He also loves to play the stock market.

Though very secretive and shy of any publicity, he is best known in the UK for his vast racing interests. He has a remarkable ability to buy likely winners very cheaply. His best-known horse is Chaplins Club, a prolific winner over sprint distances. In 1985 it won a record nine races. Savill paid just 8,000 guineas for the horse as a three-year-old at the Ascot sales. His other good horses included Wiki Wiki Wheels and Time To Go Home.

## John Seddon and family £40m

*Construction contractors and developers*

George and John Seddon were two Lancashire bricklayers at the turn of the century who formed their own company, G&J Seddon, at Worsley, near Bolton, in 1897.

Until the building boom after World War II, the company was a relatively small-scale operation. Today it is one of the ten largest privately owned contractors in the country. All the shares in the group are still held by the Seddon family, which is now in its third generation of running the business.

The company has spread out of contracting into property development, house-building and managing country and golf clubs. But it specialises in the medium-sized contracts, rather than huge but risky multi-million pounders. It was responsible for the award-winning Wigan Pier development.

With some 1,600 employees in its nine subsidiary companies, the Seddon group had a £62.7 million turnover in 1987 and after-tax profits of £4 million. If the family were to sell today, the company could fetch around £40 million.

Apart from its strong profit performance, the Seddon group is rich in assets. It owns the Tytherington Links estate in exclusive Cheshire, centred on a health and country club and golf course.

John Seddon, a third-generation member, is chairman of the business. with Christopher, another third-generation Seddon, also on the board. The fourth generation are now beginning to make their mark on the management of the firm.

Notoriously publicity-shy, the Seddons are also very downbeat in displaying their wealth. Large houses or luxury cars are rare and the family still live in the Manchester area – albeit in the Cheshire stockbroker belt. They are known to be strong supporters of local charities.

## Ian Skipper £40m

*Business man*

dob 28/11/31

Visitors to the Jorvik Viking Centre in York can see a reconstruction of a 10th-century village as they travel on an electric trolley, accompanied by a commentary from Magnus Magnusson.

This is a new type of museum and much of the inspiration for it came from Ian Skipper, a local business man and entrepreneur. Skipper ran a Ford dealership before selling up in the early 1970s to invest in high-technology companies which made his fortune.

He now runs Heritage Projects: the Jorvik Centre was his first one. Others have been developed in Canterbury and Oxford. So successful has the Jorvik Centre been that all its bank loans were paid off in 1990.

Skipper's talents in tourism development have not escaped the notice of the government and he is now a member of the English Tourist Board.

# Michael Stone    £40m

*Commodity broker*

dob 10/5/36

Stone runs one of the City's least-known yet most profitable trading companies, the Man Group. His company has been in business since 1763 and supplied ultra-potent rum to the Admiralty until the navy's grog ration was discontinued in 1970. Its principal business remains international trade – sugar, coffee, cocoa and money. Stone, who joined Man in 1957, changed it in the 1960s from a highly regarded if small produce broker into a major force in the international raw materials world.

He will be remembered in the City for his secret deal with the Russian government in 1972 to buy enough sugar to supply the whole of Russia for a year. The western world remained unaware of the operation until it was finished. In 1985 Suchard, the Swiss confectionary giant, acquired 45% of his company for a sum thought to be around $385 million, including an option to acquire the balance in 1990. Stone's personal stake in the company was believed to be around 20%, and the Suchard deal valued it at over $170 million. He is married and lives on a farm in Surrey. He lists his hobbies as shooting, fishing, farming, skiing and gardening.

In 1987 Man gave £138,000 to the Conservative Party, making it one of the biggest business contributors to party funds.

# George Walker    £40m

*Property owner and film producer*

dob 14/4/29

Son of a brewery drayman, George Walker started work as a Billingsgate meat porter, before becoming a boxer. He retired with £5,000 savings and managed his brother Billy's career as a top British heavyweight ('the Blond Bomber') before moving into business. First he owned a garage, then taxis, petrol stations and lorries. He built the Brent Cross shopping centre and is

*George Walker*

planning an astrodome at Basildon, which will be the largest indoor sports stadium in Europe.

His business has expanded into leisure and films. Walker revived the then flagging career of Joan Collins through backing films such as *The Stud* and *The Bitch* in the 1970s. He has taken over Goldcrest, the film company, and Elstree, the film studio.

The master company, Brent Walker, came to the stock market in 1985. George Walker has homes in London and Essex, and has a large yacht which is often seen on the Thames.

---

## Sir Mark Weinberg   £40m

*Financier*

dob 9/8/31

Weinberg qualified and practised as a barrister in South Africa before moving to Britain in 1961 to set up his own life assurance business, Abbey Life, with a £50,000 loan. It was remarkably successful because

he paid high commissions to brokers. He sold the business in 1970 and promptly started again with Hambro Life. In 1985 that business was sold for £664 million to BAT, the tobacco giant.

Sir Mark is now a poacher turned gamekeeper as deputy chairman of the Securities and Investment Board, policing the pension industry.

His other claim to fame is his second marriage to the beautiful Australian actress and budding millionairess in her own right, Anouska Hempel. His first wife, Sandra, was her best friend until her death in 1978. Out of a run-down Earls Court boarding house, Anouska Hempel created Blake's Hotel, one of London's most fashionable hotels. She also runs a boutique in Fulham Road. The Weinbergs live in Holland Park and have a country house in Wiltshire.

---

## Duke of Wellington   £40m

*Landowner*

dob 2/7/15

The hero of Waterloo was given a £200,000 grant by the nation to build a Waterloo Palace, similar to the Duke of Marlborough's Blenheim. But there was not enough money, so the Iron Duke made do with Stratfield Saye in Hampshire instead.

It is now the home of the 8th Duke. As well as this 7,000-acre estate, the family also has 2,300 acres in Spain, a reward for the Iron Duke's role in clearing Spain of Napoleon's troops. The house is filled with the treasures from the Iron Duke's military triumphs and major art works given to him by grateful European monarchs. The family also own Apsley House in London, though they only occupy a flat there today as the rest is a museum.

The Duke was educated at Eton and Oxford. Later he joined the army, rising to the rank of brigadier. Among his many

service appointments was that of military attaché in Spain, where he is also the Duke of Vittoria. The eldest of his four sons, the Marquess of Douro, was a member of the European Parliament, and Lady Jane Wellesley, his daughter, was romantically linked with Prince Charles in the late 1970s.

---

# James Wood £40m

*Industrialist*

Jim Wood was born a Geordie but has made his fortune thousands of miles away from the Tyne as one of America's top food retailers. The son of a building contractor, he had retailing in his blood. At 14 he became a grocer's apprentice, stacking shelves at a Co-op corner store in Newcastle; later he worked his way up the Co-op before making the move which transformed his career. In 1965 he saw an anonymous advert for a retail director in the *Financial Times*. He landed the job and discovered he was working for Sir James Goldsmith (q.v.).

For the next 15 years he was a vital part of Goldsmith's operations. When the financier bought a new company he would hand over the day-to-day running to Wood. Wood helped him buy, turn round and sell a dozen retailers and several real estate properties.

By 1980 Wood was becoming restless. For 6 of the 15 years he had been making Goldsmith a fortune running the Grand Union supermarket chain in America. He felt that he should have an equity stake in the business, but nothing materialised.

# Thomas and Gordon Black £39m

*Industrialists*

dob TB 17/11/38  GB 2/3/43

One of the finest private collections of old cars in the country – worth at least £8 million – sits in an anonymous warehouse in Keighley, West Yorkshire. Among the 200 cars on display is an 1894 German Benz, one of only 67 produced. The collection was started by Peter Black, who arrived in Britain as a 25-year-old in 1933 to escape Nazi persecution of the Jews. His first job was in London working for an uncle who built cars on a small scale under the name Sabella.

On the outbreak of war, Black moved to Keighley to join a company making webbing for the armed forces. When peace came, Black bought out the Keighley branch and shrewdly started making shopping bags out of the army surplus material. Peter Black died in 1977, leaving his two sons, Thomas and Gordon, who are joint chairmen, to run the flourishing business. It has some 3,500 employees in 17 companies making footwear, ceramics, toiletries and furniture. It is a major supplier to Marks & Spencer, with a turnover of £130 million.

The car collection was started in 1960 when Peter Black was laid up with a slipped disc, and his family doctor, a vintage car enthusiast himself, suggested that he started the same sort of hobby. He did and was hooked, reading all the books on vintage cars, visiting auctions and, dressed in old gardening clothes, supervising the restoration of his first car, a 1922 Rolls-Royce Silver Ghost. He had found it in a Scarborough orchard with a tree growing through the bonnet; the price was £30, with another £40 spent on getting it back to Keighley. Today the collection costs around £1,500 a month to maintain, and the Black brothers are keen that it should pay its way. As a result, a number of the

It took another billionaire to make Wood rich, although he was wary of the initial approach from Erivan Haub, owner of the Tengelmann chain, who wanted him to run his American business, Great Atlantic & Pacific Tea. 'I said no way in the bloody world would I be interested in another one of these rich guys who wants you to do something for him,' Wood told *Business Week*.

But, unlike Goldsmith, Haub offered Wood what added up to a 10% stake in A&P. This immediately attracted him. 'I stayed up in bed and smoked cigars all night. The next morning I called Jimmy in London and said: "You know who you're talking to? The chairman of A&P."'

At A&P, Wood bought up £600 million worth of new businesses, often poorly run family firms where he introduced strong financial discipline. Initially on a 10-year contract, Wood has signed on for another 5 years beyond the 1990 expiry date. He is described by colleagues as a quiet, serious man, not a joiner. Yet he has a reputation for being tough and uncompromising in dealing with trade unions.

In 1989 he backed an unsuccessful attempt by the management of the British Gateway to mount a buy-out of the group, which was facing a rival takeover bid.

cars have been exhibited to raise funds. The brothers regularly take part in the London to Brighton race and hire out the cars for films such as *Those Magnificent Men in Their Flying Machines*. Their cars are valued at some £4m.

# Duke of Marlborough   £38m

*Landowner*

dob 13/4/26

John Churchill, the 1st Duke of Marlborough, named his new palace after his great victory at the battle of Blenheim. Work started on the palace in 1705, though it was not completed until 1720. He was awarded a £5,000-a-year pension by a grateful nation to add to his army salary of £10,000.

Today the 11th Duke occupies the only non-royal palace in the country and owns the surrounding 11,500 acres. He has turned the estate into a thriving business

enterprise, with a conference centre and accommodation for paying guests.

For much of the 18th and 19th centuries the Marlborough family lacked the resources to maintain Blenheim properly. The 8th Duke sold off many art treasures, though his son, the 9th Duke, did much to restore the family fortunes. In 1895 he married Consuelo Vanderbilt, daughter of the American industrialist, giving the Blenheim estates access to huge new reserves of capital. The paintings which escaped the 8th Duke's sales included works by Van Dyck, Kneller, Reynolds and Romney.

Sir Winston Churchill was directly related to the Marlborough family. His father, Lord Randolph Spencer-Churchill, was the third son of the 7th Duke.

# John Delaney   £37m

*Business man*

In 1966 John Delaney married Mrs Denise Pigott, the daughter of Denys Erskine and niece of Keith Erskine. Mrs Pigott, who had previously married a partner in a firm of London tea merchants, was heiress to the Securicor fortune, controlling nearly half the voting shares in the group.

Denys Erskine was originally a hotelier, and his brother Keith was a solicitor. In the 1950s the hotel business, Associated Hotels, ran up to five hotels including the original Eccleston Hotel in Victoria, bought by their father. Securicor, which was started in 1935, was acquired from one of Keith's clients and the brothers decided to move out of hotels into what they saw as a lucrative market. By 1979 the business had 1,800 armoured vans carrying £38 billion of cash round the country.

Denise Delaney had trained as a shorthand typist. She planned the décor in the hotels and sat on the Securicor board, commuting to meetings from her Sussex farm. When she died in 1980, leaving some £3.4

million net in her will, her husband, John Delaney, who also sat on the Securicor board, took over the role of watching the family interests in the firm.

These became much more valuable in the 1980s when Securicor, in association with British Telecom, won the licence to operate a mobile phone service in Britain. Their service – known as Cellnet – became immensely profitable and had an impact on Securicor's share price, lifting it to around £8 or more a share. With over 4 million shares in the business, John Delaney's fortune now stands at over £37 million.

## Everard Goodman    £37m
*Property developer*

dob 24/2/32

Everard Goodman is the publicity-shy founder of a profitable property company known as TOPS estates, originally called Trust of Property Shares Ltd. During the 1980s the company specialised in shop-related assets, prospering through the boom in the retail sector that was a hallmark of the early Thatcher years. Goodman's roots go back to shops, when he built up the Collingwood group which incorporated County Jewellers. He sold this group in 1971/2 following a bad car smash, and stayed out of the market for a few years.

Sensing the coming boom at the end of the 1970s, he began a series of unspectacular but key purchases, of first Crawley Town Centre, then Basildon Town Centre, Dewsbury Town Centre and Corby Town Centre. Crawley benefited enormously from the boom at Gatwick, and Corby became one of the real success stories of the Midlands.

Despite the downturn at the end of the 1980s, none of these four key sites looks at all vulnerable. Goodman's approach to development is described by the trade as 'ultra-conservative', and TOPS has very

low borrowings. He is described by associates as someone who treats short-term income as irrelevant and goes for maximising rents on prime central sites while simultaneously maximising asset value.

He has never indulged in publicity on the grounds that it does not earn money for the shareholder. One of his sons is a stockbroker in London. Goodman was born in Leeds. His wealth derives from his 20 million shares in his businesses.

## Duke of Grafton    £37m
*Landowner*

dob 3/4/19

The dukedom was one of four created for the bastard sons of Charles II. The 1st Duke, Henry Fitzroy, was the son of Barbara Villiers, royal favourite and Duchess of Cleveland. The 11th Duke, who now bears the title, lives at the family seat, Euston Hall in Suffolk. The family used to own land around Euston in London but that has now gone. Their holdings are comparatively small today, consisting of just 10,500 acres.

But Euston Hall has a unique collection of late 17th-century portraits. These include works by Van Dyck, Lely, van Somer and Mytens. A famous Stubbs, *Mares and Foals*, hangs in the entrance to the hall.

The Duke, educated at Eton and Cambridge, served in the Grenadier Guards. He is a godfather to the Duke of York while his wife Ann is Mistress of the Robes to the Queen. The Earl of Euston, his heir, is married to a daughter of the Marquess of Lothian and is a director of several large City institutions.

The Duke is a fervent conservationist and is chairman of numerous preservation bodies, including the Society for the Protection of Ancient Buildings. His father pulled down two-thirds of Euston Hall, owing to the high cost of maintenance.

# Paul Judge   £37m

*Food manufacturer*

Paul Judge's formidable intellect was evident at an early age. He won an open scholarship to Trinity College, Cambridge, in 1968, graduating in 1971 with a BA in natural sciences. He then won a Thouron scholarship to the prestigious Wharton Business School at the University of Pennsylvania, where he graduated with an MBA in 1973.

He joined the British food and drinks group, Cadbury Schweppes, as a financial analyst and quickly impressed the management with his skills. Early in 1974 he was made group planning director and

later, while still in his twenties, became deputy finance director. Spells in Kenya and America broadened his career, and in 1982 he was appointed managing director of Cadbury Typhoo, best known for its famous tea and Smash, the instant potato with its robot television commercial.

In 1984 Dominic Cadbury, the new chief executive of the food group, asked Judge to become group planning director, his first task being to sell off unwanted businesses. He had no problem in selling some of the businesses such as Jeyes to existing managers, but despite a dozen enquiries from large companies he could not get the right terms for the food manufacturing business which made products such as Marvel, Smash and Hartley's jam.

By Christmas 1985 Judge was feeling disappointed with the results and went to ask Dominic Cadbury if he could mount a buy-out of the food businesses. Cadbury gave him eight days to present proposals to a board meeting. Using a business school contact, he managed to raise the necessary £97 million funding and support from eight other directors. After some protracted bargaining – with other food groups showing interest in snatching the prize from Judge and his team – they finally took over the food business early in 1986. It was renamed Premier Brands and appeared to have a tricky future loaded down with debt. But Judge was able to slash overheads and costs, and he won over the staff completely by giving them shares in the business. Using the 1984 Finance Act, which granted executives share options in a company, Judge promptly treated his staff as executives and devised a share scheme for all 5,000 of them.

Within two years trading profits had quadrupled and the group was planning a stock market flotation in 1989. But in March that year the board of Premier decided to put the group up for sale to the highest bidder. Judge disagreed with that decision and resigned as chairman, though he still remained on the board. In May the group was taken over by Hillsdown Holdings for £215 million. Judge received Hillsdown shares worth over £36 million and agreed to sell them only on a phased basis until the end of 1991. He took a sabbatical to consider his future after his decision to leave Premier.

He is a Freeman of the City of London and Fellow of the Royal Society of Arts. He lives on a farm near Droitwich in Worcestershire.

# Tom Harrison £36m
*Petrol station owner*

# David McMurtry £36m
*Industrialist*

dob 15/3/40

The secret of success in selling petrol is having a good site, such as those Tom Harrison is an expert at finding and developing. From 1965 to 1972 he worked for Burmah, developing their garage businesses, and in 1983 he entered the estate agency business, forming a partnership that specialised in road-related properties. After working in a joint-venture company with the Kwik-Fit group, he set up on his own in 1983, forming the Norfolk House group. It specialises in buying and developing petrol stations, which it either runs itself or sells to the oil majors. Growth has been explosive, and in 1988 the company was floated on the stock market.

In 1988 Harrison sold 58 stations to Petrofina, the Belgian giant, for £26.4 million. The company is also branching out into other areas of property development such as housing and industrial units. Harrison owns 16 million shares in the company, or 67% of the equity.

Growth is likely to continue with the huge development in road traffic and the ambitious road programme planned by the government.

At the age of 18 David McMurtry ran away from his Dublin home to become an aerospace apprentice at the Bristol Siddeley Engines factory. Over the years he climbed up the hierarchy, eventually becoming deputy chief designer and assistant chief of engine design for all engines made at the Filton works (by then owned by Rolls-Royce). In 17 years he created some 17 patented inventions, one of which was crucial for the development of Concorde's engines. The fuel pipes needed to be fitted with extreme precision and McMurtry came up with a 4-inch probe that measured them with great accuracy.

Rolls, though pleased with the work, which meant that Concorde could fly, was not prepared to market the device. So, in 1973, McMurtry set up his own company with John Deer, a colleague at Rolls. For the first three years, McMurtry still worked at Rolls, while Deer built up the business from a spare bedroom in his home. At night McMurtry provided the technical input needed. 'My main task was convincing Dave that there would be enough to occupy his technical mind,' Deer later recalled.

He succeeded and in 1976, with McMurtry on the board, the company moved operations to a disused ice-cream factory at Wotton-under-Edge in the Bristol commuter belt. At that time the company had five employees and sales of £200,000. Six years later it employed 150 staff, with sales of £3 million, 85% of which went overseas.

In 1983 the company came to the stock market to an enthusiastic reception, and it has been growing ever since. It has moved into robots and has set up a large research and development arm. McMurtry has 39% of the shares and Deer 19%, making a takeover impossible. The group leads the way in front of the Japanese in this market.

# Saleh Shohet £36m

*Property dealer*

dob 8/9/33

Saleh Shohet, a French citizen, has been in the property business since 1961. He is now based full-time in London. Shohet and his cousin Edward came to Europe from

Iraq in 1972 and spent the early 1970s in Spain building up a property portfolio in Madrid. They moved into Britain, aiming first at the residential property market but later going into offices.

They also have extensive American interests. They became a large shareholder in a US property company, eventually selling out and walking away with a £20 million profit. Edward, an Italian citizen, looks after the finances and administration. Their latest company, Dukeminster, has some impressive backing in the shape of American Express. It was floated on the stock market in August 1988 with a £54 million valuation.

# Sting £36m

*Singer and actor*

dob 2/10/51

Pop star turned actor turned campaigner to save the Amazon rain forest, Gordon Sumner, alias Sting, started life as a primary school teacher in his native Newcastle upon Tyne after dropping out of Warwick University. The son of a milkman, his name comes from the wasp-striped T-shirts he wore in early stage appearances as a struggling rock musician.

His first big break came in 1976 – not on the stage but when he married Frances Tomelty, the Irish actress. The marriage seemed to release a flood of creative energy in Sting and a string of hits, with his band Police, followed, culminating in the album *Synchronicity*, which sold over 7 million copies.

Sting later left his wife for Trudie Styler, a young actress, and they live in a 17th-century Highgate house, which formerly belonged to Sir Yehudi Menuhin. Sting has four children, two by each of the women in his life. Early in 1989 he splashed out

£3 million for a luxury apartment over-looking New York's Central Park.

Sting has moved into acting, though he has no formal training. He has appeared in films such as *Quadrophenia*, *Plenty*, *Dune* and *Treacle*. He has also helped his friend Bruce Springsteen by taking part in a world tour on behalf of Amnesty International.

But today much of Sting's energy is taken up with the fight to save the rain forests in the Amazon basin. After some highly successful concerts in Brazil which culminated in a show before 200,000 people at Rio's Maracana Stadium, he met Chief Raoni of the Kayapo tribe who inhabit an area of Brazil the size of Italy. The Kayapo are fighting deforestation and Sting joined them in their crusade.

Sting arranged a two-month world tour for the Chief to highlight the plight of his tribe (best known for the large wooden plates inserted in their lower lips) and he has set up the Brazilian-based Rainforest Foundation. So famous has the Chief become that he even appeared on BBC television's *Wogan*. Sting's girlfriend Trudie is vice-president of the Foundation.

He denies that his ambitions will turn to politics: 'I'm a dreamer, a Utopian. I would be no good at full-time politics. And it's exhausting. We've got to do this for the Indians. My feeling is that once they are destroyed then we all are all in time,' he recently told *The Times*.

## Franklin Van Wetzel   £36m

*Industrialist*

dob 7/9/41

Dutchman Franklin Van Wetzel was educated in Holland before going to Kenya to manage a fertiliser company. He came to Britain and in 1974 began importing running shoes from Inter, his brother-in-law's firm in Holland. His Shoeburyness home served as his office and a neighbour

worked as his accountant, with two local youngsters as packers. His first product was a pair of simple running shoes made of canvas.

Within four years Van Wetzel had designed his own squash shoe, which proved to be the foundation of his fortune. In its early years his company traded as Inter-Footwear (UK) but in 1982 he created the Hi-Tec brand name and changed the company name to Hi-Tec as well. Today Hi-Tec is the leading supplier of sports shoes in Britain with around 20% of the market.

The change of name proved enormously successful and has been used as a case study of successful marketing by the prestigious Harvard Business School. The success of the squash shoe boosted Hi-Tec turnover from £8 million to £50 million in five years and, capitalising on its success, the Silver Shadow running shoe was launched at the 1981 London Marathon.

Van Wetzel's secret has been an astute marketing campaign. This includes sponsoring Annabel Croft, and a pro-celebrity tennis tournament with stars such as Terry Wogan and Cliff Richard. In 1987 a con-

tract was signed with Mirandinha, the Brazilian soccer star, to promote Hi-Tec sports shoes.

Most of the shoes are imported from the Far East and Italy, though golf and cricket shoes come from a British plant. In June 1987 Hi-Tec moved from Shoeburyness to a new 75,000-square-foot complex near Southend Airport. A year later the company was floated on the stock market, and was capitalised at around £55 million. Van Wetzel retains over 70% of the shares. The additional proceeds from the flotation were used to fund expansion in America.

Van Wetzel lists his hobbies as all sports and travel. Married, he has a son and two daughters.

# Bill Benyon    £35m
*Landowner, MP*

dob 17/1/30

Bill Benyon, the Conservative MP for Milton Keynes, is one of the few rich men to have been educated at the Royal Naval College, Dartmouth. He is even more unusual in being a very major landowner in a prime south-east county, Berkshire.

In 1956 he left the navy after nine years' service and joined Courtaulds to pursue a commercial career. This plan went awry in 1964 when a cousin died without an heir and left him one of the finest houses and estates in the Home Counties.

This was Englefield House and estate near Newbury, acquired by his ancestors in the 18th century; in 1880 it stood at 16,007 acres spread across Berkshire, Essex and Hampshire. When Benyon inherited it, it totalled 14,000 acres, concentrated at Englefield. The house is not open to the public although it is large and contains many fascinating artefacts. It is used by the local people for school parties and events, and forms the centre of a community, linked to the local village but with the estate and its tenants at its heart.

In a revealing interview given to *The Times* in 1985, Benyon described how he had saved the local post office and store, kept the developers at bay and commuters out, and revived the local school through a merger. 'But we must get away from the old paternalism,' he told *The Times*.

In the House of Commons he has had what might be called a 'quiet' career. He was a parliamentary private secretary to the minister of housing in 1972–4 and a Conservative whip from 1974 to 1976. Normally this sort of progress should have led to a ministerial post, however junior, in the current government. But it has not, largely because Bill Benyon allied himself very firmly with the 'wets' and was a prominent member of Francis Pym's Centre Forward group which sought to reorient the party away from Thatcherite policies.

His favourite story, told to *The Times*, concerns the media mogul and Labour supporter Robert Maxwell (q.v.), whom he beat in the 1970 election. He tells how when they met years later, 'Captain Bob' Maxwell put his arm around Benyon's shoulder and said: 'Bill, that's one of the best things you ever did for me.' Maxwell, of course, went on to become a billionaire

He is a Deputy Lord Lieutenant for the county of Berkshire and a local Justice of the Peace, and belongs to Boodle's, the same club as did his ancestor in the 1880s.

# Frederick and Michael Evans    £35m
*Property developers*

The son of a Leeds tailor, Frederick Evans decided early in life that he did not like sewing and stitching. So he went into transport work around Leeds with one or two lorries. From there he went on to develop a small-scale housebuilding business. Later he moved into building tower blocks, including a 16-storey building which at the time was the highest in Leeds.

Evans, who once said he had no hobbies other than work, is still chief executive of the group though he is now in his nineties. In his mid-eighties he came into the office every day. His son Michael is deputy chairman. In 1962 they sold some businesses to a London property group, Estates Property Investment Company, for £1.4 million worth of shares.

Today Evans of Leeds is one of Yorkshire's biggest property developers, with a number of major developments in the Leeds area. It came to the stock market in 1971 and is worth nearly £70 million today. Half the shares are owned by Frederick and Michael Evans.

In the mid-1980s Evans switched from industrial property to offices and shops, neatly catching the boom in retailing and the service economy. One of the company's latest developments is a new £100 million shopping centre, planned with Yorkshire Water in south Leeds on the site of an old sewage works. Its 1989–90 results showed profits of over £7.5 million, a rise of £400,000 in a year. The company boasts that its profits have risen consistently every year since its flotation mainly because of an astute ability to find the right location for property development.

# Earl of Seafield    £35m

*Landowner*

dob 20/3/39

The Earl of Seafield's mother was reputed to be the wealthiest woman in Britain after the Queen. At one stage she owned 800 square miles of prime Scottish land, including grouse moors, salmon rivers, forestry and farms. She was able to stave off some of the death duties on the estate by transferring much of the land to her son. He inherited the title in 1969.

Since then he has sold off some of his inheritance. In 1972 he raised £1 million

by selling a 21,000-acre estate. In 1975 he sold the entire contents of Cullen House, the family seat, for £300,000. He gave a major armoury of antique weapons to the nation in 1976. But he still retains property in the Bahamas.

The Earl, known as Ginger, was educated at Eton. He has been married twice. His first wife, a City stockbroker's daughter, gave him two sons. They were divorced in 1971, and in the same year he married again. He survived a serious air crash in 1958.

# Sir Reo Stakis    £35m

*Restaurant owner*

dob 13/3/13

Sir Reo Stakis came from a poor farming family in Cyprus. His mother helped make ends meet by selling lace. To boost the sales, the family decided to export it to Britain. Reo, as the eldest of six children, was sent to act as a salesman at the tender age of 15. That was in 1928 and though he had never been further than Larnaca before, he toured Britain as a door-to-door salesman for ten years. His experience of British cooking during that time convinced him there was a market for good-quality restaurants.

He decided to start in Scotland, where he found the people particularly friendly. After the war, having saved enough money and finally married his fiancée, Annitsa from Cyprus, in 1947, he opened his first restaurant in Glasgow.

By the late 1950s the business was thriving, and he expanded after buying the freehold to his restaurant. In the 1960s more restaurants, then hotels and casinos, followed. The business went public in 1972, and today it employs 6,000 people. In the year to the end of September 1989 the Stakis group made £27.1 million pre-tax profits on a £143 million turnover. Stakis, knighted in 1988, still runs the business as chairman, with his son Andros now as managing director.

Sir Reo lists his hobbies as shooting and fishing. He lives in Glasgow and has a house in Perthshire.

---

# Duncan and Sarah Davidson   £34m

*Builders*

dob DD 29/3/41   SD 4/6/42

Duncan Davidson had a stint as a commercial trainee with George Wimpey, the construction group, before deciding to branch out on his own. From 1965 to 1972 the urbane Scotsman ran a private building company, Ryedale, with Anthony Fawcett, a tough Yorkshireman. They then sold out to London Merchant Securities for £1 million.

Davidson and his wife Sarah immediately started up Persimmon Homes, which Fawcett joined. In 1976 the company started to move out of its Yorkshire heartland by branching out to East Anglia and the Midlands. In 1985 it came to the stock market and produced bumper profits year after year. In 1988, despite high interest rates, its profits shot up by 138% to £29.5 million. In 1989, while other builders went bankrupt, Persimmon still managed to increase pre-tax profits to £32.6 million, a 10% increase which pleasantly surprised the City.

Davidson attributes his success to building in places where people want to live like York, Shrewsbury and other attractive market towns. His 1989 figures bear that out. The average price of the 1,796 homes he sold was £71,881, an increase of 23%.

Davidson, who was educated at Ampleforth, is a member of White's and the Turf Club. His mother was Lady Rachel Davidson, sister of the late Duke of Norfolk. At Ampleforth his passion was beagling, and he was master of the college prize-winning pack. He lists country pursuits among his hobbies, and has a passionate interest in horses and racing dogs. He also sits on the boards of several companies, including the Scottish Investment Trust.

His nickname is Dynamo Dunc, reflecting one description of him as a 'cool but live wire'. Duncan and Sarah Davidson live on what has been called an 'enormous' country estate in Northumberland, southeast of Alnwick. The estate is farmed by Lilburn Estates, Davidson's private farming company.

---

# Lawrie Lewis   £34m

*Exhibition organiser*

It was a case of rags to riches – quite literally – for Lawrie Lewis, chief executive of the Blenheim Exhibitions Group which, as its name implies, specialises in organising exhibitions.

Trained initially in garment production, Lewis was a sales director for a fashion company from 1970 to 1974, marketing the output of such well-known designers as Ossie Clark and Sheridan Barnett. In 1975 he branched out on his own, setting up a design company. He knew the ups and downs of the business. Three companies he was associated with in the early 1980s went into voluntary liquidation though all the creditors were paid in full and no blame was attached to Lewis.

Through the 1970s he had attended some 150 exhibitions as an exhibitor. This experience convinced him that there was a market for organising exhibitions and in 1979 he set up Blenheim Dresswell which specialised in organising fashion fairs and shows for the clothes sector. By 1982 it was becoming what *Acquisitions Monthly* magazine called 'a serious business' and Lewis called in Neville Buch, a City investment consultant, as chairman – initially for one day a week, but soon it was a full-time job.

In 1982 Blenheim organised 5 exhibitions. By 1986, when it came to the Unlisted Securities Market, that figure had risen to 36, including one for the chilled food industry. As a quoted company, Blenheim has been in the news for its hectic pace of acquisitions, particularly in Europe. It was also named as USM company of the year by the USM magazine.

The shares, which were floated at 95p, rose to over 900p within three years. Lewis is one of the few company founders who has not sold any shares when his business was floated on the stock market. Indeed, he buys Blenheim shares whenever the opportunity arises to increase his stake. Lewis now has over 3.7 million shares in the business.

Three times married, he told the *Sunday Telegraph*: 'I lost my third wife because she was away on business for six months of the year and my second because I was.'

Lewis works a 75-hour week. He lives in London's fashionable Holland Park during the week, commuting to his Wiltshire home in his American sports car on Friday evenings. He is noted for his bright bow ties.

# Roger De Haan and family £33m
*Holiday company operator*

When Roger De Haan's father, Sidney, was running the 36-room family hotel in Folkestone after the war, he began to fill the rooms off-season with elderly visitors. So popular was the idea that he founded a holiday company which was specifically designed for the over-60s. Today that company, Saga, caters for 250,000 elderly holidaymakers each year. As we are living longer and becoming more affluent and numerous, Saga's prospects are also improving year by year. Already it has noted that its clients are getting more adventurous, so it organises walking tours around the foothills of Everest or canoeing up the Amazon.

The group has had only one hiccup since it came to the stock market in 1978. In 1982 it tried to diversify into general holidays by buying Laker Air Travel from the wreckage of Sir Freddie Laker's business. After losing £2 million, Saga decided to close it down. In 1984 Sidney De Haan retired to his Somerset cottage with his wife, saying he planned to play a full role in his local community. The business is now run by his son Roger as chairman. Two other De Haans are also on the board.

One of Roger's first acts as chairman was to sell five Saga hotels, including the original Burlington in Folkestone for £4 million. The money was used to expand the retirement holiday business. In 1989 the company announced plans to diversify into retirement homes.

The family still control around 63% of the equity and, to avoid the risk of a take-over, are determined that this should never fall below 50%. At the end of 1989 they announced plans to buy the 37% of the shares they did not own and take the group private again. The unwillingness to issue more shares and so to dilute their stake had made it difficult for the De Haans to expand the business by acquisition. Roger De Haan also criticised the City's short-term approach, which is geared to making bigger profits and dividends immediately rather than investing for the long term.

# Marquess of Normanby  £33m

*Landowner*

dob 29/7/12

In 1876 the Governor of New Zealand, the Rt. Hon The Marquess of Normanby, had what was by the standards of the time a small spread of just 6,800 acres in the North Riding of Yorkshire. The present Marquess, who still lives in the same home as his ancestor, Mulgrave Castle, is understood to be the master of something closer to 50,000 acres, a considerable increase on the ancestral landholdings: a trend not much evident among the great landowners of Britain in the 20th century.

Unlike his ancestors, who were cabinet ministers and important colonial governors, the present Marquess, who was educated at Eton and Christ Church, Oxford, has confined himself to activities closer to home and to Yorkshire.

During the war he was wounded and taken prisoner in France. He was awarded the military and civil MBEs in 1943 and, at the end of the war, he was parliamentary private secretary to the Secretary of State for Dominion Affairs, PPS to the Lord President of the Council and then a lord-in-waiting. Since the war he has occupied all the customary roles of a Marquess. He is the chairman of the National Art-Collections Fund, High Steward of York Minster, Lord Lieutenant of North Yorkshire and its *Custos Rotulorum* (custodian of the land rolls).

In 1951 the Marquess married Grania Guinness, the daughter of Lord Moyne who was assassinated in Cairo in the 1940s. What should have been a quiet wedding was interrupted when an alternative claimant to the title appeared at the ceremony in the church at Lythe in Yorkshire, and objected to the nuptials proceeding. The claimant, an engineer from Newcastle called T. A. Trueman, who had four different meetings with Queen Mary in the 1930s, was later sent to prison for a month for threatening to kill Lord Normanby. He died without succeeding in his lonely cause.

The couple have seven children but one of their sons-in-law, Adam Sedgwick, was shot dead by armed robbers in Fulham in 1982. Adam Sedgwick was separated from his wife at the time.

In the late seventies the Marquess made the headlines when he sacked a farm manager on his estate for having an affair with another estate employee's wife. Politically, the Marquess moved from the Conservative side before the war to Labour in the late 1940s before resigning in 1950 to sit as an independent on the crossbenches.

# David Phillips  £33m

*Electronics engineer*

dob 31/1/45

For fourteen years David Phillips worked as an insurance broker. In 1979 he decided

petition. In August 1989 he unveiled profits of £6.1 million for the year to the end of April 1989, a rise of 18% over the previous year. Phillips said that these would improve once the computer industry had seen a shake-out of the small fry.

---

## Lord Roborough    £33m
*Landowner*

dob 4/10/03

The Roboroughs have been associated with the county of Devon since the end of the 18th century, when the founder of the dynasty, Manasseh Massey Lopes, sat as MP for South Molton. By the 19th century the family had amassed over 12,000 acres of prime agricultural land and married into three of the great Devon landowning families, the Churstons, the Bullers and the Edgecombes.

The title was created in January 1938 and the present Lord Roborough succeeded his father a mere four months later. On the outbreak of war, Massey Henry Lopes joined the Royal Armoured Corps and was wounded twice on active service. Earlier he had served as ADC to the Governor-General of South Africa, following a traditional education at Eton and Christ Church, Oxford.

After the war he returned to running the family acres, which are believed to have remained as large as they were in the late 1800s, and to the usual duties of the landed county aristocrat. These included the Lord Lieutenancy of the county, guardianship of its land rolls (*Custos Rotulorum*) and the High Stewardship of Barnstaple. Unlike some of the landed gentry, Roborough has also taken part in a whole raft of social duties, all connected with the smooth running of the upper end of the county. These include the governorship of private schools such as Kelly College and Exeter School. He is also a long-standing member of the Council of Exeter University.

to try a sideline and, working from home, began importing American microcomputers and selling them from his garage.

For two years, while he built up the business, he continued as an insurance broker. But he gave that up as the business boomed and he started selling other electronic products, particularly printers. He even flew to New York on standby tickets and bought as many printers as he could manage to bring back in his luggage.

Eventually the business – called Northamber – moved out of his front room and into new offices in Esher. In 1984, after growing at 50% a year, the company came to the stock market.

Despite the boom, Phillips kept head office costs down and there are no lavish facilities. This enables him to weather the ups and downs of the computer market. He never sells at the lowest price, preferring to offer quick delivery and a year's guarantee on his products.

Regarded as a secretive autocrat, Phillips has nevertheless managed to impress the City with his results, despite fierce com-

The Hon. Henry Lopes, his eldest son and heir, was educated at Eton, followed by a spell in the Coldstream Guards. He lives and works in Devon. His younger son is married to a daughter of Lord Astor of Hever (q.v.).

---

# Sir Terence Conran  £32m

*Retailer*

dob 4/10/31

The son of a gun importer, Terence Conran was an early rebel. He was expelled from Bryanston, the Dorset private school, despite its orientation to the arts. He went on to art college but walked out at 18 without finishing his course because he was bored. But he had developed an interest in furniture, crafts and design, and a year in Paris working as a chef's assistant developed a love for France that was to be crucial in his later life.

He came back to Britain and his work attracted attention at the 1951 Festival of Britain, but his initial interest was in catering and he founded a small chain of bistros called the Soup Kitchens. In 1964 he branched out and opened his first Habitat store in London's Fulham Road, just as the 1960s were getting into full swing.

'It was a revolutionary furniture store reflecting Conran's interest in the modern movement and his lifelong love affair with the styles of Provence. Habitat offered products, many designed by Conran, combining minimalism with a bright, youthful hedonism, that captured the spirit of the 1960s. The marketing was equally innovative: by selling small items such as kitchenware in the same space as furniture, Conran turned the utilitarian furniture store into a fun shopping experience,' wrote Jeffrey Ferry in *Business* magazine.

It was a roaring success and soon every high street had its own Habitat. In 1982 Conran extended the chain by acquiring the Mothercare group, which was three times as large as Habitat. A year later he was knighted; he was now regarded as the guru of British design.

But in 1986 the creation of the Storehouse empire, linking Habitat with the giant British Home Stores and some smaller shops, was a near disaster. The marriage never really worked, and the combined group soon became an early victim of the decline in retail spending and management inertia. In 1987, after months of internal feuding on the Storehouse board, Conran turned down a £1.5 billion offer for the group from Tony Clegg (q.v.). It only took 20 minutes to turn it down, but they were an expensive 20 minutes. The decline in Storehouse shares since that meeting has clipped some £90 million off Conran's fortune – or £4.5 million for every minute it lasted.

The idea of being a tycoon almost seems too much for Terence Conran, who would rather be cooking or gardening than running a business empire. To prove the point, in 1990 he resigned from Storehouse to concentrate on his first love, design. So stripped for cash has he become that he has been forced to sell off most of his Storehouse shares. Conran lives with his second wife Caroline, a cookery writer, in three homes:

one in the south of France, another in Belgravia, London and another on a Berkshire estate. His former wife Shirley is a best-selling novelist, while one son, Jasper, is now a successful fashion designer.

He has been married three times, his second and third wives being the daughters of army officers. He is a member of White's and Pratt's, and enjoys shooting and fishing on his 20,000-acre estate near Harrogate.

## Viscount Mountgarret £32m
*Landowner*
dob 8/11/36

The present Lord Mountgarret has a penchant for minor controversy. In the mid-1980s he was accused of blazing away with his gun at a hot air balloon which had disturbed his grouse shooting. In 1987 he exercised aristocratic privilege by having a vicar removed from a parish church within the family estate. He accused the priest, the Rev. John Steggall, of looking like the character Compo from the Yorkshire TV series: he had turned up for Sunday service having forgotten to change into his Sunday best. The bishop of Ripon acceded to Mountgarret's request and the Rev. Steggall went to a small fishing parish near Edinburgh.

Mountgarret had a classic aristocratic education, moving from Eton to the Royal Military Academy, Sandhurst and retiring from the Irish Guards as a captain. The Mountgarret title is originally Irish, going back to the 16th century. The family name is Butler, and one of Mountgarret's ancestors was the Butler Earl of Ormond, who led the Irish rebellion against Elizabeth I as general of all the Irish forces.

The rebellion was unsuccessful and led to the Flight of the Earls, in which the majority of the Irish Catholic aristocracy fled to the Continent. This deprived Ireland of a native-born leadership for almost 300 years. In 1660 the family were pardoned and by the late 18th century had established links with Yorkshire. Mountgarret sits in the House of Lords as a Conservative with the title of Baron Mountgarret.

## Christopher Needler £32m
*Quarrying industrialist*
dob 4/9/44

Christopher Needler's late father, Harold, was one of the major figures in the postwar British construction industry. He built up his Hull-based Hoveringham Group to be one of the biggest sand and gravel companies in the country. It was floated on the stock market in 1963, but in 1981 the family sold out to Tarmac for £21 million.

They decided to keep their substantial Canadian gravel and quarrying interests, acquired in 1956. The Canadian interests operate under the name TCG Materials. TCG itself stands for Telephone City Gravel: Telephone City was the home of Alexander Graham Bell, inventor of the telephone. In 1988 these interests were floated on the British Unlisted Securities Market as the Needler Group. Christopher Needler owns around 10.5 million shares, worth £10 million. The group supplies much of the Canadian industrial heartland with aggregates and has some 75 million tonnes of reserves in its 3,000 acres of land.

Needler also raised some £1 million by selling his Lloyds insurance broking business. He commutes between his London home and Canada to run the business.

Needler was educated at Repton before becoming an articled clerk for six years in 1962, ultimately qualifying as a chartered accountant. He went to Trinity College, Cambridge, in 1968 at the relatively late age of 24. Graduating in 1971, he immediately became a director of Hoveringham and was made chairman in 1975. He fol-

In 1983 Viscount Wimborne married his second wife, Mrs Venetia Barker, eldest daughter of Lady Mancroft and former wife of Captain Fred Barker, a racehorse breeder and heir to the Singer sewing machine fortune.

He became involved in controversy in 1986 over the sale of Goya's painting, *The Marquesa of Santa Cruz*, which he had acquired in 1983. Spain claimed the picture had been smuggled out of the country, a charge the Viscount vigorously denied. He claimed to have bought it in good faith. Eventually the Spanish government paid him £4.1 million for it. In 1988 he planned to set up a fighting bull farm in Bilbao, in northern Spain.

lowed his father to become chairman of Hull City football club. Though no longer chairman today, he remains a director. His hobby is golf.

# Viscount Wimborne  £32m

*Landowner and heir*

dob 2/12/39

Descended from the Guest steel family (of Guest, Keen & Nettlefolds – GKN), Viscount Wimborne divides his life between London and Paris.

The family estates, built up by his father, a Lloyds underwriter, at one time extended to 32,000 acres. These included valuable property with development potential on the outskirts of Poole. In 1972 this was worth some £26 million. In 1976 the Viscount sold a Northampton estate he owned to the British Airways pension scheme for around £2 million.

# Lord Burton  £31m

*Landowner*

dob 27/6/24

Lord Burton is a direct descendant of the Bass family, the Derbyshire brewers. Today Bass is Britain's biggest brewer though the family has long ceased to have any say in the running of the company.

The 3rd Baron Burton – named after the Burton brewing town – is a major Scottish landowner with over 58,000 acres in Inverness. He is noted for his abrupt manner: it was once said of him by a Scottish Procurator-Fiscal that he had 'a temper which seems to me at times very easily aroused and at other times ungoverned'.

The Burton fortune enabled the family to build up an extensive art collection, including works by Gainsborough and Reynolds, which were on display at the City of Birmingham Art Gallery. The gallery bought a Gainsborough from Lord Burton in 1983 for £100,000.

Lord Burton inherited the title in 1962 from his grandmother, as his father was killed on active service in the war. His grandmother was regarded as one of the richest heiresses in the country in the late

1890s and on her marriage in 1894 she received a diamond tiara for every day of the week. Lord Burton's mother was a daughter of the Duke of Devonshire and a sister of Lady Dorothy Macmillan, wife of the late Earl of Stockton, Harold Macmillan.

Twice married, Burton has often been involved in controversial issues. In 1983 he tried to block access to a marina development near his Dochfour estate, claiming that the £1 million scheme was unnecessary and would take trade away from a local shop. He also sought permission to shoot a marauding golden eagle, a protected species, which had been carrying off local lambs, but the request was turned down by the Nature Conservancy Council.

Described by one paper as an 'eccentric baron' because of such incidents, Burton has resorted to shipping lion's dung from an Essex zoo to spread over his fields in a bid to scare off herds of red deer.

# Roland Franklin  £31m

*Financier*

Roland Franklin was born into the world of finance: his family owned A. Keyser, the merchant bank. He drifted into the bank after a private school education at Oundle and three years in the navy. At first it was a civilised and agreeable job, leaving him time to pursue other interests such as holding the chairmanship of the Jewish Welfare Board. In 1962 A. Keyser merged with Ullmann to become Keyser Ullmann. Two years later Franklin's father Ellis died, leaving Roland as one of the two joint managing directors of the bank. One of their early moves was to buy the aggressive Dalton Barton bank, run by 'Black Jack' Dellal (q.v.). Dalton Barton's loans were heavily committed to the property sector, which crashed in the early 1970s. A huge support operation was required to keep Keyser Ullmann afloat.

Franklin resigned from the bank after the board criticised him for selling his Regent's Park flat to the bank for today's equivalent of £1 million. He suffered criticism by the Department of Trade and Industry over the whole Keyser Ullmann affair. But by then he had gone to America to live in New York and work for Sir James Goldsmith (q.v.), helping him with his acquisitions and – more importantly – the sale of the unwanted parts of businesses, which gave Goldsmith some spectacular profits. The pair first worked together in 1975 on the basis that Franklin gained 5% of the profits; then for 12 years they became the bogeymen of corporate America. Franklin was given extraordinary leeway to carry out the disposals, and was regarded as a very tough negotiator.

Late in 1988 Franklin decided to branch out on his own and also to return to Britain. Through a Bermuda-based company, Pembridge Associates, he built up a 29% stake in the well-respected DRG paper and packaging group which makes Sellotape. In October 1989 he launched an all-out £697 million takeover bid for the group, promising to break it up and make a handsome profit on the sale of the assets. Despite some bitter words from the DRG management about City 'short-termism', he was able to gain control because the stock market crashed, and DRG's share price fell well below the Pembridge offer.

Franklin put over £31 million of his own money into the bid. During the battle he stayed in the Savoy Hotel, surrounded by his merchant banking advisers and his 25-year-old son, Martin, an ex-Rothschild banker who worked on the bid with him.

Franklin, known for his courteous old-world charm, rarely wears a suit, preferring to conduct business in slacks and an open shirt. He often interrupts business meetings to play tennis, returning in track suit and tennis shoes.

---

# Bernard Matthews £31m
*Turkey producer*

dob 24/1/30

Best known for his appearance on his own television adverts extolling the 'bootiful' virtues of his turkeys. Bernard Matthews took a long time getting into the business. He started as an auctioneer's clerk earning 30s a week and bought a job lot of turkeys and an incubator. He could not afford to feed them, changed jobs and became an insurance clerk. He bought a second batch, but the wind blew their shelter away and the birds escaped. Third time lucky. He borrowed £3,000 in 1955 and bought Great Witchingham Hall, a dilapidated Jacobean mansion near Norwich, and 35 acres. The turkeys were hatched in the dining room, reared in the bedrooms and processed in the kitchen. Today the hall is still the centre of his business, which has extended beyond turkeys to include boneless beef, pork and lamb roasts which Matthews also enthusiastically promotes on television.

He has a holiday home in the south of France and a stylish 157-foot yacht called *Bellissima*.

---

# Jeremy Agace £30m
*Former estate agent*

dob 15/5/40

Selling houses in London and the South East proved to be a goldmine for Jeremy

*Jeremy Agace*

Agace. He followed his father to become chairman of Mann & Co., a leading estate agency based in the Surrey commuter town of Woking and founded in 1891.

In 1985, at the height of the property boom, Mann was the third largest agency in the country. Agace floated the group on the stock market, and it was initially valued at around £31 million, with Agace owning 46% of the equity. A year later, with house prices rising by 20% or more, every large financial institution was scrambling to acquire an agency.

Mann joined with Hambros and another agency to form Hambro Countrywide, with Agace as chief executive. In April 1988 he resigned from the board with his right-hand man, Paul Locke. A month later they bought two small employment bureaus. Agace, who has since retired abroad, must be feeling thankful that he moved out of estate agency work at the right time. In 1990 scores of estate agents' offices have closed, with the housing market in the doldrums.

# Kenneth and William Alexander £30m
*Chemicals producers*
dob KA 21/11/28

The two Alexander brothers own around 20% of the shares in one of Britain's most profitable yet secretive companies, Tennants Consolidated. The group, which makes chemicals for gardeners and for many other specialised purposes, produced £7.8 million after-tax profits on a turnover of £138 million in 1988. With reserves of over £20 million and small borrowings, the group could be valued at well over £100 million on the stock market.

The business was originally started by a Glasgow chemist, Charles Tennant, at the end of the 18th century. The Tennant family, now led by Lord Glenconner (q.v.), the fun-loving friend of Princess Margaret, no longer have any involvement in the business. They sold the firm in 1960.

The Alexander family's involvement with the industry started with their father, Sir William Alexander, who died in 1954. A brilliant industrialist, he was made director of administration at the National Explosive Factories in 1916, at a time when the British Army was experiencing a critical shortage of shells. A year later he became Controller of Aircraft Supply and Production. After World War I he became a Conservative MP for Glasgow Central, and served in Parliament for 22 years until 1945. He retired to Jersey, where he died in 1954.

His son Kenneth, after education at Winchester and Cambridge and army service in the Royal Tank Regiment, joined the Tennants group, where he became chairman and chief executive in 1972. His brother, Dr William Alexander, is also a director of the group. He is a retired doctor, having qualified during the war. He was head of the neurology department at the Middlesex Hospital in London for a period and now lives in Surrey.

Kenneth Alexander, who lives on a farm in Berkshire, lists his recreations as music and shooting. He married in 1957 and has a son and three daughters.

# Lord Ashcombe £30m

*Landowner*

dob 31/3/24

The thrice-married 4th Lord Ashcombe, already wealthy as heir to the Cubitt family fortune and an active director of the company, acquired, along with his third wife, one of the most elegant castles in England. The third Lady Ashcombe was the widow of an old family friend, Mark Dent-Brocklehurst, whose family owned Sudeley Castle near the Gloucestershire village of Winchcombe.

The castle was the home of Henry VIII's sixth wife Catherine Parr, who died there. Elizabeth Dent-Brocklehurst had already opened the castle to the public before she married Ashcombe in 1979. He lists himself as director of Sudeley Castle Ltd.

Eton-educated and described in the gossip columns as 'Mad Harry', Lord Ashcombe was the first member of the family to chair Cubitts for four generations. He served in the RAF during World War II and worked at the building company for several years before he took over the top post.

His first marriage in 1955 was to a former American TV hostess. His second marriage in 1973 was to a daughter of Lord Carrington, the former minister of defence and NATO secretary general, but this marriage, reported by the gossip columns to be in trouble as early as 1977, was dissolved in 1979. There are no children and the title may pass to a cousin in Ireland.

The present Lady Ashcombe has two children by her first marriage, but they cannot inherit her husband's title. They are, however, the beneficiaries of one of the wealthiest and least-known trusts in the UK, the Walter Morrison Family Trust. During the 1980s the trust sold a Poussin, a Turner, a Rembrandt and several other Old Masters to various galleries and museums, raising over £2 million in the process.

*The Times* described the founding of the Cubitt title and fortune in the following terms in 1961: 'Thomas Cubitt was the prodigious builder (1788–1855) whose massive achievements including most of Belgravia, Bloomsbury and Pimlico made him the "spec" builder par excellence and a millionaire in those far-off Victorian pounds.'

# Raffaello Bacci £30m

*Van hire entrepreneur*

dob *c.* 1938

In 1951 Raffaello Bacci, a 13-year-old working-class Italian boy, left the small Tuscan town of Lucca to come to England for a holiday. But he stayed to help in his grandfather's lamp-making business.

The business was highly seasonal and every Christmas a boom in orders would carry them through the next year. Hiring transport to distribute the Christmas orders proved progressively difficult, giving young Bacci an idea for a new company. In 1965, together with a cousin, he bought 4 vans and went into business for himself. Within 3 years he had 56 vehicles. Today the company, Salford Van Hire, has over 5,000 vehicles at depots in Manchester and Leeds. It is also involved in car hire.

It is now one of the largest commercial vehicle hire firms in Britain, with its latest accounts showing after-tax profits of over £2 million. The firm is wholly owned by the Bacci family, giving them a net worth of some £30 million.

Success means Bacci no longer needs to work a 16-hour day, though he still arrives at his Salford headquarters at 8 a.m. and works until 6 p.m. six days a week.

'Perhaps it's the immigrant thing, that we have to work harder than everybody else just to prove ourselves,' he says in his deep Mancunian accent.

His children, two daughters and a son, have all been privately educated in England and are involved in the family business. His youngest daughter Patrizia, in her early twenties, is now managing the company's latest venture in Florence.

Despite his wealth, Bacci lives modestly. His lifestyle is that of a fairly successful stockbroker. There is a Rolls-Royce, but he is most often seen in a Mercedes and home is a modest detached in the middle-class Manchester suburb of Whitefield.

'I suppose I could afford a bigger house in a better area, but where we are suits us. Anyway, what would I do with a yacht?' At the age of 52 Bacci admitted that he had often contemplated selling up or heading for the stock market, but the prospect of losing control always stopped him. 'I don't think I could work for somebody else. Even if I retained majority control I'd still be responsible to other shareholders and I wouldn't like that. I enjoy what I do and hopefully I can keep on doing it.'

*Earl of Bathurst*

encester, which was sold in 1969. In 1975 the Earl and his wife were separated and they divorced a year later. He later remarried. Lord Apsley, the Earl's eldest son, is heir to the title.

## Earl of Bathurst    £30m

*Landowner*

dob 1/5/27

A former lord-in-waiting to the Queen and junior Conservative minister, Lord Bathurst owns the 15,000-acre Cirencester Park estate in Gloucestershire which includes some of Britain's best farmland.

The Earl was a keen polo player and former Master of the White Horse Hunt until 1966. He only took government office in 1957 on condition that he could always hunt on Tuesdays. He resigned from the government in 1962. Once an escort to Princess Margaret, he married a Gloucestershire woman in 1959. In 1966 his wife Judith opened a boutique in Cir-

## Michael Birchall    £30m

*Property developer*

As a Wigan estate agent, Michael Birchall grew fed up with seeing the property developers he knew making large sums of money from their deals. He decided to join them. That was in 1979. Today Birchall is a multimillionaire from his property trading via his own company, Sibec Developments, which completes huge deals all over Britain. He has his own executive jet.

Birchall, the son of an estate agent, qualified as a surveyor in the 1960s with a Wigan architect. He first worked at his father's office, Hilton and Laylan, where he had 35% of the business. He stayed on for another 11 years after his father died in 1968, but at the age of 35 he 'didn't want to sell houses for the rest of my life', as he told *The Financial Times*.

So, with no money, he set up Sibec in a one-room office above a travel agency in Wigan. It was named after his stepson Simon and daughter Rebecca. 'My biggest decision was whether to have a telex or not. My wife would answer the phone – we had the luxury of two lines.' An old lady came in to do the books.

He needed to find some lucrative deals to make money. They came in the shape of residential land speculation and a refurbished shopping arcade. As a result, in its second year Sibec made £200,000 profit on a £300,000 turnover.

Later he was involved in a series of developments in northern and Midlands towns, costing over £100 million all told. While visiting America in 1980 he saw the potential of the new leisure shopping complexes that were then opening up. So he opened a whole series of offices in America and Canada. He is also building a huge new town for 15,000 people in Majorca, costing £400 million.

In 1988 Sibec made £12 million profits, an increase of 135% on the previous year. Birchall had been planning to float the group on the stock market, but abandoned those plans with the October 1987 crash. He now intends to keep Sibec private. He controls around 50% of the shares.

Birchall lives on a 350-acre farm near Wigan. He is noted as a generous host and entertains City property analysts lavishly. His name, *The Financial Times* reported, 'has passed into City entertainment history with an epic journey by Orient Express to Walsall'. The £50,000 jaunt for 200 guests with breakfast and lunch on board and champagne flowing all day was 'money well spent', Birchall told Julia Bright, the former diarist on *Business* magazine.

In 1990 Sibec was badly hit by the property slump and went into administration, although its properties are still worth over £30 million more than its debts.

# Alan Bristow £30m

*Helicopters and transport entrepreneur*

dob 3/9/23

The term bulldog breed could have been coined for Alan Bristow, a tough business man who made his name building the largest helicopter operation in the world.

A wartime sailor who joined the Fleet Air Arm in 1943, Bristow once described himself as 'red, white and blue to the core'. His pugnacious style was evident when he was chief test pilot for Westland after the war for three years. He quit in spectacular style by punching his boss on the nose and storming out to join the French Foreign Legion as a mercenary. For two years he flew missions for the French in Indo-China, earning a Croix de Guerre and enough money to start his own helicopter company.

Air Whaling, founded in 1953, specialised in guiding whaling ships in Antarctica. Bristow developed a technique for firing the harpoons at the whales from helicopters,

but it was so deadly that the Whaling Commission banned all whaling from the air in 1954. But Bristow by that stage had sold the invention to a Dutch company and moved on to other helicopter work.

The oil industry proved to be fertile ground for Bristow, who was introduced to Shell by an old friend, the late Sir Douglas Bader. Bristow built up a large fleet of 140 helicopters supporting the oil industry round the world, particularly in the North Sea. He found time off to run British United Airlines in the late 1960s, leading the company in an industrial dispute with its pilots. In 1977 he had another dispute with his helicopter crews resulting in a public inquiry. Lord McDonald, who headed it, said of Bristow: 'He has a turn of phrase more suited to the barrack room than the boardroom.' By the early 1980s he had reduced his stake in the helicopter business, selling the equity to British & Commonwealth Holdings, an early backer. In 1983 the sale of a 7% stake netted Bristow £10 million, leaving him with 13%, valued at £17 million.

In 1985 Bristow led an abortive bid to take over Westland, where he had first worked. But the £89 million bid (into which Bristow had put £8 million of his own money) was eventually withdrawn. Later, during the 1985–6 Westland crisis, he claimed that he had been offered a knighthood in return for supporting an American takeover for the ailing helicopter group. But he vigorously opposed the US bid.

Today Bristow lives on his 1,400-acre Cranleigh estate in Surrey, working on a new project. He has sunk an estimated £10 million into designing a revolutionary rubber-wheeled tram and has a working model hurtling round the grounds of the estate. With a strong team of high-powered professionals he developed his prototype in just 16 months. His reward: a potential £40m contract to build a system in Southampton.

In 1977 Bristow was refused planning permission to knock down the Elizabethan manor house on his Baynards Park estate, which had been built by Sir George More, cousin of Sir Thomas More. The cost of refurbishment would have been £750,000. Less than two years later the house was burnt down while Bristow was abroad, and in 1980 he was given permission to build his dream house. By 1988 he had spent £1 million on home improvements, including a helicopter landing pad. As well as owning a six-seater plane, Bristow also has *Twirlybird*, a £1 million yacht, and a £300,000 Mediterranean penthouse and marina berth.

---

# Satish, Rushmie and Jay Chatwani   £30m
*Hotel and property owners*

In 1973, having followed his father's advice and gained a professional qualification in accountancy in Britain, Satish Chatwani was barred from returning to his native Uganda by President Idi Amin. But like so many of the Ugandan Asians expelled and dispossessed at that time,

*Satish Chatwani*

Satish and his two younger brothers have thrived in Britain. All three trained as accountants – two also married accountants – and built up an accountancy practice.

In 1983 they saw middle-range hotels as a likely area for expansion and bought their first hotel, the Bedford Corner Hotel in Bayley Street, London for £1 million. They spent a further £600,000 turning it into a four-star hotel. They also bought the Waverley House hotel in London's Southampton Row for £1.8 million in 1984 and spent another £3.5 million upgrading it to four-star status. Today they own hotels worth around £30 million through their private company, Kanta Enterprises.

In the summer of 1989 they took over a quoted builders' merchant, F. Copson, as a vehicle for their future ambitions, injecting the three-star Letchworth Hotel in Hertfordshire into Copson. They plan a chain of provincial hotels and they are also aiming to start a chain of nursing homes. Their plans suffered a setback in November 1989 when a rights issue to raise £8.2 million worth of cash to fund the transformation was largely ignored by the City. Only 9% of the new shares were subscribed for, the rest being left in the hands of the underwriters.

---

# Arnold Clark  £30m

*Car dealer*

Britain's largest independent car dealer is about as far removed from the 'Arthur Daley' image of the business as one can get.

Tough, stocky Arnold Clark is an elder of the Church of Scotland, and he has an unmatched reputation for fair play with his customers. That approach has paid dividends many times over for the son of a Lanarkshire steel worker, who learned his trade as an RAF mechanic at the end of the war.

By 1955 he had saved enough to open his first motor dealership in Glasgow's Kelvinbridge area. In the 1960s he expanded to run another five showrooms, and by the time he was 40 he was rich enough to retire. But the memory of his parents' struggle to make ends meet fuelled his desire to accumulate an abundant bank balance.

By 1977 he was big enough to make deals direct with manufacturers outside Britain and he also started taking over other car dealerships.

In 1988 he had 21 branches in the centre of Scotland. He sells over 20,000 cars a year. He also has a 17,000-fleet of vehicles for hire. He recently took over the Ron Hutcheson group in a £2 million deal.

The business, known as the Arnold Clark Organisation, has 1,000 employees. Clark, the sole shareholder, is renowned for his hard work, coming in at 8.30 a.m. and staying until 8.30 p.m. five days a week. He visits several branches each day to keep an eye on the business. In 1988 its turnover reached £111 million, with after-tax profits of just over £2 million. With a healthy asset base and reserves, the business would be worth £30 million on the stock market.

Clark's obsession with work contributed to the collapse of his first marriage. He now lives with his second wife in a large mansion half an hour from Glasgow. He has four grown-up sons from his first marriage and two sons and four daughters from his second.

He has taken up sailing and owns four yachts, including Simon Le Bon's old boat, *Drum*, which he bought for £250,000 in 1987. He frequently sails on the Clyde though not always without mishap. In the Tobermory race in 1988 *Drum*, with Clark at the helm, was hit by a Royal Navy submarine.

He is expected to expand his business network into the north of England in the 1990s.

# Joan and Jackie Collins £30m each

*Actress and Authoress*

dob Joan 23/5/33   Jackie 4/10/37

The two daughters of a show-business agent have become richer and more famous than even their late father could have hoped. Joan, the eldest, was still a stunning beauty as she approached retirement age. She was a *Playboy* centrefold at the age of 50. After three years playing super-bitch Alexis in the soap series, *Dynasty*, she is now branching out on a new career in novels and film production. She has had one best-seller with her first novel, *Prime Time*, and received a £1m advance for her second, *Star Quality*.

Jackie, her younger sister, tried acting but found her talent lay in writing steamy novels such as *The World is Full of Married Men* and *Hollywood Husbands*. Her total sales to date have been 100 million, and in 1989 she received a world record advance £10 million for three books.

Joan started out as a Rank starlet, appearing in best-forgotten films such as *The Girl in Red Velvet*. Along the way she acquired husbands. To date she has had four: the actor Anthony Newley was number two. Her fourth marriage, to former Swedish pop star Peter Holm, lasted barely a year. He was 14 years her junior. Her career really took off in the 1970s when she appeared in explicit films of Jackie's novels, *The Bitch* and *The Stud*. But it is her role as Alexis that made her an international star and allowed her to make some lucrative commercials, such as the Cinzano advert with the late Leonard Rossiter.

She has a Los Angeles mansion and a £2 million home in the south of France. She gave another south of France villa to Peter Holm after a bitter divorce battle.

Jackie lives in Beverly Hills with her husband Oscar Lerner, owner of the Tramp disco. Until the early 1980s they lived in London, but then decided to pack up and leave for California. Many of the characters in her novels are based on real-life figures she knows from the film world, but she refuses to reveal who for fear of precipitating huge libel claims.

Though her novels are full of sexual antics, Jackie herself leads a quiet life and drives a battered Cadillac. She told Jean Rook of the *Daily Express*: 'People dash up to me at parties to tell me the strangest things.... What goes on in Tinseltown makes my books read like nursery school.'

# Gordon and Richard Dick £30m

*Industrialists*

Richard Dick and his father Gordon run their family-owned business, W. Lucy, which makes components for the electrical industry, from their headquarters in Oxford.

The firm began as a small iron works and flourished to become a multinational concern selling products in every English-speaking country except the US. In the 1980s the company concentrated on four lines: electrical engineering, electricity industry boards, iron castings and property.

Richard Dick, who will one day inherit the family fortune, represents the third generation of the business family. After education at Cambridge University he worked within the electrical industry before taking a job on the board of Lucy in 1977.

He is a keen sailor and travels to Cowes in the Isle of Wight three times a month to go sailing. He owns a share in a racing yacht, a Sigma 33. His other hobby is looking after his 'modest' garden in Oxfordshire where he prides himself on his mixed borders, clematis and roses. He is a governor of the local school. Married, he has young children. His father Gordon is now well past retirement age and is grooming Richard to take over the family business.

Gordon is still chairman of the group, with Richard as secretary. In its 1988 annual report the holding company, WL Shareholding, made £2.6 million after-tax profits on a £21 million turnover. With no borrowings, cash in the bank and substantial fixed assets, it would command a price on the stock market of at least £30 million.

OPPOSITE: *Joan Collins* (left) *and Jackie Collins* (right)

# Lord Egremont   £30m

*Landowner*

dob 21/4/48

Crippling death duties have hit the Egremonts three times since 1952, but they still have large estates and art treasures.

The present Lord Egremont, who succeeded in 1972, lives at Petworth House in Sussex and owns a 12,000-acre estate there. The house itself is owned by the National Trust, as are a third of the art treasures inside. But the family still own

paintings by Van Dyck, Gainsborough and Reynolds and a famous collection of Turners, who stayed at the house and painted many pictures there. They also own a 4,000-acre estate in Cumbria and Cockermouth Castle, where Lord Egremont's widowed mother lives.

His late father was private secretary to Harold Macmillan when he was prime minister. Lord Egrement was present with his father in Macmillan's office during part of the crisis following the Profumo scandal. He later went to work as a publisher's rep in Scotland. He was working for an American senator during the Watergate crisis.

Lord Egremont is married to the former Caroline Nelson, a publishing heiress. He is also a noted author and has written four books under the name Max Wyndham. These include *The Cousins*, *The Ladies' Man* and *Dear Shadows*.

# Peter Fisher   £30m
*Computer distributor*

dob 27/11/49

It is not often that a social worker ends up a millionaire, but Peter Fisher has achieved that. He was a social worker from 1970 to 1980, but he was convinced that personal computers had a bright future in Britain. So in 1980 he founded a computer company with his wife, Pam, also a social worker. At the time they both worked for the London Borough of Wandsworth.

Called Pete & Pam Computers, it operated initially out of their living room. They flew to America to bring imported Apple software home in their suitcases. At first they continued as social workers but gave up when they found they had made £80,000 profit in their first year.

They rapidly grew to become Britain's second largest distributor of personal computers. Between 1982 and 1984 turnover doubled every year, and they outgrew their original base in the south London suburb of Streatham. They then opened a second base in Rossendale in Lancashire, near to where Peter Fisher went to school.

By 1984 the Fishers felt that the company had grown so far that it was slipping out of their control. They called in a management consultant and decided to appoint professionals to run the company, taking a backseat role themselves.

In 1988 the company came to the stock market with a £50 million price tag. By then Peter Fisher was deputy chairman with Professor Roland Smith as chairman. Pam was operations director but became a non-executive director. Peter Fisher lists family and local history as his hobby.

# John Joseph Gallagher and family   £30m
*Builders*

John Joseph Gallagher runs J. J. Gallagher, a very private building and plant hire firm in the West Midlands. The shares of the group are all owned by members of his family or family trusts which he has established. He has no shares in his own name.

In the late 1980s the company has enjoyed rapid growth, with after-tax profits rising from £274,000 in 1985 to just under £4 million in 1988. Turnover has similarly risen from £3 million to £37 million, while there are large cash reserves of £15.5 million. If the Gallaghers floated the company on the stock market or sold it privately, they could get at least £30 million for it.

Its latest scheme, to develop 64 acres of the old Park Lane site near junction 9 of the M6 in conjunction with the Triplex Lloyd group, should bring even more rewards to Gallagher. The site is being turned into a business park, and Ikea, the Swedish furniture group, has bought 15 acres for a superstore.

John Joseph Gallagher lives in the exclusive Solihull area of Birmingham. Though he hates publicity, he did make the news when he took over Wolverhampton Wanderers Football Club in 1986 as part of an eleventh-hour rescue package. Wolves had collapsed with debts of £1.75 million. Gallagher now owns the team while the Wolverhampton Council own the ground. Tony Gallagher, John Joseph's son, is known to be a close friend of Ken Wheldon, the former chairman of Birmingham City Football Club.

# Robert Gavron    £30m

*Publisher and printer*

dob 13/9/30

Although he originally intended to go to the Bar, Bob Gavron now runs Britain's second largest printing company. Only Robert Maxwell's (q.v.) is larger. The company, St Ives, was in the news in 1988 when it sued the Department of Trade and Industry for libel over a damaging advert in the DTI's 'Enterprise Initiative' campaign.

Gavron's family originally hailed from South Africa and they were appalled at the thought of their son going into industry. But the young Gavron was lured there by the late Geoffrey Crowther, the editor of the *Economist*.

He went into printing and, with the help of some City backers, bought the St Ives

printing group. After years of building up the company, he floated it on the Stock Exchange in 1985. It was a huge success and Gavron immediately embarked on a hectic takeover spree, gobbling up smaller printing companies who were happy to sell up. The shares were badly hit by the October 1987 stock market crash, though the company's performance has not been affected.

Gavron owns a Georgian house in Highgate with 2 acres of garden and superb views of London. He plays tennis or swims for an hour before going to work, and he has several outside charitable interests including helping handicapped children. He also served on the literary panel of the Arts Council from 1979 to 1983. He is a close friend of publisher Paul Hamlyn (q.v.).

# Dave Gilmour and Nick Mason   £30m

*Pop stars*

Dave Gilmour and Nick Mason are two of the original members of the hugely successful 1960s group, Pink Floyd, which made an amazing come-back in the 1980s. In the two years 1988 and 1989, Pink Floyd's income reached over £35 million, making them the seventh highest-paid performers in the world. They have also had huge success in the record field. In May 1988 their album *Dark Side of the Moon* finally dropped out of the American Billboard Top 100 chart after an unbroken 725 weeks. All told, by the end of the 1980s they had sold around 60 million albums, and the entire production of a German compact disc factory is now devoted to Pink Floyd CDs.

Pink Floyd were formed in 1967 under the leadership of Roger Waters, an only child who had been raised in Cambridge by his widowed mother. Through the 1960s they were at the centre of the psychedelic

culture associated with the drug LSD. In the 1970s their live performances were dominated by sophisticated light shows, fireworks, crashing planes and inflatable pigs.

In 1983 Waters left the band after a public row with Dave Gilmour, Pink Floyd's guitarist. Gilmour and drummer Nick Mason were rejoined by Rick Wright, who had retired from the band some years previously. Despite efforts by Waters to prevent them using the name Pink Floyd, they continued to do so and made a fortune on their spectacular tours. In 1984 he took them to court over the issue and a protracted legal battle followed, with no result in sight, though there have been reports that an out-of-court settlement has been reached.

Despite the legal wrangles, the Pink Floyd members have continued to play before thousands of fans. At Versailles in 1988 they played before 80,000 people, putting on a show with £1 million worth of lasers sweeping the sky. In the summer of 1989 they held a controversial concert in Venice before 200,000 fans that left a trail of rubbish and excrement in the city.

Gilmour and Mason have done well out of the tours and record sales. In 1989 Mason bought a 17th-century house near Hampstead Heath in London for £2.5 million, beating Dave Stewart of The Eurythmics to the property. Mason owns a collection of Ferraris worth an estimated £20 million.

# Edward Harrison   £30m

*Car dealer*

Thomas Cuthbert Harrison was in at the start of the motor age. After World War I he started work in Sheffield as an apprentice motor mechanic at the age of 14. In 1931, at the height of the Depression, he took the bold step of starting on his own with £500 of capital, and soon afterwards he had a Ford dealership at his modest garage in the city's Abbeydale Road. It was tough going in the Depression and war years. But with the great expansion of car ownership in the 1950s, the T. C. Harrison Group really took off.

In 1968 Harrison decided to finance further expansion by taking the group on to the stock market. New branches were established in Sheffield, Rotherham, Derby and Peterborough. The group also began distributing Ford trucks and JCB diggers.

Thomas Harrison died in 1981 and his son Edward took over as chairman. A year later the group won the coveted Ford National Gold Award. In 1984 Edward decided to take the group private again and, using the family's 37% stake in the business, bought out the other shareholders at a hefty 26p premium on the existing share price of 48p. The move valued the company at £16.6 million.

Today the group has its headquarters in London Road, Sheffield. It produced £2.2 million post-tax profits in 1987 on a £139 million turnover. With negligible borrowings and large cash reserves, the group could now fetch £30 million if floated on the stock market.

Edward Harrison lives in an old manorial hall in Derbyshire's beautiful Peak District.

# Peter Jarrold and family £30m

*Printers*

In the 1820s the Jarrold printing firm was established in Norwich. Today it is still family-controlled, and still printing in the city though its activities have now expanded to include department stores and publishing.

The business is run by Peter Jarrold, the chairman, who took over when his father died in 1978. Peter, who was educated at Cambridge and trained as a printer, joined the family firm over 30 years ago. He was appointed general manager within a few weeks of joining. His two brothers also work with him: Richard and Antony run the retail and publishing sides of the business.

Its 1989 accounts show that Jarrold & Sons is a healthy business, reporting £3.3 million after-tax profits. Since 1984 it has invested £10 million in new plant and machinery. It employs over 10,000 people and the various members of the Jarrold family hold over half the shares between them. If floated on the stock market, it could easily command £50 million, valuing the family stake at around £30 million.

Peter has a keen interest in modern art and is active in the cultural life of Norwich. He regularly attends productions at the Theatre Royal and Maddermarket Theatre in the city. His wife Juliet is a former actress. His interest in the theatre is wide ranging and he is on the board of trustees of the tiny Norwich Puppet Theatre, one of the few in the country dedicated to that form of visual art. A keen sailor, he keeps his $9\frac{1}{2}$m Swedish yacht at Woodbridge in Suffolk where the family were originally based. He has an ambition to sail round the world and if he can't realise that he will settle for the Atlantic. He also enjoys other sports, going skiing in the winter and playing golf and tennis .

He has said that he wouldn't mind taking up painting when he retires and enjoys reading when on holiday. He lives in a former pub just outside Norwich. It's not yet known whether his own children will be entering the family business although it seems likely. His daughter works for another publisher and his son works for Granada Television.

# Tim Kilroe £30m

*Building and aviation contractor*

When the young Tim Kilroe arrived from Ireland in the late 1950s, he went to Manchester to seek his fortune. He had little

Kilroe lives in a £900,000 home in exclusive Alderley Edge, one of Cheshire's most expensive areas. But wealth has not gone to his head. A devout Catholic, he sent all his five children to local Catholic schools. A man of modest tastes and very shy, he is happiest visiting Manchester's Irish folk clubs to indulge his passion for that kind of music.

His main extravagance is the turf. He travels around the British racing circuit to follow his own runners and regularly goes to bloodstock sales. His greatest triumph came in 1985 when his horse Forgive 'n' Forget won the Cheltenham Gold Cup, an appropriate victory for an Irish owner. A picture of Kilroe receiving the trophy from the Queen Mother takes pride of place in the Four Seasons.

Kilroe has his own helicopter for getting around the North West quickly. He also drives a Mercedes; the family Rolls-Royce is mainly used by domestic staff for errands.

money but huge ambition and was regarded as 'a wonderful worker who was obviously going somewhere', according to one former employer.

He quickly made his mark in the North West. Instead of doing a traditional labouring job, he hired his own equipment and became a sub-contractor. In the 1950s and 1960s building boom, Kilroe expanded his business through regular work on small civil engineering projects around Manchester.

Today his Kilroe Group, covering all areas of building and civil engineering, employs around 1,000 staff. With a £45 million turnover, it has worked on many of the North West's largest projects.

Tim Kilroe has a number of other businesses, including two charter airlines (Air Kilroe and Air Arran) which are based at Manchester airport. He also owns hotels, including the Four Seasons in Cheshire, regarded as the north's most expensive.

Air Kilroe is doing very well and has five aircraft. In 1989 it became the first airline to order a Jetstream Super 31, British Aerospace's new 19-seater feeder aircraft. A favourite with pop groups, media stars and sports teams, it is used by the likes of Bryan Robson, Barry McGuigan and Def Leppard.

## Kurt Kilstock    £30m
*Property developer*

dob *c.* 1925

During the 1980s Yorkshire-born Kilstock became one of the major property developers in America, particularly in New York.

Starting out as a Leeds developer, Kilstock's big break came in 1972, when he sold a majority stake in his company, London & Leeds, to Ladbroke. The deal gave Kilstock control of Ladbroke's property developments. In 1982 Kilstock moved to America to head development work there; he was particularly successful in New York and Washington. After five years, at the age of 62, Kilstock decided to branch out on his own again. He sold the stake he still had in London & Leeds to Ladbroke, and formed the Kilstock Organisation with his wife Faga and his sons.

Still highly regarded in the property

world, he has worked on several developments with Elliott Bernerd (q.v.), including offices in New Jersey.

# Paul and Robin Leach   £30m
*Builders*

Hubert Leach, a World War I veteran, started his own building company near London in 1933 after participating in several speculative building projects in previous years. He started modestly with shops and houses in Enfield, before moving on to building a housing estate at Waltham Cross.

During the war, when housebuilding virtually stopped, Leach built army camps for both the British and American forces. In 1949 his son Paul joined the business after two years' national service and became a site clerk. After working in all the company's operations, he joined the board in 1952.

A year later the company was hit by financial problems when building licences, which strictly controlled development, were hard to come by. But it survived with the help of its bank, and prospered. Hubert died in 1968 at the age of 68, leaving the business in the hands of Paul and his other son Robin, who had joined in 1962.

The company now carries out work all over north London, Bedfordshire and Hertfordshire. It is particularly strong in the Lea Valley, building office blocks, factories and shopping centres as well as housing developments.

In 1976 an Acton company, Lewis and Lewis, was acquired. Today the Hubert C. Leach group has some ten subsidiaries, and in the year to the end of December 1988 it made after-tax profits of over £5 million.

The company headquarters is Hamels Mansion, a large 400-year-old house in Hertfordshire, which was extensively restored by Hubert C. Leach from 1977 to

1979. The third generation of the family is now involved in running the business. Julian Leach, Paul's son, is a director of a subsidiary. Paul and Robin Leach live in large homes in Buntingford and Bishop's Stortford respectively.

# Alan Lewis   £30m
*Textile industrialist*

dob 2/3/38

Discipline is all to Alan Lewis. A regime of karate in the morning and weight training in the evening, combined with no alcohol or smoking and a vegetarian diet, have helped him to the top in the British textile industry.

He now runs Illingworth Morris. Pamela Mason, the former wife of the late James Mason, was a major shareholder. Lewis bought her shares in 1982 and launched one of the most bitter takeover battles in the City, culminating in his victory in 1983. In July 1989 Lewis took the company private, in a deal worth some £78 million. The move was not prompted through any hostility to the City, but Lewis wanted to take a long-term view, and felt that it would not be fair to outside shareholders to see profits

269

depressed while he was busy investing for the future through moves into Europe and the like.

Success was hard fought. Lewis left school in Manchester at 15 and went to work in a printing company to pay his way through university. He built up his business interests through an Isle of Man-based company and came to prominence with the Illingworth bid.

Today he lives on the 640-acre Great Hundridge Manor estate in Buckinghamshire, and relaxes by reading poetry. He is a devout Christian.

---

# David Lewis   £30m
*Property dealer*

Timing is something that David Lewis does not need any lessons in. A chartered surveyor by training, who came into the property world in the late 1950s, Lewis built up his own property empire through the 1960s and 1970s. He sold Cavendish Land, his quoted property group, for £45 million to Legal & General in 1973, just before the property crash which bankrupted so many other property developers.

'Heath and Barber seemed hell bent on expanding the money supply and the banks were begging us to borrow money. The property companies and the banks were equally stupid and none of us fully appreciated what was coming,' he later told *The Financial Times*.

He made £8 million out of the Legal & General deal, which was invested in building up a separate private property group. This had some problems in the 1974 property crash. At the time it had some £100 million of investment properties but NatWest supported Lewis and the business survived.

Lewis lives like a tycoon. In 1972 he bought Newsells Park, the 2,435-acre estate of the late Sir Humphrey de Trafford, near Royston in Hertfordshire. Also in 1973 he bought the 18,000-acre Stra-

thaird estate in Skye unseen for 'peace and quiet'. The deal, conducted in secret, left Lewis the owner of 40 crofts and half of the 3,000-foot Cuillin mountain range. But he did not like the estate much. Ian Anderson, lead singer of Jethro Tull, bought it in 1977. Lewis had put it on the market in 1974 less than a year after buying it. He said he had paid less than £250,000 for it.

In 1984 Lewis bought into Hampton Trust, a quoted property group. He injected some of his private interests in return for a 25% stake.

In September 1987 – just a month before the stock market crash – Lewis sold out to the New Zealand Aurora Group, which bid £100 million for the whole group. In 1989 Lewis was again in the news when he took Molyneux Estates on to the Unlisted Securities Market with a value of £10 million.

---

# Robin Lodge   £30m
*Computer entrepreneur*

Robin Lodge started his business career as general manager of a computer timeshare business in 1968. That was sold in 1975 to an American company and two years

later he branched out into software, founding Metier to market Artimus, a package used for project planning. By 1985 his was a highly successful company, with sales of over £70 million in some 36 countries worldwide. He sold the business that year to Lockheed, the American aerospace giant, for £75 million.

Two years later, on the day of the stock market crash in October 1987, he resurfaced by taking a stake with a fellow entrepreneur, Brooke Johns, in a small quoted shell company called Nesco Investments, which used to supply electricity to Nigeria. They used Baytree Investments, a Cayman Islands company they controlled, to make their move. Nesco is now moving into the computer business after two acquisitions.

In 1976 Lodge married Mary Groves, daughter of Sir Charles Groves, conductor

with the Royal Philharmonic Orchestra. They have three daughters. He lives on a farm in West Sussex, and lists his hobbies as music, vintage cars, country pursuits and farming.

---

# Lindsay Masters £30m
*Publisher*

Bryanston-educated Masters joined forces with the young Michael Heseltine (q.v.), an old Oxford friend, to buy up some near-bankrupt magazines from the old British

*Lindsay Masters*

Printing Corporation. These magazines, called the Cornmarket Press, were to form the basis of a highly successful publishing empire, renamed Haymarket.

Success did not come easily even in the London of the swinging sixties. In 1962 Haymarket hit rock bottom and Heseltine had to counter-sign every petty cash voucher over 50p, and only those with a writ attached were paid.

But eventually the magazine empire prospered with Masters playing a key role. His biggest coup was to launch *Campaign*, a magazine aimed at the advertising industry, which combined a bold layout on expensive paper with well-written news and feature stories about the burgeoning advertising industry. It became a money-spinner, and more similarly styled magazines appeared, including *Management Today*, *Accountancy Age* and *Computing*. Masters also introduced a much more systematic approach to classified advertising, requiring his sales staff to make 25 calls a day to potential advertisers to solicit business. A special filing system was developed to keep track of their efforts, and it paid off spectacularly.

Heseltine, who could claim that he was a millionaire several times over by the time he was 40, left the running of Haymarket to Masters while he pursued his political career. In the early 1970s Masters' great coup was to hire the young Maurice Saatchi (q.v.) as a graduate trainee at Haymarket at three times the normal salary. Saatchi was an invaluable asset to Haymarket but also learned several techniques that served him well in building up his huge advertising agency. Masters was an early investor in Saatchi & Saatchi, but was persuaded to sell his shares back to the two brothers, a decision which he later believed could have cost him millions of pounds.

In 1980 Haymarket sold a number of its leading titles to the Dutch VNU group for an undisclosed sum. Among the titles to go were *Computing* and *Accountancy Age*. It was four years before Haymarket was allowed to set up rival publications. In 1985 it entered the accountancy field again with a new magazine called *Account* which folded two years later after losses of

£2 million. It was a rare failure for Masters.

The group is still expanding into new areas, including the European market. Masters still keeps a close and shrewd eye on the business, which could command a price of well over £90 million if floated on the Stock Exchange or sold to another publisher. He runs Haymarket from offices near Hyde Park, though many of the consumer titles are based in suburbs.

---

# Lord Middleton    £30m
*Landowner*

dob 1/5/21

In a county with more than its fair share of wealthy landowners, few come more distinguished than the 12th Lord Middleton. Based at Malton in North Yorkshire, and educated at Eton, Middleton distinguished himself in World War II. He won a Military Cross as a major in the Coldstream Guards, was mentioned in dispatches and won the coveted French Croix de Guerre. His brother, a professional soldier, retired as colonel of the regiment.

Many of his cousins and relatives were soldiers or sailors and the web of family connections spans the British aristocracy, including links to the De L'Isles and the Earls of Cromer. One notable relative was his great-uncle, Sir Alexander Penrose Gordon Cumming, who founded MI6.

In the 1870s the Middleton lands ran to 99,576 acres, scattered across Ross in Scotland, Yorkshire and the Midlands. Their holdings put them among the top 50 landowners in the United Kingdom at the time. While the precise current acreage is unknown, the huge Ross estate, covering 63,000 acres, has been sold to the Wills tobacco dynasty. Most of the Yorkshire lands, and some of those in Nottingham, Lincoln and Warwick, are still believed to be in the hands of the Middleton family.

Middleton has been president of the

Yorkshire Agricultural Society, Britain's largest, and went on to head the Country Landowners' Association, which claims to represent the owners of over 85% of the agricultural land of the country. He sat as a County Councillor for North Yorkshire, is a Justice of the Peace for the East Riding and is the Deputy Lord Lieutenant of North Yorkshire.

He married in 1947, and his wife Janet is the daughter of an army general. She formed and chaired the influential city organisation known as the Lloyds External Names Association, representing those non-professional members of Lloyds insurance whose unlimited commitment of their assets is the foundation stone of the market. She did this in response to the scandals that swept Lloyds in the early 1980s, figuring Peter Cameron-Webb (q.v.). Two of their three sons went to Eton and joined the Coldstream Guards. The third broke with tradition and went to Harrow, and from there to Manchester University where he took an MSc.

# David and Doris Padley £30

*Poultry farmers*

The death of George Padley, a 57-year-old Lincolnshire business man, in a car crash on a Majorcan holiday in 1987, left his company in the hands of his wife, Doris, and his eldest son, David.

George was the archetypal self-made man. One of eight children, he was brought up near Sleaford and his only formal education was to primary school level. At school he kept some livestock and always wanted to be a farmer. After national service, spent as a driving instructor, he came home and married Doris, a local farmer's daughter. Setting up in business on his own at the age of 21, he began with an ageing lorry as his only asset. He went round local farms, buying live poultry and

taking it to market. Three years later he invented his own processing plant which plucked the chickens. This allowed him to expand.

By 1959 he had incorporated the business as a limited company and proceeded to teach himself management techniques. He later recalled: 'I studied every book and article on general management that I could lay my hands on. I gradually learned the principles and practice and applied them to my own circumstances.' He was a millionaire at the age of 42 and the business had grown to include farms and hatcheries, making it an integrated poultry-processing, arable-farming and vegetable-processing business.

Apart from his work, he had a strong interest in his local community and financed a nature reserve in Sleaford. He also helped local schools. Though his wife was badly injured in the crash which killed him, she remains director of the family company, G. W. Padley Holdings. David Padley is managing director while his younger brother, Steven, is also active in the business. David was educated at Oundle and married in 1987. The business has had its ups and downs. In the year to the end of July 1989 its turnover was £106 million with total assets of nearly £29 million. The group could command a price tag of around £30 million if floated on the stock market. All the shares are held by the Padley family.

# Nat Puri £30m

*Industrialist*

Nat Puri arrived in Britain in 1966 from his home near the Indian city of Chandigarh as a virtually penniless student. As he recalled: 'I came with only £600 and I didn't have a rich uncle.' With a degree in pure and applied maths, he got his first job in 1967 as an engineer with a Nottingham engineering company called Skerritt.

In 1976 he left to form his own engineering consultancy and in 1983 formed the Melton Medes group, where he is chairman. He set up an ambitious programme of takeovers: his first purchase was, ironically, Skerritt itself. Today Melton has an annual turnover of well over £96 million and embraces 20 companies with some 5,000 employees, of whom 2,600 are in Britain. Puri's interests include paper mills, carpets, plastics and construction. The group makes around £2.7 million profit, and Puri intends to bring the group to the stock market.

Puri hit the headlines in 1988 when he tried to take over British Shipbuilders' Sunderland subsidiary. The bid was rejected and the yard subsequently closed. He also sought to take over the Rover group, but his bid was again rejected in favour of one from British Aerospace. He offered £400 million for Rover but the government preferred, instead, to accept the BAe offer of £150 million minus various 'sweeteners'.

Despite these setbacks, Puri has continued to expand his group, with a plastics venture in Hungary and the takeover of a French engineering company.

He lives in a mock-Tudor mansion on the outskirts of Nottingham. He is particularly shy of publicity – with good reason: in February 1989 armed raiders broke into his home, bundling him and his wife into a cupboard before fleeing with £20,000 cash and valuables. A high-speed chase down the M1 ensued with shots fired at the pursuing police, before the gang were caught and jailed.

Puri is a large benefactor of local charities. He is chairman of the Prince of Wales Trust in the East Midlands, and in July 1988 he gave £1 million to launch a Puri Foundation providing for the needy. He also helps hospitals to buy expensive new equipment.

He loves cricket and has helped with ground improvements to enable Trent Bridge to retain its Test Match status. Apart from wine, he has few passions other than working a 12-hour day. 'Business is an addiction. It is a sort of opium,' he once said. And he lives that way, rarely taking holidays.

# Lady Samuel    £30m
*Property developer*

Harold Samuel, later Lord Samuel, began his career as an estate agent, but by the mid-1930s he had devoted himself to central London property development.

During the war he acquired various central London properties, and in 1944 he bought Land Securities, a small company, for £20,000. When he died in 1987 it was the world's biggest property company with assets of more than £3 billion.

Samuel came from a comfortable middle-class background in north London and was educated at Mill Hill. In 1936 he married Edna, daughter of Harry Nedas. They lived in London near Regent's Park and on a large Sussex estate, where Lord Samuel collected Dutch paintings and grew flowers. They had two daughters, Carole and Marion, both born in the war.

Lord Samuel was a noted benefactor, donating £250,000 to Cambridge and a similar sum to London University. His own brush with controversy came in 1953, when an attempt to gain control of the Savoy Hotel Group ended in débâcle.

He left an estate of £26 million. His collection of paintings was left to Lady Samuel for her life, but was to be passed on to the City of London. In December 1987 she gave them to the City to go on permanent display, saying: 'I have had the pleasure of them for 35 years. This is what my husband wanted, that the collection should remain together and be on display at the Mansion House.'

---

# Arun, Nitin and Milan Shah £30m

*Jeans wholesalers*

dob AS 15/10/43   NS 2/2/51
MS 24/1/55

In 1969 18-year-old Nitin Shah arrived in Britain from Kenya, having abandoned thoughts of higher education and intending to make his fortune. For the first six months he found it difficult to acclimatise to his new life. After spells working in the shops of two leading retailers, he decided to branch out on his own. First he started selling jeans on commission out of a suitcase, and in 1971 he started a market stall in Notting Hill's Portobello Road, later adding another at Petticoat Lane's Sunday market so as not to leave stock lying idle.

This appetite for work did not prevent Nitin from enjoying London nightclubs into the early hours, although he got up at dawn for his market stall.

In 1973, with his elder brother Arun and younger brother Milan, he founded the Pepe group, with a boutique in the fashionable King's Road in London.

But the difficulty of getting the right clothes in the right colours and fabrics persuaded the three brothers to design and make their own. They soon found that other shops and traders wanted to buy their designs and a wholesale business mushroomed. By 1980 they had closed down the small number of boutiques they had established to concentrate on this.

Today most of their products are made in Hong Kong to rigorous Pepe standards and designs. The brothers had originally gone to Bradford to see if British mills would produce their clothes, but found them unwilling to cater for their particular designs. When the company was floated on the stock market in 1985 there were 15 times as many applications for the shares as the number available. Despite this success, the shares slipped back badly for a few months after the flotation, and it took some time to woo back City investors. By 1987 the company had expanded into America and Europe, and the shares had recovered on the back of an impressive profits record. In March 1990 it reported a fall in pre-tax profits to £10.5 million.

The company is based in the Willesden area of north London. Nitin is managing director, while Arun is deputy chairman and Milan sales director. They each have around 15% of the shares which are together worth £30 million.

---

# Earl of Shelburne   £30m

*Landowner*

dob 21/2/41

Heir to the Marquess of Lansdowne, Charlie Shelburne lives on a stately 5,000-acre estate in Wiltshire. His father now lives in comfortable retirement at another family estate of 10,000 acres at Meikleour in Perthshire.

Shelburne, who was formerly married for 21 years to the Earl of St Germans daughter, remarried in 1987. His name had been linked to the Duke of Westminster's sister, Lady Leonora Lichfield, the former wife of Lord Lichfield. But in the event, he married Fiona Merritt, a longstanding friend.

As deputy president of the Historic Houses Association, he is regarded as the coming man of the heritage movement and has turned his estate, Bowood, into a booming tourist attraction. He unsuccessfully contested Coventry North East for the Conservatives in the 1979 election and lists country pursuits as his hobby.

## Sir John Smith   £30m
*Landowner and financier*

dob 3/4/23

Friend of Prince Philip and former Conservative MP for Westminster, Sir John Smith owns large tracts of Regent Street and other lucrative London acreages. He was recently knighted for his services to charity, notably his £5 million gift to restore HMS *Warrior*, the navy's first proper ironclad ship, to full working condition.

Sir John, a director of Coutts Bank and a keen historic buildings enthusiast, loves the sound of church bells, and has personally funded the restoration of bells at 80 churches around the country. He lives on a large Berkshire estate and was once Lord Lieutenant of the county.

## Charles and Edward St George   £30m
*Lloyd's underwriters*

dob CSG 21/6/25   ESG 6/3/28

When Lester Piggott, the jockey, was seeking to raise £1 million for his bail after being arrested on tax evasion charges, one of his great friends, Charles St George, came to his rescue and chipped in £25,000. For St George, an ex-Coldstream Guards officer, the money was small beer. Together with his younger brother Edward, he owns a majority of shares in Oakley Vaughan, a leading Lloyd's underwriter, where he is also chairman.

The two men have the cash to indulge all their passions. In 1980 Charles bought Fort Belvedere, the Berkshire castle where King Edward VIII signed his abdication, for £650,000. Within six months he had sold it for £850,000. Edward lives as a tax exile in the Bahamas, where he serves as chairman of the Grand Bahama Port Authority.

Both have substantial racing interests. In 1975 Charles, nicknamed Lucky, paid $92,000 for a leading American horse. Many of his horses are trained by Henry Cecil, the top trainer; he also has horses under training in America. He is reputed to be an astute gambler, like many involved with the turf and, on the eve of his 50th birthday in 1975, he won £69,600 from a £275 bet. He lives in a Mayfair house and also owns a large spread at Newmarket, in the heart of racing country.

## John Sunley   £30m
*Property dealer*

Bernard Sunley started work at 14, 'muckshifting', but later became a prominent Mayfair property developer and builder in the 1950s and early 1960s. He also ran a thriving plant hire business based in Northamptonshire. His son John took over the business in 1964 on his father's premature death, and has found himself a regular in the gossip as well as the financial pages of the national media. In 1960, at the age of 24, Sunley broke off his engagement to an ex-debutante, Judith Lund. At the time he was working for his father and he was also a rally car driver. Six months later he was engaged again and was described in the press as 'young sporting Mr Sunley – he is keen on cricket, golf, and shooting – is regarded as one of the up-and-coming

the Arab put it on the market for £2 million, an increase in price of £68,750 per day. The Bernard Sunley group was also making a reputation in the late 1970s and early 1980s for its astute buying and selling of large blocks of London flats which were left in the hands of the financial institutions after the 1973–4 property crash. In 1977 Sunley bought many blocks from Sun Alliance, and bought 20 blocks from Legal & General for £27 million. Most were sold within a few weeks at a substantial profit.

## Countess of Sutherland £30m
*Landowner*

dob 30/3/21

powers in the building and property worlds'. He married but 13 years later the couple were divorced after they had had 4 children. John Sunley married again. But his second marriage also ended, with his ex-wife Annie receiving a £1 million divorce settlement. Sunley is a keen golfer and friend of Denis Thatcher. He lives in a large country house overlooking Sandwich golf course. He also has a town house in Belgravia. In recent years he has become embroiled in the bitter battle between Tiny Rowland (q.v.) the head of Lonrho and the Al Fayed brothers over the ownership of the House of Fraser Group. At one time he supported the Al Fayed brothers when they tried to become UK citizens, an attempt that they subsequently abandoned.

John Sunley's business affairs prospered in the late 1970s. The Sunley group won a £53 million contract in Dubai and John Sunley enjoyed close contacts with the oil-rich sheikhs. In 1977 he bought Heath House, London's highest house near Hampstead Heath, for £450,000. But in little over a year he had sold it for £625,000 to a Saudi buyer. In that time Sunley never lived there. Just 20 days later,

The Sutherland estates used to stretch over 1.3 million acres of the Scottish Highlands. Today they have shrunk to 100,000 acres.

The Dukes of Sutherland are often remembered for the Highland Clearances. In 1805 the then Duke ordered 5,000 crofters off his land to make way for more profitable tenants – sheep.

The Sutherlands have never been very successful with money. The 3rd Duke lost money on railways. The 4th Duke sold some Van Dyck paintings to buy land in Canada. It appeared to contain water so he promptly sold it but vast oil reserves were then uncovered there.

The Countess inherited the title Clan Chief of the Sutherlands in 1963. Her uncle had spent prodigiously and the Countess has been carefully trying to restore the estates ever since. They contain extensive forestry, fishing and grouse moors. In 1981 she sold a 1,000-acre estate in Stoke on Trent for £4 million.

# Sir Tatton Sykes    £30m

*Landowner*

dob 24/12/43

The Sykes family has been prominent in East Yorkshire since the end of the 18th century. The present baronet, Sir Tatton, is the eighth holder of the title and lives at the family seat and stud farm near Driffield. A previous Sykes gave his name to the Sykes Picot treaty signed in 1916, which put Lebanon and Syria in the sphere of French influence. Sir Tatton's fame comes from his racing interests: the Tatton Sykes colours of orange with purple sleeves are well known on northern racecourses, and winners have included Siegfried, Mirnaya and Exact.

In the 19th century the Sykes lands ran to over 30,000 acres. They are believed to be still largely intact. Sir Tatton was educated at Ampleforth, the prominent Catholic private school, and then went on to the University of Aix near Marseilles, before completing the traditional landowner's preparations for running his estates by attending the Royal Agricultural College at Cirencester.

# Lord Tollemache    £30m

*Brewer and landowner*

dob 13/12/39

Like a number of other titled families (see the Daresburys of Greenall fame), the Tollemache fortune is based on alcohol, in this case the Tollemache Cobbold brewing empire originally based in Ipswich.

The brewing interests were backed by enormous personal wealth. At the end of the last century the Tollemache lands consisted of the original family home, Helmingham Hall in Suffolk, with around 7,000 acres, and Peckforton Castle in Cheshire with 28,561 acres. There were also homes in fashionable parts of London. The latest indications are that the Helmingham estate is still over 7,000 acres but that at Peckforton is down to about 6,000 acres. Both estates have land worth at least £30 million all told. The present Lord Tollemache had the traditional Eton education followed by a spell in the Coldstream Guards. When he came of age at 21 he gave no less than six parties, all for his father's staff and tenants. He left the Guards after three years' service to train in estate management under the Queen's manager on the royal estate at Sandringham. And he struck up a close personal friendship with Prince Charles, who is godfather to his eldest son and heir. He married the daughter of a leading Staffordshire landowner, who is related to the Earl of Halifax. In 1977 they started accepting American tourists as visitors to Helmingham Hall.

He was quoted in the *Daily Mail* as

saying, 'We're not out to make a profit. We're just trying to keep the roof on.' He told the first group of visitors that during the Civil War one of the Tollemache women was rumoured to be Cromwell's mistress, while the rest of the household were plotting to restore the monarchy. The *Mail* reported that the Americans loved it.

Recently the Tollemache Cobbold breweries have been through several changes of ownership. In the early 1980s they belonged to Ellermans, who retained Lord Tollemache on their board. By 1989 the company had been bought by the Brent Walker (see George Walker) group. Lord Tollemache did not follow the company and, in the middle of 1989, brewing ceased at the Tollemache Cobbold site in Ipswich, breaking a link that was more than 260 years old.

# Ian Wood £30m
## Industrialist

A first class honours degree in psychology from Aberdeen University may not seem the obvious training for running one of Britiain's most successful companies in the hard and tough world of North Sea oil exploration. But Ian Wood, a tall powerful ex-rugby player with distinctive mutton-chop whiskers, has turned his family fishing boat business into the leading British offshore oil service company.

He very nearly did not go into the business at all. When his father's health was failing, he asked Ian to help out in the family business for a couple of years, after which he could leave if he did not like it. Ian did enjoy it, and quickly learned the ropes by teaching himself accountancy.

In 1964 the Wood Group had just 100 employees. Today there are over 2,000, and the group which is still family-controlled has expanded into the Middle East, the Far East and North America.

Although it has suffered sharp peaks and troughs according to the prevailing oil price and the consequent level of exploration activity, the Wood Group recently reported a surge in its profits to £4.5 million on a turnover of £82 million.

Known for his passionate commitment to Aberdeen, Wood is a considerable force in local politics. He sits on the board of the Scottish Development Agency and is bidding to head the Grampian Local Enterprise Company. He was named Scottish Young Businessman of the Year in 1979. He lives in an exclusive part of Aberdeen.

# Sir Nicholas Bacon, Bt £28m
## Lawyer and landowner

dob 17/5/53

The premier baronet of England, Sir Nicholas Bacon is a qualified barrister. He has a degree from Dundee University, where he went after Eton. A close friend of the royal family, he was page of honour to the Queen in the late 1960s. His father was the noted soldier and agriculturist Sir Edmund Bacon, and all four of his sisters have married into distinguished aristocratic families, including that of the Earl of Selborne.

One of the two titles he holds, that of Baronet of Redgrave, was the first baronetcy created in England and denoted with the letters Bt. The title was given to the eldest son of Sir Nicholas Bacon, Lord Keeper of the Great Seal to Elizabeth I, and father of Sir Francis Bacon, the great scientist.

The family seat and estates are situated near Norwich, and Sir Nicholas lives there with his wife and daughter. The estates run to some 14,000 acres.

# Remo Dipre   £28m
*Property developer*

dob 29/8/34

Italian-born Remo Dipre trained as an accountant in Italy, coming to Britain in the early 1950s to marry an English girl and make his fortune. He rapidly made a name for himself by buying a large site in Epsom. Just before the property crash in the 1970s he sold the site to William Stern, later to be Britain's biggest bankrupt. Through the 1970s Dipre built up a sprawling business empire, embracing publishing, property and housebuilding. He developed a reputation for taking on almost any project, no matter how difficult.

Extra facilities such as exercise rooms and saunas helped his houses to sell. In 1981, after a bitter takeover battle, Dipre acquired the Hawthorn Leslie industrial company for £4 million. Four years later Fairbriar, Dipre's building group, came to the stock market. In 1988 he bought the London Car Telephone Company, for £4 million.

# Cyril Gay   £28m
*Photocopying distributor*

In 1964 Cyril Gay decided that there was a market for an independent photocopying specialist and set up Eurocopy in Wakefield. With years of experience in the industry behind him, Gay, a gritty Yorkshireman, built the business into one of the largest

distributors of Japanese photocopiers in Britain. Some 80% of the business is in the south of England. In 1988 the company came to the stock market and has expanded since by acquisition. Gay holds some 70% of the shares.

Gay hates publicity, believing it will encourage beggars and burglars. But he is described by business contacts as extraordinarily wealthy, and a 'typical bluff Yorkshireman'. Early in 1989 Eurocopy paid over £14 million for the Equipu office machines company and Gay claimed that he could sort out its problems and raise margins from the feeble 7% nearer to Eurocopy's 26%.

Late in 1989 Eurocopy introduced a new combined black and white/colour photocopier from the Ricoh company. Stockbrokers who saw it on display at a Harrogate exhibition were so impressed that they immediately marked up the share prices.

# Peter Jones and family  £27m

*Industrialists*

dob PJ 5/8/36

Jones Stroud Holdings is one of those small companies that has been the backbone of the British economy for the last 20 years. With a majority of the shares held by the Jones family, this Nottingham company is in textiles and electrical insulation, making accessories and material for both industries. Originally a textile company founded in 1923, it started making parachute cords during the war. This side of the business was later adapted to the electrical industry and now it is the same size as the textile business.

With family trusts and their own interests, the Jones family have around 12 million of the 15 million shares in the group. With the group being quoted on the stock market, this stake is worth around £27 million. There are three Joneses on the board, Philip, David and Peter. They are all in their fifties.

In its results for the year ending 31 January 1990, the group made £6 million pre-tax profits on a £60.3 million turnover. The family maintain a very low profile.

# Sir Leslie and Lady Porter  £27m

*Food retailers*

dob LP 10/7/20

Sir Jack Cohen, the man who invented the 'pile 'em high, sell 'em cheap' slogan in his Tesco stores, started his business with a borrowed barrow in London's East End, using a £30 wartime gratuity. Later he went into self-service groceries and Tesco

was born. He was known as Jack the Slasher or Jack the Nagger. He had two daughters and saw them married to two business men. Hyman Kreitman, who married one of them, succeeded Cohen as chairman of Tesco. He retired in 1973.

The other daughter, Shirley, married Leslie Porter in 1949. Porter, who started as a car mechanic, went into car sales before the war. He was forced to drop this career to help his father out in his textiles business. After wartime service in the army, he came back to run the family firm,

and expanded into new areas such as furnishings and fabrics. After his marriage to Shirley Cohen, he was under steady pressure to join the Tesco business but always refused. In 1958 he finally agreed to sell some of his textile goods in Tesco, and in 1959 he became a consultant to the business, advising on non-food sales. In 1960 he surrendered and joined Tesco full-time, working to get a new division selling clothes and other similar items off the ground. Within 12 years the Home 'n' Wear division had achieved sales of £75 million and Leslie Porter had become chairman.

In 1985 Porter retired as chairman, by which time his wife Shirley was commanding the headlines. Married at 18 and with two children at 22, she found herself with time on her hands and a great deal of energy after her children left home. In

1972 she became a magistrate and in 1974 she was elected a Conservative councillor in Westminster. In 1983 she became council leader, and immediately embarked on a radical Thatcherite approach to local government. Services were put out to tender and the council pay-roll was cut by 25%. She embarked on a number of crusades such as cleaning up Soho and waging war on litter louts in Westminster.

She was dogged by controversy over a council decision to sell off three council cemeteries for 5p each. Lady Porter has vigorously denied the resulting accusations of asset stripping. Her rule in Westminster has been controversial, with many council officials finding it difficult to accept her style. Within four years of her becoming leader, 48 senior officials had left.

A recent *Panorama* television programme made further allegations about Lady Porter's stewardship of Westminster. This has not deterred her from the goals defined in her entry in *Who's Who*, where she says her hobbies are 'waste hunting' and 'cleaning London'. In October 1989

Lady Porter and her sister were left over £9 million each by their late mother. Sir Leslie also had some 8.5 million Tesco shares worth around £16 million. In 1986 he sold some £5 million worth of Tesco shares from the Cohen family trust.

Lady Porter was vindicated in the May 1990 local government elections when the Conservatives, against a national trend, increased their majority on Westminster Council.

---

# Harry Solomon    £27m

*Food distributor*

dob 20/3/37

The chickens, bacon, eggs and vegetables bought off supermarket shelves may have the supermarket's own brand label attached, but the chances are that they have been produced by Hillsdown

Holdings, a company hardly heard of in 1980. Today it is one of Britain's largest companies.

Hillsdown was the brainchild of two men, David Thompson (q.v.) and Harry Solomon. They met through their wives' chance encounter in 1964 at an ante-natal clinic in Hadley Wood, a north London suburb. Talking before their appointments, Judith Solomon discovered that Patricia Thompson's husband David was a butcher by trade but a wheeler-dealer at heart, who bought businesses and assets almost on whim. He needed a lawyer, and Judith Solomon mentioned that her husband was a newly qualified solicitor.

Thompson became his client and increasingly took a larger and larger share of his time. Solomon was quite happy with this, since the rest of his business seemed increasingly mundane, and Thompson's work was 'like a breath of fresh air', according to one recent study of Hillsdown.

In 1975 they formed a company to bring some order to Thompson's scattered interests, and called it Hillsdown after his north London house. In 1980 Solomon resigned from his law firm to work full-time for Hillsdown and the buying of new companies began in earnest. They came at a bewildering speed. In 10 years the duo bought 284 new businesses and borrowed £600 million to fund the purchases.

Some of their most successful purchases were from the receiver. They found nothing wrong with the businesses, just the way they had been managed. A new streamlined management system with speedy decision-making was installed, while Thompson and Solomon visited the factories frequently. This hands-on management worked wonders, and in the ten years from 1977 to 1987 profits rose from £116,000 to £110 million.

Thompson, who had always been the ideas man, leaving Solomon to run the business, stepped down from Hillsdown selling all his shares after April 1987. He recently sold the rest and no longer has any connection with the business. Solomon, a workaholic, who keeps fit by jogging and careful dieting, now runs Hillsdown as chairman.

# John Norgate    £26m
*Property developer*

dob 11/9/42

The 'golden corridor' along the Thames and the M4 motorway has been the base of John Norgate's fortune. He started Trencherwood Estates in 1971 by developing eight new homes in his Newbury garden. It was a business he knew well, having spent ten years as a property developer.

As high-tech firms moved into Berkshire,

so Trencherwood's building and development work prospered. In 1987 it sold 464 homes. It has now branched out all over the south of England and on the south coast. In 1990 it reported profits of over £8.7 million. Norgate himself has around 15 million shares in the business.

# Peter Prowting    £26m
*Property developer*

dob 19/12/24

In 1912 Peter Prowting's father founded a construction company in the London suburb of Ruislip. He died in 1977 and

Peter took over. He moved the company out of contracting and into housebuilding. Its first large-scale development took place in the Northwood area of Middlesex in 1953, using a modern interpretation of a Tudor design. Working mainly in the South East, Prowting built upmarket homes and managed to make twice as much as his rivals on every house he sold. The company was floated on the stock market in 1988, when it also expanded out of its traditional southern base. It was declared House-builder of the Year in that year.

Peter Prowting also has a big share-holding in Estates & General, another property group. He lists his hobbies as golf, gardening and jazz. Married twice, he has a daughter by his first marriage.

In 1966 he was in the news when he angered residents of Prah Sands, a Cornish beauty spot between Lizard and Penzance, by building a concrete cliff-top balcony in the garden of his large holiday home. The local council and the then minister of local government both condemned the balcony as unsightly. Prowting lived in Buckinghamshire at the time.

Though he remains chairman, day-to-day running of the company is in the hands of Terry Roydon, his managing director.

# Roy and Donald Richardson £26m

*Property developers*

dob 1930 (twins)

In the 1920s a couple called Richardson lived in a small house in the Black Country, paying 15s a week rent. But it was too expensive, so they moved next door where they paid just 9s a week for a two up and two down terraced house. That was where their twins, Don and Roy, were born in 1930 – in the shadow of the Earl of Dudley's steelworks.

The twins started their business career trading in ex-army vehicles after the war. They have worked together all their lives, cutting their property teeth in Stoke-on-Trent. Today they are the leading West Midland property developers and are now busy developing the old Dudley steel site into the 2 million square foot Merry Hill shopping centre, which includes a 10-screen cinema. They bought the site in 1981 for a rock-bottom price. They also have extensive interests in engineering and transport.

The brothers, who now live in Stourbridge and Halesowen, operate through their private company, Dudley, which has large stakes in two publicly quoted companies. They own all the shares in Dudley, which made £3.5 million after-tax profits in their last accounts. They also have another dozen significant private companies.

In 1969 they were locked in dispute with Alan Law, then the powerful regional secretary of the transport workers' union. Rather than bow to what they saw as pressure from Law, the brothers closed down Oldbury Transport, a road haulage business they owned. The move led Jack Jones, the T&G union leader, to brand them as 'cockroach capitalists', a charge fiercely denied by Roy Richardson, who said, 'The people I feel sorry for are the little men – and there are many in the Midlands – who are terrified of Alan Law and his regime.' In the 1970s they intended to build a new truck plant in the West Midlands with the support of the National Enterprise Board but nothing came of the plan.

Don Richardson hit the headlines before his marriage to a 24-year-old teacher when he held a stag party for 78 friends aboard the old *Queen Elizabeth* that cost £5,800 at 1966 prices. When he got married at Hagley in Worcestershire, he found a £6,100 cabin cruiser was waiting outside the church – a gift from Roy, his twin. Roy himself had had a £4,500 stag party when he was married earlier in 1966, with a £6,000 Rolls-Royce as a present from Don. Furious at the criticism levelled at them, Roy said: 'We have worked hard for seven days a week. We believe we are entitled to spend our money how we like. If others had worked as hard as us perhaps the country would not be in its present state.'

Strong supporters of the Conservative government, the brothers have had lunch at 10 Downing Street with the Prime Minister.

# Earl of Airlie   £25m

*Landowner*

dob 17/5/26

The Lord Chamberlain and a leading Scottish peer, the 13th Earl of Airlie enjoyed a conventional upper-class education – Eton and wartime service in the Scots Guards. He stayed in the army until 1950, when he went to the Royal Agricultural College at Cirencester to learn estate management. It was a wise move: the Airlie estates cover 69,000 acres in the rich farming county of Angus. He has two large stately homes on the estate: Cortachy Castle and Airlie Castle. He also has a home in London's fashionable Chelsea.

A riding accident in 1952 soon after his marriage to Virginia Ryan, the daughter of an American multimillionaire, put paid to his career of running the estates. He took up merchant banking, saying 'We all have to make a living now.' He joined J. Henry Schroder in 1953, and became a director

in 1961 and chairman 12 years later. He inherited the title from his father in 1968. Wisely, most of the family property had been passed on years previously: as a result his father's estate was valued at only £97,110. His father had also been Lord Chamberlain to the Queen Mother when she was queen.

In 1977 Airlie became chairman of the ultimate holding company, Schroder plc. In 1984 he had to give up the £168,000-a-year job to take up his royal duties.

In the early 1950s Airlie had been tipped as a suitor for Princess Margaret, but in the event it was his younger brother, Angus Ogilvy, who married into royalty. He married Princess Alexandra of Kent. Family relations with the British monarchy have not always been as close. The 4th and 5th earls forfeited their lands for joining the 1715 and 1745 Jacobite rebellions against the Hanoverian monarchy. But they were later pardoned and had their lands restored.

Airlie has six children. His heir, Lord Ogilvy, married Lord Rothermere's (q.v.) daughter Camilla in 1981. His eldest daughter married Hereward Wake, the heir of another Scottish landowner. As Lord Chamberlain, he cares for the royal residences, the royal art treasures and crown jewels. He also advises on royal warrants and titles. The only really controversial role of the Lord Chamberlain – censorship of the theatre – was dropped in 1969 to avoid embarrassment over the musical *Hair*.

# Stuart Balmforth  £25m
*Airline operator*

Stuart Balmforth helped pioneer a strategy that has since swept through British industry. As a manager of the small British Midland airline in 1978, he joined with two other managers including the better-known managing director, Michael Bishop (q.v.), to buy out the business.

Hundreds of buy-outs have taken place since, but not many can have been as successful and profitable as British Midland. Today it is one of the top airlines in Europe and challenges British Airways vigorously in the British domestic market. It has 100 arrivals and departures out of Heathrow Airport every day. Other airlines in the group include Loganair, Manx and London City, which operates from the new Docklands airport.

Balmforth had just under a quarter of the equity in the company when SAS, the Scandinavian airline, took a 25% stake of the enlarged equity, valuing the company at around £100 million.

He was born in Derby and educated at local schools. He joined British Midland in 1960 at the age of 21 as assistant to the chief accountant. He rapidly showed his flair with figures, becoming chief accountant in 1967. In 1972, after a City takeover of British Midland, he became company secretary and was appointed to the main board. Today his main responsibilities include corporate administration and keeping an eye on the 12 companies in the group.

Married with two daughters, Balmforth is a keen golfer, tennis and badminton player. He is also chairman of a leading Midlands gymnastics club.

# Viscount Bearstead  £25m
*Financier and banker*

dob 9/12/11

The Bearsted title conceals one of the most famous banking and industrial names from the beginning of the century. Marcus Samuel, created Viscount Bearsted in 1925, founded Shell Transport and Trading, one of the 'seven sisters' oil companies that dominated the industry, and often the politics, of whole regions in the early part of the 20th century.

Behind the oil company, however, and

one explanation for its creation and growth, was the private merchant bank of M. Samuel, later to become Hill Samuel.

The bank was first floated on the Stock Exchange in 1960 and the merger with Hill took place in 1965. Apart from the bank, the Samuels owned about 14 acres of Mayfair, which had been bought by Sir Marcus Samuel in the first decade of the century. The ownership was locked into Samuel Estates Ltd, in which two other rich developers, Charles Clore (q.v. Vivian Duffield) and Jack Cotton, took a half share in 1961. Most of the company, apart from the stake sold to Cotton, was held in trust for the Samuel children, and two of them became 1960s millionairesses while still at primary school.

The present Lord Bearsted succeeded to the title when his brother died in 1986. He has been a director of the family companies all his life, apart from a spell of service in the Warwickshire Yeomanry during the war, when he won a Military Cross.

Educated at Eton and New College, Oxford, he has been married three times. The first marriage ended in divorce, and the second, to a daughter of Lord Cohen, ended when his wife died in 1983. He remarried in 1984, to the widow of Michael Pocock CBE.

He maintains the family tradition of medical charity, sitting on the boards of the Royal Free Hospital, the Norwood Home for Jewish Children and the National Association for Gifted Children.

There is a small estate in Scotland and the family home is a gracious manor near Reading. In the House of Lords, Viscount Bearsted votes with the Conservatives.

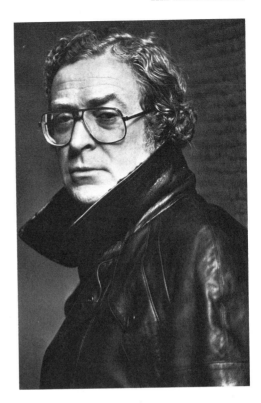

# Michael Caine    £25m

*Actor*

dob 14/3/33

Son of a Billingsgate fish porter and a charlady, Michael Caine (born Maurice Mickle-

white) was born and raised in two rooms in London's Elephant and Castle. He was an evacuee during the war. When he was just six he stayed with a policeman's wife who beat him until his ears bled and locked him in a cupboard. But he was rescued by the NSPCC and sent with other evacuees to a big country house.

He first became interested in acting as a 16-year-old pupil at Wilson's Grammar School, Peckham. He peered into a drama class to gain a closer look at a girl he rather liked and fell through the door. The teacher, who was short of boys in the class, immediately enrolled him. His interest in acting was further heightened by regular visits to the cinema.

A series of dead-end jobs followed – mixing cement, making pies and working with a pneumatic drill – before he did his national service. He saw action in Korea and was later one of the British army's best marksmen before wangling his first job as a tea-boy on a film set. In 1953 he became a general dogsbody for a Sussex repertory company. In 1955 he came to London to work under Joan Littlewood, the leading theatre director of the day, learning new acting skills all the time.

After ten years in bit parts on stage and television, his first starring role came in the film *Zulu*, where he played an upper-class officer, a role far removed from his Cockney background. He had changed his name to Caine after seeing the film, *The Caine Mutiny*. His big break came when he starred as Harry Palmer, the Cockney agent and womaniser, in the 1965 film of Len Deighton's book *The Ipcress File*. Later his role in *Alfie*, also as a Cockney womaniser, made him a star.

Throughout the swinging sixties he lived in London, enjoying flings with starlets and revelling in his reputation as a ladies' man.

In 1979 he moved to Hollywood, complaining he could not exist under a Labour government that had taxed his earnings at 98%. He bought a £10 million Beverly Hills mansion but returned to Britain in 1987 as he missed his old haunts and he wanted his daughter to be educated at an English boarding school. He bought a £2 million house at Henley, overlooking the Thames, where he settled with his second wife, Shakira Baksh, a Guyanese beauty queen.

Caine has made over 60 films and while some were savaged by the critics, there have been memorable ones such as *Educating Rita* and *The Fourth Protocol*. In 1986 he won an Oscar for *Hannah and her Sisters*. He can now command well over £1 million a film and two films in 1987 earned him £3.5 million. He also made £1 million for his part in the television serialisation, *Jack the Ripper*.

Apart from his films, Caine also owns a third of Langan's Brasserie, founded by the late Peter Langan. In 1976 he put £25,000 into the venture. He is also developing multi-screen cinemas in Britain, and has a flourishing wine business. In America he has invested in shopping malls and bowling alleys.

# Michael Carr and family £25m
## *Industrialists*

The chances are that a British car – be it a Jaguar or a Rover – will be coated in Carr's paint. Carr's is one of the leading suppliers of high-quality paints to Britain's engineering industry and takes pride in its innovation and technical excellence. Up to 10% of the company's turnover is spent on research and development. It is particularly renowned for its body priming paints and top coats for the car industry.

But its position today is a far cry from the original Carr's factory founded in 1892 in Artillery Street, the heart of Birmingham's industrial belt. Founded by a local man, Arthur Carr, the company made coatings for bedsteads and tin boxes. He shared the factory with his brother William, who ran a paper-making business, Carr's Paper.

Today the combined group operates from two sites in Birmingham, although it at one stage nearly moved out in its search for bigger premises. Its headquarters is a 4-acre site bought from Courtaulds in the West Heath area. Carr's is regarded as one of the top ten industrial paint groups in Britain and has over 500 employees.

The firm is highly profitable, making £2.9 million after-tax profits on a £39.5 million turnover in the year to the end of March 1988. With little debt and large cash reserves, it could easily command a price tag of over £40 million on the stock market.

The Carr family still have a majority shareholding in the business. Chairman Michael Carr is a grandson of the founder Arthur Carr. His brother David is managing director, and son Nicholas is a works director.

The brothers Michael and David, who are close, live in the same village near Coventry. Both are very publicity-shy, though they are known to have raised thousands of pounds for charity. David

Carr said: 'We just get on with our business quietly. We don't want to make a song and dance about it.'

## Sir Ivar Colquhoun (of Luss)  £25m

*Landowner*

dob 4/1/16

The present Laird of Luss is the 8th Baronet and the chief of Clan Colquhoun. The family were once among the largest land-owners in Dumbartonshire with over 40,000 acres. The Colquhouns are related to the Seafields (q.v.) who are still the fourth largest landowners in modern Britain. More recently Sir Ivar's daughter married the Marquess of Lorne, now the Duke of Argyll (q.v.). But the family have not been without their share of controversy and tragedy.

As a boy Sir Ivar was said to wander the estates around Loch Lomond, barefooted and in a kilt. Later he was educated at Eton and then joined the Scots Guards. Before World War II he was the lightweight boxing champion of the army. During the war he led units of his regiment in bayonet charges and raids. After the war he took part in a polar expedition.

In 1963 tragedy struck when the heir to the title, Torquil Iain, was found dead in bed at the age of 19. Torquil's brother, Malcolm, was once prosecuted by his father for allegedly stealing £300,000 worth of family heirlooms. Like his father, Malcolm was educated at Eton, and like many old Etonians, provides plenty of interest for the gossip columnists.

In 1974 the Laird was beset by yet other problems, this time in the form of an American claimant to the title. Bill Colquhoun, a former American naval officer, said that he was a direct descendant of a Colquhoun brother who fled the battle of Culloden, at which the English defeated Scots rebels in 1746. The American provided the *News of the World* with some racy copy, to which Sir Ivar did not respond.

Sir Ivar won a legal victory when, after 5 years' wrangling, the courts recognised his claim to 300 yards of foreshore at Finnart where BP had built a large oil terminal.

## Tom Farmer  £25m

*Tyre fitter*

dob 10/7/40

The youngest of seven children from a staunchly Catholic family, and raised in a three-room tenement, Tom Farmer had his first job, cleaning cookers, while he was at school in Leith, Edinburgh's run-down port area. When he left school he started work in the stores of a local tyre depot. He graduated to collecting old tyres and finally became a tyre salesman.

He left in 1964, at the age of 23 and he started his own tyre and car accessory business in an old grocer's shop in Edinburgh with an initial investment of £200. He opened the shop seven days a week and, in the era of strict resale price maintenance, started a discount operation. It was an immediate success and by the time he was 29 he was a millionaire.

Retiring to San Francisco to enjoy life with his family, Farmer soon became homesick and bored. Within three months he was back in Edinburgh, recruiting his old fitters and starting two new tyre and exhaust centres, which he called Kwik-Fit. He had been impressed by Californian muffler shops which fitted new exhausts while the driver waited, and he determined to try the same in Britain. Within 10 years he had 52 branches, and today there are over 600, which he oversees with an eagle eye.

Kwik-Fit, which came to the stock market in 1982, now employs 2,200 people and services 175,000 cars a month. In 1989 turnover was expected to top £200 million. Recently the large West German tyre maker, Continental, bought a 10% stake in the company.

## Maurice Hatter    £25m

*Industrialist*

In 1948 Maurice Hatter left the Army's Royal Signals regiment, where he had worked as a radio mechanic, with just £100 in his pocket. 'I had a lot of ideas about electronics. I got a few off the ground and started a nice little electronics company,' he recalls. Ten years later he sold that nice little company for £30,000. Two years later he founded IMO Precision Controls, based in north London, which markets electronic components for leading companies. In 1989 it made £4.03 million post-tax profits on sales of over £32 million. In the same year the Growth Companies Register singled out IMO Precision as a company with great potential. Hatter himself also made the news because his salary was over £1 million that year.

Hatter lives for his work and claims that 'money is a by-product'. He starts work soon after getting up at 7.00 a.m. After reading documents, he usually has a working breakfast with colleagues at 8.00 a.m. before driving to his factory off the North Circular Road at 9.30 a.m. He keeps going until 8.30 p.m. He lives in Regent's Park, London, and drives an Aston Martin. A father of four, Hatter is divorced. He supports charities, giving away £100,000 a year.

## John Lelliott    £25m

*Builder*

dob 3/4/35

Born in Teddington, south-west London, John Lelliott went to school locally and to the nearby technical college before being called up for national service. After two years in the Royal Engineers, he came back to 'civvy street' and went into the building industry, working in a small works department of a private firm. His crucial move came in 1963, when he joined a company called Winter & King as manager of their small works department. When the parent company went into liquidation in 1964, he bought the business and changed its name to John Lelliott. It has grown to become one of London's leading building contractors, with an annual turnover of £250 million.

After a disastrous foray into property development in the early 1980s, the company recovered to build a solid reputation, particularly for its refurbishment work. It aborted a stock market float at the time of the October 1987 crash, but could go for one again soon, if the property market picks up.

Lelliott has been married for over 30 years, and is a keen supporter of Wimbledon Football Club, where he is vice-chairman. In the mid-1980s he was involved in a project to build a new stadium for Wimbledon in south London, but difficulties with raising the £20 million finance have held it up.

Despite the recession in the building industry, particularly in the south-east, Lelliott managed to secure some £42 million worth of orders in December 1989,

including work on stands at Lords cricket ground. The group has plush headquarters in exclusive South Audley Street, Mayfair.

---

# Paul, John and Michael Madeley   £25m

*Ex-DIY business men*

Paul Madeley was best known as the Leeds United and England footballer who made his name in the late 1960s and early 1970s. He played in every position for Leeds except in goal, helping them to two league titles, the FA Cup, the Football League Cup and, twice, the UEFA Cup.

The late Don Revie described Madeley as his gilt-edged security, saying, 'wherever I ask him to play, he just nods his head and says "Right." We don't get much conversation out of Paul. He comes in, says "Good morning," stays at the forefront of training and goes home as quietly as he came.'

Madeley, who signed from Farsley Celtic in 1962, made a record 708 appearances for Leeds before retiring in 1981. He also won 24 England caps, despite telling Sir Alf Ramsey, the then England manager, that he did not wish to play in the 1970 World Cup.

On retirement he began helping his two brothers in the family wallpaper business. The Madeley brothers started their chain in 1969 with a single store in Otley, just when Paul was making his name as a footballer. By 1987 they had built it up to 27 stores, mainly in Yorkshire, but with a strong presence in Wales and the West Country. In 1984 it made the transition to out-of-town superstores and the business grew fast. By 1987 the brothers had built up a £30 million annual turnover and £2.4 million profits. They planned to sell the chain to their managers for around £25 million, but Philip Birch, then the boss of the Ward White group, pipped them at the post by offering £27 million for the Madeley business, £2 million more than the managers' price.

The deal left Paul Madeley with his own sports shop in Leeds, which he had opened in 1980 with his wife Ann. They live quietly in a four-bedroom detached house on the outskirts of the city with their two sons.

# Anthony and Nicholas Marmont and family   £25m

*Drink manufacturers*

In the 1920s the Marmont family bought out a Leicestershire drinks company called Carters, which had been established way back in 1894. Today the Marmonts still control most of the shares in the flourishing business, which makes its own drinks, bottles and vending machines. Its drinks are sold under a variety of labels, including Lemontime, Diet Lemontime, Zzipp, English Royal and Sunspel, as well as the Carters name.

The group has enjoyed good growth in recent years. In 1986 it reported after-tax profits of £1.1 million on a £26.3 million turnover. This rose to £2.4 million profits in 1989 on a £45.6 million turnover. The number of employees also rose from around 420 to around 600, spread over three sites in the East Midlands. Two of the sites are modern complexes, including a new packaging plant at Long Eaton, near Nottingham.

The Marmont family still keep a close eye on the running of the company. Anthony Marmont is president; his son Nicholas, as chairman, is responsible for day-to-day operations. Other members of the Marmont family, including Anthony's wife Angela, are also large shareholders in the business.

The Marmonts are a proud family, proud of their success in business and of their Leicestershire roots. They live within a few miles of the businesses in Loughborough.

# Kenneth Maud   £25m

*Industrialist*

dob 10/5/44

South African-born Maud started life as an investment analyst before going into merchant banking. He later joined Allied Technologies, a tiny 'shell' company, and turned it into South Africa's largest electronics groups, with 12,000 employees.

In 1986 he left South Africa and his 2,000-acre game reserve to come to Britain. With his clipped and precise tones, he sounds more English than the English. At the time he said, 'After the problems faced in South Africa, not least exchange controls, one can't help but feel that the world is your oyster from a UK viewpoint.'

Maud's first move in June 1986 was to take over an ailing grain storage company, Peek Holdings. Within three years he had transformed it through a series of takeovers into a high-technology electronics group, with interests in computers and global positioning systems relying on satellites. In the year to April 1989, profits trebled.

| £ Area | % | Number | Value £m | % |
|---|---|---|---|---|
| Landowners | 21.25 | 85 | 18,057 | 33 |
| Property | 10.75 | 43 | 3,161 | 5.7 |
| Builders | 5 | 20 | 1,137 | 2.0 |
| Hotels | 2.75 | 11 | 1,279 | 2.2 |
| Food | 4 | 16 | 1,428 | 2.5 |
| Brewing | 1.5 | 6 | 436 | .7 |
| Shops (retail) | 8 | 32 | 7,824 | 14.2 |
| Publishing & authors | 6 | 24 | 2,636 | 4.7 |
| Music & acting | 5 | 20 | 1,178 | 2.0 |
| Trading | .5 | 2 | 124 | .1 |
| Shipping | .25 | 1 | 930 | 1.6 |
| Finance | 6.75 | 27 | 3,326 | 6.0 |
| Shoes | .5 | 2 | 368 | .5 |
| Industrial (gen) | 26 | 104 | 10,728 | 19.7 |
| Others | 1.75 | 7 | 1,710 | 3.1 |
| Total | | 400 | £54.322 bn | |

Since bursting on to the British business scene Maud has made a reputation for spotting and hiring top executives, and one rival has commented on his skill in recruiting top managers.

Maud returns to his native South Africa at least four times a year to keep an eye on his game ranch and other assets left behind because of the strict exchange controls. Wildlife conservation is a major interest and back home he can watch giraffes, zebras, antelopes, leopards and baboons in his back garden in the Northern Transvaal.

He is a regular at the RAC golf club in Woodcote, South Oxfordshire. A self-confessed workaholic, Maud also spends much of his life in aeroplanes jetting across to his official home in San Diego, California, where his three children are being educated and to South Africa where he maintains citizenship. His English home is in Abingdon, Oxfordshire, where he lives with his wife Janice, and he also has interests in the Caribbean.

# Lord Mostyn    £25m

*Landowner*

dob 17/4/20

Lord Mostyn's horses have performed a good deal better than their owner, who has clocked up only five wins out of the 100 races he has ridden in over the years. From time to time both he and his wife have taken tumbles that have hospitalised them. His horses, in the hands of professional trainers Nicky Henderson and Richard Shaw, have won well over 30 races.

A well-known landed family in Flintshire, the Mostyns have been based at Mostyn Hall for generations. Previous Mostyns served as cabinet ministers and MPs for the county in the 19th century.

Educated in the traditional way at Eton and at the Royal Military Academy, Sandhurst, the present Lord Mostyn saw action with the 9th Queen's Royal Lancers in the Middle East in World War II. He was

wounded, mentioned in despatches and won the Military Cross before leaving the army as a major. He succeeded to the title in 1965, when his father died aged 80 after a distinguished career in World War I and thereafter as a Justice of the Peace and a Deputy Lord Lieutenant of Flintshire.

Mostyn's son and heir, the Hon. Llewellyn Lloyd-Mostyn, was also Eton-educated. He began his career as a barrister with the Army Legal Services and now practises from chambers in the Middle Temple.

# Neville Oldridge and family    £25m

*Sand and gravel merchants*

Four brothers run Britain's biggest private sand and gravel company, Sandtoft Tileries, which is also a major supplier of concrete and clay tiles. Its major plant is in Doncaster, but there are also five other works in the north, in Humberside and Nottinghamshire.

Sandtoft was established in the early part of the century, initially based at Briggs near Scunthorpe, and is entirely owned by the family. Neville Oldridge, the chairman, lives in one of the more upmarket areas of the Nottingham town of Retford. He bought his six-bedroom home in the early 1980s and has spent many thousands of pounds improving it. He is regarded as a brilliant business man, and is credited with the company's expansion.

He was struck by tragedy when a rare cancer, neuroglastoma, killed his adopted son. Today he is a very committed fundraiser for research into the disease.

In its 1989 annual results, Sandtoft produced £4.3 million after-tax profits on sales of £25 million. With large reserves and small borrowings, it could command a price of at least £25 million if floated on the stock market, turning the Oldridge family into millionaires many times over.

# Lionel Pickering £25m
*Ex-journalist and publisher*

The manor house in Derbyshire complete with tennis court and 50 acres is a far cry from Lionel Pickering's early days as a junior reporter on the *Burton Chronicle*. But this ex-journalist established one of the largest chains of free newspapers in the country, the Trader group, which he sold to the Thomson Group for more than £25 million in the summer of 1989.

Starting as a junior reporter in 1952 after his national service, Pickering (58) later became a sports reporter and sub-editor with the *Derby Evening Telegraph* before emigrating to Australia. He worked first with a news agency; then he moved from job to job, including a spell working for Rupert Murdoch, developing his skills.

Fed up with the rat-race in Australia, Pickering came back to Derby in 1966, bringing his Australian wife Marcia with him and moving into a terraced house bought for him by his parents. Having seen the success of free newspapers in Australia (82 in the Sydney area alone), he decided to try his luck in the East Midlands. For Christmas 1966 he started a free eight-page paper in Derby. 'I did the lot – sold the advertising, wrote the copy, did the layout and headlines and even delivered the bloody thing,' he later recalled.

It was a struggle at first. Despite living on just £5 a week, the paper was consuming his £800 savings and a lot of money from his parents. But in the end he survived and prospered by ploughing the profits into the business and expanding into other areas. In 1974 he opened a purpose-built factory to produce the papers. Learning about sales and management from reading teach-yourself books, Pickering eventually turned the group into a thriving business and the offers started coming in. He did not want to sell but in the end, he says, 'I thought of a number, doubled it and added 50% and Thomson said okay. My bluff was called.' In 1989 the

Trader group profits topped £2 million.

Though he has stayed on for a year to help Thomson with the takeover, Pickering says he has no intention of going back into free papers, but will develop the news agency, Raymonds, he bought 2 years ago.

# Malcolm Potier £25m
*Property developer*

The owner and laird of the Isle of Gigha, or God's Isle as it is called, is a property developer from Sevenoaks in Kent. After attending the City of London School, Malcolm Potier trained as a surveyor before working with a series of leading estate agencies. In 1982 he founded Tanap Investments and started building the office blocks that made his fortune, naming them after his daughters Tay and Tara. The name Tanap came from the first two letters of his elder daughter's name, Tay Nathalie Potier.

Gigha, 2 miles off the Kintyre coast, cost Potier £6 million, and he beat off challenges from Arab interests and Mick Jagger (q.v.) to become the new owner. The 6-mile-long, 2-mile-wide island had been expected to fetch about £3 million, but the level of interest doubled the price. The island boasts 160 inhabitants, a nine-bedroom hotel, six farms, a nine-hole golf course and Achamore House, surrounded by a famous rhododendron garden. Warmed by the Gulf Stream, the island boasts palm trees and a seal population.

Potier fell in love with Gigha during his first visit on a family holiday in 1981. 'When we left, I remember standing on the ferry and looking back at Gigha and thinking, "This is it. I'd really like to be able to own a place like that."' He came back every year for holidays and got to know the locals before submitting his bid to buy Gigha. 'Some people want to own a train set, but I have always wanted a Scottish island,' he said after the sale was completed.

Potier claimed that the island was the first possession he had ever bought for himself. He drives a battered D-registration car to prove his point. He lives near Sevenoaks, but has said he would not move permanently to Gigha, restricting his visits to six weeks a year. He also plans to keep the island much as it has always been, with as few changes as possible. He said he might expand the hotel by six bedrooms and turn it into a conference centre.

'I voluntarily entered into restrictive covenants that I would not change the island. But as far as I am concerned, there is no more beautiful spot on earth, and there is no way I would want to spoil it, or affect the pace of life led by our many friends there,' he told the *Daily Telegraph*.

revolution. The son of a prominent international lawyer who married the daughter of a well-known Cambridge boat-building family, Eddie spent several years of his childhood in India, before embarking on a thoroughly English middle-class education, which he did not take to at all. He was 'suspended' from Gordonstoun, and then went to a Reigate grammar school before finally ending up at a Haywards Heath secondary modern school. He led a self-confessed 'wild' life, and left school without O levels. His real love was sport and at Gordonstoun he held nine athletics records.

After his education Shah worked as an assistant stage manager in a theatre and had a small walk-on part in one play. This character was called Eddie, and the name has stuck with him ever since, replacing his real name, Selim Jehane. He went on to become production manager on *Coronation Street*, the hugely popular soap opera.

After a spell working as a space salesman on a free newspaper published by the *Manchester Evening News*, he decided in March 1974 to start on his own. With £3,000 raised by mortgaging his home and a further £6,000 invested by two friends, he launched the *Sale and Altrincham Messenger*. In the first year he lost £10,000 but built up a 35,000 circulation and went from strength to strength. By 1983 he had built up profits of £600,000 on a £5 million turnover, and enjoyed the fruits of success

# Eddie Shah £25m

*Publisher*

dob 20/1/44

Eddie Shah's roots gave few clues to his later role as architect of a British industrial such as a large BMW car and his own private plane – registration mark G-BOSS. A golf addict, he collects antique clubs and at one time played off a handicap of three.

But in 1983 he rose to national prominence when he had a huge battle with the then all-powerful National Graphical Association over union recognition at his Stockport works. Thousands of pickets attempted to besiege his plant, while he was subject to a number of death threats. Coffins were even delivered to his home for his family. In the end he won the battle and determined to break the grip of the print unions nationally by opening a new non-union national newspaper called *Today*. Despite its brave campaigning style and a bold use of colour, it was a financial disaster and had to be taken over by Lonrho. Eventually Lonrho sold *Today* to Rupert Murdoch.

Shah then retreated back to the north, and continued to run the Messenger group. But in 1988 he decided to enter television production, sensing that the television industry was about to undergo the same transformation as newspapers. He also had another go at launching a paper, but the *Post*, a tabloid without sleaze, was not a success and folded after just 33 issues. The experience seems to have left a scar on Shah, who at the same time sold the by then 20-strong Messenger chain to Reed International for £25m. He has retained the Messenger assets, valued at around £7 million and has said he intends to concentrate on television production, property development and providing seed-corn capital for small businesses.

# Rod Stewart £25m

*Pop star*

dob 9/9/45

'Do ya think I'm sexy?' Rod Stewart asks as he belts out the repertoire on stage that has earned him a £25 million fortune since

his first top ten hit 'Stay With Me' in 1970. Several of the world's most glamorous women may have the answer, including Joanna Lumley, Britt Eklund, Alana Hamilton and his latest love, top American model Kelly Emberg.

Stewart's love life has made him a natural target for the tabloid press and the gossip columns. But the brash Londoner, who is a fanatical supporter of the Scottish national football team, started life in very different circumstances.

Though his father bought Stewart a guitar as a birthday present, his first job was as a gravedigger. But as a guitarist with the Hoochie Coochie Men, who backed Long John Baldry, Stewart's pop career was born. He later became a lead singer with The Faces, and was with them when they made their breakthrough.

'Maggie May', his first solo hit in 1971, established Stewart as an international star, and from then on he was rarely out of the news. He was banned from British Airways flights after smashing up a plane in a drunken brawl. Heavy drinking, he felt, was part of the image of the hell-raising pop star. In 1981, after taking a special cure in Barbados, he managed to kick the

habit, and today rarely drinks more than a glass of wine. 'I don't think I live a rock'n' roll lifestyle any more. I don't smoke, don't take drugs, don't drink a lot. I don't even go out much,' he told the *Sunday Express*.

The old Stewart loved partying through the night, so much so that he exhausted Alana Hamilton, his first wife. She suffered from a debilitating fatigue syndrome, but Stewart wanted her to go out to parties even when she was pregnant. They separated in 1983 after just four years of marriage. They had two children, Kimberley and Sean, who live with Alana in California. Stewart lives there too but says he misses England enormously.

In recent years he has also tried to change his image as a womaniser. 'I don't want to be a sex symbol any more. I've proved that and it's so silly really. If George Michael wants to take over the sex symbol crown he can. I've given up all that.'

# Alfred and George Tack   £25m
*Sales trainers*

Alfred Tack has proved to be a workaholic throughout his life. At the age of 60, when most men would be thinking of retirement, he was presiding over 16 companies and writing best-selling novels before starting work. From 7.30 to 8.45 a.m. he would write 1,000 words in his neat long-hand before going to the office to preside over the affairs of his successful sales training organisation. By 1967 he had written a dozen crime novels and a further nine books on marketing and salesmanship. One book, *Sell Your Way to Success*, sold over 90,000 copies. Many of his novels cover murder and intrigue in the boardroom, which, he claimed, 'does go on, though not of course in my companies'.

Tack's energy was apparent on a trip to South Africa, where he managed to com-

plete a novel in six weeks, as well as delivering nine lectures and three radio talks and attending a number of business meetings.

Writing had been in his blood from an early age. Though he started out as a door-to-door salesman for ladies' wear at the age of 16, he also worked as a freelance journalist, getting articles published in various magazines. He later joined his elder brother George in running the Tack organisation, which in the late 1960s could boast a £3 million turnover from training salesmen from 7,000 British firms. They even managed the equivalent of selling coal to Newcastle by offering courses for American companies to train their salesmen.

Today Tack Industries still embraces sales training and printing but the company has also expanded into making heating and ventilation equipment. The two brothers, though now in their eighties, still control virtually all the shares in the group, and Alfred Tack remains as chairman. In the year to the end of March 1989, Tack Industries made over £2 million post-tax profits on a £34 million turnover. With negligible borrowings and substantial cash reserves, the business would be worth at least £25 million if floated on the stock market.

# Earl of Wemyss and March   £25m
*Landowner*

dob 19/1/12

When the two earldoms of Wemyss and March were created in the 17th century, the Wemyss family were already great landowners in Scotland. The 1st Earl built the harbour at Methil with his own money. By the late 19th century the lands ran to 57,000 acres in five Scottish counties and a further 5,000 acres in Gloucester and

Worcester. Most of those lands are now held in trust in the Wemyss and March Estate Management Co. Ltd, of which the present Earl is a director. He sits in the House of Lords as a Conservative.

A nephew of the Duke of Rutland, Francis David Charteris succeeded to the title in 1937. Educated at Eton and Oxford, he served as a major in the Middle East during World War II with troops from Basutoland where he had been a colonial administrator. After the war he took up his position as a leading Scottish aristocrat, serving as a Justice of the Peace and as Lord Lieutenant of East Lothian. A strongly religious man, he is a Lord High Commissioner of the Church of Scotland and was for a time the president of the National Bible Society of Scotland. His other activities include membership of the Queen's bodyguard in Scotland, the Royal Company of Archers, and acting as the Lord Clerk Register of Scotland and Keeper of HM Signet for Scotland.

In 1954 tragedy struck the Earl's family when his first son, aged eight, was killed in a car crash on the Croshill Dailly road in Ayrshire.

His son and heir, Lord Neidpath, was page of honour to the Queen Mother and is married to a Guinness heiress. He is extremely bright, with a doctorate from St Antony's College, Oxford.

Today the landholding has dropped to around 17,000 acres.

The present holder of the title is the 11th Baronet. Educated at Eton, he served in the 1st Royal Dragoons. A prominent huntsman, he is Master of the Flint and Denbigh Hounds. His father, also a soldier, had a distinguished war record. At the outbreak of World War II, he was a major in the Royal Horse Artillery and took part in the evacuation of Dunkirk. Sent to Singapore, he was captured by the Japanese and spent three years on the Siam–Burma 'death' railway, from 1942 to 1945.

The family is descended from a Welsh chieftain called Cadrod Hardd (Cadrod the handsome) who lived in Llanfaithley around 1100. The title is English, from Gray's Inn in London, and originated from the fact that a Williams-Wynn was Speaker of the House of Commons from 1679 to 1685 and sat as the MP for Chester through three parliaments. The same Williams-Wynn fell victim to a modern disease in that he was fined £10,000 for libel. In modern terms, this is about the equivalent of £10 million. After the revolution in 1689 the judgement was quashed.

Sir David's younger brother was killed in Ulster in 1972 while serving in the Army with the 14th/20th King's Hussars.

# Sir David Watkin Williams-Wynn, Bt   £25m

*Landowner*

dob 18/2/40

In the 1880s the Williams-Wynns were the 20th largest landowners in the whole of the United Kingdom and Ireland. Their estates were concentrated in three Welsh counties, Denbigh, Montgomery and Merioneth, but there were holdings in four other counties. The total then came to 145,770 acres.

# John Wolfe   £25m

*Airline operator*

In 1978 John Wolfe and Stuart Balmforth (q.v.) joined Michael Bishop (q.v.) to take over the then small British Midland Airways. They were in the vanguard of the management buy-out revolution which was to boom in the Thatcher years.

They were unable to find backing in the City for the takeover, so an American bank put up the £1.5 million needed, and they have never looked back. Initially they had

75% of the company, but were able to gain virtually all the equity later. Bishop had around half the shares, with Wolfe and Balmforth having just under a quarter each. At the end of 1988 they enlarged the equity by 25% which they sold to SAS, the Scandinavian airline. The deal put a price tag of £100 million on the business as a whole. This growth continued through 1989, despite the tragic M1 air crash.

John Wolfe, one of the original trio, is the man who runs British Midlands' day-to-day operations. He also buys and sells the aircraft in its expanding fleet. All this is grist to his mill, as he was in the RAF for three years. During his RAF career, he had a good grounding in the Far East where he was responsible for the movements of service personnel and their families in Singapore, then still a major British base.

He joined BOAC in 1961 and was responsible for ramp and traffic arrangements at London's Heathrow Airport. He later went to work for British Midland in 1965 as assistant charter manager at a time when British tourists were just discovering Spain in large numbers. In 1972 he joined the board, which enabled him later to participate in the buy-out.

Married with four children, he lives near Nottingham, where he grew up, and is a keen sportsman, listing golf, football, cricket and tennis as his hobbies.

---

# David Gestetner and family £24m

*Office equipment suppliers*

dob DG 1/6/37

In 1881 David Gestetner produced the first stencil by applying wax coating to some special long-grained paper he found on a Japanese toy kite. Thus was born the Gestetner duplicator and a business that grew to employ some 17,000 people in 1,300 offices worldwide in its heyday in the 1970s.

The first David Gestetner ran the business until the 1920s, when he was succeeded by his son Sigmund. By then an ex-employee had set up the rival Roneo company, but Gestetner still prospered. Sigmund died in 1956, while his son David was doing national service. David took a history degree at Oxford before joining the business.

It was not until 1972 that David and his younger brother Jonathan became joint chairmen. By then David had worked his way round the business, starting on the shop floor in the firm's Tottenham factory; he later worked for the American sales operation in 1963. He joined the board in 1967 and became export director.

Gestetner's profits peaked at £30 million in 1977. Five years later the company was reporting a loss of around £3 million and was struggling to find new products in an age when photocopiers were replacing duplicators. It suffered a severe blow in 1981 when a deal with the British Technology Group to market its Nexos word processor fell through.

In 1986 an Australian group took over the running of Gestetner in an agreed deal with the Gestetner family which owned around 28% of the shares. In return for injecting badly needed capital, the Australians undertook some severe cutbacks. The 14-acre Tottenham site was closed, sold and replaced by a new streamlined head office. New products were brought in and by 1988 profits were back up to nearly £28 million. David Gestetner remains a director of the company.

---

# Tony Travis £24m

*Timber merchant*

dob 18/5/43

In 1899 a timber-importing company called Travis & Arnold was founded. Today Tony Travis, a Harrow-educated barrister, runs the business, which has expanded to become a builders' merchant.

In 1989 it merged with Sandell Perkins, another builders' merchant, after a bitter takeover battle. The merger was nearly spoilt by the intervention of another group, Meyer International, which offered a much higher price for Travis & Arnold shares. But in the end the support of the Travis family, holding 38% of the Travis & Arnold shares, proved decisive, and the Sandell merger went through.

Tony Travis is now chairman of the enlarged group which is based in Northampton. Married three times, he lives in Fulham, London. His first wife was the daughter of Lord Pritchard, and his third is a daughter of Sir Peter Foster.

# Harry Goodman £23m

*Airline and tour operator*

The son of a machinist in London's East End, Harry Goodman left school at 15, an orphan with no qualifications. His father had died when Harry was two and his mother when he was eleven.

The man who today is one of the leading British tour operators had a hard time breaking into the business. Thomas Cook refused him a job as he lacked the necessary qualifications. After his national service, where he learnt to fight as a welterweight boxer, he did a spell as a travel clerk in Holborn. Then, at the age of 22, he bought his way into a travel agency in the London suburb of Sidcup along with two partners. They each put £500 in to the business and later branched out as tour operators, changing the name to Sunair. In 1971 Goodman sold his stake in the business for £70,000 and then took a two-year sabbatical to establish good contacts in the Spanish and Greek hotel businesses.

He then bought Intasun, the holiday firm, for £25,000, selling off its travel agencies to concentrate on package tours. The early days were tough but the big break came in 1974 when the Clarksons holiday business collapsed. Within 40 minutes of the news breaking, Goodman had hired three private jets and had them airborne with a buying team on board to approach the overseas hoteliers, who had panicked. 'We got reductions of 40% on room rates because we could assure them that their beds would be filled,' he told *The Sunday Times*. The move doubled his business that summer.

He repeated the move eight years later

when Sir Freddie Laker's operation collapsed, and made £1.5 million windfall profits. In the early days stories about Goodman's rise were legion. At one time he wanted to impress some business men by driving a Rolls-Royce but lacked the money to buy one. So he simply took one out on approval from a show room, then returned it after the meeting saying he did not want it.

He also developed a reputation both for his punishing working hours and, in the evenings, for his party-going. His lifestyle cost him his first two marriages, as he once told the *Daily Express*: 'A business like this can be disastrous for relationships. In my first marriage, if I saw my wife a month a year, it was a lot.' He proposed to Yvonne, a blonde air hostess on his private executive jet, the first time they met, asking her to be his third wife.

In 1982 Goodman was fined £200 for possessing a small amount of cocaine. But after that he successfully kicked the habit and is now a fervent anti-drugs crusader.

In 1987 he realised that he had no time to spend on his luxury yacht, *Europa Sun*, so he sold the 172-foot gin palace just two years after buying it, having only managed to spend four days on its decks.

That year, disenchanted with the stock market, he decided to take his company private so that he could concentrate on building it primarily into a new airline rather than a tour business.

---

# Don Lewin   £23m
*Retailer*

After he left the armed forces, Don Lewin worked in a variety of jobs, including one as a Kleen-eze brush salesman, knocking on countless front doors. He answered an advert offering an agency to sell greetings cards for a firm in Leeds, and he went to work with enthusiasm, finding a ready market in newsagents and chain stores. He even expanded and employed some sub-

agents. But he believed that there was a market for shops selling a wider range of better-quality cards and hit on the idea of specialist shops. He borrowed £100 from his father to open a bank account and establish his credentials.

In 1968 he opened his first shop in Essex selling American Hallmark cards. Named after his son Clinton (who was christened after the 1960s cowboy star Clint Walker), the group began to expand and soon there were seven shops, requiring Lewin to work 18 hours a day for seven days a week. He sold up on his 40th birthday, intending to take life easy.

But he soon became bored and before his next birthday was in business again with a new venture called Clinton Card Shops. When it came to the stock market in 1988, there were 72 shops and some 7 million customers mainly in Essex and London.

The British market for cards is worth £600 million annually, with large numbers sent every Christmas and St Valentine's Day. In the first half of 1989 Clinton Card sales rose by 66% to over £12 million, while the number of shops had risen to 135. Valued at around £30 million, Lewin and his family hold 75% of the shares, worth £23 million. Married for almost 40 years, he drives a Rolls-Royce.

---

# Allen Lloyd   £23m
*Chemist*

dob 9/5/49

As a Coventry schoolboy, Allen Lloyd was good at science and had a passion for cars. But lacking the cash to run his Mini Cooper, he sought a career that would earn him enough to fund his hobby.

A Boots chemist at a school careers meeting convinced him that he should become a pharmacist. Having worked in his mother's newsagent's shop at week-ends, he reckoned he knew a thing or two about retailing.

an aggressive takeover policy, expanding its range to nearly 500 shops, making it second only to Boots in the British market.

Peter Lloyd, Allen's younger brother, works in the group as development director. Allen Lloyd, an earnest chap, continues to indulge his passion for cars and drives a vintage Jaguar. He still has the original Mini Cooper whose upkeep propelled him into a career as a chemist.

---

# David Parker £23m
*Clothing wholesaler*
dob 18/5/38

David Parker's Sherwood group is one of Britain's largest bra makers and the main rival to the giant Courtaulds. Sherwood was established in 1947: it makes exotic ladies' lingerie and nightdresses. Worn by glamorous models, all these products are advertised in the annual report, making it almost a collector's item in the City.

Sherwood numbers the Burton Group, Asda, Littlewoods and British Home Stores among its clients. Parker was a former management trainee with Boots who moved into the textile industry. In 1968 he branched out on his own and took over Sherwood (then named Debfor) for £12,100 with the backing of a sleeping partner who has since sold out. In those days the group made golfing clothes as well as bras, but Parker abandoned them to concentrate on underwear.

Through the 1970s Parker expanded the business from its Nottingham base and in 1986 he took the group to the stock market. Since then it has made sizeable acquisitions, including a Dutch company. He holds just under 60% of the shares, worth around £23 million.

His strategy appears to be working. In the year to the end of June 1989 Sherwood reported pre-tax profits of over £4 million, a 36% rise in a year, while turnover rose by 52% to £33.4 million.

Initially Lloyd worked in Boots on Saturdays and in his holidays while he qualified as a pharmacist at Leicester Polytechnic. In his first year after graduating (the pre-registration year) he bought a house with the help of a £500 loan from his father. After 18 months he sold it, making an £8,000 profit. With money from his family and a NatWest bank loan, he bought his first shop. This was at Polsworth, near Warwick, and it opened on 4 February 1973. His wife Marilyn (they had met while he was a scout and she a guide) did the books. Today she is data-processing controller for the group.

'The early years were a struggle, although I had support from my family. I had to sell everything to get enough money – my car, my home, everything. I worked and worked and luckily everything began to take off from there,' he told the *Sunday Mercury*.

By 1986 there were over 100 shops. They offered self-service but, unlike some other cut-price drug stores, all had a pharmacist attached. The group is based mainly in the West Midlands, but after coming to the stock market in 1986 it has pursued

## The Stuart-Liberty family   £23m
*Retailers*

The Liberty shop in London's Regent Street is one of the West End's better-known and loved landmarks. It stands on the site where Arthur Lasenby Liberty opened his first store over 115 years ago, and it is one of the very few stores of any size still to have a significant family involvement. Two Stuart-Liberty brothers head major divisions of the company, which is publicly quoted, and Arthur Stuart-Liberty, son of the founder, sat on the main board as a non-executive director until his death in July 1990. The presence of the two brothers, Richard and Oliver, should ensure continuity of the Liberty family talent at the firm.

Generally, the family have kept a very low public profile, in sharp contrast with the store itself, which regularly promotes special offers in conjunction with papers like *The Times*. In the late 1960s and early 1970s Arthur's only daughter, Francesca, had a brief fling with the gossip columns who followed her long-legged, miniskirted moves through various other stores with intense interest. They had very mild things to report, especially after she was fired from Harrods after just five weeks because so many of her friends came to visit. She hung around for a brief period with the jet set, cruising on the Mediterranean on a huge yatch hired by Michael Pearson, heir to the Cowdray title and the Pearson fortune. She did not pursue her interest in stores and is not on the board of the company.

The store, with 21 branches all over the UK and one in New York, is noted for its distinctive clothes and for the wide range of its merchandise. Long before green issues became popular, Liberty was practising an early form of third-world awareness by selling goods from the poorer or more remote parts of the globe. They removed all golliwogs and related merchandise from the store after a single complaint.

## Robin Thistlethwayte   £23m
*Landowner*

In August 1988 a quiet and unassuming 52-year-old chartered surveyor had the shock of his life. Robin Thistlethwayte discovered he was the major beneficiary of his great-aunt's will. Mrs Eva Borthwick-Norton, who died at the age of 97 in February 1988, had left him the bulk of her estate, valued at £23 million. Her husband had died 38 years previously and they had no children.

The bequest, which was a 'complete surprise' to Thistlethwayte, came in the form of a 7,700-acre estate containing the village of Southwick, near Portsmouth in Hampshire.

Thistlethwayte moved from Oxfordshire to the manor house with his wife and three children to become the local squire. He promised to keep Southwick – which dates back to AD 40 – much as his great-aunt had kept it. There were no yellow lines or parking signs to disfigure the pretty village, with its 67 houses, two churches, farms, pub and post office. This delighted local villagers.

Mrs Borthwick-Norton left the estate to Thistlethwayte because she believed it should return to the family from which her late husband had inherited it. She also left the Thistlethwayte diamonds to his wife.

The estate comprised other farms in Hampshire and Somerset. Mrs Borthwick-Norton also left paintings and books to the Inland Revenue to cover death duties, and some £182,000 to her staff and friends and to charity.

In April 1990 four paintings worth over £6.5 million were accepted by the government in lieu of inheritance tax on the estate. The paintings included a Rubens

*Robin Thistlethwayte*

and two Gainsboroughs. In her will, Mrs Borthwick-Norton directed that the pictures should be displayed at the Royal Scottish Academy.

# Phil Collins   £22m

*Pop star*

dob 31/1/51

Raised in the London suburb of Hounslow in a classic three-bedroom semi with bay windows, Phil Collins now has a £1 million mansion in the Sussex village of Loxwood, complete with a £50,000 garden pond. Known locally as the Squire, he is extremely popular with the villagers, often nipping down to the local pub for a pint. His fortune is based on his role as drummer and singer in the group Genesis, which has sold over 50 million records in 15 years.

Acting and performing have always been in Collins' blood. His mother jointly runs the Barbara Speake Stage School, while his sister runs her own theatrical agency.

He started as a drummer with his own drum set at the age of three. Later his mother paid £3 an hour for him to have lessons. An aunt taught him to play the piano. His first professional role came when he was a child actor in Lionel Bart's musical *Oliver*, playing the Artful Dodger. After Chiswick Grammar School he was in a band called Flaming Youth and later joined Genesis as its only non-private school member.

In 1981 he developed a solo career – first as a singer with hits like 'You Can't Hurry Love' and 'No Jacket Required'. The latter won three Grammie awards in Los Angeles in 1987.

His acting career has also been successful, starting with a guest appearance in the American television series, *Miami Vice*. His feature-film debut was in *Buster*, where he played the great train robber of that name.

Despite his superstar image, Collins admits that he is 'no Don Johnson [the star of *Miami Vice*]. I think fans can relate to me rather than having someone just to admire because they're fantastic-looking.'

He is close to his family, particularly his elder brother Clive, who is a renowned cartoonist, winning the Cartoonist of the Year award in 1984, 1985 and 1987.

Known as a workaholic, Collins split up from his first wife, childhood sweetheart Andrea, which greatly depressed him. She lives in Vancouver with their two children, Joley and Simon. Collins has since remarried. His second wife, Jill, is an American and they have had a daughter, Lily.

# Tony Gartland   £22m

*Industrialist*

dob 23/6/41

Halifax-born and bred, Tony Gartland was an unlikely partner for Lord King, the chairman of British Airways, former boss of the Babcock Power business and friend of the prime minister.

But Lord King accepted the takeover of the Babcock business by Gartland's company, FKI. Based in Sowerby Bridge, FKI was floated on the stock market in 1982 and acquired a reputation for taking over under-performing engineering companies which would then be made to work by ruthless surgery.

When Babcock was taken over for £415 million in August 1987, there were 23 plant closures and 4,000 job losses in six months. Up to 30% of former Babcock executives left the enlarged company. But the 'marriage' was not a happy one and the two companies 'divorced' in August 1989. Gartland is now non-executive chairman of FKI plc.

Gartland started out as a chartered accountant who took over a small car park meter company in 1974. Since then 26 companies have been bought. He is never happier than when making a loss-maker profitable, cajoling his staff with engineering metaphors such as 'We're trying to get the flywheel to build up some more speed.'

# Kevin McDonald   £22m

*Plastic pipe manufacturer*

dob 20/10/33

Kevin McDonald started early in the plastics business and founded a small company, Bartol Plastics, which was taken over by

Hepworth Ceramics. McDonald became managing director of the plastics division but, by the late 1970s, he was convinced that he could undercut the major companies in this field by as much as 50%.

So, in 1979, he teamed up with Geoffrey Harrison and Brian Leesing to start a new business, pooling their different expertise. McDonald knew all about running a plastics business, Harrison was the technical and engineering expert, while Leesing handled the finances. The business was called Polypipe.

The three took a 125-year lease for £25,000 on land owned by Doncaster Council. They put their own money and funds borrowed from the bank into building a brand new 5,000 square foot factory, complete with the best tools and moulding machines.

The aim was simple. Polypipe was to grab as large a share of the market as possible by undercutting its bigger rivals on price by cutting out all the frills. Within two years they had expanded the factory to 25,000 square feet and a year later it doubled again to 50,000 square feet.

In 1985 the company came to the stock

market, and then embarked on a series of acquisitions to expand into different parts of the country. The strategy paid off. In March 1990 the half-year results rose by 34% and McDonald said that the results reflected continued expansion of the core business.

In March 1987 McDonald sold 4 million shares netting him £9 million. That still left him with 37% of the shares.

---

# Leonard Steinberg £22m

*Bookmaker*

dob c.1938

Belfast-born Steinberg first started in the bookie's business in Northern Ireland as a schoolboy. On Derby Day in 1954, at the age of 16, he took £3 of bets off his sixth-form colleagues.

Before the Irish authorities legalised betting shops in 1957, his optician father ran an illegal betting shop, and young Leonard added another. Though he trained as an articled clerk to a firm of accountants, the relaxation of the gaming laws convinced him that he could make more money as a bookie than by doing the books. In 1958, at the age of 21, he founded Stanley Leisure with two betting shops in the then quiet city.

In the mid-1970s he decided to expand to the mainland after an IRA terrorist blasted him with a shotgun when he opened his front door. His first mainland shop was opened in Stockport in 1976, but his big coup came in 1978 when he bought 109 shops from Ladbroke all in the north of England. Despite the high unemployment rate in the 1980s, the northern shops boomed. Steinberg also expanded into casinos and floated the group on the stock market in 1986.

The late 1980s saw Steinberg consolidate his base on Merseyside and other

Europeans go. Then we provide Chinese food and chopsticks,' Steinberg told the *Daily Mail*.

---

# David Brown £21m

*Truck designer*

dob *c.* 1925

Born and bred in Wensleydale, throughout his life David Brown has displayed the sort of dogged determination that Yorkshire cricket teams once had in abundant quantities.

Leaving school at 17 without any formal qualifications, he went to work in his father's logging business after ditching an engineering apprenticeship in Leeds. At the age of 32 he took his first salaried job in the Congo, where he set up a company involved in timber extraction and road building. During his African sojourn he took out the first of many patents.

In 1958, when his wife became ill, he sold up in Africa and returned to Britain. First he worked for the Leeds company

areas of the north. The number of betting shops passed the 200 mark, while in February 1989 Steinberg bought five casinos from George Walker's (q.v.) Brent Walker group for £25 million.

Steinberg learnt his management skills off his father, and pays his staff well. He has tried to remove betting shops' Andy Capp image by introducing carpets and television. An experiment of offering soft drinks ended after Stanley lost money on them. He introduced novel forms of betting, including how many goals Maradona would score in the 1986 World Cup Final. No punter managed to get it right and Stanley was reputed to have cleared £100,000 on the bets.

Steinberg himself is well respected in the betting world for his encyclopaedic knowledge and is a firm friend of the father of modern bookies, Joe Coral. Coral gave Steinberg his first cigar, and he is rarely seen without one today.

The group expanded into casinos – all in the north – and was floated on the stock market in 1986. The casinos are a world away from the top London gaming places frequented by Arab oil sheikhs. 'In Liverpool our clients are European and Chinese until half-past-midnight, and then the

Hunslet, where he designed tractors for use in mines. Then he became a chief designer for another company. Within two years he was chief executive but then switched to a competitor as managing director. This company was eventually taken over by Babcock and Wilcox, where Brown became director of engineering and market research. He left in 1973 at the age of 48, armed with nothing more than a briefcase full of patents and the determination to start his own business in the North East.

He sold his Gloucestershire house for £20,000 and moved into a council house in his new Peterlee base, using the proceeds of his house sale as capital. DJB Engineering exploited his own patents in four-wheel drive technology in a new dump truck. Initially, it was a struggle. The factory was so sparsely equipped that the drawings had to be done on the floor. There was not even a packing case to serve as a desk – and no phones to boot. Despite the oil crisis, Brown was a millionaire in four years. 'It did become rather embarrassing living in a council house with a Rolls-Royce and a Mercedes parked outside and an executive jet at the airfield,' he later told the journalist Chapman Pincher.

In 1985 he gave Caterpillar exclusive rights to sell the dump truck – now called the Artix – in a deal which netted him £30 million. That money enabled Brown in 1987 to buy the Bedford Trucks operation of General Motors, based in Dunstable, for an estimated £20 million. The new group, renamed AWD, makes trucks and a range of cross-country vehicles.

Brown has moved out of the council house and now lives in a luxury home near Thirsk, with three cars.

£ Some 215 of the 300 have declared a political allegiance
2 Labour
1 Green
4 Liberal
3 SDP
206 Tory

# Lord Home of the Hirsel £21m

*Landowner and politician*

dob 2/7/03

When Sir Alec Douglas Home lost the 1964 General Election to Harold Wilson, few people realised that he had been the last true Conservative aristocrat and grandee to occupy 10 Downing Street.

He had pipped R.A. Butler to the post of prime minister in 1963. But even within

the party the manner of his selection, by appointment rather than by any election, set in motion a process that led to the election by Conservative MPs first of Ted Heath and later of Margaret Thatcher.

Despite losing the election and later resigning as leader of the opposition in 1965, Home returned to high office as foreign secretary in the Heath government in 1970. When Ted Heath lost the 1974 election, Sir Alec resigned, and for the second time became a full member of the House of Lords. He had resigned his earldom in 1963 so that he could become prime minister, and in 1974 he was created a life peer as Lord Home of the Hirsel.

Born the son of the 13th Earl of Home, Alec Douglas Home was heir not only to a title but to vast Scottish estates. In the late 19th century the Home acreage, 106,550 scattered across six counties, made the family the 40th largest landowners in the UK. Today there are about 20,000 acres, much of it prime farming land.

At Eton, Home was noted more for his enthusiastic cricket than his brains. He went up to Oxford, continuing his cricket career. Conservative MP for Lanark from 1931 to 1945, he had the unfortunate task, as a joint Under-secretary of State for Foreign Affairs, of accompanying Neville Chamberlain to sign the Munich pact with Hitler in 1938. He was always more interested in foreign affairs than in domestic politics.

Outhwaite has encountered problems over huge losses incurred by his syndicates from the early 1980s.

Merrett has become a specialist insurer of satellites in space. Ex-President Reagan decorated him for organising and financing the rescue of a stray American satellite.

Oxford-educated, Merrett is a member of the Lloyd's ruling council. He is married to Helen Fearnley, a vivacious journalist who works for *Financial Weekly*. They first met when she went to interview him, and she later became Mrs Merrett the second.

In its accounts for 1989, Merrett Holdings made £5.8 million pre-tax profits on a turnover of over £2.3 million. It is quoted on what is called the over-the-counter market, though Stephen Merrett has indicated that he would like to go for a full stock market quotation.

## Stephen Merrett £21m

*Lloyd's underwriter*

dob 30/5/39

Stephen Merrett's father Roy was considered to be one of the great figures of the Lloyd's insurance market. He brought young Stephen into the market. In 1962 his father sold his underwriting agency for £500,000 though Stephen bought it back in 1976 for £3 million. Stephen has turned Merrett Holdings into the second largest underwriting agency at Lloyd's and he has over half the equity, which is worth well over £20 million.

As a young man in his father's agency, Stephen Merrett was often overshadowed by another rising star, Dick Outhwaite. Outhwaite broke away to establish his own business and a deadly rivalry ensued. It has lasted until the present day, with both running their own businesses, though

## Alan Prince £21m

*Ex-chemist*

dob c. 1944

In 1971 Alan Prince, a pharmacist based in Southampton, was fed up with managing shops for Boots or Westons. 'I wasn't pre-

success. By 1980 he had 25 shops, and by 1984 there were 50. That year Sharedrug, as his group was called, came to the stock market and was well received by investors. A year later, with profits rising strongly, there were 74 stores. The business also began to expand out of its Solent heartland into the Midlands and the West Country. Early in 1988 Prince decided to accept an offer from Woolworth for the chain, which was 145-strong by this time. The £32 million price resulted in Prince and his wife netting some £20 million. At that point he announced that he was retiring, at the age of 44.

pared to sit there and count the days to my retirement.' So he and his wife Sylvia, a legal secretary, sold a plot in their back garden for £3,000 and opened their own chemist shop in the Bitterne area of Southampton.

Prince had seen how cut-price chemist shops worked while on a trip to America. He determined to try the same in Britain, cutting out the wholesaler and having self-service in the stores. It was an immediate

# Shami Ahmad    £20m

*Clothes retailer*

dob *c.* 1962

By the age of only 27, Shami Ahmad was managing director of the Manchester-based 'Joe Bloggs' jeans and other trendy clothes businesses that he built up from

nothing to something worth £20 million in four years.

In the pursuit of his ambition – 'to turn Manchester into the new Milan' – he exudes style but hesitates to flaunt his £108,000 Ferrari Testarossa (market value £200,000) which he usually keeps locked in his garage. He makes do with his £100,000 Bentley Turbo, while his father, Nizam, who started a market stall when he arrived from Karachi in 1962, potters around in an £80,000 Rolls-Royce Silver Spirit.

After school each day as a youngster, the fashion-conscious Shami would travel 90 minutes by bus from Burnley to Manchester to help his father in his shop. He often heard him say: 'If you are going to aim, you might as well aim for the stars in the sky.' Friends describe Shami as hungry for success.

---

# Yaqub Ali £20m
*Retailer*

Yaqub Ali left Pakistan soon after the partition of India and arrived in Glasgow in 1952, with just £4 10s in his pocket. He started work as a door-to-door salesman. Today, with his brother Taj, he owns Europe's largest wholesale warehouse in the notorious Gorbals. It is called, appropriately, Castle. They also have an off-licence chain.

Despite being awarded the title of Scotland's most successful Asian immigrant by the *Scottish Business Insider* magazine, Ali lives a simple life with his Scots wife, apart from his one indulgence: a Jaguar. In 1989 his business made a £1.9 million profit on a £90 million turnover. A strong supporter of Mrs Thatcher, Ali organised a dinner for her on one of her visits north of the border. He also reckons the British economy would benefit from an influx of Hong Kong Chinese: 'New people work harder and new blood is good for business,' he said.

---

# Julian Askin £20m
*Industrialist*

Suffolk-born Askin was finance director of a British company at the age of 25. But he left after a year to seek his future elsewhere. Later, a little down on his luck, he tried to become a novelist and wrote *The Gold Connection*. Though it was no blockbuster, it encouraged Askin to start work on two further novels. But he never managed to finish them. Instead, in partnership with Hugo Biermann (q.v.), son of a senior South African admiral, he built up a computer and reinsurance business in Johannesburg between 1980 and 1983, when the pair moved to Britain to make their fortune.

In 1985 they made their first move by launching a takeover bid for Askin's old company, Energy Services & Electronics. The bid narrowly failed, but six months later they acquired a 61.5% stake in Thomson T-Line, then a loss-making timber merchant based in the Scottish town of Falkirk. The stake cost them just £500,000. A hectic series of deals and takeovers followed, as they traded assets and revitalised the group. In 1988 they bought Robert Sangster's (q.v.) Vernon's Pools business for £90 million. They left the running of T-Line to a professional manager, while they worked from their headquarters in St James's, London, planning new takeovers and disposals. They claim that they never argued and loved working together, so much so that they shared an office and an old-fashioned partners' desk.

In 1989 Thomson T-Line was taken over for £186 million after a bitter battle with Cyril Stein's Ladbroke Group. The deal netted over £21 million for Askin and Biermann, whose original controlling stake in Thomson T-Line had been whittled down by the issue of new shares to finance their expansion.

The pair resigned from Thomson in February 1989, saying they planned to concentrate on their overseas business activities. But, in fact, in October that year they emerged as a major new shareholder in George Ingham, a Halifax textile company. Chelsworth, a Guernsey company whose shareholders include family trusts of Biermann and Askin, took a 25% stake in Ingham.

## Lord Astor of Hever   £20m

*Heir and director*

dob 16/6/46

John Jacob Astor, 3rd Lord Astor of Hever, is a great-grandson of the 1st Viscount Astor, the fabulously wealthy 19th-century American entrepreneur. He sits with his cousin, the 4th Viscount Astor (q.v.) in the Lords, and both vote with the Conservatives. Lord Astor's grandfather, the 1st Lord Astor, was a long-serving Conservative MP and the title was created for him in 1956.

Apart from his service as an MP, the present peer's father was best known as the proprietor, later the life president, of *The Times* newspaper when it was still the voice of the ruling establishment in Britain. His connection with the paper continued through the ownership of Roy Thompson and only ended when Rupert Murdoch bought the paper in 1981. Educated at Eton like his father, Lord Astor did a spell in the Life Guards before retreating to tax exile in the south of France. In 1970 he married an heiress to the Harvey sherry fortune. The wedding took place at Hever Castle, one of the two homes owned by his father at the time, the other being at the 8,000-acre Tillypronnie Estate in Aberdeenshire. Hever was sold in 1983, a year before the 2nd Lord Astor's death, for £9 million. The contents, including a very valuable art collection, were not sold with the castle.

While in France, Lord Astor ran a property development business, and he was also a director of a company in New York which made Aids-testing kits. He has set up a company in London called Astor Enterprises, and intends to establish it as part of the London property scene. He lives in Kent with his wife and three children only 15 miles from the ancestral home, Hever Castle.

## Trevor Baines   £20m

*Entrepreneur*

Trevor Baines has an unusual background. His father owned a mine in Wales, while his mother was one of the first white women traders in Africa. After education at Stowe, he went to Liverpool Tech to do his O levels. He took time off to go to America for a couple of years, selling clothes and acting as caretaker on Errol Flynn's yacht in Jamaica.

At 21 he joined the family's African trading business – selling beads and the like – and was made a director at 25. In 1969 the business moved from Britain to the Isle of Man. Trendy Trev, as he is known, inherited £3 million from his father in 1972 and has been involved in several property deals on and off the island. In 1982 he also made a cheeky bid worth some £56 million for the exclusive Beverly Wilshire hotel in Los Angeles, but nothing came of it. He was also part of a consortium that at one stage owned the Miss World competition, but he sold out complaining that television had spoiled it.

Baines lives for much of the year on the Isle of Man with his wife Wendy, one of three sisters who make up the Brazil pop group, now called Press the Flesh. They have been married since 1979 and Trevor is heavily involved with the business, going to live concerts and even enduring a 13-hour flight to the Falklands when they went to entertain the British garrison. His wife, formerly Condessa Wendy Nicolau de Almeida Reid, is also a Portuguese port heiress.

A thirst for adventure and travel had led

Trevor to ride the Cresta sleigh run every winter since the mid-1970s. He has also been made a Fellow of the Royal Geographical Society for his inspired travel. He took a camel racing team to the middle of the Arabian desert on one occasion.

Known in the island for his charity work, he helps deprived Manx children with special treats such as visits to Disneyland. He celebrated his 50th birthday with a weekend of 1940s-style celebrations, culminating in the world's largest birthday party for 10,000 people.

# Major John Berkeley £20m

*Landowner*

dob 24/7/31

The Berkeley family, now headed by Major John Berkeley, own two of the largest estates in the west of England, both of which have survived intact despite severe estate duty problems in the late 1960s.

The first is the Spetchley Park estate of over 4,500 acres in Worcestershire. The other is the Berkeley estate in Gloucester. The latter contains Berkeley Castle, where the Berkeley family live. It is described as the oldest inhabited fortress in Britain and was first opened to the public in 1956. It was the scene of the murder of King Edward II on 21 September 1327. The occupant, Lord Thomas Berkeley, who was the King's custodian, was charged with the murder but acquitted. At one time or another the Berkeley family have held the titles of Viscount, Earl and Marquess. The earldom became extinct in 1942 and silver sold in 1960 to meet death duties on the Earl's estate made a world auction record of £207,000 at Sotheby's. A cousin of the Berkeleys sits in the House of Lords as Baroness Berkeley, one of only 20 hereditary female titles.

The army title sported by the present occupant of Berkeley Castle derives from his position as a company commander in the Queen's Own Warwicks and Worcester Yeomanry. His professional military experience was as a lieutenant in the 10th Royal Hussars. He was educated at the Oratory, a Catholic private school, and then went to Magdalen College, Oxford. He is the Deputy Lord Lieutenant of Hereford, Worcester and Gloucester, and was High Sheriff of Worcester in 1967 and of Gloucester in 1982. He still runs one of the very few private foxhound packs in the country, first started in the 12th century to hunt deer on the estates. He married the daughter of a landowner from Scotland in 1967 and they have two sons. As well as the two estates, the castle contains a magnificent art collection and many other priceless treasures.

# Hugo Biermann £20m

*Industrialist*

dob *c.*1950

Son of a South African admiral, Hugo Biermann started up a computer and reinsurance business with his partner, English-born Julian Askin (q.v.), in 1980. But in 1983 the duo decided to leave Johannesburg and move to Britain to make their fortune.

In 1985 they made their first move in Britain by launching a takeover bid for Askin's old company, Energy Services & Electronics. The bid narrowly failed, but six months later they acquired a 61.5% stake in Thomson T-Line, then a loss-making timber merchant based in the Scottish town of Falkirk. The stake cost them just £500,000. A hectic series of deals and takeovers followed, as they traded assets and revitalised the group. In 1988 they bought Robert Sangster's (q.v.) Vernon's Pools business for £90 million. They left the running of Thomson T-Line to a professional manager, while they worked from their headquarters in St James's, London, planning new takeovers and disposals.

They claimed that they never argued and loved working together, so much so that they shared an office and an old-fashioned partners' desk.

## David Bowie £20m

*Pop star*

dob 8/1/47

Born David Jones in the tough inner London district of Brixton, David Bowie's early life was as exotic as his pop career. His father ran a Soho wrestling club, while his mother was a cinema usherette. He learnt the saxophone and began playing with local groups while working in a West End advertising agency as a copy clerk. He moved out of his parents' tiny Bromley house into digs to pursue his musical career, but with little success.

Keen to hit the big time, Bowie wrote to David Bloom, the washing-machine magnate, seeking financial backing. Bloom, who later went bust in spectacular fashion, booked Bowie for his wedding anniversary party. But after two numbers, he told Bowie to clear off, complaining that the party was being ruined.

Undaunted, in 1969, after five flops, Bowie achieved his first hit with 'Space Oddity'. By them he had met Angie, the American model who was to become his wife. He was also playing every Sunday night at the Three Tuns pub in Beckenham, where he had a huge cult following. He changed his appearance, cutting his hair short and spiky and dyeing it orange, to create the character Ziggy Stardust.

The tabloid press was full of minute details of his sex life and drug-taking in the late 1970s. He parted from Angie and became a recluse, living in Berlin's Turkish quarter. He became the first pop star to admit publicly to being bisexual.

Turning to acting helped to rescue his career and life. He has appeared in a number of films including *The Man Who Fell to Earth*, *Just a Gigolo* and *The Hunger*. But it was his role in the 1980 Broadway production of *The Elephant Man* which really won him critical acclaim.

Today Bowie is linked in the gossip columns to Melissa Hurley, a ballet dancer. His relationship with his former wife Angie is bitter. They have both used the media to castigate each other and Bowie charges that she has no interest in their son Joe who, at Bowie's insistence, was educated at Gordonstoun.

In the late 1960s and early 1970s Bowie's 19 albums sold 19 million copies, while one tour in 1987 grossed £3 million. He has a £3 million Swiss château where he lives as a tax exile, and a £1 million apartment in Japan. He now lives a much healthier life, having kicked drugs and drinking very little.

## Barbara Taylor Bradford £20m

*Author*

A real Yorkshire lass born in the Leeds suburb of Armley, Barbara Taylor Bradford

is one of the world's highest-paid living authors. Before she even began to write her last three books she had received a $9 million advance from her three English publishers. Her books are described as 'romantic fiction' and have sold over 50 million copies worldwide, in 32 languages. Her first book, which she wrote when she was in her forties, was called *A Woman of Substance*, and dealt with the rags-to-riches story of a young Yorkshire girl at the turn of the century. In many of the regular interviews she has given, both here and in the USA where she lives, she has emphatically denied any connection between her own life and the life of the leading character in that first book.

She was the only daughter of middle-class parents who enrolled her in Armley library where she had read most of Dickens by the age of 12, and then bought her a typewriter. She earned her first pay cheque, 10/6d, at the age of 12 for a children's short story. Her formal education ended early and she was working in the typing pool at the *Yorkshire Post* by the age of 15. However, a year later she was a cub reporter and at 20 had become the women's editor of the paper. She then moved to London, where she was first

fashion editor of *Woman's Own*, and then worked on the *London Evening News*, *Today* magazine and finally the *London American*.

On Christmas Eve 1963 she married the American film producer Robert Bradford in London. They had been introduced by the press officer at the Savoy Hotel. Early the following year she left with him for New York, where she has lived ever since. She was always a working wife and initially wrote books on interior design. In an interview with Linda Lee Potter for the *Daily Mail* in 1984, she said, 'I kept starting novels but never getting past chapter five.' Then she gives a very important clue about her writing: she told Potter that she read an interview with Graham Greene in which he said 'character is plot'. Her books are based on very strong personalities.

Beginning with *A Woman of Substance*, all her books have been made into TV mini series which have been sold and shown worldwide. Her parents died in 1981, a traumatic event for her, but she still visits Yorkshire and her interviews are littered with references to her roots and the importance they hold for her.

---

# Marquess of Bristol £20m

*Landowner*

dob 15/9/54

'Johnnie' to his chums, the 7th Marquess of Bristol is one of the more colourful members of the British aristocracy, and one of the few in modern times to have had their collars held by the long arm of the law.

In September 1989 he was fined £3,000 on drugs charges at a court in Bury St Edmunds, after admitting that he had a habit costing him £1,500 a week. Five months earlier he had been released from prison in Jersey after serving seven of a twelve-month sentence imposed for smuggling cocaine. While in La Moye prison, Bristol loved to lord it up, according to a fellow prisoner, even to the extent of having a personal monogram on his uniform. More practically, the Marquess claimed to have made £4 million in property deals while a guest of Her Majesty. He was visited regularly in prison by his business manager.

Bristol has known wealth all his life. His Suffolk home, Ickworth House, is one of the finest mansions in the country. Though it is managed by the National Trust, Bristol lives in one luxury wing, surrounded by servants. He also has 4,500 acres surrounding the house. Shrewd investments in the early 1970s in oil speculation, money broking and sheep farming in Australia (where he has a 59,000-acre farm) helped increase his fortune from the £4 million he inherited to around £20 million today.

He was estranged from his late father, who disapproved of his fast and extravagant lifestyle, which included stunts such as flying to London by helicopter for a haircut. In the late 1970s he lived in

Monaco as a tax exile. He married a property magnate's daughter in 1984, and they celebrated their wedding with a £100,000 reception. Francesca, his wife, had been married before to an American rock musician and was a former Oxford Street shop assistant. But the marriage ended after two years when she fell for a Brazilian house guest.

His business manager said of Bristol once: 'John needs a close family unit and wants children so that he can pass on Ickworth.'

He once told the *Daily Mail*: 'I am scared to death of going broke. I am petrified at the thought of ever being poor and think about it every morning when I wake up.'

Controversy has never been far from Bristol. In 1986 a house guest at an Italian villa he had rented was found dead in his bed. The Italian police were called to investigate but the guest had died from a brain haemorrhage after a fall.

# Rose Bugden and Richard Gabriel  £20m

*Courier service operators*

dob RB 24/10/32

The mother-and-son team of Rose Bugden and Richard Gabriel run Interlink, one of Britain's fastest-growing courier companies. It was Gabriel who had the vision of a computerised delivery service that would take on the Post Office and British Rail. But it was his mother, Rose Bugden, who supplied the initial funding and who later kept the company from falling into outside hands.

By his own account, Gabriel was a failure at school, managing to pass only one O level (in maths), though his mother takes some of the blame: 'I moved him to a different school and he didn't stand an earthly.' Once out of school her son (the second of seven children) discovered a new motivation: 'I decided that I was going to do work I enjoyed doing.' He loved being a motorcycle dispatch rider but after an accident on his bike he spent some time in the office, where he discovered the clients were charged three times what he was paid. He then knew he wanted to run his own show.

With his mother, he did the rounds of several banks using as security the deeds of her little cottage in mid Wales. Richard bought a computer and learnt to program it from a book. But in 1982 the business he and his mother were building suffered a major setback when a fire destroyed the new computers at their Bristol headquarters.

A period of serious cash flow problems followed, during which the cottage in Wales again came in handy. Each weekend, Rose would take the deeds to the bank and get the money to pay the staff. The following Tuesday she would get the deeds back after paying in the company's takings. At one stage, she remembers, everything was staked on the business. 'Even the family home was mortgaged to the hilt. If it had all gone under I would not even have had the price of a caravan.'

Since then, Interlink has developed into a national service controlling 120 area franchises. When they started, they charged £8,500 for a local franchise. Today they cost around £250,000. The company joined the Unlisted Securities Market in 1986, and the family's 70% stake is now worth around £20 million. Rose Bugden still runs the company's Bristol franchise and has the job of keeping in contact with the others. She says her new wealth means she can have a larger garden and she intends to travel more in future, 'but neither of us ever worked for the money'. Before Interlink, she managed a nursing home for 15 years.

Richard drives a Bentley, an Aston Martin and a Range Rover when he is allowed to: he has frequently been banned for speeding. Meanwhile he has taken to the air in his Piper Dakota. 'There's no such thing as speeding up there,' he says.

# Earl of Carnarvon £20m
*Landowner, racing manager*

dob 19/1/24

The Carnarvon family are rich and aristocratic: the present Earl, the 7th, is said to be one of the closest family friends of the Queen and Prince Philip. He is also the Queen's racing manager, a post he has held since 1970. The Carnarvon title was originally created for a grandson of the Earl of Pembroke and its first holder had equine links with the royal family even then, as the Master of the King's Horse. In the 1880s the family had land in six English counties, totalling over 35,000 acres. The family seat, Highclere, is one of the few castles in the country not regularly open to the public. The current estates, including land in Somerset, are thought to be around 10,000 acres.

The royal connection has made the present Earl a deal more discreet than his father, who turned self-parody into a minor art form. *The Times* obituary did him generous justice with one of the most colourful and indiscreet pieces that it ever printed. It variously described him as 'a most uncompromisingly direct ladies' man', and 'an inveterate stage-door johnny'. Predictably his first two marriages, the second to the Viennese dancer and singer Tilly Losch, ended in divorce. He was widowed in 1985. *The Times* said of his routine in London that 'he held court at White's (which excluded women) and played bridge at the Portland Club, but his metropolitan base was the Ritz Hotel in Piccadilly. At the hotel the canny Carnarvon's chief concern was to find a suite, not so much overlooking the Park as overlooking the rent.'

The telegram he sent to Sir Jock Delves Broughton when he was acquitted of the murder of the 22nd Earl of Errol in Kenya in 1941 (on which the film *White Mischief* is based) is framed in White's and reads, 'Hearty congratulations on winning a neck cleverly.'

In his later years, the 6th Earl wrote

two books of racy memoirs, *No Regrets* and *Ermine Tales*, and he became an outrageous chat-show celebrity.

His father, the 5th Earl of Carnarvon, is best remembered as one of the people directly responsible for the discovery of the tomb of the Egyptian god king Tutankhamun. His sudden death gave rise to the legend of the 'Curse of Tutankhamun' which certainly did not affect his son who lived to the ripe old age of 88.

The present Earl has come in for some pointed comment in the gossip columns over the performance of the Queen's horses, but not apparently from his employer. Yet it is said that one of the Queen's real regrets is that she has never had a Derby winner.

# Barbara Cartland    £20m

*Author*

dob 9/7/01

Novels such as *The Wings of Ecstasy* or *Cupid Rides Pillion* have propelled Barbara Cartland to fame as the world's top-selling living author (her claim). With over 480 novels under her belt, total sales now exceed 500 million, and they flow at the rate of 23 a year.

Barbara considers herself to be queen of romantic fiction, and in an age of increasingly explicit erotica, she adheres strictly to old-fashioned chivalry. When asked to review Joan Collins' book, *Prime Time*, she responded in characteristic style: 'I couldn't believe my eyes when I started to read this sordid attempt at authorship. It sickened me – it's quite evil in the debauchery it portrays,' she said.

Twice married, first to Alexander McCorquodale and then, after she divorced him in 1933, to his cousin Hugh, her greatest claim to fame in recent years has been her link to the royal family. Her daughter, Raine, Countess of Spencer, is stepmother to the Princess of Wales. Her son, Ian, is chairman of Debrett's Peerage.

Her family background was wealthy, from a long line of Birmingham industrialists, though her father was killed in World War I, serving in the Worcestershire Regiment. But it is the novels that have really made Barbara Cartland wealthy.

Every day, fortified by a daily intake of 70 vitamin pills, she sits for two hours on a sofa with a hot water bottle on her feet and dictates around 7,000 words to one of five secretaries. One secretary told *Daily Express* readers that 'she goes into a trance. She sees it all happening before her.'

Her house, Camfield Place, near Hatfield in Hertfordshire, used to be the home of Beatrix Potter. It is decorated in the famous pink that has become a byword for Barbara Cartland. She is chauffeured in a vintage Bentley and entertains her friends and guests to afternoon tea. She also makes frequent appearances on television extolling the virtues of old-fashioned love and romance.

Outside her books, she campaigns for a variety of causes, including wages for wives and retaining prayers in school. 'The country is being divided. Only children who go to paying schools are being taught the wonder of prayer,' she once said.

Her entry in *Who's Who* at 15in is the longest, and catalogues all her novels and voluntary activities.

---

## Alan Clark   £20m
*Politician and landowner*

dob 13/4/28

In the 1990 House of Commons register of Members' interests, the Hon. Alan Kenneth McKenzie Clark, Conservative MP for Plymouth Sutton and a defence minister, states that, 'I own Saltwood Castle in Kent and farms in Wiltshire and Devon. My family own Eriboll Estate and Harbour in Sutherland.' Clark is a cousin of the Earl of Seafield (q.v.), the fourth largest landowner in the United Kingdom. He is the son of

Lord Clark, famous for his book and BBC TV series on Civilisation, and for being one of the great popularisers of high art. He was also exceedingly rich, having inherited a thread manufacturing fortune, Sudbourne Hall in Suffolk, a house in Grosvenor Square, London, and another in Scotland. He bought Saltwood Castle in the 1950s.

Alan Clark had a classic upper-class education – Eton, Oxford and the Household Cavalry, but is seen as a very unconventional Conservative in some ways. Totally devoted to Green causes, he never eats anything that has been killed in an abattoir, he dislikes nuclear power and he almost succeeded in getting a law on the statute books that would have labelled fur with the means used to trap the animal from which it came. None the less, he is pro capital punishment. He is also rumoured to be very critical of American influence in the UK. He says he is a rock-solid Thatcherite and he has held office long enough to prove it.

He really does live in Saltwood Castle, one of only four in private hands in the UK. It was restored in the 1940s. First constructed in the 11th century, it was from Saltwood Castle that Henry II's four knights rode out to Canterbury to murder Thomas à Becket. Five centuries later Elizabeth I dined there regularly.

The castle contains many of Lord Clark's papers and Alan himself is a military historian. His wife Jane is the daughter of a former colonel in the Duke of Wellington's Regiment.

actors – and one of the richest – thanks largely to the part of James Bond in the films based on Ian Fleming's books. At one stage in the 1960s he was earning the sum £1,000 an hour, 24 hours a day.

But his roots were far from the upper-class world portrayed by Bond. He left school at 13 during the war and took a series of temporary jobs on building sites, before learning a trade as a French polisher, for an undertaker polishing coffins.

After three years' service in the navy he was invalided out because of ulcers, but the experience left him with an abiding hatred of the snobbery and prejudice of officers. A spell of body building led him to London to win a bronze medal in the Mr Universe contest. He was captivated by the bright lights and stayed.

He made it into the infant British television industry, winning parts in *Dixon of Dock Green* before making his debut in films in 1956. But it was not until 1962, at the age of 32, that he was cast as Bond in *Dr No*. The film was an instant hit and the Bond legend grew. The third Bond film, *Goldfinger*, took $10 million in 14 weeks, a cinema record up to then.

After he tired of Bond, he went through a lean spell in the 1970s, but has re-emerged as a big star in the 1980s, winning his first Oscar for best supporting actor in *The Untouchables* and having a major role in the latest *Indiana Jones* blockbuster.

Cautious with his money, Connery lives in Marbella as a tax exile. He was careful always to claim his overtime on the Bond set and, in the last Bond film, *Diamonds Are Forever*, he demanded, and got, 12.5% of

# Sean Connery £20m

*Actor*

dob 25/8/30

If the ship that was supposed to be evacuating Sean Connery to Australia in 1940 had not been sunk, he might have gone there, stayed and become a clerk or waiter. Instead, he is one of the world's best-loved

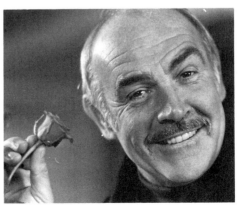

the profits. He has also been astute in developing outside business interests, including his own private bank, Dunbar & Co., based in Pall Mall.

After his first marriage to the actress Diane Cilento broke up in 1973, he married his second wife, Micheline, a year later.

# Catherine Cookson   £20m

*Author*

dob 20/6/06

If it had not been for a secretary in a publishing house, Catherine Cookson's career as a writer might never have taken off. She sent her first novel to a publisher who read three pages and then passed it to his secretary, saying 'This is no good.' But the secretary took the manuscript home and read it through in bed. 'The next day, she came back to the office and told her boss he was wrong, and that if he had any sense, he would go back to this book and look at it again,' Catherine Cookson told her friends at her 80th birthday party when she proposed a toast to all secretaries.

Some 80 novels followed, with 85 million copies sold worldwide, in 17 languages. Cookson is also Britain's most borrowed author. Of the top 100 titles taken out of libraries, at least a quarter are her works.

But success has only come after a hard and painful life. Born in Tyneside, the illegitimate daughter of an alcoholic mother who pretended to be her sister, she left school at 13 to work in domestic service. Later she moved south to run a laundry and then the workhouse in Hastings with 20 to 30 inmates. It was only in 1940, after she met and married a local schoolmaster Tom Cookson, that she was able to take up writing as a full-time occupation. She had developed an incurable blood disease, lost four babies through miscarriages and suffered a nervous breakdown. She started writing to recover from the breakdown. Her first novel, *Kate Hannigan*, was not published until she was 44. Her novels – usually set on Tyneside – are meticulously researched social histories rather than romantic novels.

She moved back to the north-east and lives in a large house in Northumberland, still with her husband Tom. In 1986 Bantam Press bought the rights to her next ten novels for £4 million. She is a generous supporter of charities and donated £800,000 to Newcastle University. 'I enjoy my money by helping sick children,' she says. Equipment she has donated to hospitals in Newcastle has helped turn desperately ill children into healthy ones.

# Norman Draper   £20m

*Industrialist*

dob *c.*1921

Norman Draper started with his father's firm of tool suppliers in 1936, and was paid just a few shillings a week. Norman, then 15, began his first day with the company as a van boy, but by the end of the week he was already selling tools from the back of a second-hand van.

The company was founded by Norman's father, Bert, in 1919. He started supplying hand tools after learning the skills of engineering in an aircraft factory after World War I. In the 1950s the company expanded so rapidly that it outgrew its original premises in Kingston-on-Thames and moved to Chandler's Ford. It is still privately owned and very much a family concern. Norman, who always sports a bow tie, is joint managing director of the firm with his son John.

Draper Tools packages and supplies tools from the UK and all over the world, offering a nationwide delivery service. It boasts a product range of 14,500 items, including power tools, gardening tools, hand tools and other specialist equipment.

The company, which started in little more than a shed, now has more than 180,000 square feet of warehousing and offices at Chandler's Ford. Norman, who lives near the complex, is known in the area for his great love of sport.

The name of Draper Tools is emblazoned over the shirts of Southampton Football Club. Over the last five years the company has paid out around £400,000 in sponsorship to the first division team.

In its latest available accounts, the company made after-tax profits of £3.3 million on sales of £27 million. If it were floated on the stock market, the group would fetch a price of around £20 million.

up pop groups such as the Sex Pistols and Blondie and many key 1970s artists.

Ellis's original job with the company took him to America for six years and he signed up many of the best American groups. Establishing a reputation as a dealmaker, he was elected chairman of the Record Industry Association of America in 1981, the only foreigner ever to hold the post. By the mid-1970s both Wright and Ellis were millionaires and in 1984 Wright bought out Ellis for £17.4 million before taking the company public the following year, making himself a multimillionaire in the process.

After splitting with Wright he set up his own Ellis Corporation. Chrysalis moved into a period of very erratic results, often disappointing the City; but Ellis moved on to greater things, running Ellis Corp. as an investment rather than entertainment company.

In May 1989 he was elected chairman of British Phonographic Industries, the representative body for the whole UK record business. The post is an important one, as Ellis now has to face increasing demands for a reduction in the price of compact discs where market growth has been artificially constrained by high prices. He must also manage the vital relationship between BPI and the Prince's Trust, for which it is a major and significant fundraiser.

## Terry Ellis   £20m
*Music promoter*

Terry Ellis' fortune derives from his highly successful partnership with Chris Wright (q.v.) in the Chrysalis record company. Educated at Welwyn Garden Grammar School, he took an honours degree in maths and metallurgy at Newcastle University, before converting his part-time work as college social secretary into a full-time occupation in 1967. That was the year he got together with Chris Wright, who was also running an artist's booking agency. They quickly converted the Ellis Wright Agency into Chrysalis and signed

## Lord Feversham   £20m
*Landowner*
dob 3/1/45

Peter Duncombe inherited his title when a distant cousin, the last Earl of Feversham, died in 1963 without a direct heir. Eton-educated, Feversham now lives at the ancestral home in Helmsley, after recovering it from a girls' school which had occupied it for 60 years. The estate, which once ran to 39,000 acres, is still an impressive 12,000 acres and the house, burnt down in 1879, is now open to the public.

Unlike many landowning peers, Feversham sits on the crossbenches in the House of Lords and does not take any party whip. He is very active in local affairs in Yorkshire and has chaired both the Yorkshire Arts Association and the Standing Conference of Regional Arts Associations. He is a past president of the Yorkshire and Cleveland Local Council Association.

After Eton, Peter Duncombe began a law course but gave this up in favour of a job on a yachting magazine. In 1967 he published a novel, *A Wolf in Tooth*, and followed this with *Great Yachts* in 1970. His maiden speech in the House of Lords caused a stir. He said 'I do not feel I am trespassing. I have a hereditary right, which cannot be defended, to talk here. I do not think the hereditary principle can be defended in any way.' He went on to argue for the regionalisation of government and for reform of the House of Commons. The *Sun* noted that he made his speech at the age of 23; the average age of the other speakers in the House was 67.

Feversham's first wife, the model Shannon Foy, died in 1976. The daughter of a local Yorkshire landowner, she met Lord Feversham at the age of 16. He remarried in 1979, again to a local Yorkshire girl, art student Pauline Aldridge. There are four children from the two marriages.

# Lord Glenconner £20m

*Landowner*

dob 1/12/26

The Tennant family fortune goes back to the end of the 18th century when a Glasgow chemist, Charles Tennant, invented a new bleach which revolutionised the industry. He became a powerful industrialist and was later a Liberal MP and baronet.

Today the family have no interest in the business but are well-known Scottish landowners, with 9,000 prime farming acres in Peebles, owned by Charles Tennant, 3rd Lord Glenconner. There are also extensive land holdings in Australia, and Glenconner used to own the exclusive West Indies island of Mustique which he developed into a millionaire's paradise. He sold it in 1977 and went on to spend £3 million building another exclusive resort on an old plantation in nearby St Lucia. The Glenconners also have one of the most desirable properties in Kensington.

In 1986 he organised a 60th birthday party in the West Indies which cost a reputed £500,000. Among the guests were Princess Margaret, a long-time friend of Glenconner, Mick Jagger, Jerry Hall and Raquel Welch. In 1960 Glenconner had given the newly married Anthony Armstrong-Jones and Princess Margaret a 10-acre plot on Mustique, which helped raise its profile as an exclusive resort.

Glenconner married the daughter of the Earl of Leicester, who is a lady-in-waiting to Princess Margaret. But despite their 30-year marriage, their children have caused enormous problems. Eldest son Charlie was a heroin addict, their middle son Henry dropped out to teach transcendental meditation. He died of Aids, while their youngest, Chris, suffered horrific head injuries when he was in a motorbike crash in central America. Expected to die, he was in a coma for four months.

Despite his lifestyle, Glenconner has a good business brain and has managed to protect his fortune by shrewd property deals. The family frequently appear in the gossip columns of the tabloid press.

# George Harrison £20m

*Musician and film producer*

dob 25/2/43

Ex-Beatle George was the youngest member of 'the fab four'. He later graduated to Indian sitar music and to films as a successful independent producer.

An ardent supporter of the Green movement, George grows his own organic vegetables on his £3 million estate near Henley-on-Thames. Built in 1889 by the millionaire Sir Frank Crisp, Friar Park had formerly been a religious retreat. George rescued and lovingly restored it. The house boasts an Alpine rock garden complete with 20,000 tons of Yorkshire rock, hauled to the site by train.

With his second wife Olivia (his first, the celebrated 1960s model Patti Boyd, went off with Eric Clapton, his best friend), George takes his Green commitment seriously. The couple avoid chlorine-bleached paper and also use the local bottle bank for their empties. They even have a shredder to convert newspapers into garden fertiliser.

Handmade Films, the production company he founded, uses predominantly British casts, crews and studios to produce low-budget but usually highly popular films. Successes have included *Life of Brian*, *The Long Good Friday*, *Mona Lisa* and *A Private Function*. The only failure was *Shanghai Surprise*, starring Madonna.

George still keeps up his interest in music. When the Beatles split, he topped the charts with his own work 'My Sweet Lord' in 1971, and has since worked with a galaxy of famous stars. His most recent musical venture was to form the Travelling Wilburys – a group which embraced Bob Dylan and the late Roy Orbison. It was set up – in part – as a protest against computerised music.

George's relations with the other ex-Beatles are not always cordial. He refused to join Paul McCartney and Ringo Starr in a reunion for the Live Aid concert. He had been overshadowed by John and Paul, who wrote and sang most of the Beatles hits. He also lacks the royalties that have made Paul (a fellow Green supporter) even richer. But George enjoys considerable wealth. His house includes a recording studio and private cinema. He also has holiday homes in Hawaii and on Australia's Great Barrier Reef. As a treat for his eleven-year-old son, he recently splashed out £10,000 to bring a top American skateboarding team over to Britain.

# Kumar brothers    £20m
*Fashion and football wholesalers and promoters*

Bimal, Ramesh and Samesh Kumar came to Britain from India as small boys in the 1960s with their mother, Chanchal Kumar. Their father, Bawa Ram Kumar, joined them later and the family settled in Manchester. They went to school locally and later all went to Salford University, where Bimal graduated in maths, Ramesh in biochemistry and Samesh in economics. They were keen followers of Manchester United football team.

Their father had started a market stall business in 1974, and when he died in the late 1970s they took it over. The three pitches at Orsmkirk, Ellesmere Port and Skelmersdale were selling £4 million of textiles a year, but the brothers decided to expand. They started importing goods from the Far East and developed a new sideline in supplying them to large stores like Top Shop, Dorothy Perkins and C&A. Today they are one of the country's largest importers and wholesalers of fashion goods, and they have developed their own team of designers in London.

One of their clever moves was to spot the potential of fashions tied to football club colours. They signed deals with Everton, Middlesbrough and QPR, and later an exclusive tie-up with Manchester United. This latter deal was expected to generate an extra £2 million of sales for the Kumars.

The logic of the football fashions was spelt out by Bimal Kumar to the *Manchester Evening News*: 'It is becoming a very lucrative area of our business because it is less risky than other areas of fashion. Manchester United always play in red and white and Everton in blue and white. Therefore if the goods don't sell this month, they will sell next month, whereas some fashions become obsolete.'

They have extended their operations to include cash and carry warehouses in Manchester and retail outlets in London. They also own the C&A building in Manchester and of other city-centre sites.

In April 1989 their interest in football was extended even further when they took control of Birmingham City Football Club, paying around £1.5 million for an 80% stake.

They also enjoy playing football themselves and at the end of their 12-hour days in London they often take part in 90-minute friendly matches. Samesh, the youngest of the Kumars, is mainly responsible for running Birmingham City, leaving the business interests to his two brothers.

industry, not finance. In 1970 he set up the Moving Picture company, specialising in television commercials and special effects. Thirteen years later he sold the company to Carlton Communications, the media group, for £13 million of Carlton shares but stayed on with the company. Three years later he left, and made a fortune of £25 million by selling his Carlton shares. At the time it was felt by the City that the entrepreneurial Luckwell could not work within the confines of a large group.

Luckwell himself is a quiet and unassuming man, far removed from the glamour of the media or the image of a business tycoon. His office was once described as a cubby-hole that 'would probably be rejected by the average product manager as being too cell-like'. He received 128 proposals about how to spend the money from the Carlton sale. Instead, he went on holiday for six months, indulging his passion for travelling the world.

It was two years before Luckwell emerged in television again (a condition of the Carlton sale) when he took a 5% stake in the TV-AM business.

# Mike Luckwell   £20m

*Television commercial executive*

dob 31/5/42

Though his first job was as a junior Stock Exchange dealer, Mike Luckwell was to make his fortune out of the entertainment

# The McLean family £20m

*Property heirs*

The former chairman and chief executive of CSE Aviation, Murray McLean, made his fortune running his own business in his native South Africa. He left the country in 1976 after the breakup of his first marriage and went to France with his new wife, gaining a degree at the Paris School of Economics.

He spent a year working for a charity in Cambodia during the aftermath of the Pol Pot regime and then came to England, settling in a manor house at Begbroke, Oxfordshire.

In 1981 he gained control of the plastics company Robert Moss Ltd, of Kidlington, Oxfordshire, with a bid which valued it at £3.2 million. In four years the company's value rose to £26 million and McLean made £4.5 million when he sold his shares to the Bunzl group in 1986.

In 1985 he became a non-executive director of CSE Aviation, which, with its air training school at Kidlington, is the largest general aviation organisation in Europe. The following year he became its chairman and chief executive in a boardroom shake-up. In 1988 a new holding company, Oxford Airport Holdings, was formed to control all the issued share capital of its principal subsidiary, CSE Aviation.

McLean devoted a lot of his time to charity work, spending one day a week helping the trading side of Oxfam's operation. He died aged 54, never having recovered from a heart attack in 1988 shortly after marrying his third wife, Sophie. Control of the company was left to a family trust. In February 1990, the trust members decided to sell after reaching the conclusion that their future did not lie with aviation. The airport is valued at some £20 million.

# Raymond Mould £20m

*Property developer*

dob 8/12/40

Raymond Mould qualified as a solicitor in 1964, winning the Newcastle Law Prize. Three years later he founded Askew Cunningham Limited, a company which specialised in tax planning. In 1981 the company ceased trading following a House of Lords decision which effectively cut the market away from tax planners and advisers.

But by then Mould and two colleagues had formed Arlington Securities to undertake property development. Specialising in up-market business parks, Arlington went from strength to strength in the 1980s, developing sites such as the Solent Business Park at Fareham in Hampshire, complete with lakes and fully grown trees liberally planted around the site. In May 1986 Arlington came to the stock market with a price tag of £55 million. In those heady days of the bull market its shares were snapped up and the share offer was 34-times oversubscribed.

In 1988 pre-tax profits rose 59% on the 1987 figure to reach £23.4 million. In 1989 Mould and his fellow directors agreed on a friendly takeover from Birtish Aerospace, valued at some £278 million. Mould received nearly £20 million from the share sale, and stayed on to mastermind the development of British Aerospace's considerable land portfolio of industrial sites. Under the terms of a unique deal, Mould and his directors will share 10% of any development profits from BAe's property holdings.

Mould is an enthusiastic follower of the turf and owns six brood mares. He keeps his horses with four trainers, and races under emerald green and white colours. He also enjoys shooting and fishing.

# Richard Northcott £20m

*Business man and film maker*

dob 24/9/47

Charged with sorting out his father's ailing paint and wallpaper shops in Scotland, Richard Northcott visited America in 1973. He came back with plans for Dodge City, a chain of cut price DIY shops. They were to be out of town, with parking, refreshments, late night shopping as well as Sunday opening. In all, he built 32 stores and, in 1980, he doubled the size of the business by building 500,000 square feet of space – more than any other UK retailer.

'Not bad when you consider I never invested a penny myself. It was all borrowing from the bank, very low profit margins and high stock turnover,' he later recalled. In 1981 he sold the business to Woolworth, pocketing £17 million.

Educated at Blundell's, the West Country private school, Northcott later trained as an accountant and worked as a financial investigator before his Dodge City experience. But even after he had sold up, he was not finished with retailing. A year later he started a new chain, Brown Bear, selling home furnishings and kitchens. He sold that in 1984 to Gerald Ronson's (q.v.) Heron group for £5.5 million, only to see Ronson sell it on within an hour to Sir Phil Harris (q.v.), the carpet tycoon.

He then tried his hand as a farmer and lotus-eater. 'I thought it would be wonderful. I could relax and look at the farm. But I was just bored,' he told the *Sunday Times*. He decided on a new career as a Hollywood film producer, with Lord Anthony Rufus-Isaacs, the Marquess of Reading's brother. Their biggest success was the controversial film 9½ *Weeks*, starring Kim Basinger.

Northcott has been frequently spotted at fashionable parties and often graces the gossip columns. He was a long-time friend of Davina Phillips, a prominent London hostess and property tycoon in her own right. She sold him her London house worth some £1.25 million. In 1985 he married Kirsten Lund, a Canadian model, whose sister married Lord Anthony Rufus-Isaacs. Northcott lives in a £3 million white mansion overlooking Los Angeles and, apart from his London house, he also owns a 900-acre Sussex farm.

# Robin Phillips £20m

*Industrialist*

dob 4/4/33

Robin Phillips's fortune is built on the hand dryers found in virtually every public lavatory. His company, Warner Howard, in which he is the largest shareholder, rents out hand dryers by the thousands and makes a fortune as a result.

In the early 1960s Phillips worked in Canada for a local company which owned a British offshoot, Coinamatic. In 1964 Phillips (Kidderminster Grammar School, first class honours in Economics from the London School of Economics and a qualified chartered accountant) was sent to become managing director of Coinamatic in London. The company specialised in renting coin-operated washing machines.

By 1980 the Canadian parent was losing interest in the business, and a management buyout was launched, backed by a venture capitalist. A year later the Warner Howard hand drying business was bought and the combined group was renamed after it. In 1987 the group came to the stock market, and today Robin Phillips has over 11 million shares. The company produced record profits of £2.3 million in the first half of 1989.

Though ill-health has forced him to take a back seat, he is still involved in strategic decision making. He lists his hobbies as cricket and swimming.

## Viscount Runciman and family £20m

*Shipowners*

dob 10/11/34

Few British sociologists make it to the House of Lords or become multi-million-aires. Viscount Runciman has done both. As chairman of Walter Runciman & Co, a shipping group founded by his great-grand-father in 1887, Runciman has spent much of the late 1980s and 1990 trying to fight off predators keen to acquire the company where his family owned 30% of the shares. In the end the fight was unsuccessful, and the Swedish group Avana took over Run-ciman for around £65m in April 1990.

It had been a valiant fight, with Run-ciman boasting a 34% average annual increase in profits in the five years up to the takeover.

But Lord Runciman, educated at Eton and Trinity College Cambridge, can console himself now with more time to enjoy the academic world he left in 1976 to run the family business. He remained a part-time reader in sociology at the University of Sussex and a visiting professor at Harvard. Though he has all the qualities and pedi-gree of the great and the good – national service in the Grenadier Guards, a member of Brooks's Club, a former president of the General Council of British Shipping and a member of the Securities and Investments Board, he is also treasurer of the Child Poverty Action group. Runciman has written several books including a *Critique of Max Weber's Philosophy of Social Science* and *Relative Deprivation and Social Justice*. He first took up sociology while studying history at Cambridge, continuing his studies while working as a clerk in the firm's Newcastle office. He started work there in 1964. Today, he lives in London's exclusive St John's Wood.

## Roy Sandhu £20m

*Industrialist, property developer*

Roy Sandhu left Delhi in 1962 as a 14-year-old and settled in the East End of London. The crowded, tenemented area still contained the working docks which provided much of the community with a livelihood, either directly or indirectly.

In the 1970s, when the docks were in decline, Sandhu began his own textile manufacturing business, following a family tradition. He also began to acquire property and with it a taste for development.

His timing was excellent. The vast new Dockland development scheme including the Wapping site of News International and the 850-foot tower at Canary Wharf had begun to take shape, just as his first really big project, Aliffe House on the corner of Mansell Street in London E1, was opened by the Trade and Industry Secretary, Lord Young, in 1988.

In 1986 Sandhu had made a formal application to Tower Hamlets Council for permission to create a 60-storey, 1.4m-square-foot project on the corner of White-chapel High Street and Commercial Road, also in E1. He received a mixed reception. Some Labour and Liberal councillors wanted to abolish the planning committee so that he could be given the go-ahead for the project, which would bring valuable new jobs and a new look to a very run down area. The Royal Fine Arts Commission, whose acquaintance with E1 must be thought to be slight, said that the case for such a large development 'had not been proven'. Sandhu, now with his entire family over from India and working in the company, instead built 73 flats a little further east, at Narrow Street and Shoulder of Mutton Alley.

In an interview with the *Estates Times* in 1989, when he revived and restarted his plan for the big project, though with the height scaled down to 40 storeys, he said that 'success in a building lies in how you design the outer skin'. His buildings are both decorative and imaginative, with echoes of Indian Moghul architecture.

His Roy Properties group made £7.2 million after-tax profits up to the end of December 1987. There are three Sandhus on the board.

---

# Ian Skelly  £20m
*Former car dealer*

Motherwell-born and bred, Ian Skelly worked with his two brothers, Billy and Sherwood, in their father's Ford dealership, which they expanded enormously until a bitter dispute in 1974. Ian set up on his own and on American Independence Day, 4 July 1976, he opened the Ian Skelly Group in derelict premises in Glasgow's Rutherglen district.

It was at the height of a recession and a fuel crisis, but Skelly reckoned that high-technology, fuel-efficient German cars would prove winners in Scotland. He developed an impressive sales technique developed from numerous visits to America, and he expected all his staff, from top to bottom, to wear the blue company pullovers, blazers and overalls. He fitted coffee bars, television rooms and children's play areas to keep his customers happy during a sales pitch. In 1981 he had expanded into Liverpool and, in May 1989, a £5 million centre opened in Manchester.

By then he had Europe's highest volume VW-Audi network, with annual sales of nearly £100 million. At this point Skelly decided to sell up, and netted £18.3 million from the Leeds-based Appleyard group. He chose Appleyards because they promised to look after his 490 staff.

Skelly sold because he had been working seven days a week on the business, rarely relaxing, apart from playing tennis at his luxury Carluke home. The death of his father hastened his decision, as did the fact

that he had no son to take over. 'I reckoned we had become too big for me to give that personal touch,' he told the *Glasgow Herald*.

Skelly and his wife Rita owned all the shares in the business. They are regarded as generous supporters of charity. He is also a large shareholder and sponsor of Motherwell, the Scottish football club.

With the money in his pocket from the sale, Skelly said, 'I don't know what I shall do in the future but right now I am going to have a rest. I want to travel and do what I want to do before I am too old. One thing is sure – I'll remain in Scotland. I have never considered becoming a tax exile. I'm happy to stay and pay my taxes and enjoy my football, despite the weather.'

---

# Christina Smith  £20m
*Property owner*

When Christina Smith moved to Covent Garden in 1963 it was still the traditional fruit and veg market. Today she is a large landowner in the area and, almost single-handed, saved the much-loved old buildings and narrow streets from 1960s developers.

Her early working life gave no hint of property dealing. She did several jobs 'of the type well-brought-up girls do', as she told the *Daily Telegraph*, including working for a City broker. In the late 1950s she joined Sir Terence Conran as a personal assistant in his Fulham exhibition-fitting business. She left in 1962 to work in America, and saved enough money for a round-the-world trip. It was here that she developed the idea of selling ethnic merchandising.

But it was chance that took her to Covent Garden. She was calling on an engineer but fell in love with the busy streets and market atmosphere. After seeing a To Let sign, she borrowed £1,500 from her father and bought the lease on 26 Neal Street.

Here she established Goods & Chattels, specialising in South American crafts and furniture. For ten years she catered for the 'swinging 60s' generation, but in the early 1970s closed down the shop and turned to importing goods from China, then newly opening up to the West.

At the same time, with the old Covent Garden Market closing, the developers were getting ready to move in. They were halted by pressure from Christina through the Covent Garden Forum on the Greater London Council and also by a collapse in the property market. She began buying leases and freeholds. Within 10 years, she owned or leased eleven properties, with a total floor space of approximately 120,000 square feet.

Today she owns Smith's Restaurant and a whole host of other enterprises in Covent Garden. She also lets out workshops to local artisans, adjusting the rent according to their means. She lives in large flat in the area, where she is a well-known figure. She loves art, has a large picture collection and attends sales regularly at the local auction houses. Her great fear, now that Covent Garden has been saved from the developers, is that it will be submerged by an army of tourists. 'Why', she once asked, 'do tourists always spoil everything in the end?'

---

# Bob Sperring £20m

*Retailer*

Starting out in his father's newsagent's shop in a suburb of Southampton in 1965, Bob Sperring built up a chain of convenience stores open for 12 hours a day, 7 days a week. By his early 30s, Sperring was a millionaire, and Sperrings, as the chain was called, was a big success. At the age of 42 he decided to sell the business and pocketed nearly £20m to add to his considerable fortune. But the company's growth had nearly cost him his health and

he suffered a heart attack from the huge strain of work.

Today, Sperring lives in a luxury house in Southampton, and lists his hobbies as property consultancy, travel, skiing, tennis and shooting. He has also supported the Solent Stars, the highly rated local basketball team. He is also a director of the local radio station.

---

# Dave Stewart £20m

*Pop musician*

dob 9/9/52

Born in Sunderland of 'respectable lower middle-class' parents, who separated when he was 14, Dave Stewart left home at 17 to make his fortune in London.

He formed his first band, Longdancer, which signed the first ever record contract with Elton John's Rocket label in 1973. It was not a success and Stewart moved into a Crouch End flat, parted from his wife and got caught up in the pop drug scene, abandoning hope of a music career.

But a chance meeting with a waitress in a north London restaurant in 1977 changed his life forever. It was love at first sight for Stewart and Annie Lennox, a drop-out from the Royal College of Music. They formed their own band, The Tourists, which achieved a number-one hit with a new version of 'I Only Want To Be With You'. A year later The Tourists disbanded, but the duo kept together and in 1981 achieved a hit as The Eurythmics with 'Love is a Stranger'. Though the pair ceased to be lovers in 1980, The Eurythmics survived and prospered. Some 16 million LPs have been sold.

Stewart has also moved into record production and set up his own recording studio in an old Crouch End church. Superstars such as Bob Dylan, Mick Jagger and George Harrison have had records produced by Stewart, making him one of the world's top producers.

331

In 1987, he set up his own record label called Anxious. He recorded a song by his old chauffeur, but that was a flop.

Today Stewart has abandoned drugs for a healthier life and he has large homes in London and Los Angeles. He enjoys the company of other pop stars such as Mick Jagger and has been linked with a string of girl friends, the latest being Siobhan Fahey of Bananarama. 'I rang her up and said: "I can't get you off my mind and that's the top and bottom of it. What are we going to do about it?" '

# John Upson    £20m

*Builder*

dob 6/3/44

The son of a Southend builder, John Upson is every inch the self-made man as this portrait in *Contract Journal* shows: 'Diamonds glint from his cufflinks and ring; a goldplated Rolex nestles against sharply-cut suit and powerful cigars are a constant companion.'

Ten years ago, he was just another manager in the construction business. He was working for David (now Lord) Young, the former Secretary of State for Trade and Industry, as construction director for his Greenwood Homes property business. But in 1979 Upson left after a boardroom battle and decided to branch out on his own with his wife. He bought the Erostin company for £100 and immediately started housebuilding in Milton Keynes, one of the fastest growing areas of Britain. He describes himself as 'a child of the city. We've grown together.'

He is also active in developments round the West Midlands, and is working on a large office project at Birmingham Airport. Upson has learnt his lesson from the 1974 property crash, when he 'worked for a building firm which went bust and I got burnt', as he told the *Sunday Express* recently. With house prices falling and house builders in some difficulty, he has channelled resources into commercial development and civil engineering. He sold his surplus land last year before the bubble burst and has also cut back his house building from 180 houses to just 80 in 1990.

Upson, who lists his hobby as shooting, also has widespread bloodstock interests. He has just been granted his trainer's licence and has 22 horses in training. Last year, when his horses were being trained elsewhere, he had 19 winners. His horses race in his white and green colours.

'My aim is to keep Erostin nimble footed. If I don't keep making more money for Erostin shareholders, I won't be able to buy any more racehorses,' he told the *Sunday Express*.

# Value Index

## Name Index